GERMANY, RUSSIA, AND THE BALKANS
PRELUDE TO
THE NAZI-SOVIET NON-AGGRESSION PACT

Marilynn Giroux Hitchens

WITHDRAWN

EAST EUROPEAN MONOGRAPHS, BOULDER
DISTRIBUTED BY COLUMBIA UNIVERSITY PRESS NEW YORK
1983

TABLE OF CONTENTS

PREFACE

The history of the Nazi-Soviet Non-Aggression Pact, indeed the history of the coming of World War II, has been dominated by a discussion of Poland. This is so primarily because war's initiation saw its first battlefield in Poland, and because the Non-Aggression Pact promoting that explosion is generally explained in terms of the territorial revisionism agreed to in Poland. And yet, logically, the interests of both Germany and Russia ranged along the whole of their frontiers which to the south included the Balkan states. This monograph basically sets out to answer the question of whether or not the Southeastern states were not also important in driving the Non-Aggression Pact to its culmination.

The scope of this book is naturally limited by the materials available and by the number of facets of the topic which can be logically accounted for at one time. In the case of materials, while the archives of Yugoslavia are partly accessible for the period of 1939 and some native historians have been admitted to the Rumanian archives, the Greek, Turkish, Bulgarian, and Russian archives are not generally accessible.[1] Limited but useful were the U.S. Archives, whereby a certain candor displayed to the then neutral United States diplomats, authenticated impressions gleaned from other sources. In this regard, U.S. sources include U.S. State Department papers, Post Files, and Military Intelligence Reports. Published documents by the Germans, Americans and British were directly accessible and used, while the Italian documents were broached through a secondary medium. The *Greek, Polish* and *German White Books* and the *French Yellow Book,* due to the selective nature of their contents, were only partially useful, and in any case often redundant. Memoirs like the *Ciano Papers* were, of course, helpful, but naturally interpretive. Beyond these primary records, there is a wealth of secondary material, the bulk of which speaks only indirectly to the topic.

With regard to the materials used in this study, there are several points to be made. Since the primary sources available are oriented almost entirely toward diplomatic history, social, economic, and political history, all of which bear on the events of the period, are taken into account only as they influence diplomacy. Furthermore, the dispatches of the German, Italian, and Russian diplomatic corps only partially represent the true attitude of those governments, as the ultimate policies were made by Hitler, Mussolini, and Stalin, whose thoughts and motivations, even were the archives available, are nowhere recorded as such. Thus, in the case of these three dictatorial states, the actions rather than the motivation has become the stuff of history, with the historian at the least guessing and at best piecing together the rationale of an often irrational tide of events. But, while materials to an extent circumscribe the parameters of this topic, they are not the ultimate dictator either. The theme itself is basically a diplomatic one, and history ultimately is made, not by debate, but by action.

With regard to the workability of the topic, the triangular threads, even though limited to a diplomatic focus with the Nazi-Soviet Pact as the ultimate point of orientation, are not always easily isolated either diplomatically or geographically. For instance, in many cases, it is impossible to discuss Germany in the Balkans without also discussing the role of Berlin's cohort Italy, or of discussing the Soviet role in the Balkans without bringing Great Britain and France into the picture.

From the Balkan point of view, geographical and political isolation is complicated still further. Traditionally the Balkan states have been considered as Bulgaria, Rumania, Yugoslavia, and Albania, with Austria, Hungary, Czechoslovakia, and Poland referred to as the Central European states, and Greece and Turkey as the Mediterranean states.[2] But during the 1920s Hitler invariably used the term "Southeast Europe" in which he included the Central European states (except Poland) until they were absorbed and thereafter Turkey and Greece as well. Meanwhile the Soviets tended not to separate out the Balkans from the other East European states invariably using the term "East Europe" which emphasized in a defensive sense the whole line of states along the Soviet western frontier. Likewise, the British and French attempted to link the Balkans diplomatically with the other East European states in their so-called "peace front." The Balkan countries themselves went outside a classical geographic framework joining in alliances with Czechoslovakia in the Little Entente, and Turkey and Greece in the Balkan Entente. Moreover, they were fiercely nationalistic and found it difficult to assume any "Balkan" attitude or identity.

Consequently the Balkan component, like the German and Soviet ones, tends to escape absolute and static definition. Nevertheless, history in many ways justifies the extraction of this Southeastern group of states from the rest of the states in the Eastern area. First, the Balkans actually began to emerge as an entity in 1939 once Germany had absorbed Austria and Czechoslovakia, satellitized Hungary, and turned to the isolation of Poland. In the German mind the program for all of these states was the same—neutrality, economic exploitation, and control. Once the Germans had embarked on this road, the British, French, and Soviet counter-offensive was colored by it. Their program involved linking the Balkans together and then tying them to Poland and the Baltic states.

From another point of view the Balkan component justifies study. As has already been mentioned, because Poland is specifically mentioned in the Nazi-Soviet Pact, historiography has been dominated by the Polish question. Yet, not only was the situation in the Balkans as powerful a force as Poland driving the Nazi-Soviet Pact to its conclusion, but precisely the failure of Berlin and Moscow to reach a stable agreement over so important an area, makes it desirable for study.

Finally, the very geopolitical position of the Balkans, which throughout history has assumed such importance as the "link" or "bridge" between three continents and was in 1939 at the confluence of disparate German, Soviet, and British interests, elevates the area to a rank deserving serious historical consideration. Once in the early 20th century the Balkans were the "powder keg" for a Great War. This paper seeks to answer the question of whether or not that was not basically true in the second of those great 20th century conflicts as well.

The format of this paper follows the organic development of the situation, that is, the three threads of the theme, Germany, Russia, and the Balkans are drawn into the picture as their importance brings them to the forefront. German dominance in the area came first. This was followed by a resurgence of Balkan activity due to the reintroduction of the West resulting from the British and French guarantees. Finally, the Soviet Union is brought to the front stage as Moscow becomes the key to the balance of power and fate of the Balkans.

In a study of this kind, there is felt, of course, enormous gratitude for all those whose work has preceded one's own, for the librarians at the University of Colorado and research specialists at the National Archives in Washington, and for numerous colleagues and friends. Above all, unending appreciation is especially felt for Professor Stephen Fischer-Galati of the University of Colorado who suggested and oversaw the development of this topic through its various phases. In addition, I would like to acknowledge the spiritual and intellectual support of Professors Libor Brom of the University of Denver, Frederick S. Allen of the University of Colorado at Denver, Edward Rozek of the Univeristy of Colorado at Boulder and Francis J. Kelly of Loretta Heights College. Finally, I acknowledge the patience and support of my husband, Benjamin, my children Marguerite and Marilynn, and my parents, Mr. and Mrs. Joseph P. Giroux.

INTRODUCTION

> It must never be forgotten that the Balkans
> ceased to be the Balkans only when they have
> freed themselves from the all too anxious pro-
> tections all over Europe.
> The Czech Press, *Venkov,* January 20, 1939.

> It is hard to realize, sometimes, how little the
> Balkan countries really know about each
> other, preoccupied as they are with mutual
> suspicion and ancestral hate!
> MacVeagh, Secretary of State, No. 3394
> September 13, 1939, File 508, U.S. National
> Archives, *Post Files,* Record Group 84.

The Rhineland, Anschluss, Munich—by early 1939 Hitler's shadow was creeping all over the Balkans. The West had turned its back, the Central European states had submitted, the Russians were watching in silent retreat, and the Balkans, without alternatives, were preparing to go along. But Western idealism and pride had been struck a blow at Munich and the counterswell was already in the making when the dissolution of Czechoslovakia exposed the rapaciousness of Hitler's imperialism, and then the Italian invasion of Albania thrust a dagger toward the heart of the British Empire at Suez. The question for the British now was not whether there would be a conflict, but when and where. They made their stand in Eastern Europe for many reasons, some honorable and some self-serving—to keep Germany from access to Rumanian oil, to divert the battlefield east, to halt Hitler's march by confrontation or the threat of it, and to honor a commitment to

1

freedom in Eastern Europe. Hastily they guaranteed first Poland, then Greece and Rumania, and finally successfully allied themselves with Turkey.

The front, timing, and format were ill-chosen from the point of view that neither the British nor the French were prepared physically, geographically or diplomatically to open a front in Eastern Europe without the aid of a united Balkans and/or the Soviet Union. The one was as incompatible with the other as were the Balkan countries to each other. The Balkans were reluctant to abandon their neutrality until the West reached agreement with the Soviet Union outlining the parameters of the Soviet contribution. The Soviets were reluctant to involve themselves without a sufficient quid pro quo presumably meaning extending their frontiers at the expense of the East European states. And both feared Hitler's wrath and wished not to be involved. Thus began the wooing of Moscow by both Berlin and London with the Balkans silently contemplating that for their part, control by Berlin might not be as bad as either London's war or Moscow's occupation. Two decades earlier the eyes and interests of Berlin, Moscow, and London had been focused in the Balkans. It was a scenario recreated as if the tremendous changes wrought by the Communist Revolution, the Treaty of Versailles, the shrinking British Empire, and the demise of the Ottoman Empire had not mattered at all.

In the end Berlin's olive branches to the Soviet Union proved more tantalizing than London's. What had London to offer but war, while Berlin promised neutrality and territory. The territory concerned involved only Poland and Bessarabia which left the entire southern Soviet frontier with its key strategic and historical positions along the Black Sea at the Straits exposed. But exposed to whom? The whole long road to conclusion of the Nazi-Soviet Pact suggests that the reintroduction of British interests in East Europe, which focused more strongly in the Balkans than in Poland, provided a threat equal to if not greater than Hitler's to the Soviet Union. In guaranteeing the Balkans, Britain had, in effect, agreed not to abandon them, and so faced the Kremlin not one but two enemies. The classical Russian answer to such a dilemma was to let a war between two enemies advance the power of the Soviet Union to the degree that the Balkans would be theirs. In the meantime the West's wooing gave the Soviet Union the power it needed to meet the Germans at the negotiating table on a par basis.

In the diplomacy of the months between the guarantees and conclusion of the Nazi-Soviet Pact, the ghosts of Versailles came back to haunt its authors. The very Balkan states created by the victors refused to abandon their new found liberty to the British efforts to ally one with the other under a British-Soviet umbrella of sorts. They were bolstered in this by the unilateral nature of the guarantees and in German tactics which played skillfully on ancient Balkan antagonisms to thwart any such alliance. Meanwhile, the Soviets did nothing to secure the Balkan minds of their pacific intent. It is easy to blame the Balkans for the tragedy which resulted in the signing of the Nazi-Soviet Pact if the fate of the Balkans is perceived as within their own making. In fact, the making and unmaking of the Balkans was, in very great measure, in the hands of the Great Powers whose interests had one thing in common, primary allegiance to their own best interests. Thus, the Nazi-Soviet Pact was made on the Balkan conception of their own best 'interest and the temporary merging of Nazi-Soviet interests in the Balkans which above all in 1939 was based on the Balkan status quo.

In the view of this study, while Poland was the issue which dominated the diplomacy surrounding the Nazi-Soviet Pact, the Balkans were of paramount concern, for any Balkan eruption, which because of the complexities of Balkan politics was more likely, would bring the interests of both the Soviet Union and Germany into play in an uncompromising format. Such Soviet involvement in league with the West or even alone would have been disastrous for the Germans and the Soviets alike. Therefore, it was the very conflict of interests which made a communality of interest in Balkan neutrality possible, thus it was the common purpose not the conflicting Balkan spheres which brought the Nazi-Soviet Pact to fruition.

It is hoped that this study will, in surveying Germany in the Balkans, the Soviet Union in the Balkans, and the Balkans vis-a-vis themselves, unravel some of the mysteries surrounding the Nazi-Soviet Pact, increase our understanding of the forces at work in the immediate prewar months, and deepen our appreciation for the delicate relationship between Great and Small Powers in keeping the peace.

CHAPTER I

GERMANY AND THE BALKANS—PRELUDE

With Hitler's rise to prominence in 1933, Germany's military and economic power steadily began to mount. Meanwhile, the Depression-ridden West, preoccupied as it was with its internal problems, increasingly lost interest in its obligations preserving the territorial integrity of the small Eastern states it had created at Versailles. The West's weak link, Eastern Europe, soon became the object of Hitler's gaze and actions. By skillful planning and opportunism, Hitler created and then exploited crisis after crisis, which by 1939 led to the annexation of Austria, the satellization of Hungary, and the near collapse of Czechoslovakia. Once the first line of Eastern defense, the Central European states, had moved into the Nazi orbit, the Balkans and Poland lay open and exposed.

This chapter will examine the process by which Hitler moved successfully against East-Central Europe, a process intimately involving the Balkans both in terms of Hitler's long range aims and in terms of Balkan reactions themselves. The results of the remilitarization of the Rhineland, Anschluss, Munich, and Prague largely determined the next phase of Hitler's moves in the East which were directed against Poland, not the Balkans, an indication not of Hitler's disinterest in the Southeast, but rather of his already accomplished victory there.

Aims, Interests, and Economics

The basic aims, interests, and polices of Germany in the Balkans were largely evident and secured before April 1939. In assessing these aims and interests both ideological and empirical evidence can be cited, and in the case of the Balkans, it is startling how closely aligned these two factors are.

In historical terms Hitler's theoretical aims have often been likened to the recreation of the Holy Roman Empire of yore. Certainly the very term "Third Reich" implies this connection as does his referral in *Mein Kampf* to "the march along the road of the Teutonic Knights of Old."[1] Likewise, Hitler told Hungarian Foreign Minister Csáky on January 16, 1939 that in Hungarian complaints of Vienna, "Hungary was thinking only of the 1,000 year old realm of St. Stephen which he would override in the name of the ancient Germanic Empire."[2] But allusion to the Holy Roman Empire could only carry Hitler's thinking so far, as the Holy Roman Emperors, in their quest for religious Germanization, never reached the Balkans. Presumably Hitler sought to improve on their performance, using the moral and nationalist sentiment of the Emperors to legitimize his move eastward.

This historical sentiment reappears in the ideological form in *Mein Kampf* were the drive and settlement Eastward is a dominating theme in Hitler's basically geopolitical philosophy. It presupposes both empire and settlement of the Balkans incidental to which was the exorcism of the French threat to Germany's rear. Specifically, in terms of settlement Hitler talks of "Russia and her vassal border states." The strategy Hitler proposed to achieve these ends was an offensive against the West which "will come first." In this connection he defended Bismarck's policy of alliance with Italy "in order to finish off Austria the more easily," and treaty with Russia which Bismarck welcomed as a "rear cover which gave him a free hand in the West." But while Hitler saw the validity of neutralizing Russia, he did not support an alliance on the grounds that a Nazi-Soviet war against Europe would be fought not on Russian but on German soil, that as a technical factor Russia would be out of the picture in part due to Poland and in part due to backwardness, and on the grounds that Russia was not to be trusted.[3]

He saw Great Britain and her propensity to help France as his only valid opposition, but he relied on Britain's concern for her Empire to bring London to an accommodation, which would in turn bring on U.S. neutrality. He discounted the tactic of allying with Britain's enemies and vassals like "various Balkan States, Egypt, and India" in order to bring down the British order on the theory that alliance with weak nations would weaken Germany much as the link with the Dual Alliance had weakened the Kaiser's Germany. Hitler's ultimate vision was a world divided between Germany,

Britain, and Japan whereby the Balkans would rest well within the German sphere.[4]

Hitler also had some observations to make in *Mein Kampf* regarding German policy in the Balkans. He recognized the usefulness of the process of Balkanization, that is of the divide-and-rule principle which he noted the British had used effectively before World War I and the French after it. Coincidentally he suggests that mobilization of these states could be dangerous if the perceived enemy was Germany and that a positive response on Germany's part to heterogeneous desires and aims could prevent such a single offensive front.[5] Thus, as the German program began to evolve, it called for emasculation or destruction of Balkan alliances and until the British and French were finished off, avoidance of war in the Southeast at all costs. German hegemony in the area became a necessity, not just to provide an interim resource area and a political and strategic buffer, but to prevent extension of the war through unplanned internal explosion or external intervention. As one German foreign officer commented in July 1940 as Russia prepared to enter Bessarabia, "The Führer earnestly seeks peace as Hitler has always wanted in *Mein Kampf*."[6]

No economist, Hitler does not mention specifically an economic drive into the Balkans, but his emphasis on German settlement of Russia gives some credence to the idea that the riches of Russia, not the Balkans was to be the ultimate object of economic exploitation and that any economic program in the Balkans was politically motivated, that is aimed at tying the Balkans to Germany. But, while Germany must have envisioned rule of the Balkans within an empirical framework once the conquest of Russia was completed, her need for Balkan peace and chauvinism in 1939 prevented this. Therefore, her main stated aim was economic, that is assurance of a steady flow of raw materials for the German war machine. That the economic value of the Southeast became increasingly important and was a large factor in Hitler's decision to disturb the area by occupation rather than in preparation for the long cherished *drang nach osten*, was due to a failure of events in the Western area to move according to the timetable set up and to Soviet incursions.

The German emphasis on economics was, perhaps, aimed at reducing Balkan, Western, and Russian political fears, but whether it was just a political tactic on their main purpose in the Balkans becomes irrelevant in terms of the way they went about the Balkan economic drive, for the net result was that it somewhat tied the countries to the Reich politically. The

German economic conquest of East Europe was mapped out by President of the Reichsbank and Minister without Portfolio Dr. Hjalmar Schacht. His plan was to increase German self-sufficiency in primary products and to foster manufacturing by converting Southeastern Europe into a kind of hinterland. Germany estimated that about one-third of her foodstuffs and raw materials had to be imported and that East Europe could provide up to 50 percent of these requirements. It was calculated that if the Reich had access to the total exports of these countries, Germany would be self-sufficient in cereals, livestock, meat, vegetables, fruit, tobacco, timber, leather, and bauxite, and would obtain substantial quantities of iron ore, steel, copper ore, manganese, chrome, fats, petroleum, wool and cotton. In the case of ores it was calculated that by 1937 the Balkans would be in a position to meet 20 percent of the German requirements and with exploitation that percentage would increase.

The fulfillment of German economic aims in the Balkans was facilitated by inherent Balkan weaknesses that made it ripe for a German trade assault. The French system was a diplomatic arrangement with no basis in economic support. The Depression brought ruin to France and made her incapable of taking agricultural products as were Russia and other other Western countries. Germany, therefore, was the predestined market.

That the German economic program was aimed at political control as well as economic benefits is clear from the nature of the agreements signed. They were in no sense based on the principles of Western mutual and just exchange.[7] For example, one technique was to offer high prices for the sale of Rumanian and Hungarian wheat, and for Yugoslav and Rumanian timber, and Greek, Bulgarian, and Turkish tobacco. This in turn caused the accumulation of frozen balances and monies owed them by the Germans and as a result Balkan denial of import licenses to Britain and others. Political influence was obtained by the necessity of maintaining good relations with Germany in order to insure payment of debt.

Another technique was tying economic agreements with arms sales largely of old type weaponry which Germany would export immediately on credit. The political influence was obtained by the consequent continuity needed for the supply of spare parts. Still another technique was the long-term credit formula. For instance, Rumania sold for cash and bought on credit, but the clearing in Berlin did not take place for ten years. If the Balkan country met their liabilities well and good, and if they defaulted, that was better still since it meant the accumulation of frozen balances in Germany owning the Balkans which placed them in a state of commercial and then political dependence.

A final technique was exploitation agreements whereby Germany promised to develop resources and build plants in return for use or produce. (From 1937-1940 German investments in the Balkans rose from one percent to 20 percent.) All of these devices, originally resorted to when Germany was weak and needed to expand her trade, ultimately secured 40 to 50 percent of the Danubian and Balkan states' trade, so that Germany could then afford to threaten the Balkans against diverting their trade elsewhere.

Little opposition to this creeping economic and political strangulation came from either Russia, Britain, or the Balkans themselves, Russia because trade with the Balkans was complementary and Britain because the spectacular gains of Germany were not at the expense of British trade, and for both because they did not aim to control Balkan politics through trade. Prime Minister Neville Chamberlain even bowed to German economic domination of the area admitting that geographically, "Germany must occupy a dominating position there."[8]

Up to 1937 Hitler was indiscriminate, buying and selling as much as he could. But after that the economic drive increasingly took on political overtones whereby Germany began organizing Southeast Europe as a complement to her own. The plan called "Grossaumevirtschaft," which was outlined in the Munich period by Nazi Economics Minister Dr. Funk during a swing through the Balkans, was never quoted in full in Balkan papers.

Yugoslavia, Bulgaria and Turkey, which are our political friends form a kind of Balkan Axis which reaches from the German border to the Black Sea. This fact makes it possible to negotiate great economic reconstruction plans.

Noting the Danube's great importance for the Southeast, he said, "there is being created an economic area from the North Sea to the Black Sea . . . which possesses everything Germany needs especially ores," and by negotiations and long-term credits Germany would increase productive power of the area so that Germany might make extensive purchases. And he noted, "Incorporation of the Sudeten German economy will only increase the German share."[9] The political overtones of Funk's "Four Year Plan" were not lost on statesmen of the time. U.S. Charge Gilbert noted that from confidential sources he had learned that it was a German effort to bring together an "autarkic block in Southeast and East Europe including Turkey."[10]

The German "Four Year Plan" was not popular in the Balkans for the obvious reasons that German could not provide some of their needed tropical fruits, because large German imports stifled domestic manufacturing, and because of the realization that higher prices for agricultural goods ultimately fell on the Balkan consumer.[11] But the cycle, once started, was difficult to break, and little help came from outside. Balkan requests for weaponry from Britain and France were continually denied as were Balkan requests of the West to absorb Balkan agricultural products. When the British and French did begin to respond in 1938, it was for political reasons that is to counter German influence and to woo the Balkan countries toward the encirclement front. For example, in August 1938, France offered a credit to Bulgaria under the condition that an accord between Bulgaria and the Balkans states would be signed.

However, as the German need for raw materials and political control of the Balkans increased in 1938-1939, the economic importance of the trade decreased commensurately with the result that Berlin often found itself in the undesirable position of signing economic treaties which had little economic benefit to Germany at all. German documents suggest, for instance, that the benefits of the Rumanian-German Economic Treaty were exaggerated.[12] In the case of Yugoslavia, economic negotiations were opened in 1938 to "facilitate" and "expedite Yugoslav withdrawal—in preparation for a number of years—from anti-German political combinations in the Danube region."[13] After Munich when German industrialist Krupp asked the already overextended Reich for a guarantee of an arms transaction credit of 100 million RM, Minister Wiehl, though reluctant to arm Yugoslavia, answered in the affirmative noting that the "transaction is desirable for political reasons, but political interest does not go so far as to justify an economic loss."[14] The story was repeated in the case of Bulgaria. In 1939 Ribbentrop urged that negotiations go as far as possible in granting Bulgarian requests for long term loans for "political reasons," and when the deal was finally consummated, Germany had agreed to a war materiel grant of 30 million RM in two years while acquiescing in the Bulgarian refusal to shorten the period of repayment.[16]

Because of Hitler's plans for economic and political control of the Balkans, the Danube became the most important geographical feature of the area, above and beyond the Dardanelles. In the long view, it was to be the route into Russia, particularly should Britain maintain control of the Mediterranean and North Sea as planned. But importance turned into dependence and need for control, once the war dragged on in the West. For, with the North Sea blocked, Turkish refusal to give way to benevolent neutrality, the increasing need for access to Balkan resources, and lack of roads vital to German mechanized warfare in Hungary, Rumania and other Balkan countries (a situation Hitler did little to correct for defensive reasons) the Danube's importance was magnified beyond Hitler's original conception.

One of the ironies of the German economic offensive in the Balkans was that as the German political offensive in East Europe gained momentum, so too did the German need for raw materials and for conservative use of their own weaponry. Neither inflation nor taxation were popular alternatives, but the reality was that exploitation and the economic techniques used until then to capture Balkan trade had reached an optimum point. Likewise the Danube began to lose its value, increasing the importance of the Dardanelles commensurately. This situation not only diminished the Reich political bargaining power accordingly, but left Hitler fewer political alternatives. Having lost the economic lever, the Nazi-Soviet Pact was the next logical step in Balkan coercion.[16]

* * * * *

Thus, theoretically Hitler's interest in the Balkans was as a road to the settlement of Russia and as an object of settlement itself, and in his perception of these states as Soviet vassals, he defined Russia as his main Balkan enemy—hence the importance of the Danube and Baltic rather than the Dardanelles and North Sea. At the same time he recognized that the road to Moscow went through Paris first, and that during this phase of the action, Germany's rear must be protected by destruction of the French security system, the prevention of anti-German Balkan alliances, and if need be an agreement which would neutralize Russia without alliance with her. One convenient tool of Balkan control came to be economic satellization, which served the dual purpose of providing Germany with needed resources on an interim basis and masking the political aims upsetting to the West, Russia and the Balkans alike. On the road to Nazi control of the European heartland, Hitler fully expected Britain to negotiate, but

British obstinacy, idealism, and pragmatism in the defense of Europe, made the British stand in the Balkans the key factor altering the projected relationship with Russia, vastly increasing the importance of the status quo of the area and then its control.

Following closely his blueprint, Hitler very largely transformed his theoretical presumptions into fact prior to 1939. The Rhineland, Anschluss, and Munich turned Germany into a Holy Roman Empire ready to drive East. In the process of this consolidation, the French security system in the East was destroyed and the Balkans neutralized by a process of Balkanization and economic satellization. In effect, by 1939 and particularly after Prague in March and Albania in April, the Balkans had moved into the German sphere. This in turn paved the way for the isolation of Poland and then the turn against France. A brief look at this process is necessary as a framework for the events which occurred from April to August 1939.

Strategy and Effects of the Rhineland and Anschluss

March 7, 1936, in outright defiance of the Versailles Treaty, German troops moved into the demilitarized zone between Germany and France. This remilitarization of the Rhineland was a turning point in the defense of the Balkans for as French Foreign Minister, Pierre Étiènne Flandin pointed out, thereafter there was no hope of giving assistance to Yugoslavia or Rumania or preventing German domination, and it rendered the Little Entente valueless.[17] France, in the face of Germany's military and economic resurgence, wished only to husband her human material in her own defense and to rely on Great Britain who was disarmed. German Ambassador in Austria, von Papen, in a dispatch to the Führer dated January 12, 1937 pointed out that the effect of the Rhineland was the ad hoc creation of a Berlin-Vienna-Rome Axis. Now, wrote von Papen, Germany was ready for the vindication of German historically based rights in the Danube Basin.[18] German Minister in Czechoslovakia, Eisenlohr, concurred, writing that now there was no hope "of erecting a dam against the German need for expansion toward the Southeast."[19]

For the Balkans, there were other, perhaps more impairing effects of the Rhineland move besides Frances' inability to defend them. One was the danger which was now posed to the only other principal route into Central Europe (through Yugoslavia) brought on by the creation of the

Berlin-Rome Axis and the consequent crumbling of the Stresa Front. Though the reorientation of Italy away from England and France and toward Germany had been in the making since the Italian invasion of Ethopia the previous year, the Rhineland move further defined the similarity of interest between Rome and Berlin and it laid the groundwork for the subsequent trade-off whereby for Italian acquiescence and support of German moves in Central Europe, Italy would gain a sphere in Southeast Europe.

Equally devastating was the dashed hope of the Stresa Front that a general settlement of intra-Balkan relations directed toward bringing the revisionist states of Bulgaria and Hungary into line could be achieved.[20] For German power reawakened the hope that Bulgaria and Hungary could, on German coattails, obtain the national goals denied them at Versailles, Trianon, and Neuilly. Along with this deteriorating political and strategic situation, went the growing economic dependence of the Balkans on Germany. In effect, French strength, Italian self-interest, and the ultimate power of Great Britain until then had rendered the decisions made in 1919 effective, but now the whole basis of status quo maintenance seemed in jeopardy. And, intra-Balkan rivalries and aggressions were awakened, threatening not only the Balkan peace, but the extension of squabbles beyond their frontiers.

The Balkans altered their policies in accordance with the threat posed, that is the power and Southeastern ambitions of Germany and Italy (and suspect intentions of Russia)[21] versus the growing unwillingness and inability of the West to defend them and the ascerbation of their own internal tensions. Yugoslavia, Rumania, and Greece decided to take Poland's cue and pursue a policy of "balance" between the Axis and the West hoping thereby to reduce pressure on them without sacrificing their political and economic interests.[22] They tended to lay increasing emphasis on the associations with the Balkan rather than the Little Entente in order to avoid entanglement in the apparent threat to Czechoslovakia. Turkey, meanwhile, watching the Mediterranean situation and particularly Italian aspirations alongside apparent British acquiescence, turned an eye toward obtaining more direct control over the Straits and her littoral.

As Anschluss approached, threats to the Balkans centered around Rumania and Yugoslavia. The direct threat was that absorption of Austria would place Germany on the Yugoslav frontier and in a position to threaten Czechoslovakia and therefore Rumania. The indirect threat was posed by revisionist Italy and Hungary. Presumably, for acquiescence in the move against Austria, Italy would claim coveted parts of Yugoslavia around Trieste and Fiume, and Hungary would press claims both against Rumania in Transylvania and against Yugoslavia in the Voyvodina. The economic threat was that German absorption of Austria would mean the loss of the only other major Balkan trading partner besides Germany. In effect, this would place almost the entire Balkan economic exchange in the hands of Germany.

Although Balkan fears centered around the indirect threat, Hitler's revisionist intentions in this regard were tactical only. Hitler did not wish to unsettle the Balkans by any sort of revisionism which had the danger of turning the area once again into the Powder Keg of Europe. Nor did he wish to provoke formation of a Balkan coalition against him, increase the power of Italy and Hungary, or disturb the trade area upon which completion of the Nazi Four-Year Plan depended. Essentially Hitler desired peace in the Balkans and Anschluss without a price, at the same time provoking enough fear of revisionism in Balkan capitals that economic and political subservience on a unilateral basis would follow.

Hitler's strategy was to dangle the threat of revisionism before Rumania and Yugoslavia in order to pressure them into appeasement, at the same time posing as a friend who would restrain Italian and Hungarian appetites, champion anti-Bolshevism, and provide the Balkans with the needed arms refused them by the West. For example, German Minister to Yugoslavia, Heeren, communicated to Yugoslav Premier Stoyadinović on January 17, 1938 the Führer's sentiments which were to the effect that Hungarian-Yugoslav boundaries were guaranteed along the present lines there being absolutely no sympathy in Germany for Hungarian revisionism, and that the German drive to the Adriatic pushed by the Habsburg Empire had been abandoned because

> . . . as Yugoslavia in her relations with Germany had now renounced the French spectacles, Germany too, in her relations with Yugoslavia was now no longer using the Viennese spectacle.[23]

In the German view Yugoslav foreign policy displayed a new "interpretation" and "independence" as a result. In an unsigned memo dated January 3, 1938, a German official refers to the fact that Yugoslavia had avoided commitment to the Great Powers, had refused to develop the

Little Entente into a treaty of alliance, had responded positively to German economic negotiations, had continued her policy of nonrecognition of Russia, and had concluded a Pact of Friendship with Bulgaria in January 1937 and of Mutual Recognition of Boundaries with Italy in March 1937.[24] With an eye on their own precarious Serbo-Croat conflict which Germany could well exploit, the Yugoslavs gave the green light to Hitler in Austria. At Sinaia, Stoyadinović proceeded to make a statement to the effect that the Yugoslav Kingdom was based on the principle of Yugoslav unification and consequently Yugoslavia could not oppose the German doctrine. But desperately trying to still follow a policy of balance, Foreign Minister Stoyadinović also made trips to London and Paris as well as to Rome and Berlin in 1937 and 1938, and in Rome he made efforts to keep Italy from going to the German side by representing to Rome that like Italy, Yugoslavia did not support Anschluss.

Like pressure was exerted by Berlin on Rumania with the same results. Recognizing that the question of the security of her frontiers was vital and that the key to this now lay in Berlin, the new Rumanian President, Goga, addressed a message to the Führer in January 1938 expressing the hope of cordial relations and implying German approval of the present Rumanian boundaries.[25] A favorable (in Rumanian eyes) reply was subsequently forthcoming and with it, a new economic treaty serving to increase the volume of trade between the two. Soon after (February 10, 1938), a new Constitution designed to shore-up government control in the face of possible antagonism to the growing pro-German shift, gave King Carol a virtual monopoly over foreign policy formulation and implementation. In both capitals freedom of choice in foreign policy was slowly being chiseled away and growing in its place was a fearful, stoic, and deadly acceptance of neutrality.

Hitler's posture as Rumianian and Yugoslavian defender against Hungarian revisionism seems to have been sincere from the point of view that he valued Balkan peace and neutrality. Secretary Mackensen informed Hungarian Minister Sztójay in November 1937 that the Germans agreed only to "discuss and support" Hungarian proposals for the Hungaro-Yugoslav boundary settlement not to "guarantee it," and Berlin made Budapest aware that Hitler did not intend to unleash a European war over Hungarian aims.[26] On the other hand there is ample evidence that the Hungarians sold out Austria to Germany in the hope of revisionism, a hope which

Hitler often nourished by intimating that only through Germany could Budapest realize her foreign policy aims.[27]

Hitler's Balkan policy during Anschluss was also directed toward the destruction of the Little and Balkan Ententes. Thus he encouraged not only Hungary, but Bulgaria and Italy to reach unilateral accommodations with Yugoslavia in order to weaken the internal cohesion of these groupings. In the case of Yugoslavia, a Bulgarian Treaty of Friendship was signed in January 1937, and in the case of Italy a Pact of Mutual Recognition of Italo-Yugoslav Boundaries in March 1937. But he stopped short of guaranteeing the frontier changes resulting from such agreements in the belief that a guarantee would discourage dependence on Germany. Hitler also attempted to frustrate any other Balkan groupings which might connect themselves with Austria or Czechoslovakia. Successfully shelved was a Czech plan for a Danubian economic federation (Hodža Plan) and a plan for a coalition of succession (to the Habsburg Empire) states.

The capitulation of Italy to Hitler's plans for Anschluss put added pressure on the Balkans to remain neutral during the assault. Notice that Italy would not oppose Anschluss was apparent as early as 1937 when Italian involvement in Africa and Spain effectively tied Rome's hands. Then in January 1938, German General Göring told a cool and irritated Mussolini that he must accept German claims in Austria,[28] effectively destroying the Rome Protocol pledging a concordant policy on the part of Hungary, Austria, and Italy. British policy played its part too, for London's original disinterest caused the Balkan countries to seek their own solutions, but when the Prime Minister reversed himself in late June saying the reorganization of the Danube was of interest to Great Britain, the Balkan countries became fearful that this would bring war and other powers like the Soviet Union into their territories. Both interpretations drove them toward appeasement and neutrality vis-a-vis Germany.

As the absorption of Austria moved forward, it became increasingly clear that Nazi aims were directed toward Balkan vassalage. Article II of the Austro-German Protocols of November 21, 1936 pledged prevention of Danubian economic coalitions and the joining of the two greatest Balkan trade partners thereby assuring Balkan economic dependence on Vienna and Berlin. German Ambassador in Austria, von Papen, opined that Anschluss prepared the "striking power of the Reich in Southeastern Europe," and that due to Austria's history and experience, she could be used as a "mediator" in the Danube area[29] which now fell within the German sphere (the Mediterranean for Italy). The Italians did not like having to bow to Anschluss and to the loss of a Southeastern sphere, and so they attempted to outflank Hitler after the fact by inviting the Hungarian officials Imrédy and de Kánya to Rome, whereupon they attempted to persuade Budapest toward closer relations with Yugoslavia to the end that Yugoslavia would fill the place occupied by Austria in the Rome Protocols. But increasing pressure on Hungary occasioned by Germany's new position in the Balkans and her own jockeying for position, made Hungary reluctant to give the impression of joining any bloc for the present.

Surrounding much of the success of German policy in the Balkans was the question of Russia. The Germans constantly played up the anti-Bolshevik theme as a reason for interest in the Balkans, as a reason for opposing revisionism, and as a reason for the linking of all Teutons against the Slavs. It had a remote meaning with regard to Anschluss, but a terrifying one in its aftermath. For should an assault on Czechoslovakia be made by Berlin, implementation of the Czech-Soviet Mutual Assistance Pace would very likely take place, which was certain to bring Soviet troops onto Balkan territory. In this regard, it was recognized everywhere that with Austria gone, Czechoslovakia would be the next victim, and the fear of Russian involvement imposed across Balkan territory was just one more reason for the Balkans to shift toward Berlin.

Repercussions of Anschluss were felt everywhere in the Balkans especially concerning the security of frontiers. The Yugoslav Minister suggested that a German statement regarding frontier inviolability be made as did the Hungarian Minister (after being rebuffed on the suggestion that former Hungarian territory incorporated into Austria by the Treaty of Trianon be returned). German Foreign Minister Ribbentrop's reply to the Hungarian request was along the lines that assurances were ad hoc only, "that is applicable to the period during which German troops were moving into Austria."[30]

Besides concern with frontiers, there was skepticism that Balkan neutrality could be safeguarded either from within or without. Henceforth King Carol of Rumania told the German Minister in Rumania that though he regarded Anschluss as inevitable, he feared its manner could lead to complications with England and France. He, therefore, warned against direct pressure on Czechoslovakia and pressed for a German disavowal of the Iron Guard. At the same time, however, it was recognized that a blow had been struck by Anschluss to the Little Entente and that there would be little interference from these countries. In this regard the Rumanians told the German Minister that in effect the fate of Czechoslovakia was doomed due to Yugoslavia's declination of an invitation to a meeting of the Little Entente.[31]

*   *   *   *   *

German reoccupation of the Rhineland laid the basis for Hitler's subsequent moves East. The resulting French inability to defend their interests in Central and Southeastern Europe, not only set up the framework for Anschluss, but altered the position of Italy. The resultant crumbling of the Stresa Front turned Rome from friend to foe, and it dashed hopes of a general settlement in intra-Balkan affairs, reawakening revisionist impulses which Hitler could so diabolically exploit. The Balkans altered their policies accordingly, maneuvering as best they could via policies of "balance" and capitulating when they had to in March of 1938.

Thus, the annexation of Austria, which was the cornerstone of the Central European arch and the heart of a historical unity embracing the Balkans, initiated the Nazi drive to the Southeast. Geographically, Anschluss was intended to and did surround Yugoslavia on three sides, for Greater Germany was now on the Italian, Hungarian and Yugoslav frontiers and within a hundred miles of the Adriatic at Trieste and Fiume. In so doing Czechoslovakia was isolated, geographically by being encircled and politically by the impotence of the Little and Balkan Ententes, both of which were dysfunctional without Yugoslavia, in turn making Rumania unlikely to act in Prague's behalf. In addition, Germany gained a key position on the Danube and economic control of the second largest Balkan trading partner.

Ancillary to the Reich's successful strategy were Hungary and Italy. Unable to act herself, Italy had given in to Berlin on the Austrian adventure, getting in return promises of Mediterranean interests and guarantees of the border at the Brenner Pass, hence a direct link to the Balkan states of Yugoslavia and Albania via the Adriatic. Hungary's role was more obtuse. In encouraging Hungary to reach a unilaterial accommodation with Yugoslavia, the Nazis had not only weakened the Little Entente but the Balkan Entente as well, as Hungary could now direct her attention to pressuring

Rumania. But Germany stopped short of any revisionist promises to Hungary not just because she would lose needed leverage in the divide-and-rule policy being pursued in the Southeast, but because of fear that a general explosion in the Balkans or any weakening of Yugoslavia or Rumania would involve the Soviet Union and threaten access to raw materials in the Balkans. With Germany on Hungary's frontier, it was impossible for Budapest to obtain revisionism except through German patronage, in effect satellitizing her and turning her into a surrogate state.

The German diplomatic emphasis on anti-Bolshevism also met warm response in the Balkans especially in Rumania, Yugoslavia, and Hungary for domestic as well as strategic and foreign policy reasons. Also, not lost on the Balkans was the absence of Western support for Austria. Thus, German control of revisionism, the Soviet bogey, and German strength versus Western appeasement made it clear in the Balkans that the most advantageous arrangement possible must be made with Germany which increasingly began to appear as a policy of neutrality, of vassalage if necessary, and of a unilateral rather than multilateral Balkan policy.

Munich and the Turkish Problem

In the move against Czechoslovakia, Germany had to reckon with support from three possible directions—Russia, the West and the Balkans. The Germans were fairly certain the Soviet Union would not act in Czechoslovakia's behalf. They based their assumption on French reticence to act which was a necessary precondition to bringing the Soviet-Czech Pact into play, the reluctance of Rumania to allow Soviet troops to transit her territory, Soviet military and political weakness, Soviet ideology which viewed all European conflicts as capitalistic wars from which, they, from a neutral position, could benefit, the pressures of Japan on the Soviet eastern flank, and the very antipathy itself of Czechoslovakia for the Soviet Union.

With regard to the West, it can be said that it was well observed and understood by the Germans (and Czechs as well) that by 1937 all post-World War I props supporting Czech independence were partially if not completely eroded away. Statements in the French press like "what do the Czechs matter to us?" or the Franco-Czech alliance should be "put to sleep" were noted in both Prague and Berlin. In fact, it was the German view that the visit of Lord Halifax and Delbos to Berlin freed Czech President Beneš to do what he had been unable to do before, that was to deal directly with the Reich in the hope of establishing better relations which would lead to the maintenance of Czech sovereignty, rather than to bow to a settlement between the Great Powers.[32]

What seemed true of the Soviet Union and the West also seemed true of East Europe and the Balkans. German Minister in Czechoslovakia, Eisenlohr said that the dysfunctionality of the League of Nations left Central Europe no hope of "erecting a dam against German need for expansion toward the Southeast." He also noted the failure of the Hodža plan, poor relations with Poland, the failure of the Little Entente to transform itself into a military alliance and to follow a common line of foreign policy, the fact that the Yugoslavs had improved relations with Italy, and that Rumania was taking a more conciliatory position toward Hungary and a more distrustful approach toward Prague and Paris. Hungary, meanwhile, was turning a deaf ear, finding it

> . . . impossible to conclude a pact of friendship with Czechoslovakia due to their wholehearted attention to revisionism from the point of view of the rights of the Crown of St. Stephen.[33]

German diplomats also noted that ethnic, historical, and cultural differences made both Austria and Czechoslovakia unpopular sentimentally in the Balkans. The Bulgarians said of the Czechs—they are the "Jews among the Slav peoples," and Bulgarian King Boris even accused them of collaboration with the Russians in the subversion of Bulgaria.[34]

In a speech on February 20, 1939 and then in directives on April 22 and May 30, Hitler moved to destroy Czechoslovakia. The military aim was to "help increase the total war effort" and in conversations with the Hungarians he referred to territorial aims.[35] From the political point of view, Hitler aimed to divide East Europe north and south not only isolating Poland but the Balkans as well, for he planned to keep the Carpatho-Ukraine not in the interests of a drive against Russia, but as a "pawn" to satisfy Hungary and isolate Rumania. Hitler's confidence that the conquest would be conducted with the facile aid of Balkan paralysis, was not entirely enjoyed by the German diplomatic corps who worked tirelessly to assure Rumanian neutrality and Hungarian complicity as well as to blunt the often undesirable effects of Hitler's abrasive style.

German diplomatic strategy was based on the idea that the Czech problem was only "part of the problem of the Central European area" and that too much pressure on Czechoslovakia would only alienate the Czechs and alarm the West. Isolation would be the key to Czech dependence on Germany for guarantees of security, and Poland, Rumania, and Hungary were to play important roles in the scheme. As Eisenlohr envisioned:

> . . . like the Middle Ages whereby Germany should not try to lead Czechoslovakia against France, but make her dependent on the Holy Roman Empire in foreign affairs.[36]

The neutrality of Rumania was essential in order to prevent implementation of the Czech-Soviet Mutual Assistance Pact whereby Soviet troops would cross Rumania en route to Prague.[37] Using the carrot and stick approach, the German diplomats on the one hand assured Rumania that Germany had no territorial aspirations in Rumania. They arued that increased trade and especially weaponry sales would result from a Czech rape, and they approved additional sales of weaponry in August (in return for much needed Rumanian gas supplies.) They showed reserve toward the indictment of Fascist Iron Guard leader Codreanu and wherever possible, they sought to emphasize the Bolshevik threat to Rumania and the place Germany could play in Rumania's defense against this. On the other hand, Hitler expressed to the Rumanians his "disinterest" in the "territorial problems between the Balkan countries," thereby raising the dreaded prospect that for Hungarian collaboration against Czechoslovakia, revisionist claims against Rumania would be promised, or equally dangerous, a German guarantee of the Czech-Hungarian frontier which would free Hungary to pursue claims against Rumania.[38]

In the case of Hungary Germany faced the ticklish problem of wishing to utilize Hungarian revisionist aspirations against Czechoslovakia and Rumania without unleashing the Little Entente, massive revisionism, and a World War. Seasoned German diplomats like State Secretary Weizsäcker and others were clearly worried about the explosive potentialities of encouraging Budapest. The Yugoslavs had made it clear that an attack from Hungary on Czechoslovakia would indeed by a *casus foederus* for the Little Entente,[39] and German Minister in Italy, Mackensen, had reported Ciano as saying that:

> Stoyadinovich must not be manuevered by Budapest into a position which would enable the Yugoslav opposition to remind him justifiably of obligations on the part of the Little Entente.[40]

Ribbentrop and War Cabinet Minister Göring, however, who presumably represented Hitler's view, believed the pot must be kept boiling. Göring, therefore, suggested to Hungarian Minister M. Sztójay that Hungary join in the German-Czech conflict, and aboard the "Patria" at Kiel on August 23, 1938, Hitler told Prime Minister Imrédy and Foreign Minister Kánya that those "who desired revision must seize opportunity by the forelock."[41] Likewise, Ribbentrop discouraged Hungary from coming to any accommodation with the Little Entente scolding Csáky for carrying on "negotiations with the Little Entente to which, of course, Czechoslovakia also belonged." On the other hand, Hitler welcomed any accommodation Hungary could come to individually with members of the Little Entente to lessen the prospects of their involvement should Hungary act.[42]

Before Munich Hitler encouraged Hungarian verbal bellicosity and threats of revisionism against Balkan neighbors in order to pressure Czechoslovakia into a bilateral agreement and to neutralize the Little Entente. But he did not intend for Hungary actually to act for he told Hungarian Regent Horthy that "in this particular case, he required nothing of Hungary."[43] However, after September 15 when it became clear that a negotiated settlement with the Great Powers was in the making, Hungary was pressured to take some revisionist action on her own to forestall a settlement on purely ethnic grounds. In an interview with Sztójay on September 16, Göring belittled the Hungarian press for its quietude and the minorities for their calm, and he berated the Hungarian ministers for their failure to visit the allied ministries two or three times a day and for not demanding in clear terms the detachment of the Hungarian region of Czechoslovakia.[44] Hitler, exasperated with the way the situation was developing, reproached Hungary for not joining in and "if she did not, he would not be in a position to put in a word for Hungarian interests." Hungary, he said, should demand plebescites in the areas she claimed and not guarantee any new frontiers.[45]

Another reason Hitler began to pressure Hungary into action involved the about-face in the position of the West. Before September 15, Hitler had gained a certain confidence that the Balkans, Russia, Poland and the West had been neutralized vis-a-vis Czechoslovakia[46] and, therefore, there was no need to invoke Hungarian action at the risk of a runaway Balkan war. After, when it became clear that the Sudeten putsch was endangered by the reassertion of Western interests and that pressure tactics had failed, Hitler stepped up pressure on Hungary to threaten action on her own behalf, certain now that any such Balkan action would be localized by the will of the West to avoid war, even at the expense of the Balkans, and that any such award to Hungary would not be to Germany's detriment.

It has been written that Munich was the low point in the allied history of pre-World War II Europe. What is often not considered is how Munich was Hitler's own defeat in that he received much less territory than he had anticipated, in fact it was a defeat that he even had to make a settlement at all. In this regard, it is noteworthy that the very Balkan antagonisms which Hitler played upon to isolate Czechoslovakia, acted as a brake upon him, for he was unwilling to go allout in backing Hungarian action before Munich in fear of his own inability to delimit the field of a Balkan war.

Because in the Munich settlement the West abdicated any responsibility for settlement of minority revisionist issues outside of the Sudeten area, the primary meaning of Munich for the Balkans was that revisionism was completely in the hands of Germany; for Germany it was the recognition that revisionism, particularly based on minorities was a Pandora's Box which once opened, ran the risk of a runaway Balkan situation, easily defying delimitation and that greater control might be needed; and for both was the recognition that revisionism could bring outside intervention and war.

The Rumanians, for instance, believed that any solution which might avert war would promise an unhappy precedent for Rumania with her large minorities,[47] while the Poles saw the situation wherein if German troops moved into Czechoslovakia, Poland would seize Teschen and Slovakia, in turn causing Russia to attack with the French and English then taking Stalin's side.[48] In other quarters there were worries that the Czechs might provoke intervention by Hungary, thus bringing Yugoslavia and Rumania into it,[49] and the *Papulo D'Italia* published an article attributed to Mussolini to the effect that the solution could not be limited to Sudeten Germany, but must be extended to Hungary.[50] Even the Soviets in an article in *Pravda* entitled "A Game of Fire" noted the danger of French and English support for a minority settlement based on the number of racial population involved.[51] Adding fuel to this unstable situation, was the fact that the major brake on Hungarian revisionism, the Little Entente, had been largely destroyed by the assault of one of its members, Czechoslovakia.

The other meaning of Munich was that fear of German power in the absence of Western defense, caused the Balkans to be bludgeoned by the Germans into further economic concessions and then into neutrality when the West did begin to assert itself. In Greece, for instance, when British, French, Italian, and German propaganda was vying for the Greek heart by means of institutes, fairs, trade missions, theater presentations, and fleet visits, no subsidized propaganda could match the tremendous impression made on the Greeks by Anschluss and the Czech settlement, the Greek having gained, according to U.S. Minister MacVeagh, a fearful respect for German "cunning and her might on land."[52]

In reviewing the events of the Munich period, the question of why Hitler came to an agreement with the West, which was obviously distasteful to him, is a salient one. German documents suggest that while Berlin was certain of Little Entente neutralization, Western inertia, Soviet self-interest, and Hungarian chauvinism in the isolation of Czechoslovakia, there was surprise at Czech resistance, a hesitation when it came to going all out in the use of revision, and lurking unease with regard to Turkey. It is very possible that Hitler regarded the isolation of Czechoslovakia as complete, except for the very important Straits region which yet could bring Soviet and British interests into play and through which help could be brought to Rumania and Czechoslovakia, and it was this insecurity which drove him to his own appeasement at Munich. Turkey gained even greater importance after Munich, in that with the Little Entente destroyed, any Balkan collective action now rested with the Balkan Entente of which Turkey was a key member.

The remilitarization of the Rhineland had had a special meaning for Turkey in that it threatened the collective security system of the Straits as embodied in the Lausanne Agreement. Turkey, therefore, took steps to gain greater control over the Straits and littoral by the working out of a new agreement, the Montreux Convention (July 20, 1936) from which Germany and Italy were excluded because of their aggressive policies. While Germany found the provision giving Turkey permission to remilitarize the

Dardanelles during time of war threatening, it was at the same time recognized that the Convention was not altogether to Germany's disadvantage in that it had somewhat disengaged Turkish actions from the West.

On January 5, 1937 the Germans emphasized to Turkey that Germany's naval position had deteriorated since the Convention as the Russian Black Sea fleet could not pass easily into the Mediterranean while her coast was safe from attack, and then they threatened not to abide by it. The Turks replied on March 9 to the effect that they were only trying to serve their own cause of order and security and not to discriminate. State Secretary Weizsäcker then suggested dropping the threatening tone toward Turkey and replacing it with one which followed the Turkish line of reasoning stressing equality by seeking to obtain equal rights via a separate agreement with Turkey. To this initiative the Turks were evasive citing "legal obstacles" to German accession to the Montreux Convention by way of a bilateral agreement. Ankara, however, did not exclude the possibility of revisionism without consulting the other powers, but intimated this would be dependent on a quid pro quo.[52]

The Italians took a positive view of Turkish evasiveness pointing to unstable Russo-Turkish relations as the reason for Turkish truculence, but the Germans seemed less convinced that the Soviets offered threat enough to safeguard a favorable Turkish attitude toward Germany. Due to Turkish dilatory tactics, it was not until just before Munich, July 17, 1938, that the two sides again met. This time German Foreign Minister Ribbentrop, in a conversation with Turkish Ambassador Menemencioglu asked not accession to the Convention or revisionism of it, but simply a promise of neutrality and a promise not to enter into any diplomatic combination against the other even in peacetime. But the Turks hedged again stating that so far, any such agreements were only with her neighbors.[53] Even economic pressure, which could have been considerable since about 47 percent of Turkey's exports and 35 percent of her imports was engaged with Germany, did not produce the desired political results.

The primary reason Turkey could hold out against Germany was its relationship with Russia which had been warm and friendly in the 1930s despite some differences at Montreux. But there were other reasons too, for instance—the lack of revisionist aspirations or minority problems, the strength of the Turkish-Rumanian-Yugoslav-Greek coalition against Bulgaria, the straddled position of Turkey between Mediterranean and

Balkan interests and hence between the interests of Italy and Britain on
the one hand and Germany on the other hand, and last but not least the
superb Turkish capacity for, as von Papen put it, *"paz arlik"* or prolonged
bargaining and just plain audacity.

* * * * *

There is a certain irony in attempting to answer the question of what
part the Balkans played in the Munich agreements, for though they all,
except Turkey, in some measure played to Hitler's tune by placing their
neutrality and revisionism above support for Czechoslovakia, it is unlikely
that their actions had any real effect on the key decision of the West to
dissolve Czechoslovakia on the basis of ethnic principles, a decision which
was based on military unpreparedness and a misplaced morality. Given this
position, it it unlikely that the West, even if the Balkans had settled their
disputes and collectively supported Czechoslovakia, would have taken any
road other than the one they chose, for they wished above all to avoid
war. On the other hand, Balkan instability and Turkish truculence may
have given the West the leverage it needed to impose on Germany its compromise solution to the Czech problem.

Though Hitler did not like the Munich solution, it had benefits enough
in the Balkans for the moment. The Little Entente had been destroyed,
the Hungarian position vis-a-vis Rumania and Yugoslavia had been strengthened, the common Hungarian-Polish frontier idea had been put to rest,
Russia had become embittered, the Yugoslav internal situation had become aggravated, and the Balkans had been impressed that the West was
so uncertain of the moral position it had created at Versailles, that revisionism was threatened now by the West itself. Impotent, the Balkans
watched while Hitler set into motion the machinations leading to the total
dissolution of Czechoslovakia, placing Germany on the frontiers of the
Balkans and Poland.

Victory of Divide and Rule—Prague

That Hitler did not intend to be content with the settlement reached at
Munich is clear in his Directive to the Wehrmacht shortly after Munich in
October 1938 outlining the final dissolution of Czechoslovakia "to secure

the German frontiers and occupy Memeland."[54] As had been written in *Mein Kampf,* the aim of the Czech maneuver was not as a prelude to an invasion of Russia or Poland or any of the Balkan countries, but in the interest of securing Germany's rear in order to make war against France. The hope was that control of Czechoslovakia would cut Poland off from the Balkans, promote the occupation of Memel cutting Poland off from the West, further encircle Yugoslavia, immobilize the Balkan Entente countries by threat of Hungarian and Bulgarian revisionism, and create a benevolent buffer between Germany and Russia, thus moving all of East Europe into the German camp, without the necessity of occupation, the latter move being unnecessarily provocative to Russia and the West.

The dissolution of Czechoslovakia was to be consummated along the same lines as Anschluss and Munich, that is by political pressure capped with a military solution. To bring the political aspect about, Hitler used the same tactics in the Balkans he had so successfully used before during Anschluss and Munich, that is Hungarian, Bulgarian and Polish revisionism, and to this he added Slovak and Ruthenian nationalism. Since the Munich Agreement pertained only to the Sudetenland, the West had given a blank check to Hitler to settle minority problems now pressed upon Czechoslovakia from other quarters.

Poland and Hungary had hoped to enrich themselves at Czechoslovakia's expense and protect themselves against German encroachment by creating a common Polish-Hungarian frontier, a plan which was wholeheartedly supported by Italy, bitterly opposed by Rumania and the other Balkan states, and unacceptable to Hitler until Czechoslovakia had been destroyed. Therefore, only Teschen was ceded to Poland, but this revisionist reward and the support Warsaw gave to Italy and Hungary during the Munich crisis rather than to the Little Entente, resulted in Polish isolation from the Balkans. Though Polish Foreign Minister Colonel Beck stated that he did not collaborate with Hitler in taking Teschen, merely demanding equal treatment regarding the ethnic settlement,[55] it was not lost on the Balkans that Polish security was seen in terms of access to the Baltic and the West, in friendship with Hungary, and in balance between Germany and Russia, not in its connections with the Little or Balkan Entente countries.

Hungarian revisionism was not so simple, directly affecting every country in the Balkans and Russia, for should any parts of the Carpatho-Ukraine

(Ruthenia) or Slovakia fall to Hungary, there was danger of a general Balkan revisionist explosion led by Bulgaria with counteraction from Rumania, Yugoslavia, and Greece, and Russia too would likely be involved. German documents make it clear that at no time during the German-Czech and Hungarian-Czech border negotiations did Germany have any intention of relinquishing either Slovakia or the Carpatho-Ukraine, that both were to be used for the following aims—the destruction of the Czech state, as an enticement to keep Hungary in the Axis orbit, to threaten Rumania and Yugoslavia into dependence, and to prevent creation of a

> . . . compact block of succession states on the German eastern frontier with lines of communication to Southeast Europe, and to dissolve the relationship of Czechoslovakia with the USSR as early as possible.[56]

Though Hitler commented that Slovakia and the Carpatho-Ukraine had values as a nucleus for further development in the East and Foreign Minister Ribbentrop noted that it was the point of least resistance possessing rich timber, mining and armaments, for the moment the basic idea of German policy, said Hitler, was to keep both irons in the fire and to shape matters vis-a-vis Czechoslovakia, Hungary, and Rumania in the German interest "according to the way the situation develops."[57] Therefore, rather than creating two weak independent states, or autonomous states oriented to Poland or Hungary, it was decided that autonomy within Czechoslovakia oriented toward Germany would best further German aims.

This was not the situation on the Hungarian-Czech border, however, where revisionism seemed safe and acceptable. At first, in order to take German interest out of the world's eye and to indirectly pressure Czechoslovakia into a more dependent position vis-a-vis Germany, Berlin encouraged a direct Hungaro-Czech border settlement. Hitler advised October 12, 1938 that "should Hungary mobilize, it is not our intention to hamper the Hungarians . . . or even advise them in moderation."[58] But the Hungarian inability to limit her demands, the resistance of Yugoslavia and Rumania, and the breakdown of the Hungarian appeal to the Great Powers for a solution, caused Germany and Italy to promote their role as mediator on the condition that Hungary accept the conditions as final.

The resultant Vienna Awards of November 1, 1938, according to Ribbentrop, were based completely on ethnographic principles though they failed to include Pressburg (which Göring saw as a bridgehead), Neutra (the old capital of Slovakia), and Sevljusch in the Carpatho-Ukraine.[59] Hungary readily accepted the Award, Czechoslovakia less so as Germany refused to guarantee the new frontier. Poland, meanwhile, was deeply disappointed at the failure to create a common Hungarian-Polish frontier, but the fact that Poland blamed Hungary rather than Germany, had the advantage to Hitler of furthering Balkan-Hungarian antagonisms while creating a Polish-Hungarian rift (later intensified by the guarantees).

Having reached the saturation point in the dissolution of Czechoslovakia by means of Hungarian revisionism, Germany now looked to a nationalist solution. Encouraged by Berlin were the Slovak and Ruthenian separatists.[60] But instability in the area only served to whet Hungarian appetites once again. This time Hitler moved visibly to block any such Hungarian claim in order to bring Slovakia and Ruthenia to the realization that only with Germany could the two areas achieve their aims of more national independence from Prague and security from Hungary.

However, when the nationalist clamor failed to raise the Czech mood to a pitch sufficient to cause an incident attendant to the German invasion, and further, when Prague appealed to Rome, Paris, and London on the guarantee question, Hitler reverted back to Hungary to bring the desired crisis about. In an obscure exchange referring to "operation spare parts," Hungarian Regent Horthy wrote to the Führer that plans were already laid "for a frontier incident on Thursday, March 16, 1939, to be followed on Saturday by the big thrust," and he expressed to the Führer his happiness, "for this headwater region is, in fact, for Hungary—I dislike using big words—*a vital question.*"[61] Recalling that their timidity at Munich had left them with nothing, Hungarian Minister Baron Bessenyey, with characteristic Hungarian bravado and an apparent lapse of memory regarding Germany's role, informed the diplomatic community that Hungary had decided to occupy the Carpatho-Ukraine and thereby confront Germany with a *fait accompli,* adding that was the only kind of action Hitler respected and that it was useless to negotiate with men of Hitler's caliber who "do not understand the ordinary language of diplomacy."[62]

With Hungary poised on the Ruthenian border, Hitler proceeded to promise Slovakia independence and to soothe Italian fears. When Hungarian troops did cross over and Slovakia proclaimed her independence, the Reich announced to the world that to carry out the Munich agreements and secure the peace of Europe, Germany would move her troops across the border on March 15, 1939. On the same day and for the same reason —to safeguard order and peace in Central Europe, Czech President Hácha, said he had "placed the fate of the Czech people and country in the hands of the Führer of the German Reich." The payoff for Hungary was the Carpatho-Ukraine which the Reich softened for the Ruthenians by the stipulation that it would be granted autonomy under its own viovoide, an acceptable solution in the face of Rumanian pressures.

Rumania, meanwhile, was pacified by the German promise that no Hungarian advance would be made east of a line running north from Huszt and that the status quo would be maintained. The need for pacification efforts may have been more immediate than appeared on the surface, for according to U.S. Minister Hibbard, there could have been an all-out Hungarian-Rumanian war and the consequent dangers of Russian involvement.[63] Apparently, when Poland took Teschen and the Carpatho-Ukraine was established, Beck had offered Rumania a small strip of land embodying 14-15 kilometers inhabited by Carpatho-Rumanians, but Rumania refused, partly due to loyalty to the Czechs, but also in order to avoid offering to Hungary a revisionist example. Rumania seems later to have regretted the decision, and when Rumanian Foreign Minister Gafencu visited Poland in February, both agreed that if further revisions occurred, Rumania would get this strip of land.

The opportunity came at Prague when German objection to the occupation of the Carpatho-Ukraine was removed. Rumanian troops moved to the border, but Hungarian troops were more prompt, and at this point both Germany and Yugoslavia urged Hungarian restraint. Fully in control of the situation, Hitler guaranteed the new border, so that when the Carpatho-Rumanians petitioned Rumania for reannexation, the Rumanians abstained from taking action. The volosin then petitioned Berlin for a free Carpatho-Ukraine like the Slovaks, but the Germans simply directed the petition to Mussolini as a gesture, pretending Roman control. Among the advantages to Germany was the fact that a strong anti-Russian front had been created by the new Polish-Hungarian frontier while pacifying the Kremlin, for Hungarian rather than German occupation of the Carpatho-Ukraine indicated Nazi disinterest for the moment in a thrust into Russia.[64]

To the rest of the world, the German occupation of Bohemia and Moravia flew flat in the face of all Hitler's promises and principles. For them, it was the end of appeasement and the beginning of resistance, but there was disquiet and uncertainty as to Hitler's intentions. Debate centered around the question of whether Hitler would drive east into Poland or Rumania or west into France, and that speculation centered around Rumania and her oil fields was only natural, for Munich and Prague were for Rumania what Anschluss had been for Yugoslavia.

There was another reason besides oil why it appeared Rumania might be the next victim and that involved the national minorities in Rumania which were well organized and supported by their mother countries. And as several Balkan military attaches put it, supporting irredentist claims suits Hitler, and "nowadays what Hitler says goes."[65] The extent and nature of Rumanian paralysis in this regard was well illustrated during the Hungarian-Czech border rectification and then during the grant of the Carpatho-Ukraine, and it was an even more persuasive tactic after Prague when Rumania found herself surrounded.

Hungary was Rumania's major threat and Germany used this vulnerability skillfully. After Munich, Hungary had made it clear to Rumania that Budapest expected the other members of the Little Entente to remain neutral in Hungary's dispute with Czechoslovakia which was in their view of a bilateral nature and dependent on the reaching of a minorities agreement.[66] When Rumanian Minister in Germany, Petrescu-Comnen expressed concern over Hungarian attempts to obtain territory occupied by Slovaks and Ruthenians, German Minister Fabricius replied that while his Government did not support such claims, Germany would not intervene.

This position, King Carol's acknowledgment that the possibility of aid on the part of the West and Russia to Czechoslovakia was remote, and then the October 31, 1938 meeting between Yugoslavia and Bulgaria at Nish threatening Yugoslav defection from Rumania's side, increased the feeling in Bucharest that Rumania must find her place at the side of Germany in order to survive in her present form. The Rumanians, therefore, sought closer ties with Germany via trade negotiations committing Rumania to increased grain deliveries, and then King Carol went to Berlin to kowtow before Hitler.

During this encounter which took place on November 24, 1938, Hitler again successfully used the tactic of threat and assurance regarding Rumania's frontier. Hitler told King Carol that all German foreign policy problems were now solved and that the only German aim in Southeast

Europe was to increase trade, but he did not make any concrete commitment regarding the Rumanian wish to keep Hungary out of the Carpatho-Ukraine. Because King Carol was well aware that Germany was spending large sums to stir up agitation against him and his regime largely among the minorities, Hitler was able to obtain a pledge that while Rumania would not be openly anti-Russian "because the vast Russian state was her neighbor," she would pledge never to permit the passage of Russian troops.[67]

Meanwhile, the Vienna Awards and news of King Carol's visit to the Führer caused tremendous internal pressure to mount in Bulgaria against the Kiosseivanov Cabinet for what was labeled a timid stand on the question of revisionism. The opposition called the Salonika agreement with the Balkan Entente as weak-willed for it allowed Turkish fortifications along the Bulgarian-Turkish frontier, and it pointed to the loss of prestige suffered by the attempt to consolidate the Friendship Pact with Yugoslavia by means of border revisionism and to the new trade agreement with Greece which appeared to have no tangible advantages. This caused the Bulgarian Minister President to bring up revisionist claims against Rumania, Greece, and Yugoslavia, and particularly to record with Berlin in November 1938, Bulgarian interest in Dobruja and in December interest in a Bulgarian outlet to the Aegean Sea. In January 1939, Sofia went a step further approaching Hungary with the idea that the two countries run parallel action in pressing claims against Rumania in Transylvania and Dobruja, but Hungary declined.[68]

Berlin's response until Prague was to maintain reserve toward Bulgarian revisionist aspirations and not to press adherence to the Anti-Comintern so as to prevent antagonizing and alarming Rumania, or in any other way endangering the fragile Balkan peace. This position was strengthened by the Greek response to Munich and its aftermath. German Minister in Greece, Erbach, reported in early October 1938, that while the Metaxas Government wished to remain neutral, Greek public opinion and the press were hostile to Germany during the Czech crisis and therefore they found salvation in collaboration with the European Powers. After the First Vienna Awards Metaxas was adamant in stating that "Greece would fight if Bulgaria attacked any one of the Balkan powers, and Turkey would aid her."[69] But, under pressure of a French loan to Bulgaria, certain of Rumanian paralysis, and with Bulgaria's economic and military potential in mind, Germany supported on the day of the Prague occupation an extension of arms credits to Bulgaria.[70]

While the external Yugoslav position had been fairly well neutralized by Anschluss, the Czech crisis had repercussions internally, threatening the carefully worked out German Balkan peace. Pressured by increasing anti-German sentiment and a more vociferous Croat independent movement, Prince Paul sacrificed the pro-German anti-Croat Foreign Minister Stoya-dinović, ousting him in early 1939. The Germans watched the situation closely, but in the end concluded that foreign policy was not affected particularly after the new Foreign Minister, Cinkar-Marković, told Ribben-trop that the Yugoslav aim was to adjust Yugoslav policy still further to-ward Germany.[71] It was also hoped that the personnel shift might even help Germany in that it signaled the end of Serbian influence and more power to the Croats who had close ties with the German culture. Specula-tion turned to reality when Yugoslavia, without a murmur, acquiesced in Czechoslovakia's dissolution. Thus did Hitler successfully orchestrate the dissonant themes of Balkan politics to produce the revised and more use-ful harmony he sought.

* * * * *

The events of the Munich to Prague period served to enhance the strangle-hold Germany held over the Balkans. At first direct German penetration seemed to threaten, but when the Carpatho-Ukraine passed to Hungary, it was the indirect threat of Hungarian and Bulgarian revisionism, the strings of which were controlled in Berlin, which was uppermost in Balkan minds. Meanwhile, the Yugoslav position had deteriorated to the point that Belgrade abandoned Czechoslovakia, sought a unilaterial accom-modation with Bulgaria at Nish, kowtowed at Berlin, refashioned the makeup of its internal political system, and looked for salvation in the shady and dubious game of playing off against each other, Axis partners Germany and Italy. But less than a month after Prague, Belgrade had lost control of this diplomatic scheme too when the Italians, with Berlin's acquiescence, invaded Albania.

Meanwhile, Rumania was endangered on all sides. In the south loomed threats of Bulgarian revisionism whose voice had been strengthened by Munich, the first Vienna Awards and Prague. In the west, Hungary, streng-thened by the Awards and then by occupation of the Carpatho-Ukraine, was rapidly surrounding Rumania's vulnerable Transylvanian frontier. In the north, Poland's balancing act between Russia and Germany provided little security.

And, the path to western Europe had been wiped out. Though Turkey's position remained independent enough to allow allied weaponry through the Straits, it was apparent at Munich that there were no such armaments available. Adding to the tragedy was the fact that the threat to the Balkans looming on the horizon was uneven, so that while those close to Germany and Italy trembled, those in the second ranks, Bulgaria, Greece, and Turkey, remained passive and undisturbed. In Greece, for instance, while the rest of Europe was in turmoil, the people lived quietly and prospered in 1938, uncertain of who was the enemy or of which way to go. Meanwhile, the Turks, certain of their place at Britain's side should there be a war in the Mediterranean were unconcered with Rumania's problems and fearful of a Slavic bloc.

The Soviet Union, insulted and threatened by the Western failure to include them at Munich, withdrew to pursue the buildup of her own defenses, and with it the possibility of Soviet-Western restraint on Germany vanished. Surrounded, Rumania signed an economic agreement with Germany which both the Germans and the world saw as synonymous with political dependence. With the Little Entente destroyed and two partners of the Balkan Entente under threat of strangulation, the other two Balkan Entente powers, Greece and Turkey were preparing their own path to neutrality.

Conclusion

By April, 1939, the Rhineland, Anschluss, Munich, Prague, and the German southeastern economic offensive made clear in Germany, in the Soviet Union and in the world what had already been well learned in the Balkans, that is, they must "make their own peace in time with the new masters of Europe." The *Balkan Herald* struck the theme noting that:

> Only neutrality—and their own closer unity in such a firm bloc as the Balkan Entente—can preserve (the Balkan States) from a future full of uncertainty.

And Rumanian Foreign Minister M. Grigore Gafencu's paper the *Timpul*

(Bucharest) said "Germany has her plans; have other countries their plans? If other powers have no plans we must perforce go with Germany." From Great Britain came Chamberlain's appeasing words, "Geographically, Germany must occupy a dominating position in central and southeastern Europe."[72] The Balkans had become hostage to Berlin.

Germany had played a skillful hand in obtaining what she wanted in the Balkans—resources, peace, isolation, and neutralization, in short a string of benevolent and benign buffer states able to shield her from Russia when she turned on the West. Meanwhile, Poland was cut off from the Southeast and hence Western aid. By preferential trade, currency and arms agreements, by playing on internal divisions and claims, by malevolent use of Hungarian, Italian and Bulgarian irredentism and revisionism and then posing as defender of the status quo, by the coalescing of German minorities, she had destroyed the Balkan alliances and so paralyzed the Balkans that they became silent accomplices in the destruction of Austria and Czechoslovakia. The Balkans, in turn, abandoned by the West, flanked by a distrustful Russia, faced with a powerful Germany, and consumed with a nationalism which stood firmer than Balkan federalism, fell back upon their own unilateral resources to come to the best terms possible with the Reich. They operated from the assumption that any deviation from strict neutrality would bring war to the Balkans and the certain destruction of their sovereignties, while cooperation in the German plan for the Balkans and Poland, which for the moment paralleled their own, could save them.

But the tide turned when Germany forgot to adequately cultivate her own backyard. In April, Italy invaded Albania, and Britain, by the reintroduction of her power, threatened the carefully worked out Balkan peace, ultimately reintroduced Soviet power, and invoked the specter that Poland might not capitulate. The Italian drive was a direct territorial threat as well as a revisionist one, and all Balkan states, status quo and revisionist alike, looked to the other Axis power, Germany, to dilute this threat. The nature of the British guarantees, meanwhile, served only to enhance Russia's importance, shore up Balkan nationalism to the point that hopes for a common Balkan defense were destroyed, and increased the Balkan predisposition for neutrality.

The story of Germany in the Balkans from April to August 1939 is largely the continuation of an ongoing process, but with an increased tempo and a more primary focus. It included threats that British promises of defense could not be fulfilled, support for Bulgarian and Hungarian revisionism in order to thwart any enlargement of the Balkan Entente, and continuation of the economic offensive in order to tie the Balkans to Germany as a source of supply and to ensure their neutrality in the war against the West. But they were not entirely successful and, therefore, Germany shifted from a unilateral to a bilateral system of Balkan control in the East which embraced the Soviets.

CHAPTER II

GERMANY AND THE BALKANS
MARCH TO AUGUST 1939
HEGEMONY DISRUPTED

In the years following Hitler's rise to power, we have seen how the Balkans were set adrift by the West and as a result, how they gradually moved into the German orbit of economic and then political domination. With this, the Germans had what they wanted in the Southeast, making unnecessary direct attack and occupation or extensive revisionism, either of which would have brought the interests of the Soviet Union, Italy, and Great Britain into play and very likely a second World War along with it. Such a situation was not incompatible with Balkan aims in that national existence was preserved, there was protection against Italy and the Soviet Union, and a symbiosis of economic interests was assured. This was not true of Poland, however, where size, geo-political positioning, nationalism, and a stronger and more diversified economic base made resistance to domination more possible and hence likely.

The dissolution of Czechoslovakia (and Hungarian occupation of Ruthenia) on March 15 and then the invasion of Albania on April 7, however, abruptly ended the complacency into which the Balkans had drifted. Balkan national survival was suddenly placed in jeopardy, for it appeared that Germany, or more likely Axis partner Italy, might actually invade, that any such move might threaten Soviet Black Sea and Danubian interests to the extent that the Soviets would become involved, or that uncontrolled Balkan revisionism might be unleashed. For these reasons, the

36

British guarantees of frontiers were welcomed. But the reintroduction of British power threw the whole German program into limbo, for Balkan loyalties were put in question and the unilateral control Germany had wielded over Balkan revisionism was now dissipated. A new German program of Balkan unification was the result, a program which sought one avenue after the other to neutralize the area. The German-Rumanian Economic Agreement, the Pact of Steel, and the anti-encirclement were the foundations of the new German effort, which was really an effort in counterpoint to offset the guarantees, the invasion of Albania, and the Anglo-Turkish Declaration. The effort proved insufficient, not because it did not work its will on the Balkan states, but because Western resistance brought the interests of the Soviet Union into play and hence the need to deal with the Balkans on a new level, that is within the framework of Great Power politics. The final juxtaposition in preserving the Balkan status quo came when the West threatened to bring Russia to its side, with the resulting Nazi-Soviet Non-Aggression Pact.

The German-Rumanian Economic Agreement and the Guarantee to Poland

The action taken on March 15, 1939 against Czechoslovakia confirmed that Hitler's aims were not confined solely to the German ethnic group, and that:

> In light of what has taken place in Europe in the past year no small state or group of states would dare resistance to a German attack without the certain immediate and effective support of these two countries. [Great Britain and France.] [1]

Likewise, the West began to realize that East Europe held a key defensive position for them and that this defensive line was already in a precarious position. The Hungarians[2] and Germans sought to soothe the West back into complacency, saying that:

> A definite development is occurring in all Southeastern Europe and this development would be hindered by German interference in Rumania and Hungary.[3]

But the Western nations by now were suspicious that Hitler was simply seeking to counteract war rumors, and in any case they had had enough of appeasement.

The focus of Hitler's intent in the view of Paris and London began to center on Rumania for a number of reasons. First, there were reports of German pressure for a trade agreement. Second, there were indications that Germany meant to use Hungary as a catspaw against Rumania or as a base for invasion. In this connection it was feared that Hungarian revisionism in Translyvania would be touched off by Hitler's move into Ruthenia, and in this case Rumania had no assurances of support from her Balkan neighbors who had pledged help only against Bulgaria.[4] At the same time Bucharest and Budapest had made known their determination to defend against the other, the danger being that a Rumanian-Hungarian explosion would give Germany reason to step in.

In London, the Rumanian Minister, Tilea, aroused fear that Germany was about to gain control of Rumanian oil, and ultimately of Ukrainian wheat, as well as access to a base of operation on the Black Sea. Tilea intimated that Rumania had been presented with an ultimatum by Germany despite King Carol's and Foreign Minister Gafencu's insistence that this was not so.[5] Though some authors emphasize the importance of Tilea's assertion in directing British thinking toward extension of guarantees to Rumania,[6] it is more likely that Britain's own considerations were paramount. On March 18, 1939 the British Chief of Staff's assessment was that if Berlin controlled Rumanian oil, a wartime blockade would be nullified, directly threatening Greece, Turkey, and the eastern Mediterranean.

On the other hand, Tilea's activities may have had a great deal to do with the direction in which British diplomatic efforts thereafter proceeded, for while the idea of organizing the Southeast into some sort of defensive peace front was already prevalent in Western thinking, Tilea, in reiterating it, gave the impression that this too was the Balkan hope. In his interview with the British Foreign Office on March 17, Tilea requested the British Government to consider whether it might be possible to "construct a solid block of Poland, Rumania, Greece, Turkey, (and) Yugoslavia with the support of Great Britain and France." Tilea went on to note that the idea had added appeal because it was believed that under these circumstances Russia would help them out, and then he went on to suggest that in the first place Rumania and Poland might be asked to make their treaty of mutual assistance applicable to the case of Rumania being a victim of German aggression (it was presently applicable only against the Soviet Union), and then that the members of the Balkan Entente would be requested to proclaim their "joint determination to guarantee each other's frontiers."[7]

The weaknesses of this approach were immediately evident. Poland preferred to safeguard Rumania by urging conciliation in Hungarian-Rumanian relations rather than by an outright pledge of aid if Rumania was attacked. Then, when British diplomats in Warsaw, Athens, Ankara, Belgrade and Moscow (the latter had not been on Tilea's list) tried to ascertain what the attitude would be if Rumania were attacked, the results were unsatisfactory in that the small states felt that was putting the cart before the horse, as the small states would decide in accordance with Great Britain and France who must first define their own attitudes. They also feared economic and political censure by Germany, particularly after the British told Gafencu among others that they could not supply "anything approaching the quantities of weaponry requested." Unsatisfactory also was the reply received from Moscow in which Soviet Foreign Minister Litvinov asked the British whether they wished the USSR to undertake and help Rumania while keeping their own hands free.[8]

Noting the rejection of the smaller states to commit themselves in front of the Big Powers, Great Britain and France groped for some multilateral commitment particularly on the part of Poland through whose territory allied supplies and troops could come. Having rejected a Soviet proposal for a Six-Power Conference (France, Poland, Britain, Rumania, Turkey) to discuss joint action (the Soviet bogey was as pertinent to the British program in East Europe as to the German),[9] March 20 the British proposed a Four-Power (France, Poland, USSR) statement to the effect that there would be immediate consultation and joint action should Rumania be threatened. On March 21 Colonel Beck had a conversation in Berlin with Ribbentrop during which considerable pressure was exerted on Warsaw with regard to Danzig, the Corridor, and the Anti-Comintern Pact. It is not surpising, therefore, that on March 22 Beck rejected the proposal on the basis that for Russia and Poland to appear as cosignatories, would be tantamount to serving notice in Berlin that Poland had abandoned her policy of balance, thus provoking immediate and disastrous action against Poland. Back to square one, the British turned to the idea of limiting the question of Polish assistance to Rumania recognizing that Britain and France must make a smilar pledge to Rumania and Poland, and it was hoped that under those circumstances Poland and Rumania might not object to Soviet help.

Beginning on March 21 three events occurred which shifted the British-French focus of concern from Rumania to Poland. The first was the German occupation of Memel on March 21 giving Germany a direct line of attack on Poland through Lithuania. The second was the placing of Slovakia under Germany's protection, allowing Poland to be surrounded by Germany on three sides. The third was the publication on March 24 of the Rumanian-German Economic Agreement. While this treaty indicated to Germany and the West that Rumania's foreign policy had been completely neutralized since March 15, it also indicated that, for the moment, if Rumania would capitulate, Germany's interest in Rumania was economic only. A quasi-settlement with Rumania also meant that all German forces could be turned against Poland.

In the successful conclusion of this treaty, the Germans had played a skillful hand against Rumania, utilizing Rumanian fears of her avaricious neighbors and directly applying pressure against Rumanian contacts with the West. On the signing of the treaty on March 23, Wohlthat noted to Göring that the Rumanians were forced to leave the deliberations due to the critical situation at home. According to the Polish Minister in Hungary, this had been due to a German-Hungarian plan worked out on March 19 whereby Germany approved Hungarian seizure of Ruthenia on the condition that Hungary place an army on the Rumanian border to pressure Hungary into signing the trade pact, and that Germany then suggested Hungary take an additional slice of Slovakia when Rumania refused to sign.[10]

Also threatening to Rumania were the Bulgarians on the Dobruja frontier, and Russian forces were straddling Bessarabia. Despite the potentially explosive nature of the situation, the Germans were well in control, assisting the Rumanians to halt the Hungarian advance into Slovakia *after* Rumania's signature of the treaty. Meanwhile, the Germans gave no encouragement to Bulgaria, thereby blocking action of the Balkan Entente,[11] while Rumanian capitulation stalemated the Russians.

The treaty terms were within the framework of German economic plans for the Southeast, that is for a long-term reorientation of the Rumanian economy to complement the German economy. The provisions provided for an increase in and pro-German orientation of Rumanian agricultural production, the establishment of mixed German-Rumanian companies for exploitation of ores and petroleum, industrial collaboration, establishment of a free zone for trade, delivery of arms to Rumania, development of land and water communication, and public utilities, and collaboration of banks.

In German eyes, the Wohlthat Treaty had affected a beneficial symbiosis between the two countries in all areas. Hitler, in a conversation with Gafencu on April 19, 1939 said, "You give us food, we give you machines." With regard to Hungary, he told Gafencu that he would not encourage any claims against it, as long, as course, as "I may count on your friendship."[12] The point about supplying Rumania with arms which could be turned against Germany seems not to have troubled Berlin and was even seen as an advantage in the future defense against Russia. German Minister Fabricious commented:

> The arming of the Rumanian army by Germany, rather than threatening Germany, constitutes a decisive factor in the shaping of Rumanian relations with the Reich and the implementation of the Wohlthat Treaty.[13]

The Germans saw in this treaty not only an economic victory but a complete political victory as well, for it had been signed amidst Western negotiations which ended in nothing more than a unilateral guarantee, unsupported by any other Balkan or Eastern European nation or Russia. Wohlthat concluded that "rightly or wrongly the Rumanian people felt peace was assured by the treaty."[14]

The Rumanians tended to agree with the German assessment that it was not the text of the economic treaty which gave it weight, but rather its political implications. In remarks to the American Minister in Bucharest, Gunther, Rumanian Foreign Minister Gafencu admitted that concessions had been made to Germany now in order to prevent giving reason for arresting them by force later. While noting that Rumania as well as Germany benefited from the provisions of the treaty, particularly with regard to offering Rumania a steady market, the doubling and tripling of agricultural products and technical aid, he admitted it would be difficult to accept German economic aid and maintain independence.[15] A similar view surfaced in Ankara, where it was stated that an ultimatum had been substantially if not literally tendered. This subservience had farreaching consequences for the future of Balkan solidarity, the Bulgarian Prime Minister saying that it was now too late to negotiate on the question of Bulgarian adherence to the Balkan Entente as the Rumanian-German accord would nullify all obligations under the Balkan Pact.[16]

The Western view that Rumania had become by the treaty a vassal state, turned its attention in London and Paris from Rumania to Poland as the bastion of Western defense in East Europe. Having failed in an attempt at a collective or four-power guarantee, suspicious of Beck and of Russian interest, and increasingly anxious that Germany would strike before a general security system could be formed, Britain decided to act unilaterally. On March 31, 1939 Prime Minister Chamberlain went before the House of Commons to say that Britain would extend an interim guarantee until other arrangements could be resolved.[17]

The tragedy of the guarantee was soon apparent, for the very nature of the guarantee, in protecting Poland's national sovereignty, doomed hope of its extension and the formulation of "other arrangements." In the period of April 4-6, Britain tried to extend its reciprocity to Rumania, but Poland, while accepting reciprocity with Great Britain, refused to commit to Rumania due to complications with Hungary (Poland calculated that in a war with Germany, Hungary would turn against the Polish Central Industrial District), because Rumania would be of little help if Poland was attacked, and because Poland preferred Rumania, not Poland, be attacked. Stalemated, Great Britain converted an interim guarantee to a permanent one.

As far as the Balkans were concerned, the Bulgarian Prime Minister was quick to point out the fallacies to the American Minister in Sofia, Atherton. He noted that the guarantee did not in any way shift the balance of power in East Europe, and that it served only to frustrate Balkan attempts to come to any solutions among themselves as a way to avoid any revisionist concessions either to Hungary, Bulgaria, or the Soviet Union. In Kiosseivanov's view, it only served to accelerate Hitler's preparation for self-sufficiency, and it gave Hitler a new tool with which to propagandize his expansion (before it was Germany for the Germans, now it was self defense against encirclement).[18] Hitler said as much in a speech on April 1 at the Wilhelmshaven when he warned all East Europe that, "Whoever declares himself ready to pull the chestnuts out of the fire for the Great Powers must expect to get his fingers burnt in doing so."[19]

* * * * *

In retrospect, the period from March 15 to April 7 established the basic pattern of diplomacy in East Europe which brought the Nazi-Soviet Pact into being. This pattern involved Axis pressure to control the area before a turn West, Western unilateral resistance in the face of multilateral failures, and Soviet exploitation of the interplay. The Nazi move into the rest of Czechoslovakia, March 15, adroitly carried out by East European factionalism, brought the end of British appeasement and the beginning of resistance. Fearing Hitler's next move would be into Rumania, Britain and France groped for some sort of multilateral support from the Balkans and Poland. The responses were unfavorable because all were fearful of Germany, war, and consequent action of the Soviet Union and Balkan neighbors. The Soviets, meanwhile, seeing an opportunity to reenter European politics, proposed a conference composed of states key to their own defense, but the West, cautious in its relations, asked instead for a promise of aid to Rumania.

In the meantime, using Hungarian and Bulgarian revisionism and direct pressure, Hitler obtained Rumanian signature on an economic pact which appeared synonymous to vassalage. This had the effect of hardening the Bulgarian position against Rumania in the belief that the Balkan Entente had been destroyed, and it destroyed the possibilities of a link between Poland and the Southeast. Believing that Rumanian acquiescence meant that for the moment Rumania was not the target, Britain turned its attention to Poland which now appeared to be the next victim, and after unsuccessfully trying to obtain Balkan support and unwilling to bring in Russia, they extended a unilateral interim guarantee on March 31. The results for any future multilateral Balkan program were disastrous, for the guarantee in supporting the status quo, hardened the position of revisionist Bulgaria and Hungary, gave Hitler a reason to exact further political and economic concessions from the Balkans to maintain Balkan control, and took away any propensity Poland might have had to link itself with the Southeast.

At this point, it was not Hitler's desire to in any way disturb the Southeast, which he believed, he had well under control and which would be quiescent in his next move against Poland. But, his naked aggression against Czechoslovakia, had aroused not just the British, but the Italians as well, and so Rome made the next move, a more precarious one since it was directed toward a British interest more important than Rumanian oil and the North Sea, namely the Suez. In raising the ante, the importance of the Soviet Union to both sides was also elevated, and with the entrance of Italy into the Southeast, German diplomacy was vastly complicated.

The Invasion of Albania and the Gurantees to Rumania and Greece

On March 28, the war in Spain ended, freeing, in fact forcing (as no gains were made in Spain) Germany's Axis partner Italy into action elsewhere. The Spanish failure was compounded by the gains Germany and Hungary had made in Czechoslovakia, giving a sense of urgency to the growing Italian need for compensation and expansion. In Albania, the Italians, like the Germans, used Balkan factionalism and fear of Germany (as Germany used fears of the Soviet Union) to their advantage.

The Italian scheme for the invasion of Albania was apparently hatched by Foreign Minister Ciano to enhance his personal position and as a reaction to Anchluss. There were some long-term objectives as well. First mention of the idea occurred in a written report by Ciano to Mussolini on May 2, 1938 on his return from witnessing Albanian King Zog's marriage whereupon he observed that the finest wedding present came from Hitler and that the new Queen Geraldine's Hungarian relations served to bring Albania even closer to Germany.[20] During this visit the idea of using Albania as an avenue of revenge against the compliant attitude Italy had had to bear during the Austrian annexation seems to have become implanted in Ciano's mind. To the ambitious Foreign Minister, occupation of Albania would reinsure against German expansion in the Balkans, tip the Balkan balance back to where it had been before Anschluss, give Italy resources and a place for colonization, simplify the Italian naval problem by making the Adriatic a continental lake, protect Italian oil fields behind Valona, and provide a base for irredentist and separatist agitation against Yugoslavia and Greece and for military operations along the old Roman road (Via Agnatio) into Macedonia.[21] Strategically it would keep the British and French out of the Adriatic and Yugoslavia bottled up. Practically speaking, Italy could gamble where odds were in her favor, for while Tunis, Corsica, Dibouti, and Savoy raised French ire, this descended when the shouting was pointed elsewhere on a small unarmed kingdom.

In the face of uncertainty as to the limits and nature of Hitler's aims in Anschluss and Munich, and due to continued involvement in Spain with hoped for gains to offset Germany, the idea appears to have been dropped temporarily. But it reappeared again in Ciano's January 8, 1939 diary entry in a more subtle form, whereby Ciano suggested instigating a revolt by a spontaneous offer of the Albanian crown to Italian King Victor Emmanual, or a partition scheme among Hitler's hostages and enemies which would round off the Greco-Albanian frontier opposite Corfu, give Yugoslavia control over Lake Scutari, and renounce the Albanian claims to Kossovopolis.[22]

The idea of an inducement to Greece seems to have been dropped, but Yugoslavia appeared to welcome a chance to assert a little independence from Germany by playing Italy's game. According to Ciano, who met Stoyadinović on January 18-23, the Yugoslav Prime Minister suggested that problems with unrest in Albania could have two solutions—1) replacement of Zog, or 2) partition of Albania between Yugoslavia and Albania, the latter of which could be discussed more concretely and confidently at a later date. Evidently without the Regent's consent, Stoyadinović told Ciano that Belgrade accepted the Italian view that Germany was the real threat whereupon Ciano promised not to act without telling Yugoslavia, and as added inducement, he offered territorial concessions and demilitarization of the Albanian frontier, suppression of Albanian agitation for Kossovo, conclusion of a military alliance, and support for Yugoslavia when she decided to secure an outlet to the Mediterranean by occupying Salonika.[23]

Ciano concluded after his talk with Stoyadinović that Italy would encounter no difficulties with Yugoslavia as her claims were not exaggerated nor excessive. The fall of the Stoyadinović Government on February 4, 1939, which was a direct result of Prince Paul's irritation at the unauthorized liberties Stoyadinović had taken in advancing Italy's Albanian scheme,[24] served to hurry on the preparations without and if necessary against Yugoslavia who must not, in Ciano's view, have time to contact England and/or France. "With the removal of Stoyadinović," he wrote, "the Yugoslav card has lost 90 percent of its value."[25]

Ciano contemplated between April 1-9 for action. In the meantime, the Italian Ambassador in Berlin, Attolico, warned that Germany had designs on Albanian oil. Ciano suspected that Zog, warned by Yugoslavia, had attempted a countermove, but the German Ambassador in Italy, Mackensen, rapidly disclaimed any such action, reassuring Ciano of Germany's consideration for Italy. The events of March 15, 1939 lent urgency to the Italian schemes for now that the racial barriers of German expansion had been removed and the disparity of power between the two Axis powers acknowledged, Italy feared German expansion into Italy herself and into the Adriatic. For the Italian Fascists, even more to be feared was the likelihood that war would begin before Italy was ready, thus cutting her out of its benefits, and that any effort to dissociate herself from Germany might turn Germany into an enemy without any compensatory gains from the West.

Italy was not formally informed of German action until March 15, and while officially the Italians greeted it as "inevitable" and "logical," ballasted by German assurances of Italian spheres and plebiscites for non-Czech nationalities, inwardly Mussolini sulked, stating that "every time Hitler occupies a country, he brings me a message." When Ribbentrop then informed Attolico of Germany's intention to give Hungary the right to occupy the Carpatho-Ukraine while Germany occupied Bohemia and Slovakia, Mussolini again endorsed the first idea (as a bulwark against Germany) but was against the second believing that there had been sufficient gains for Germany already.[26] Resentful and worried that all German promises had been destroyed, Ciano's Albanian scheme at last found a fertile field in Mussolini's mind.

But Hitler, sensing the Italian mood, moved quickly sending a message to Rome in which he warned the Duce to put off any large-scale operations for a year or two. Thereupon Mussolini moved back into his former ambivalent state, fearing that any Albanian operation might undermine Yugoslav unity and throw Croatia into German hands, and so he countermanded the Albanian operation on March 16. But in a March 20 letter, Ribbentrop assured Ciano that Germany had no aims in the Mediterranean and he denied German interest in Croatian affairs saying that this time it was Germany's turn to be completely disinterested.[27] Added to this carte blanche, was the arrival of Croat leader Maček in Rome and with it real hope of adding Croatia. The Western attempt on March 21 to form a democratic bloc stiffened Mussolini against any appeal to the authoritarian states of Rumania, Poland, Turkey, and Greece, and finally the Italian Council's affirmation of adhesion to the Axis sealed Mussolini's course of action. Only Italian Ambassador in Germany, Attolico, voiced concern, pressing for an agreement with Germany prior to any action which would clearly define Italo-German spheres, but his pleas fell on deaf ears.

It is unclear whether Hitler really intended for Mussolini to move against Albania given the impunity with which he approached the Kaiser's "blank check" in *Mein Kampf.* On the other hand there seemed gains enough, for it would compromise Italy so she would not be against Germany in a general war, it would weaken the prestige of Italy in the Balkans making German economic and political influence more feasible, and it would provide the sop for Mussolini which he had long desired to show he had gained from the Axis. It also held the possibility of further intimidating the West and diverting attention from Poland.

At any rate, after a week of indecision after the Czech coup and without any concrete promises, Mussolini decided to push on with preparation against Albania, and on March 25 an ultimatum amounting to virtual annexation was dispatched to Tirana. When King Zog, whose wife was expecting to give birth momentarily, unexpectedly refused, a revised version was sent on April 1 with a warning of what refusal would mean. Zog skillfully jockeyed for time with counterproposals which Mussolini refused, and on April 7 the Italians invaded.

The Germans appeared to have known of and by default supported the Italian plans for action, for on April 4 Ciano told von Mackensen that "something was in the wind,"[28] and on April 6 the German Military Attache in Yugoslavia said that Italy had "not yet" occupied Albania but that it was expected at any moment.[29] When the Albanian Minister inquired of the German Under Secretary on April 5 as to what the German reaction would be to a land invasion of Albania by Italy, Woerman replied that Germany had no interest in the Adriatic and that any intervention against Italy was out of the question.[30] On the same day, Ribbentrop conveyed to Ciano the German position that "in principle" Germany "welcomes wholeheartedly any strengthening of Italy and of Italian influence," and he noted that it served to strengthen the Axis and to diminish the importance of Greece, which in any case would be easier for the Axis to influence. In a de facto circular to German missions abroad on April 7, State Secretary Weizsäcker said that the Italian action had "our complete approval and will be wholeheartedly supported by us . . . . ."[31] Meanwhile accolades poured in from missions abroad, von Papen in Turkey writing:

> The occupation and military consolidation of Albania as a 'bridge-head' is of great value for the Axis powers, as from there, the 'neutrality' of the Balkan States can in any case be assured.[32]

Clearly unfolding was the disunity of the Balkan nations, and with this the further isolation and immobilization of Yugoslavia, the erosion of the Balkan Entente, and now more important, the prevention of a multilateral Balkan defense system. Balkan antagonisms centered around Yugoslavia whom the other Balkan states accused of complicity with Germany in the Albanian move. In their own defense the Yugoslavs argued that the whole thing was German inspired, and with the Germans on their northwestern frontier, six Hungarian divisions moving to the northeastern border, and the Croat question threatening, their only hope was in siding with Italy. In addition, they pointed out that the British themselves had said that a move against Albania did not constitute a direct threat to British interests, allowing Hitler to consolidate the Axis in the area.

In this capitulation, the olive branch seems to have been tendered, for Ciano remarks in his *Diaries* on April 6 that Belgrade had inquired as to what attitude Italy would take if Yugoslavia occupied certain points on the Albanian-Yugoslav frontier. And Foreign Minister Cinkar-Marković admitted that four days before the invasion he had been advised that if Albania refused terms, Italian military action would result, and that subsequently Italy had promised "a guarantee of Yugoslav interests" meaning inviolability of frontiers. While a seeming empty concession in view of the guarantees contained in the Italo-Yugoslav Friendship Treaty of March 25, 1937, Cinkar-Marković noted that no such guarantee had been given to Greece. The local reaction to the Government's policy teetered between a philosophical acceptance based on trust that Italy would keep its word not to take action against Yugoslavia, and outright indignation over what was called a "craven and cowardly" Government policy of acquiescence.[33]

When tempers had cooled, it was certainly acknowledged that Italy had not taken Yugoslavia frankly into its confidence regarding Albania despite the Yugoslav-Italian accord, but at the time the other Balkan countries pounced all over Yugoslavia for her actions. The Turkish Minister expressed dismay at "the lies told by the Yugoslav Government previous to Italian occupation despite obligations as an ally of Turkey to keep her informed." In his opinion, Yugoslavia, having done nothing to date, could do nothing now but accept the Italian action as agreeable. The Greeks shared the Turkish resentment at not being informed as was required under the Balkan Pact, though they were charitable enough to note her precarious position.[34] Even Bulgaria, fearing a German-Italian move into the Balkans, found Belgrade's silence a most disquieting feature.[35]

Though the propensity of Greece and Turkey was to find in Yugoslav actions a scapegoat for their own fears and frustration, their own actions were no more sanctimonious. U.S. Minister in Albania, Grant, reported on April 4 that King Zog had appealed to all the Governments of the Balkan Entente whose security would be threatened to make a collective statement with a view to stopping the contemplated action. In the opinion of the Turkish Assistant Secretary of the Ministry of Foreign Affairs, Bati, such a statement was well within the purview of the Balkan Entente since the aggressive act by Germany or Italy against one of the Balkan Entente members was "projecting the aggression into the Balkans and therefore making it a Balkan state within the meaning of the Pact."[36] But no response was forthcoming. Confidentially, the Greeks said that the appeal was, perhaps, too late, while the Turkish view was that there were other questions of equal importance (particularly Bulgaria) and that Turkey would not commit herself to any policy until her vital interests were at stake which obviously did not include Bulgaria.[37]

There was also a broad divergence of opinion regarding the motivation and consequences of the move into Albania.[38] The Yugoslavs believed it was Nazi inspired, a reaction to the Polish guarantee and a sop to Italy, and they generally regarded their position now as immobilized. On the other side were the Hungarians and Rumanians who saw it as Italian in inspiration and a sign of Italo-German discord. Most, however, viewed it as a coordinated act. The Bulgarians, for instance, saw it as a definite Axis plan to prevent formation of a Balkan defense bloc. The Soviets at first followed the West's interpretation that it was a concerted Axis act, simply reproducing dispatches from abroad. But in a lead editorial in the *Journal de Moscou* on April 11 they proferred the opposite view, characterizing the invasion as an act of Italian absurdity and cruelty, saying that Albania was not an end in itself but to obtain a foothold in the Balkans to ensure its share of the spoils in case Germany took action against Yugoslavia or another Balkan country.

In the end, it was the British attitude which proved decisive and unsettling to Hitler. In London it was a call to action for it was feared that "Hitler had led from dummy" and that the real status quo in the Mediterranean had been altered threatening Corfu, Greece, and even Egypt and Gibralter.[39] Therefore, attention shifted from Poland to the Balkans where it was noted that British hesitancy in sending a fleet to the Adriatic and Greek waters had done damage enough, irritating and alienating the Southeastern states. At first aid to Yugoslavia and Bulgaria was contemplated but Yugoslavia's position was considered too precarious and it was believed Bulgaria would not accept a guarantee. Therefore, British policy began to focus on Greece and Rumania.

The Italian occupation had caused a decisive shift in the Greek attitude. The Greek reaction to the British inquiry of late March regarding the German threat to Rumania had been evasive and to the effect that everything depended on Yugoslavia, as Yugoslavia was in the "lion's mouth" due to possible attack from Germany and Bulgaria. The Greek Minister President at that time also noted the strong attraction of Greece to a like totalitarian state, and he acknowledged Greek dependence on the German tobacco market. Now, however, the decidedly anti-Italian (but pro-German) sentiment of the Greeks had been aroused, and the apparent imminent attack on Corfu, the fact that Italy gave a guarantee to Yugoslavia of their frontier but not to Greece, and the British interim guarantee to Poland which seemed to reflect some Western resolve, prompted the Greeks to send an urgent message to London regarding the security of Corfu, and ultimately to accept the guarantee.

Despite the fact that, in order to avoid complication with Britain, Italy quickly sent assurances to London and Athens that Greek integrity would be preserved, public opinion in Britain forced Chamberlain into a stronger position (in part to offset the failure of Britain to denounce the 1938 Agreement with Italy) than a mere show of British sea power off Corfu. On April 10 the British Cabinet met, and on April 11 it became known that the Prime Minister intended to announce guarantees to Greece when he spoke to the House of Commons on April 13. Berlin, learning what was in the wind, warned Greece against acceptance of the guarantee. This served to renew Greek fears to the point that when the text was received on April 12, it was with mixed feelings, and so Metaxas wanted emphasized by Chamberlain the spontaneous character of the agreement. Chamberlain bowed to this request in his speech of April 13 saying nothing to suggest that it was not a unilateral act.

Behind Greek reluctance to join anything approaching a multilateral anti-Axis front, was concern that the British and French seemed to have no policy, that the policy of encirclement would only incite Germany to further offensive action and eventually war, and that it was really a substitute for British will and a display of force. In addition, they were still concerned about the Yugoslav attitude which they regarded as of utmost importance, for if there was some assurance of military action from Belgrade, Greece could face the Italian threat with some degree of confidence. But it was realized that Yugoslavia was hemmed in on all sides, and it was feared that the Italians would quiet Yugoslavia by promises of Salonika should Italy move through this vital area en route to Greece. Though Turkey was regarded as a reliable ally, Greece doubted her willingness or ability to come to Greece's aid in an area so distant as Epiris where hostilities were certain to begin. And Bulgaria, it was expected, would be tempted by totalitarian promises of revisionism. Athens had no confidence in Rumania's ability to defend herself in view of her having no close ties with Hungary and Poland, unless she ceded back Transylvania.[40]

On the other hand, the Greek felt they had to do something to thwart not Germany but Italy, whose move into Albania had been "the first step in a totalitarian program to obtain Italian predominance in the eastern Mediterranean."[41] Thus, while the Italian factor had a positive effect on bringing Greece to a neutral position vis-a-vis Germany and a pro-allied position vis-a-vis Italy, it was a negative factor in terms of bringing Greece around to the ultimate British vision of the creation of a Balkan front. For the Greeks tended to see the Italians behind Yugoslavia and so this set the stage for the Greek anti-revisionist stand against Bulgaria, the dissipation of which was a necessary first step in federalizing a Balkan effort.

The problems facing Rumania in regard to acceptance of a British guarantee were even more acute than those the Greeks faced due to the proximity of Germany and Russia, and poor relations with Hungary, Bulgaria and Poland. After the Albanian invasion, Gafencu had received a pressured invitation to Berlin, reiterating fears of German economic and political pressure. He therefore said that Rumania desired a "spontaneous" guarantee like the one to Greece which they could represent to Germany as not of their seeking. And they desired a guarantee which was not dependent on nor reciprocal with Poland, as they mistrusted Beck's policies which might eventually lead to an understanding with Germany and which were aimed not to antagonize Hungary. They also argued that reciprocity with Poland, which the British wished tied to the guarantee would have an adverse effect on Rumanian relations with the Balkan Entente in that they too would be bound to aid Rumania if she were attacked by Bulgaria, the likelihood of which increased in the event that Rumania was to participate in a war on Poland's behalf. Above all, they wanted a guarantee which would secure integrity as well as sovereignty (the Polish gurantee referred only to the latter) especially against Bulgaria.

By April 13 the British were becoming increasingly reluctant to even guarantee Rumania due to the uncertainty of Polish-Rumanian relations the fact that Rumania no longer seemed in danger, and the need to clarify relations with Turkey and the USSR upon whom the means to help Rumania depended. On the othe hand, Gafencu asked on April 12 (and again on the morning of the 13th with great urgency) that Rumania be part of the Greek guarantee to be announced the next day, for it seemed to Rumania, whose alliance system had always been based on the status quo (the Balkan Entente against Bulgaria, the Little Entente against Hungary, and the Polish-Rumanian treaty against Russia), that the British guarantee was the best protection against Germany and her surrogates, and it would strengthen his hand in his forthcoming visit in Berlin.[42]

Likewise the Admiralty was concerned about the effects of a naval blockade if Hitler could lay his hands on Rumanian oil and wheat, and so they wished a guarantee as did Turkey and France, the latter fearing that Rumania was in great danger from Hungary and because of oil. The Foreign Office rightly argued that by guaranteeing Rumania, the lever to bring Poland and Turkey into the system or to enlarge the Balkan Entente by the inclusion of Bulgaria would be lost. But the absolute insistence of the French, who intended to announce their own guarantee to Rumania, and the British fear of the results if Germany were allowed to play on Franco-British dissension, won the day, and so it was agreed in the afternoon of April 13 to include Rumania.

Chamberlain's speech in the House of Commons on April 13 dealt mainly with the background and implications of the Italian coup in Albania and with his defense of the decision not to denounce the Anglo-Italian agreement of April 16, 1938. With regard to Greece and Rumania he said that his Government attached "the greatest importance to the avoidance of disturbance by force or threats of force of the status quo in the Mediterranean and the Balkan Peninsula." Consequently, he said, any threat to "the independence of Greece or Rumania" or a threat which

> . . .the Greek or Rumanian government considered it vital to resist with their national forces, His Majesty's Government would feel themselves bound at once to lend the Greek or Rumanian Government . . .all the support in their power.[43]

The French issued parallel guarantees on the same day in the form of a statement to the press.

The official reaction to the guarantees in Rumania and Greece was guarded. Rumania, under pressure of talks in Berlin, repeatedly insisted that the guarantee was not directed against Germany and that she would accept a German guarantee also, and then Bucharest offered non-aggression pacts all around, but there were no takers.[44] The Greeks were frightened by rumors that Mussolini was taking an interest in the Macedonian question, believing that the Axis approach to Salonika would bid strong attraction for Yugoslavia and Bulgaria to join the Axis to secure Macedonia and Thrace. They also realized that Italian forces in Albania were large, that there were limitations to British sea power to prevent attack on land, and that Turkey would be of little help, involved as she was in defense of the Straits.

Therefore, in the April 13 edition of *Messager d'Athènes* Metaxas sent a message to Britain giving "profound thanks" and "deep satisfaction" for the guarantees, but at the same time "thanks" were given to Italy for assurances of the integrity of Greece. As U.S. Minister MacVeagh noted, thanks for not attacking were more profuse than those for helping. This caused the general public, who greeted the guarantee warmly, to mistrust Metaxas, and to view the Italian pledge as a satanic repeat of what had been handed out to Albania, and to imbue them with a spirit to fight.[45] In Rumania, the people also greeted the news with surprise and enthusiasm, particularly after no dramatic consequences resulted from the guarantees.

The reaction in Berlin to the guarantees, at first cautious, soon became victorious as one after another of the guaranteed states pledged loyalty to Berlin, and the others failed to join the guarantee system. Ribbentrop's circular of April 12 instructed his missions abroad to handle the whole affair with composure and that Berlin expected no further states to be "hoodwinked by the British." But he also warned any other states against falling prey to British entreaties, reminding them of Hitler's April 1 speech (that he who is "ready to pull the chestnuts out of the fire for the Great Powers must expect to get his fingers burnt in doing so"). In Berlin on April 19 Gafencu took pains to describe the guarantee as a diplomatic move not characterized by a policy of encirclement. Hitler, while agreeing it had not altered German-Rumanian relations, reminded Rumania that her real enemies were Hungary, Russia, and Bulgaria, and that Britain was unable and would not do anything for her on those scores. Meanwhile, Greek Minister Mavroudis assured Berlin that "she was firmly resolved not to go beyond that limit," and the Turks refused the British suggestion that they also guarantee Greece. By April 22 German State Secretary Weizsäcker had concluded that the whole British initiative had been a sign of weakness.[46]

Balkan countries, fearful of Germany and Italy, and of her power over Balkan neighbors, could not risk Axis wrath, and so had sought and accepted guarantees for whatever good they would do in safeguarding their frontiers and emboldening their position vis-a-vis Germany, Russia, Italy, and each other. The wholescale guarantees given by the British and French had devastating consequences for future efforts to form a peace front in that they fortified Greek and Rumanian determination not to come to any accommodation with Bulgaria or Hungary or to join a peace front which might encourage Germany or cause war. On the Bulgarian and Hungarian side, the guarantees, in supporting the status quo, left these states nowhere to turn for fulfillment of their aspirations except to Berlin, and it inhibited rapprochement efforts. And it destroyed the hope of extending the Rumanian-Polish alliance. Perhaps it was sour grapes, but the Polish Ambassador in London and Paris, Count Raczynski, said that if the allies had not been in such a hurry to guarantee Rumania, a Rumanian-Polish alliance would have been possible, but that now that Gafencu was confident of aid if she were attacked, she had no need of Poland and wished not to be obliged to go to Poland's aid if she were attacked.[47]

The guarantees were never considered a threat to Germany nor should they have been in their announced format. In fact, it can be said that the Nazis more than the West were their architect in that the witches brew had already been done with sufficient impunity to destroy the British efforts at East European collaboration and support for Poland. The thrust of German policy thereafter was the blunting of the guarantees by continued pressure in the Balkans to adhere to strict neutrality, the prevention of any new guarantee or the formation of a peace front joining the Balkans together and then tying them in with the Soviet Union.

But, there were indirect results of the guarantees which cost Germany heavily, ultimately threatening her Balkan position and leading to the next moves by each side. One of these was open American support for the allies. On April 14, the day after announcement of the guarantees, U.S. President Roosevelt sent messages to Germany and Italy requesting reassurances that neither power contemplated military aggression. In this message, he said that the possibility of conflict "is of definite concern to the people of the U.S.," and then he asked for assurances that 31 named countries would not be attacked. All of the Balkan countries were included as was Russia. While the message carried no material weight as the Congress had rejected revision of the neutrality legislation, the moral effect, particularly among the Balkan peoples was instantaneous and applauding, though official reaction was guarded and based on calculated German response.[48]

Hitler's wrath at the Roosevelt initiative was evident. He did not answer Roosevelt's appeal directly. Instead, he spoke to it in ridicule in his April 28 Speech to the Reichstag. Point by point he answered Roosevelt, particularly the one regarding assurances against attack to thirty named nations saying he himself had ascertained whether this inquiry was addressed to Germany with their consent. In all cases, he said, the reply was negative.[49] In such a way, Hitler make it clear that since he had no designs on the Balkans, any resultant war must be measured in terms of Western interference.

Hitler's speech was received in the Balkans with enthusiasm proportional to the proximity to Germany. In Yugoslavia it was printed on the front page in total and hailed as a great step toward peace, while in Turkey the official press opinion was that it changed nothing, and that Hitler did not secure the Europeans but only justified his acts which continued to be gluttonous and obstructive to formation of a Balkan union. There was also marked resentment over offers of guarantees on terms which were construed as implying status of protectorates over lesser powers. In Greece and the USSR the speech was printed without comment, while the Bulgarian press said it was less onerous than expected, but it noted that the absence of reference to Russia in the speech was significant.[50]

The Bulgarians had rightly perceived that U.S. entrance into the picture had altered the German position to Russia significantly. Hitler had no illusions about the power of the U.S. or regarding the fact that he would sooner or later have to deal with Washington. But, as with Great Britain, he hoped European victory would give him the power to negotiate. In the meantime, he believed U.S. interests were greater in the Pacific than in Europe and that a deal with Japan would sufficiently engage a benign U.S. and Russia, that his European plans would be protected. Instead, a show of U.S. resolve had the effect of distracting Japan, as did the guarantees, due to the Japanese wish not to alienate Great Britain and France until the Chinese and Russian situation was clearer, thus removing a major Nazi pawn in the neutralization of Russia.

The third indirect result stemming from the guarantee was that two weeks later, British resolve stiffened along concrete lines. Implementation of the guarantee would mean war, and so on April 27 military conscription in Britain was introduced. French President Daladier made an impassioned plea for this before Hitler's April 28 speech and the British Ambassador in France agreed that conscription was essential to prove to the people of Central and East Europe that Britain was in earnest. The act was greeted with a sigh of relief by all the allied nations and by the Balkan countries as well. And Japan now hesitated to join Hitler for fear of tangling with Britain. But Hitler was displeased, for his theory that the British could be bought and that this enormous factor would not have to be reckoned with until the end, seemed to be crumbling. Hitler answered the new British program in his April 28 Reichstag Speech, denouncing the Anglo-German Naval Agreement and the German-Polish Peace Declaration.

* * * * *

Thus, faced with a British guarantee to Poland, Hitler countered with a crippling trade pact with Rumania and then a green light to Italy in Albania. This, in turn, caused Britain and France to extend guarantees which, in and of themselves, were not damaging to Hitler's program for the Southeast in the unilaterial form in which they were offered and the apologetic manner in which they were received. But indirectly the counterpoint was damaging, for it brought previously neutral countries like Greece and the U.S. into the ranks of adversaries, it began the rearming of Britain, it shifted the Japanese and therefore the Russian position, and it planted the seeds of Balkan disloyalty, necessitating a firmer German policy in the Southeast. Finally, the very failure of the guarantees for Britain, caused her to look south and to take the next step in resistance by linking up with strategic Turkey. Germany countered with the Pact of Steel.

The Anglo-Turkish Declaration and the Pact of Steel

The failure of Britain to form a defense bloc in the Balkans and the obligations incurred in the East by the guarantees, caused her to look to Turkey as the best bastion of defense both of her Mediterranean interests and as the nucleus of the anticipated peace front linking Turkey, the Balkans and the Soviet Union. Meanwhile Turkey's attitude had changed significantly as a result of the events of the intervening six months. In 1938 Turkey had seemed singularly unconcerned with the position of Rumania in the face of the German move east,[51] but increasingly pessimistic about the ability of her neighbors to put up any kind of defense, confident of the strength of Turko-Soviet relations, recognizing similarly threatened Mediterranean interests with the British who now had proferred concrete evidence of resolve, and hopeful that the new relationship would help transform her present precarious trading system into a free exchange of goods, Ankara decided to move forward in discussions with London.

While German policy was directed toward stalemating such an agreement, there seemed some disparity of view between the German diplomatic corps and Hitler as to the nature of the danger. At the base of the disagreement was the difference between the view at the Wilhelmstrasse that Great Britain was Germany's major enemy and Hitler's view that Britain could be bought, and it was the difference in view as the importance to Germany of control of the Straits versus the Danube. Von Papen, German Ambassador to Turkey and representative of the former view, worked tirelessly to keep Berlin informed and to thwart conclusion of the talks. In a dispatch on May 20, he noted the danger to Germany if Turkey went with Britain, for while a British base in Greece could be answered with countermeasures, and the Dardanelles could be closed via Salonika thus excluding Britain from the Black Sea and Russia from the Mediterranean if the Turkish mainland was controlled by Germany, even if Italy controlled the whole Mediterranean, Britain could not be defeated unless Germany acquired the "landbridge to India." Turkey, he said, will "always be in a position to prevent this with the main part of her forces south of the Taurus."[52] Hitler, on the other hand, was blasé about the Turkish position believing that he could come to terms with Britain, that Turkey, who had done little to fortify the Straits, would not bleed for Britain or attack Hungary, and could be pressured, and that Russia could be swung around against Turkey if need be.

On the day of the occupation of Bohemia and Moravia, the Germans learned that the Turks were negotiating with the French over uniting Hatay in return for a pact of mutual assistance. Upon inquiry the Turks told the Germans that Turkey would continue to cooperate economically if Germany would refrain from pressing the Balkans into taking an ideological stand, and that they would maintain neutrality except to honor obligations under the Balkan Entente against Bulgaria.[53] On March 21, however, the Turkish Ambassador in London, Aras, told Halifax that "Turkey would go to any lengths with Great Britain" if it was known that Britain was generally with them, and if Turkey was attacked, that they would benefit from direct assistance.

In negotiating with the Turks, it soon became clear to the British that, like the other Balkan countries, Turkey was not anxious to work within any multilaterial framework involving reciprocal obligations in the East. Aras told Cardogan on March 31 that under the Turkish-Soviet Treaty of 1925 and 1929 neither party could make arrangements with an immediate neighbor of the other party without the latter's consent, which stymied the idea of a bloc with Poland. To entreaties that Turkey go beyond obligations of the Balkan Entente in giving assistance to Rumania, Ankara was noncommittal. On April 10 when the British asked Turkey if she was prepared to extend her obligations to Greece under the Balkan Entente, the Turks replied that they could not sacrifice their neutrality without some "definite guarantee of their own security." The Germans, therefore, were delighted when the Turkish Ambassador reported to them that British encirclement plans were without foundation.[54]

Like the other Balkan countries the Turks were profoundly affected by the heavy inroads the Axis had already made into the Balkans and realistically had written off any kind of Balkan defense. Everything, in their view depended on the degree of support Turkey received from Great Britain and France. So once more abandoning their peace front hopes, London decided to go ahead and give Turkey help on the condition it would be reciprocal. In the meantime they hoped that such aid would bulwark the Turks enough that they would aid Rumania or neutralize Bulgaria, but by April 15 the Turks still refused to go beyond the scope of the Balkan Entente Pact. The German Charge voiced some surprise that Turkey had rejected the British demarches but attributed this to "cold and sober considerations," to a desire to remain neutral as long as possible, and in recognition of the importance of economic ties. Confident, the Nazis contented themselves with threats to the effect that the slightest deviation "would be regarded by Germany as a defection to the enemy camp," and to encouragement to Italy to make a clear statement of aim similar to the one to Greece feigning benevolency.[55]

As time progressed, it was becoming clear in the West that as Poland was the key to East European defense, Turkey was the key to Balkan defense, and in both cases the Soviet Union could not be ignored. The Turks nourished this idea along, suggesting on April 26 that parallel negotiations with the Soviet Union take place, and pledging to exert themselves to bring Russia into a common front and because of her association with Rumania under the Balkan Entente and friendly relations with Poland, to bring "about an understanding which would effectuate a common eastern front."[56]

In the Balkans, where there was historical mistrust of Russia, fear of the internal and political consequences of Bolshevism, and reluctance to be in any way linked with the Soviet Union which could be represented in Berlin as "encirclement," the idea of approaching Moscow by means of Turkey as a group had some appeal. Gafencu, for instance, said that while he could not enter into an agreement with Russia and would be embarrassed if Great Britain and France did as it might provoke Hitler, he at the same time believed

> that to insure the necessary support of the Soviet Union for a broad system of security, it would be better to rely on the office of the Balkan Entente than those of the 'border states' which separated the Reich from Russia—as while Berlin should increase its irritation over an agreement that might be interpreted as an act of 'encirclement,' it was difficult to raise objections to the active participation of Russia in defense of peace of the Balkans.

"If it were possible," he continued "to set a united Balkan region whose independence was guaranteed by the Great Powers against the Reich, Hitler would not be able to disturb it." "Turkey," he concluded "was a better point than Poland where the West and the Soviet Union could meet."[57]

Despite misgivings about the Soviet Union, the idea gained substance when, in the midst of the Turko-British talks in Ankara, Russian Minister Potemkin arrived in Istanbul (April 26). The Germans seemed shaken by this, appointing a new Ambassador to Turkey, von Papen, who arrived a day later. After reviewing the situation, von Papen concluded that Turkey's "alleged neutrality" was a "mere fiction" in that Turkey saw the Axis alone as the enemy, that she strove for solidarity of the Balkans and cooperation of the Soviet Union, and had requested British assistance. But he predicted that Turkey would remain neutral until the Axis powers took the offensive in the Mediterranean or the Balkans. On April 29, therefore, he called on the Turkish President and combined threats with reassurances of German good intent. He said that Germany expected strict neutrality from Turkey in the event of war in the Mediterranean, which meant closing the Straits to everybody, but that Germany also supported the Balkan Pact as peaceful conditions were necessary for economic collaboration.[58] The Turks for their part tried to play down the exchange with the Soviet Union saying it had been on Soviet initiative and British suggestion.

When Potemkin's visit failed to produce an agreement, State Secretary Weizsäcker confidently sent a circular to diplomatic missions abroad (May 2) in which he stated that according to information in his possession, the Turkish Government had replied to the British offers of a pact to the effect that its conclusion depended on results of negotiations with the USSR who were as yet uncommitted. He went on to point out that conditions of the Turkish agreement were that it be concluded at the same time as an Anglo-Soviet mutual assistance pact and a corresponding Russo-Turkish mutual assistance pact, that it was predicated on settlement of Bulgarian-Rumanian differences to insure Bulgarian neutrality, and that the British must pledge immediate consultation to insure Turkish defense, all of which made an agreement unlikely.[59]

The confident air assumed in Berlin was not shared by von Papen who energetically tried to ward off conclusion of an Anglo-Turkish agreement. He was matched by an obtuse, audacious and skillful Turkish game designed to maintain her quasi-neutral role vis-a-vis Germany. For instance, when von Papen inquired as to why Turkey had such hostile feelings toward Germany, the Turks inquired as to why Germany had her ally Italy seize Albania. When von Papen then offered to guarantee their security and to see to it that Italy withdrew her troops from Albania, the Turkish Secretary General remarked that German guarantees were worthless. When von Papen inquired as to the Turkish attitude if Germany guaranteed the Dodecanese Islands, the Secretary-General retorted, "What would Germany do if we guaranteed to her the cession of Alaska?" What they were interested in, he said, was to know if Turkey was going to get the military supplies which had been ordered in Germany, and if Germany could not guarantee delivery, Turkey could not guarantee further deliveries of chrome to Germany.[60]

The Turks, for their part, as early as April 23 were thinking about a treaty of alliance for fifteen years as the goal, and then at the end of April upon receipt of British proposals for a four-stage agreement of a far-reaching nature,[61] they definitely accepted the idea of a mutual assistance pact, and one which hinged on no prior agreement with the Soviet Union. Ankara, however, was like the Balkans in one important respect. She refused to tie herself to a collective scheme of Balkan defense objecting to the British definition of *casus feodaris* as "leading to war in the Mediterranean or Balkans," desiring instead the phrase "to threaten the security of Turkey." The British acquiesced in this request so as not to prejudice Turkish negotiations with Bulgaria and the Soviet Union.[62]

But, while wishing to limit the scope of her involvement to situations which directly threatened her interests, Turkey did not in any sense consider herself neutral. In the final version of the Declaration the absence of the word "neutrality" was significant, and Turkish Prime Minister Saydam on May 12, when he announced the Pact to the Turkish Parliament, noted that neutrality no longer served Turkish purposes as they wanted to associate with "those countries which were united for peace but not shrinking from war if necessary," and that negotiations would continue with the Balkan Entente and with Russia. Now that trouble had spread to the Mediterranean and the Balkan regions, he said, for Turkey to remain neutral could be to jeopardize her own security.[63]

The Declaration,[64] which was announced simultaneously in the British House of Commons and the Grand National Assembly in Ankara on May 12, stated both country's intent to conclude a definite long-term agreement of a reciprocal character (Article two), and in the meantime their intent to lend each other aid in the event of war in the Mediterranean area (Article three). The agreement also recognized the need to ensure the establishment of security in the Balkans (Article six), and it was noted in Article seven that any of the arrangements would not preclude making agreements with other countries. Article four noted that the agreement was not directed against any country, but designed to assure Great Britain and Turkey of mutual assistance and aid should the necessity arrive.

After the Anglo-Turkish Declaration was signed, von Papen continued to view the Pact with alarm characterizing the losses if Germany did not detach Turkey as "twenty years of hard work," equipment, outstanding debt, and Turkish youth, eighty percent of whom were in German universities. And he believed that Turkish policy would change if the Italian threat were disapproved.[65] Why von Papen continued to emphasize the Italian threat is unclear given the nature of articles in the Turkish press clearly justifying the alliance in the face of German not Italian aggression. In an Istanbul-German paper, the *Turkische Post,* a Turkish deputy in justifying the alliance to German readers wrote that Albania had been "the drop which caused the glass to run over," and that German irritation of the Pact was due to the obstacle it presented to the realization of German aims. In *Yeni Sabah* of May 11, it was stated that:

> It is the Germans themselves who have driven Turkish statesmen to conclude an alliance with Great Britain. Germany destroys Czechoslovakia, menaces Rumania, and supports Italy and her conquest of Albania.[66]

While the emphasis on the Italian threat may have been tactical only, it was also most certainly connected with Papen's view of the British danger and, therefore, that Turkey disengaged from Britain might be worth the price of estrangement from Italy.

In Berlin there was no duplication of the panic felt by von Papen. Among the reasons was the Balkan reaction which soon dispelled the fear that, in domino fashion, the rest of the Southeastern countries would swing to Britain. Saracoglu's statement that his Government had found favorable reaction among the Balkan states,[67] belied the actual state of affairs whereby the more threatened by the Axis, the more negative the

official reaction. In Greece, for instance, the Declaration was headlined
and translated in full in the papers of May 13 but with no editorial comment. Three days later the official opinion was guarded noting that the
Declaration was "not directed against any third party." Metaxas urged
that Greece make it "her sacred duty to say no single word which could
be interpreted as a mark of hostility" by the other powers.[68] The most
negative impact of the Declaration was felt in Yugoslavia where press
statements were made against it, and it was feared that Yugoslavia would
leave the Balkan Entente as a result. Even Bulgaria felt extremely threatened because a German response might mean war. Only Rumania made a
positive statement and that was because of its impact on Bulgaria, not
Germany.

As terms of the Declaration gradually became known, there were other
reasons for German confidence as well. One was the failure of Britian to
gain a simultaneous French pact, signalling division in Western ranks.[69]
However, six weeks later when the Hatay issue was resolved, the French
declaration was made in an unexpurgated form, once again giving Hitler
cause for concern. The other more important concern was the willingness
of Turkey to tie the Balkans to the Anglo-Turkish agreement through
Article six which stated:

> The two governments recognize that it is also necessary to ensure
> the establishment of security in the Balkans and they are consulting
> together with the object of achieving this purpose as speedily as
> possible.

Though it was far from clear to the Germans (nor to the British for that
matter) exactly what this meant in terms of collective security, it at least
implied Turkish interest in the Balkans and in British efforts to tie the
Balkan Entente together.

Therefore, the Germans began directing their efforts toward preventing
implementation of Article six. Berlin's approach was to use their "trump
card" (threats of arms withdrawal), a tactic which von Papen reported met
with only partial success, the Turks pledging not to become engaged in an
Anglo-Polish-German conflict unless it was extended to the Mediterranean
and her Balkan allies attacked. (Von Papen noted, however, that he could
not imagine a conflict with Great Britain that would not involve the

Mediterranean.)[70] But Saracoglu refused to modify Article six saying it only laid down that the Balkans were a sphere of Turkish interest and conflicts might arise there not covered by intra-Balkan obligations. At the sametime, he noted that, while Turkey did not want any collective security and did not wish "the Balkan Pact to be used by the Western Powers in any way as an instrument for encirclement and for a possible automatic entry into the war," the Balkan Pact was an instrument sui generis and, if there was Bulgarian participation or an attack through the Balkans which brought the aggressor to occupy the Black Sea coast, that Turkey's sphere would be violated. Later in a speech to the Congress of the Republican Peoples' Party on July 8, he pointed out that Hitler in *Mein Kampf* had recommended alliance with England and why, therefore, should it be so bad for Turkey?[71]

The thrust of German policy after the Anglo and Franco-Turkish Declarations inclusive of Article six, was to keep Turkey from implementing Article two pledging conclusion of a definitive agreement with the West and to prevent Turkey from joining a Balkan or expanded encirclement program and by summertime there seemed some signs of success. In mid-June Saracoglu assured Berlin that the Balkans would not be included in a final Anglo-Turkish treaty, and on June 30 von Papen reported that the British wished Turkey to guarantee Rumania's non-Balkan borders in return for a British guarantee of the Thracian frontier, and that Saracoglu had assured him Turkey would do no such thing. Saracoglu added that if Rumania was threatened and supported by Britain, the Turkish treaty would come into play, but if Hungary attacked Rumania without German participation, there was no *casus feodaris*. On the other hand, when von Papen asked the Foreign Minister whether in the event of a Mediterranean conflict in which the Balkans were neutral with the British occupying Greek ports, would Turkey stand by her allies, there was only, he reported, "embarrassed silence."[72]

Apparently, threats of economic censure and political pressure were not enough to detach Ankara from London and that a new policy must be found. Von Papen alluded to this new policy in early June when he offhandedly observed to Saracoglu that Britain appeared to be handing over leadership in European politics to Russia, and then on July 5 he reported that rumors of a Berlin trip to Moscow in order to paralyze British policy caused a great sensation in Ankara.[72] U.S. Ambassador to Turkey

MacMurray had already speculated at the time of the Anglo-Turkish Declaration that Russia might turn out to be Germany's next move against
Turkey when he noted Berlin's cool reception to von Papen's suggestion
to disengage Turkey from Britain at the price of Italian estrangement. Obviously, wrote MacMurray, a pact with Russia was already being envisioned
in Berlin as the necessary check against Turkey without loss of Italy who
might turn to London.[73]

On balance, the Germans could look to pluses and minuses in the outcome of their policy to prevent an Anglo-Turkish link. The pluses were
that the link was bilateral only and did not extend to the Balkans, that the
Balkans themselves seemed severely threatened by it, enough so to weaken
the Balkan Entente, and Italy had not been sacrificed in the process. Indeed, Italy was sufficiently threatened by the Declaration that a pact with
Rome was now probable. The minuses were much greater, however. Turkey
had abandoned neutrality joining Britain and then France in a declaration
which was to be followed by a military alliance; Article six linked Turkish
interests directly to the Mediterranean and obliquely to the Balkans; and
Soviet acquiescence, which had been key to Turkey's decision to go ahead
with the Declaration, signaled the possibility that Turkey would become
the nucleus of the anticipated peace front linking Turkey with Britain and
then with the Soviet Union and the Balkans, forming the encirclement ring
Germany so greatly feared.

Hitler must have been already envisioning at this point a link with the
Soviet Union to bring Turkey back to neutrality, but since such a move
might in itself throw the Italian Fascists into the arms of Britain, it was
necessary that Italy be more tightly tied to Germany. But there were other
reasons too why Hitler wanted the Pact of Steel. In this respect the need
to control Italy was an important factor, for Balkan and Soviet pacification were the foundations of German plans against Poland and then France,
both of which could be threatened by a precipitous Italian act. Also, it
would thwart British efforts to win Italy as they had in World War I and
it would offset the Turkish turn to Britain. And there were a host of other
advantages; it would put pressure on France and the Balkan Entente, pacify
Italy regarding their suspicions of German interest in Croatia, add an element of power to Hitler in his war of nerves against the Anglo-French
policy of guarantees, and assure Italian acquiescence in the assault on Poland. Finally, on April 24 the Germans received a negative reply from the

Japanese regarding a tripartite pact, spurring Berlin on to tie down the pact at least at a bilateral level.

The German need to control the Balkan situation had become more important as Italian interests began to focus there rather than the Mediterranean, which was in part due to Western efforts to tie a ring around Italian and German expansionism. In May Ciano told Gafencu that "the Danube flows into the Black Sea which only a prolongation of the Mediterranean . . . ,"[74] while Mussolini adopted the attitude that since the democracies were planning a war of exhaustion, "we must not be satisfied with declarations of Balkan neutrality, but must occupy the territories and use them for supply of necessary food and industrial war supplies," and in securing the Axis area, "we can count on two favorable pawns—Hungary and Bulgaria."[75] But increasingly Italian claims began to come into conflict with German aims as for instance when Italy began to support Hungary's passive resistance to Berlin's attempts to force Budapest into a customs union, and when Berlin began contemplating a move toward Moscow which Mussolini warned should be limited to preventing Russia from adhering to the Western bloc.

All of the Italian ambitions in the Balkans, Germany agreed to verbally in order to get the Pact signed, with the presumption that the Italians were too weak militarily to press any claims for some time. Germany had proposed such a treaty of alliance as early as October 20, 1938 (to include Japan also), but it was rejected on the basis that Italian public opinion was not yet ripe for an alliance. Ribbentrop continued to pressure along those lines prior to the March 1939 moved against Czechoslovakia. What made the Italian Government (not the people whose traditional hatred and suspicion of the Germans lingered) finally amenable, were the events of March and April 1939, and finally the Anglo-Turkish Declaration.

On the heels of the guarantees (April 15-17), Mussolini met with Göring who promised that Germany would not encroach on the post-Albanian definition of the Italian sphere (which was an ephemeral line drawn somewhere along the Danube), that Italy had complete dominance in Yugoslavia and was "in charge of a solution of the crisis" (Serbo-Croatian conflict), and that war would be later and that it would be a synchronized effort.[76] But, continued fear of the Polish adventure made the Italians propose further talks, and on Germany's part an unpromising communication from Japan on April 24 induced Ribbentrop to acquiesce. On May

6-7, Mussolini, Ciano, and Ribbentrop again met. During these talks their respective positions were further defined. They agreed that the status quo in Yugoslavia should be maintained and the Italian action regarding Turkey, France and Yugoslavia be postponed, that both would support Bulgaria, that Greece was in the Italian sphere, that the Italian wish to bring Hungary and Spain into the Axis camp (as reinsurance against Germany) would be honored, that relations with Russia should be increased due to the danger that the British might bring Moscow into the allied alliance (despite the fact that the Italian Government used Anti-Communism as an excuse for the Axis alliance), and that as a result of the Pact, the West would be so intimidated that it would abandon Poland, allowing German designs on Danzig to be fulfilled without war.

On both sides, the conversations verged on the ethereal. Ribbentrop had not even brought a draft continuing to hope for a Tripartite, while Ciano was not confident of Mussolini's position which still leaned heavily on anti-German public opinion. During this period, the astute Italian Ambassador in Berlin, Attolico, continually urged Rome to get concrete promises of German intent not to begin the war early and of rights to spheres, while Ciano continually urged Mussolini that the best way to restrain Hitler was through an alliance.[77] Mussolini seems to have ridden the fence for quite a while, but the friendly reception Ribbentrop received in Milan, the latter's demeanor, Ciano's report of the conversations which seemed to assure Italy of German consideration of her interests, caused Mussolini to ring up Ciano and to tell him to make a public announcement of a bilateral pact which he had always preferred to a tripartite anyway. Ribbentrop, caught at a disadvantage due to the Japanese communication, reluctantly agreed pending Hitler's approval, which was immediately forthcoming. On May 7 a communique announced the perfect identity of views of the two governments, and that it had been decided to establish relations between the two in the definitive form of a political and military pact.

By this time, the influence of allied pressure and particularly of the Anglo-Turkish talks was becoming apparent in the promulgation of the Pact. The Italian *New Chronicle* on May 4, 1939 suggested that an alliance was "a possibility only in the event of Great Britain and the USSR coming to an understanding," and for Ribbentrop's part, announcement even before there was a pact draft, most certainly was in some measure to deter the Turkish Government in their ongoing negotiations from joining the democratic bloc. On May 12, the day of the Anglo-Turkish Declaration, Ribbentrop gave Attolico the Nazi draft of the Pact which Ciano said contained "real dynamite," but neither he nor Mussolini, to Attolico's distress, wished to make any modifications.

The Preamble reaffirmed the common policy already set down. The Pact provided for consultation, military support, collaboration on economic and military affairs, and the secret additional protocol called for joint cooperation regarding the press. On May 17 Mussolini approved the final text and on May 22 Ciano visited Berlin for the signing. During this visit Nazi leaders gave him the impression that there had been no change in the German view regarding the need for three years of peace and moderatin regarding Turkey and Hungary, and he sensed qualified approval of Italian designs on Croatia, but there were no written promises to that effect. Diabolically, on the very day the Pact was signed, Hitler expounded on plans to isolate and attack Poland, along with which he explained the need for secrecy from both Italy and Japan.

* * * * *

If there was any predisposition on the part of the Balkan countries after the Anglo-Turkish agreement to drift away from neutrality toward the allies, there was very little after the Pact of Steel, because it appeared now that Italy could not be won over to the allied side and that Italy and Germany had a common policy and an agreement regardin spheres in the Balkans. The impact of the Pact fell particularly on Yugoslavia, for as Gafencu noted Italy no longer controlled her own destiny, her chief role now was in pressuring Yugoslavia so as to break up the Balkan Entente.[78] Certainly the Yugoslav hope of playing Germany off against Italy to obtain sovereignty had vanished, and the Serbo-Croat internal conflict became more precarious as Italian interference increased. The right to move toward Hungary and to use her as a surrogate awarded to Italy in the Pact (which Hungary was only too ready to accept to protect herself from Germany and build her own Balkan sphere) put added pressure not just on Yugoslavia, but on Rumania and Greece to do Hitler's bidding and to maintain the strictest neutrality.

In a larger framework, the Pact was dangerous for the Balkans for it implied an Italian sphere there and German support for it without clearly spelling out the parameters. Uncertainty led to increased revisionist-anti-revisionist threats, stalemating the latent hope of a Balkan collective security system. All the while, it secured Germany's southern flank for action against Poland and in this way, encouraged war in general and Italian imperialism in the Balkans in particular. And in elevating the Fascist threat, it eliminated in those countries a much more anti-Bolshevik faction than the Nazis, thus in its own way preparing the Balkans for the Nazi-Soviet Pact. On Russia's part, the realization of how far the Balkans had been taken along the road to German satellization was made even clearer, and thus her southern defense was more obviously exposed, while the absence of the Japanese in the Pact was conspicuous. For the British part, having lost the Italian card, they had to look to Russia, with the obvious result that Nazi attention turned in that direction also and, the ante was raised.

From the Pact of Steel until the Nazi-Soviet Non-Aggression Pact, German policy in the Balkans focused on attempts to counter continued efforts by the British to form an encirclement front whose nucleus was now the Anglo-Turkish link. In this counter-offensive, the familiar tactics of divide-and-rule politics, threats of invasion, and economic and military censure were only marginally successful for the Nazis who, by late August after considerable effort, regarded the Southeast with suspicion and only conditionally loyal to their stated neutral position.

German Anti-Encirclement in the Balkans

As a result of first the Anglo-French guarantees and then the Anglo- and Franco-Turkish Declarations, the Germans began to look at the Balkans with distrust. As early as April 13 Ribbentrop formulated the basis of the German anti-encirclement policy, sending a circular to German diplomats abroad in which he instructed them on how to behave in the face of Anglo-French "efforts at encirclement directed against Germany and Italy." They were to refrain from making any demarche, but if a discussion arose they were to answer to the effect that "we do not expect any further States to be hoodwinked by the British," and he warned, "We would regard any participation in, or connection with, such a combination as being directed against us and would react accordingly." He advised his diplomats in conversations to treat "the whole affair with great composure and ridicule the nervous zeal with which the British are trying to harass other states to serve their own ends."[79]

The German anti-encirclement program operated on two levels in the Balkans. The first was on a unilateral basis whereby Berlin dealt with each Balkan country individually according to its particular fancies, needs, and aims. The other was on a collective basis whereby Berlin tried to break up or make dysfunctional Balkan alliances and alignments, particularly the Balkan Entente, and to prevent the Soviet Union from joining any such Balkan alignments or the West. The second of these will be taken up in the next chapter and the question of the Soviet Union in the last two chapters. For the moment, focus will be directed toward Germany's singular approach.

The German program was designed to prevent fulfillment of the Anglo-French program which sought an intra-Balkan alliance tied to the West and possibly to the Soviet Union as well. That the allied program failed was due not so much to the brilliance of Nazi diplomacy and an astute conceptualization, as to the fact that Balkan and German designs for the Balkans coincided in their desire for neutrality in the Southeast, to the overwhelming power factor in Germany's favor (fattened by Italy making threats of invasion and internal disruption powerful weapons in their coercion), to the inability of the Balkans to settle their own disputes and to agree on the common friend and foe, and to fear of the Soviet Union and a Nazi-Soviet war (on their territory) against which Germany provided the best shield (even by the Nazi-Soviet Pact). Nevertheless, the German Balkan program was ingenious in the way it tapped this very strong desire for neutrality, and in its attention to and exploitation of intra-Balkan grievances.

Italian anti-encirclement (except for over-encouragement of Hungary) aided the Nazi effort, particularly in Yugoslavia and Greece, though the motivation was different, for while Germany wished a benign Southeast in order to insure a steady source of supplies, stalemate Balkan support for Poland, and prevent Soviet action, Italy wished to preserve the neutrality of the Southeast until she was strong enough to move in herself. Her tactics were much the same as the Nazis, using a heavy dose of revisionist threat laced with invasion rumor. Gayda, writing in *Giornale d'Italia*, warned the Balkan countries that if they wished to avoid classification as being among the enemies of the Axis, they should take steps to that end, and he held Yugoslavia up as the model of true neutrality. Gayda said that while refusing to take a "dramatic" view of the attitude of the guaranteed states, Italy was keeping a watchful eye on Balkan developments "with their conflicting interests and the trends toward revisionism for the sake of greater justice and enduring peace." He added that Italy is "now the greatest Balkan power" and did not lack friends in the peninsula.[80] In Italian pursuit of Balkan neutrality, the Fascists had a strange bedfellow—the Vatican. Since the Church considered its main enemy communism, it stood against both Axis aggressive moves and British-French encirclement, particularly the talks with the Soviet Union. Exploiting this, Hitler and Mussolini both pressed the Vatican in June to renew "peace" efforts particularly as it involved the Anglo-Soviet talks and later Poland.[81]

The two most tractable of Germany's Balkan pawns were Bulgaria and Hungary for the simple reason that they were revisionist states who stood to gain nothing from the Western program of guarantees and other intra-Balkan security systems. On the other hand, it gained Germany nothing to promote that very revisionism which would lead to the same place the British guarantee system led, that is to war in the Balkans. Besides, promising revisionism to them would alienate the other Balkan countries (Yugoslavia, Rumania, Greece, and Turkey) who were of equal interest to the German program.

Therefore, the German program in Budapest and Sofia stressed the availability of German arms in exchange for neutrality, the danger of war if they did not go along with Germany rather than the West, the folly of the Balkan defense system for the same reason, and only as a last resort, the fulfillment of revisionism in the long term if they stuck by Germany. To the status quo states, Hitler promised support against Hungary and Bulgaria, as for example when he told Cinkar-Marković that Germany would not be a party to return of Dobruja to Bulgaria and would not encourage Yugoslav-Hungarian intimacy because of the Polish situation. As U.S. Minister Lane speculated, such a policy was designed not just to woo Rumania and to safeguard Germany's own economic interests, but to cut across the Italian desire to control the Balkans by strengthening Bulgaria and encouraging Yugoslav-Hungarian friendship at Balkan Entente expense.[82]

Hungary, due to her unfortunate geographical position, was little likely to participate in the allied encirclement, but her benevolent attitude toward Poland, her penchant for revisionist disturbances which increased now that Greece and Rumania were guaranteed and Yugoslavia domestically divided, the anti-German attitude of the Magyar people and aristocracy which the Italians were encouraging, the personal animosity between Hitler and Ribbentrop on the one hand and Teleki and Horthy on the other, the support Budapest was giving to the Italian scheme to make Hungary the basis for a Balkan front under Italian aegis, and the betrayal the Hungarians felt for the First Vienna Awards, altogether made Hungary a constant concern to Berlin and its plans to pacify the Balkans while assaulting Poland.

On April 29 Ribbentrop told Hungarian Prime Minister Teleki and Foreign Minister Csáky not to be overawed by the British campaign and that Germany had no intention of attacking Poland, but if she did attack, Hungarian intervention would be futile. In a conversation on May 1, Berlin urged improved relations with Yugoslavia and Rumania, and gave no promises of satisfaction of her revisionist claims against Rumania and Yugoslavia. Nor did the Germans acknowledge Csáky's protest in Berlin to the effect that he could not understand why the Germans continued to supply Rumania with immense amounts of armament, and they encouraged the Hungarians not to take cruel liberties with the Ukrainians, suggesting that Hungary stabilize the situation by granting the Carpatho-Ukraine autonomy. Nazi pressure appeared to have the desired effect, for in a Report to the Foreign Relations Committee soon after, the Hungarian Foreign Minister made a laudatory reference to the Axis, stressing the identity of views and that friendship with Yugoslavia was desired and rapprochement with Rumania sought as Germany desired. Csáky added, that Germany would back Hungarian revisionism but at a later date.[83]

Subsequent events, however, made the Hungarians shift position and to attempt not to be sucked into the Axis orbit and to remain neutral. On the one hand the Anglo-Turkish Pact and then stepped up Balkan Entente activity threatened Hungary who feared that Turkey was trying to bring Yugoslavia and Rumania into an anti-Hungarian combination and that Bulgaria must be induced to join the Balkan Entente. On the other hand, Hungary was equally worried about the Axis after the Pact of Steel, particularly as it seemed to undercut the Italian policy to move independently into the Balkan coalition with Hungary, and as it seemed to signal a German policy change regarding Yugoslavia which Germany now intended to carve up like Czechoslovakia.

Thus, to protect herself and to ensure her part in the spoils, Hungary on July 28 suggested tripartite negotiations with Germany in the field of war economy, and when this was rejected, Budapest (in light of the German policy of supplying Rumania) vehemently reiterated the Hungarian policy that if Germany requested troop passage to Rumania, Hungary would resist with force. Meanwhile, she continued the policy of close relations with Poland and on July 24 Teleki wrote to Hitler that in any general conflict Hungary's policy would conform to that of the axis but that she on "moral grounds could not take action against Poland." Hitler did not receive this kindly, nor was he pleased by Csáky's visit to Rome on August 18, particulary when Ciano reported Csáky as saying that in the event of conflict, Hungary would "first bide her time and reinforce her frontier guard."[84]

But, on the heels of a pressured trip to Berlin amidst rumors that Hitler was attempting to remove Horthy and Teleki, and in the face of Italian neutrality and the Nazi-Soviet Pact, on August 25 Hungary reversed herself again saying she would be on the side of Berlin. However, the Hungarians proceeded to adopt a pro-Polish attitude during the sports tournament on August 28 between the two countries, whereupon the Germans ordered a cessation of deliveries of certain war material and Ribbentrop apparently used the ultimate weapon suggesting that it was quite possible for Hungary to secure the ancient prefect of Halicz if Hungary desired, and that Hungary could attack Transylvania at the time Germany attacked Poland. On September 1, therefore, Hungary expressed loyalty to Berlin.[85]

With regard to Bulgaria, one of the constant aims of the British and agreed to by Gafencu and Saracoglu at their meeting on April 8-9, was the idea of bringing Bulgaria into the Balkan Entente. During talks with Ciano in early May, Ribbentrop referred to the need to prevent this, whereupon the offer of Czech war stores was used as bait with the Germans agreeing on April 21 to increase arms deliveries to Bulgaria. In June, German State Secretary Weizsäcker instructed his Minister in Sofia, Richthofen, to ascertain whether Bulgaria would join the Anti-Comintern. Richthofen considered that it was possible if she received enough arms and if Yugoslavia were to denounce the Balkan Pact.[86] Unable to persuade Yugoslavia to leave the Pact and fearful that an armed Bulgaria would precipitate a Balkan conflict, the Germans had to be content with a neutral and hopefully benevolent Bulgaria. Meanwhile, the Bulgarians had become dissatisfied with Geman equipment and so were tempted by French low bids. This flirtation with the West so infuriated Berlin that she threatened Bulgaria with non-delivery of all war material.

Unfettered, Bulgarian Premier Kiosseivanov in early July made a long talked-of visit to Berlin, but it did not result in adhesion to the Pact as Germany desired. During a conversation in Berlin with Hitler on July 5, Kiosseivanov observed that Bulgaria exported 80 percent of her production to Germany. Well appreciated, the next day Ribbentrop promised to "do everything to expedite as much as possible the delivery of the 2,000 machine guns" mentioned by Kiosseivanov to the Führer, and that all deliveries of arms would be speeded up, and at the Führer's wish, Bulgaria was to receive modern German howitzers. Playing German interest for all it was worth, Kiosseivanov then requested thirty to forty Czech tanks for equipping a motorized division.[87]

Back in Sofia, on July 11, King Boris emphasized to German economic expert Clodius, that theough the trip to Berlin had been satisfactory, "it was a source of great anxiety to him that Bulgaria was lagging behind her neighbors in armaments," and he asked him to convey to the Führer an urgent "personal desire that two small Geman submarines should immediately be transferred to the Bulgarian Navy" due to the threatening attitude of Turkey and Rumania. During this interview with Clodius, King Boris defined his country's positions in the following terms: Bulgaria had striven for years to improve "her political relations with Yugoslavia and Turkey, in order to concentrate more effectively on directing her territorial aspirations against Rumania and Greece." The reorientation of Turkey had now put Bulgaria in a difficult position and the Turkish attitude had had "a more unfavorable influence on Rumanian foreign policy." At any event, Boris concluded that "Bulgaria must always remain at Germany's side."[88]

This was a pragmatic conclusion not an endemic one, for there was no love for the Germans on the part of the Bulgars and a predisposition for neutrality above all. The Bulgarian Military Attache confided to U.S. Military Attache Reily that the people were not kindly disposed toward Germany or what it stood for, remembering how brutally and arrogantly they were treated in the last war, and were it not for markets and the Turkish threat, revisionism and fear of a fate like Czechoslovakia's, they sould be ill disposed to position themselves on the side of Germany.[89] But just a few days earlier, at Bled, on July 9-10, Bulgaria had failed in its attempts to get Yugoslavia to denounce the Balkan Entente (and Yugoslavia had failed to persuade Bulgaria to join the Entente), and a month later Rumanian King Carol visited Istanbul, giving rise to Bulgarian fears of a Turkish-Rumanian agreement. On August 21, the Bulgarian Minister in Berlin, Draganov, told the Germans that his country might receive an ultimatum from Rumania and Turkey and possibly from Greece also.[90]

Hitler's statement at Obersalzburg in August that "the only one of the Balkan countries on which the Axis could entirely depend was Bulgaria," belied the fact that reliability was based not only loyalty to Germany but Bulgarian self-interest, making it not altogether without cost to the Germans, nor particularly reliable. No wonder that Hitler (despite pressure from the OKW to the contrary), wary that a war might be started too soon or that Bulgaria's Slavic sympathies might push her toward Moscow, played the pressure game up to the last deciding on August 11 that submarines could not be handed over for the moment. Only on August 26 did war material begin to arrive much to Kiosseivanov's satisfaction.

The steps the British and French were taking in Bucharest, Athens, Ankara, and Belgrade and the receptivity to it experienced in those capitals, made the Germans begin to look with distrust at the status quo Balkan states. Because of its oil, control of the Danube, and its proximity to Poland, the new Rumanian turn was of special concern to Berlin. As far as oil was concerned, not all of the weight was in Hitler's favor. On May 13, the German Minister in Bucharest, Fabricius, urged Berlin to give Rumania military supplies from Czech stores in return for additional petroleum, and he pointed out that the inability of Germany to supply uniforms had caused the Rumanian Government not to break off economic negotiations with Britain.

In the last weeks of peace the petroleum question became even more crucial to Germany. On July 22, Economic Director Wiehl said it depended on Rumania whether petrol rationing would have to be introduced in Germany. Hard bargaining between the two countries, therefore took place, and more than once Hitler gave instructions that arms deliveries should cease even though Clodius noted the economically dependent position in which such agreements placed Rumania.The Germans often tried to obtain crucial oil deliveries without tangible quid pro quos, and the Rumanians for their part stood firm, refusing shipment until arms deliveries were made. By September all German departments agreed that armaments deliveries should be made to Rumania under all circumstances.[91]

Such was not the case when it came to revisionist threats. There it seemed Germany had nearly total control over Hungarian and Bulgarian appetites, and soon it appeared over Soviet appetites as well. Rumanian Foreign Minister Gafencu was told starkly by Ribbentrop on April 18 and by Hitler on April 19 that the guarantees would not benefit Rumania, and it was intimated that though Hitler was "not interested in an alteration of frontiers in favor of Hungary," if Rumania participated in the policy of encirclement, Hitler would unleash Hungary.[92] As far as Bulgaria was concerned, Gafencu complained bitterly to Fabricius on July 7 that articles in the German press reproduced in Rumanian newspapers were to the effect that Germany was supporting Bulgaria's claim to Dobruja.[93]

Endangered on the southern and western frontiers, the Rumanians had to contend with the Russians as well, and in this respect the Nazi-Soviet Pact was Hitler's ultimate weapon. Fears of Russian designs on Bessarabia, enlivened after the Pact, caused Gafencu to tell Fabricius on August 27 that Rumania would not support Poland or become involved in war even if Britain and France took part, and that her relations with Turkey extended only to the limits of the Balkan Pact. King Carol himself admitted to the German Air Attache that, fearing attack from Bulgaria, he had not formed an alliance with Britain and had rejected a British plan to sabotage her oil fields in event of war. In late August as Hungarian and Rumanian troops moved to their respective frontiers, it was Hitler who called Budapest off.[94]

Hitler regarded Yugoslavia as the second most unreliable of the Balkan "neutrals" despite his many trump cards against her—her surrounded geographical position, unstable domestic situation, fear of Italy, need for arms, and vulnerability to revisionist pressures from Italy, Hungary, Greece and Bulgaria. What he feared was the Slavic link to Russia, Belgrade's ability to find sanctuary in Italy, and the key role Yugoslavia continued to play in the life of the Balkan Entente. Because Hitler needed Balkan stability, he was willing to support Yugoslavia at least to the extent he supported the status quo. In regard to both Hungarian revisionism and Italian aspirations, Berlin took Yugoslavia's side. During the Steel Pact signing, Ciano recorded in his *Diary* that Ribbentrop had hesitated to encourage Italy's designs on Yugoslavia and the fomenting of unrest in Croatia. "Ribbentrop approves, but I can see that he really prefers to maintain the Yugoslav status quo," wrote Ciano.[95] As far as Hungary was concerned, Ribbentrop told Cinkar-Marković that Hungary was prepared to make no claims against Yugoslavia and Hitler hoped that Yugoslavia would come to terms with Hungary, though he did not encourage intimacy as this would weaken Rumania where German interests were now paramount.[96]

On the other hand, the Germans continually pressed for Yugoslavia to accede to the Anti-Comintern, leave the League, and dissassociate herself from the Balkan Entente. Along with this, they began to increase their presence in the area, establishing new German consulates, airfields, and politically active groups. However, the Yugoslavs hedged, pledging only neutrality. On June 1 in Berlin, Prince Paul refused to join the Anti-Comintern on the grounds that Yugoslavia was the only European country not to recognize the Soviet Union and that such a stand would be unpopular in his sentimentally Slav country, but he half-heartedly agreed to leave the League. On July 8 Andrić explained that Yugoslavia must move cautiously in regard to leaving the Balkan Entente and that it was better to be in than out to keep watch on and if need be to direct its development.[97] Then from July 12 to August 2, Prince Paul visited London alledgedly for personal reasons (his son was in school there), which convinced Hitler of Yugoslavian perfidy.

Therefore, on July 25 Andrić was again pressured to leave the League and back orders of war material were held up. Neither of these threats moved Belgrade to change her position, causing Hitler to complain to Ciano on August 12 at Obersalzburg that "Yugoslavia would only remain neutral as long as it was dangerous to go over openly to the side of the Western democracies." On September 1, however, Andrić stated that Yugoslavia would remain neutral and that she was trying to induce other Balkan Entente states to follow suit. When pressed, Andrić finally accepted the German position that Yugoslavia's neutrality must be benevolent.[98] By this time the German economic experts had their way too, deciding that oil contracts for arms and aircraft agreements with Belgrade should be signed.

The pro-German Greek attitude which the Germans had carefully exploited,[99] was severely threatened by the Italian invasion of Albania. But the Germans showed little perturbation at the Greek acceptance of the British guarantee. When Simapoulos, the Greek Minister in London, told the German Charge that his Government had not sought the guarantee,

Kordt's only reply was to the effect that he was glad Greece had received a guarantee from both sides, though Goebbels seemed relieved during his early April visit to learn that Greece had made no commitments beyond those already in place with Turkey and those flowing from the Balkan Pact. Two days before the Turko-French Declaration of June 20, the Germans pressured Greece (as they did Rumania) to refrain from being drawn into any extension of the Balkan Entente as a result of paragraph six of the Anglo-Turkish Declaration. When the Greeks proceeded to explain that paragraph six contained a declaration only to the effect that consultation was to take place regarding security of the Balkans and that there were no new obligations and commitments, German Minister Woermann remarked only that he was aware of this interpretation and that it differed markedly from the Turkish interpretation.[100]

Apparently the Germans felt that the Greek predisposition to join the encirclement was slight, for Ribbentrop told Ciano on May 6-7 that now that Albania was occupied, the importance of Greece had dwindled and in any case, it would be easy for the Axis to control her though it would probably mean deposing the present King.[101] Besides the pressure of Italy, Germany believed she had an arms and economic stranglehold on Greece sufficient to neutralize her. Greece requested an arms credit, but Germany treated the request in a dilatory fashion. Besides Greece's untenable position economically, militarily, and geographically, Germany considered that strong revisionist pressure from Bulgaria and longstanding border problems with Yugoslavia would make it impossible for her to give active assistance to Germany's enemies.

Turkey, of course, was somewhat outside the Balkan framework due to her geographical position and the absence of revisionist problems, so she was not vulnerable to the same pressures as were the other Balkan countries. Having failed in their efforts to stave off conclusion of a pact with the British and French, the Germans and especially von Papen who believed that Turkey was "looking for a way out," tried to "influence everybody toward strictest neutrality."[102] The Turks, like the other Balkan countries, were receptive to this tack, particularly in the face of the attack on Poland. She was, therefore, willing to go to the defense of other Balkan states only if her own interests were threatened, for instance, if Germany had marched into Rumania or threatened through Rumania, or if Bulgaria had brought the Balkan Entente into play. But, the Turko-

Russian and Turko-British connections were another thing, and against this the Germans had to find a new weapon, in Moscow.

To the Italians, the Anglo-Turkish agreement was more obnoxious than the guarantees, and so when Ciano visited Ribbentrop on May 21, he played up the Turkish threat, afterwards flattering himself that he had, "with original Turkish documents intercepted by our secret service," convinced Ribbentrop that Turkish hostility was directed against Germany as well as Italy. Italy also hoped to use the fear of Turkish hegemony backed by Great Britain in the Balkans as a bogey to frighten Greece and Rumania, "both of whom still remember the stench of the Turks." He added, "it is always worthwhile to revive certain old hatreds."[103]

But the Germans were not ready to abandon Turkey completely, in part due to the German concern for the essential raw materials she needed from Turkey, especially chrome. On May 25, the Turkish Ambassador in Berlin was informed by the Germans that all of seven or eight missions in Berlin to buy German weaponry were given to understand their presence was no longer needed and that no further work would be done on the Turkish orders. Then all during the summer, Berlin treated Turkish requests for war materials in a dilatory fashion, though von Papen's view was that the inability of the West to supply Ankara could turn the tide in Germany's favor. The Turks for their part hoped that the Anglo-Turkish Declaration would put pressure on Germany to change from a clearing basis to free exchange. Both sides held firm, however, and in the end Turkish audacity won the day. On August 24 Saracoglu told von Papen that "Turkey might be a hundred times weaker than Germany," but she must reject the German economic proposals of August 21 and she would export her product "to other countries by paying premiums."[104]

While the Turks alone seemed able to meet German revisionist economic and political threats with some degree of sovereign obstinance, their concern was for their own neutrality and national existence, but their parameters, unlike the other Balkan states, reached into the Mediterranean, the Near East, and toward the Soviet Union enabling them to go futher with Britain than did the other Southeastern states. On the other hand, they too begged the question of reciprocal aid in the Balkans and were careful to maintain their neutrality. On September 11 in the first official statement on the war, the Prime Minister before the Grand Assembly said, "We are outside the present war. We hope that the war will not lead to developments which will reach our country."[105] And so, by carefully orchestrating

the neutrality of the Balkan countries (and the Soviet Union), Germany
was also ultimately able to gain Turkish neutrality in the Southeast as
well.

* * * * *

Ultimately, therefore, on a unilateral basis, German-Balkan diplomacy
was successful in neutralizing the allied encirclement drive. Not one more
Balkan country accepted a Western guarantee, nor did any sign any sort
of mutual assistance pact during the summer of 1939. That the Germans
were successful in their diplomacy is the result not so much of German
genius, but the facts of Balkan existence in 1939 and German power.
Though it is true the Germans displayed a certain shrewdness in their attention to the individual aims and interests of the Balkan states, skillfully
playing on the revisionist-status quo antipathies and the need for arms and
desire for neutrality, it is also true that in 1939 Germany and the Balkans
were essentially marching in the same direction, that is toward neutrality
and a mutually beneficial economic meld. German genius that there was
lay in the fact that Germany convinced the Balkan countries that she
would not invade, and that she would and could control revisionism and
the Soviet threat. Since fear of invasion and revisionism had been the main
reasons for Balkan acceptance of the guarantees, confidence on that score
in part prevented further slippage into allied ranks.

As important as the Balkan element of Germany anti-encirclement was,
the overriding fear in Berlin was of encirclement involving Britain, France
and the Soviet Union (and ultimately the United States). Therefore, during
the summer as the lanes of communication between Berlin and Moscow
opened up, the need for German pressure on the Balkans was diminished.
As a result of the Berlin-Moscow link, the Balkans, and particularly dissident Turkey, were exposed to the most powerful of reasons to stay within the German fold, the fear being that should war move to the Balkans, a
link between these two countries would expose them to excesses of both
German and Soviet-Russian perfidy. On the opposite side of the coin, a
Soviet-German rapprochement and Nazi-Soviet competition in great measure protected them from a potential source of war on their territory.

But even with the Nazi-Soviet Non-Aggression Pact as ballast, the Germans paid particular attention to localizing the war against Poland. In an

unsigned memo of August 22, advance propaganda to be used in the individual countries were formulated.[106] The neutrality of the small countries was to be safeguarded. Hungary was to be treated with friendliness, but warned that her revisionist aspirations would not be backed by Germany. Yugoslavia and Rumania were to be given less friendly warnings to remain neutral. The Germans even continued to hope that Yugoslavia might join the Anti-Comintern Pact on the assumption that the Pact was really directed not against Russia, but against Britain. In fact, control in the Southeast remained a policy of Hitler's right up to the moment of German invasion, in August 1940, Germany exerting pressure on Rumania and Hungary to prevent armed conflict. Hand in hand with Balkan neutrality went Russian neutrality secured by the Nazi-Soviet Pact, and Italian neutrality in the early stages, after which Italy would join Germany in the West (not the East).

Conclusion

The dissolution of Czechoslovakia and the grant of Ruthenia to Hungary resulted in the continuation of the successful German program practiced in the preceding years whereby the Balkan states hastily submitted to Nazi will. This was very apparent in the ensuing German-Rumanian Economic Agreement, which was a statement of not just economic, but political submission to Hitler. The control the Germans displayed over the limits of Hungarian revisionism was a significant factor in the Rumanian decision to protect herself by appeasing Germany, and the same was true of other Balkan states particularly Yugoslavia.

The submission of Rumania, with the inherent meaning it had with regard to the destruction of any propensity Rumania might have had to go to Poland's aid, increased German pressure against Poland. Here at last the British took a stand, but in the process of the Polish guarantee, the link between Poland and the Balkans was finally severed, for neither Poland nor Rumania (and her sister Balkan states) agreed to any sort of reciprocity in each others' defense. Thus, for the Germans the cause of Balkan pacification was served as was the Balkan quest for neutrality, and, as had been intended, Poland was cut off.

The turning point for the Germans in the Balkans came not with the Polish guarantee, but the invasion of Albania. This assault threatened the

Balkans with direct invasion, and for the first time turned them against Germany. It appeared in Bucharest, in Belgrade, in Athens, and in Ankara that Germany either could not control her Axis partner or did not want to. Likewise, British interests in the Mediterranean at Suez were imperiled. This similar anti-Axis interest brought the Balkans and Britain together, providing the framework for the guarantees. But the substance of any further agreement was lacking because the British desired creation of an interlocking Balkan-Polish-Soviet peace front, while the Balkan concern was limited to the interests of frontier security. Berlin for the moment seemed victorious.

There was an uncomfortable exception however, when British attention turned to the Straits. Turkey, on May 12, declared herself ready to assist Great Britain, a move which sowed the seeds for development of the peace front sought after by Britain and France. For Turkey was a key member of the Balkan Entente and the nexus of a relationship with the Soviet Union. Under threat of having their whole Balkan program and with it designs against Poland and then France destroyed, the Germans moved quickly to repacify the area. The first step was to gain control over Italian actions, a move designed not only to prevent any other Italian Fascist moves in the Southeast or defection to the British, but to dilute anti-Italian sentiment and neutralize the area, particularly Yugoslavia. The next step was unmitigated anti-encirclement pressure in Balkan capitals, pressure which took the following forms—threats of Bulgarian and Hungarian revisionism against status quo Balkan states Yugoslavia, Rumania, and Greece, promises of weaponry, and arguments to the effect that British aid would produce results counter to Balkan interests (German invasion).

In short, Hitler's supreme victory in control of the Southeast was at Prague, when rearrangement of frontiers to Hungary's advantage cut Poland off from the Southeast and threatened the other Balkan states. Rumania bowed down as a result, signing an economic agreement synonymous to satellization. It was a Pyrrhic victory though, for advancing German power caused Italy to act, this time in the direction of the Balkans. Britain was finally aroused and as a result, the contest was on between Britain and Germany for the Balkans, and in the wings were two other interested participants, Italy and Soviet Russia. In the chess game that followed, Britain countered the Albanian move with guarantees to Rumania and Greece and then a mutual assistance declaration with Turkey. Germany moved against this with the Pact of Steel and an anti-encirclement offensive. For both, the Soviet Union soon began to hold the key to Balkan control, for Germany to frighten them back to Berlin and to counter British efforts to link up with Moscow, and for Britain to create an eastern front linking the Balkans, Poland, Turkey, and the Soviet Union with the hope then of detaching Italy.

In this battle to swing the Southeast in the desired direction, neither side really won, for Britain was unable to persuade the Balkans to form an interlocking defense agreement among themselves against the Axis, and Germany was never able to again be certain that the Balkan countries would be benevolently neutral. In fact, the complexity of Balkan politics provided a challenge to both sides, for knitting the Balkans together was as complex as was the German problem of divide-and-rule. Missteps by the British prevented harmony thus playing into Hitler's hands, while excessive revisionist/anti-revisionist machinations ran the risk of a Balkan explosion and destruction of Hitler's plans for delimitation of the war.

There are some who think that had the Balkans linked together and then tied up with Britain and the Soviet Union, war might have been avoided, while others believe such a vision was so unconnected with the realities of the area that this was not policy or vision, but a dream. In fact, the Balkans had their own program and this in itself influenced the course of events. Balkan efforts at collective security, why they ultimately failed in the allied sense but succeeded within their own framework, and why, perhaps, they would not have kept the peace anyway are the next salient questions in the British and Nazi move toward Moscow.

CHAPTER III

THE BALKANS—FACTIONALISM AND NEUTRALITY

Hitler needed a neutral and loyal Balkan area in order to ensure a steady flow of raw material supplies and to prevent a Balkan conflict or the creation of an allied Balkan front which would involve the Soviet Union. In his immediate aim, which was to isolate Poland, Hitler needed in addition, to prevent a Balkan-Polish link. Among other things, he dealt on an individual basis with each Balkan state in his attempt to win their loyalty and if not that, their neutrality. By arms supplies, economic domination, and threats of revisionism he was largely successful in his quest for Balkan servility to the Nazi program.

The Western unilateral guarantee policy helped rather han hindered his program, for it perpetuated the age-old dictum of divide-and-rule by freezing the frontiers. However, both the Balkans and the West sought to counter Hitler's successful Balkan fragmentation by schemes of Balkan unity, with the thought that a viable Balkan front would either deter Hitler from a move east or create a deterrent in the East sufficient to prevent Hitler's turn on the West. Viewed strictly in Balkan terms, the benefits of unity were enormous, for it would protect the Balkans against what they feared most in the oncoming European conflict, that is an internecine Balkan war. In the Balkan mind, the first enemy in war was not the West, Germany, Italy or the Soviet Union, but boundary rectification, which was for these small states at the heart of national destruction or survival.

In terms of the Second World War, history has put the question to the Balkans as to whether or not successful Balkan unity might have provided a deterrent to Hitler sufficient to have prevented his march against Poland, and hence the holocaust which resulted not only in the destruction of Europe, but in the loss of Balkan freedom to Bolshevik tyranny. This is a salient question when assessing responsibility for World War II and even in a more limited framework, in approaching the question of the preservation of Balkan freedom. Winston Churchill himself told Rumanian Foreign Minister Gafencu during his trip to London in April of 1939 that "If they (Balkans) stand together, they are safe,"[1] But even if the Balkans were safe from each other could this, without attachment to one Great Power or the other, have provided armor sufficient to ensure their survival?

The History of Balkan Unity

Based on the historical record, prospects for Balkan solidarity would have appeared dim to the prognosticator in 1939. The hope was that an outside threat of sufficient magnitude and the remodeling of Balkan statism on the basis of national self-determination as had occurred at the end of World War I, would give the Balkans the necessary framework within which to work out a federalist scheme heretofore lacking. In theory, freed of Ottoman, Habsburg, and Russian imperialist oppression, and having gained throughout the Balkans an equality of nation-state status, the Balkans would find the desire and the means to develop an interlocking political and economic system which would better serve their needs, particularly in the face of the perilous economic and political abyss into which they had fallen by 1939. The theory did not match reality because there was not unanimity as to the nature and magnitude of the outside threat posed, because the problem of the Great Power interference continued to exist, and because nationhood brought national rivalries and insecurities rather than unity and stability.

The idea of a unity of the Balkan people is as old as a coordinated effort against the Ottoman Empire, but it only gained practicality in the twentieth century when, according to historian Douglas Dakin, "the Balkan States began to develop their own military power demanding that the Great Powers take them into account."[2] But, he concludes, while on the one hand arms gave the Balkan powers more freedom to pursue their national interests, it also ascerbated the relations between them. Stated in other terms, the national self-determination and Western liberal policies from which they were born, turned into nationalism with all its attendant chauvinism, autarky, and jealous rivalries.

The magnitude of territorial disputes provided unlimited potential for intra-Balkan friction. For instance, there was Hungarian and Rumanian rivalry over Transylvania, Rumanian and Soviet rivalry over Bessarabia, Bulgarian and Greco-Yugoslav rivalry over Macedonia, Albanian and Yugoslav rivalry over Voyvodina, Yugoslav and Austrian rivalry over the Banat, and Bulgarian and Turkish rivalry over Salonika. To these territorial disputes must be added long-standing political, social, and religious tensions, for example between democracies like Czechoslovakia and dictatorships like those which evolved in Bulgaria, Greece, Albania, and Rumania during the interwar period, or as a result of unstable political systems like in Yugoslavia which evoked outside intervention, or between social classes whereby the upper classes identified with Germany the peasant classes with Russia, with the Jewish middle class in between.[3] Then, too, there were the economic realities whereby the artificially created autarky of Versailles served to break up the symbiosis of the Danubian Basin, making the East European states competitive rather than complementary in the quest for markets for their grain and jealous of the one industrialized state, Czechoslovakia.

Added to the veritable political, economic and territorial difficulties, was the reality of the Balkan geopolitical position in international politics. The very bases of the Versailles, Trianon and Sévrès treaties perhaps doomed forever Balkan solidarity, for a host of controllable little countries were set up as a barrier against German expansionism and then as a *cordon sanitaire* against Bolshevism. Thus, from the beginning the Balkans were not entirely sovereign in the sense that the West, having given birth to these Balkan states for their own purposes, carried the burden of their sustaining life and could oversee their destruction should their purpose for being vanish. In addition, the validity of the whole Western concept of states in the East as protection for France, hinged on Russia and Germany in collapse and a strong France and Great Britain willing and able to protect this front in the East.

Yet, it was in this untoward milieu that the seeds of Balkan federalism took root. Haunted by a longing for collective security and the conception that an ongoing organization of East Europe could liberate these countries from the domination of any Great Power, two Balkan organizations, the

Little and Balkan Ententes, were formed with the blessings of France, who saw in them an instrument of the preservation of the status quo. The Little Entente, composed of Rumania and Yugoslavia, who both signed on with Czechoslovakia in 1921 (and with France in 1926 and Rumania and Yugoslavia with France 1926-27), was designed as a balance against Italian friendship and bloc formation with revisionist states like Albania, Hungary, and Bulgaria. As such, the Little Entente was a punitive rather than an ameliorative Balkan organization, which secured some but alienated others of the East European states, setting up a situation whereby the chances for Great Power interference on the side of the disenfranchised were greatly increased. Unless, therefore, the composition and purpose of the body was altered, the organization was not a truly federal one leading to Balkan unity. On the other hand, by threat rather than persuasion, the prospects for stability of the area were enhanced due to the united front formed on behalf of the status quo states.

The sequence of alliances leading to formation of the Little Entente serves to illustrate the anti-Hungarian rather than federalist nature of this grouping. On August 14, 1920 Czechoslovakia and Yugoslavia signed an alliance pledging to come to each others' aid in case of an unprovoked attack by Hungary. On April 23, 1921 Czechoslovakia and Rumania promised aid to each other in case of Hungarian attack and consultation on all matters of foreign policy. On June 7, 1921 Yugoslavia and Rumania signed an alliance directed at both Hungary and Bulgaria. During the next eight months military alliances were signed, and in the next years cooperation in foreign trade and matters of foreign policy exclusive of Hungary were affected. Soon France, although never formally joining it, became an ardent patron of the Entente as all four were against revisionism. Thus, out of Balkan feudism and Great Power interests was the Little Entente formed. Basic to its conception was the idea that the first enemy of the members was a fellow Balkan state.

Nevertheless, Little Entente development along progressive lines appeared hopeful as the Axis threatened. Two weeks after Hitler came to power, the Little Entente strengthened itself by creation of a permanent council, increasing its economic relations, and refusing Mussolini's proposal for a Four Power Pact to rule Europe. Yet, the Little Entente did nothing to bring Hungary into the pact or to dilute the anti-Hungarian nature of the pact, thus giving Budapest little choice but to turn to the

Axis for support. In return, Hungary rather than the Axis, became the focus of Little Entente activity, Budapest providing for Germany the key to unlocking Entente support for Czechoslovakia and destruction of the Entente.

The Balkan Entente was the product of a series of conferences beginning in 1930 between Yugoslavia, Rumania, Greece, Turkey and Bulgaria,[4] for the purpose of shoring up a flagging economic situation brought on by the 1929 depression and reinsuring against Balkan revisionism. At the Fourth Balkan Conference, from November 5-11, 1933 everything looked hopeful. Even the chief of the Bulgarian delegation in his closing speech said it had been the most fruitful of the conferences to date, the Bulgarians being given the right of full equality in its relation with other countries, and plans being made for a bridge over the Danube between Rumania and Bulgaria, uniformity of maritime, extradition and other laws.[5]

But political difficulties, especially between Bulgaria and Yugoslavia largely centering on control of Macedonia, could not quickly be overcome despite peacemaker Alexander of Yugoslavia's efforts in 1933. As a result, a pact was signed on February 9, 1934 between Rumania, Yugoslavia, Greece and Turkey but not Albania and Bulgaria, whose absences were conspicuous in that the Pact provided for the mutual defense of frontiers of any of the four, and a Bulgarian signature would have meant renunciation of all hope of territorial gain. At the time the members were pained to declare that the Pact was not directed against any nation and aimed only to protect Balkan frontiers against Balkan agression, but the omission of Bulgaria (and Albania), the failure to solve the border questions, and claims (by Bulgaria) that this Balkan grouping was calculated to have European consequences, weakened the Entente once it became the seatbed of Great Power political play. And it had the serious consequence of preventing the fusion of the Little and Balkan Ententes, the possibility of which was discussed in the fall of 1934 but abandoned when it was concluded that the adhesion of Bulgaria was necessary.[6]

Though there were grave weaknesses in this Pact which called itself "Balkan," for example the refusal to listen to Bulgarian claims, the Greek refusal to abandon hopes of acquiring Albanian territory, and the failure to guarantee against outside aggression, it was a signal of a limited nature that the participants were willing to act collectively on a restricted basis against aggression. Thereafter, there was established a Permanent Council and an Economic Advisory Council. The links of both Rumania and Yugoslavia to the Little and Balkan Ententes, some feel successfully deterred Mussolini's entry into Southeastern Europe in the early 1930s. The assassination of King Alexander of Yugoslavia in 1933 and the politics surrounding the assassination (it was blamed on Hungary), however, in some measure removed the heart and soul of a collective Balkan spirit which was based on a dialog with the states left outside the Pact. From then on, the Balkan Entente increasingly took on the aura of an anti-Bulgarian coalition.

The other problem besides intra-Balkan rivalries hampering efforts to effectuate a truly federal Balkan organization was that their fate had always been tied directly to that of Central Europe, the Straits, and Poland, which was in turn tied to the fate of the Great Powers. And the Danube and the Straits, in turn, have always been connected, as the Straits are the exit for the Danube and since 1956 the precedent had been that the Straits should be internationalized, that is administered by a combination of riparian and nonriparian states. The same was true of the Danube in the interwar period, as control of the mouth was handed over to a League-based International Commission. The questions for the Balkans involved how far Balkan solidarity should extend, the benefits such unity contained, and whether or not unity should be accompanied by the extrication from Great Power politics.

During the 1930s, progress was made in turning over the Straits and the Danube to Balkan control. By the Lausanne Convention of 1923,[7] the shores of the Dardanelles and Bosporus were demilitarized, and an International Straits Commission was formed to administer the Straits. Some of the problems emerging out of this agreement were that Germany was excluded, and Russia was dissatisfied at not having gained greater security by a special provision concerning exit of her warships and the closing of the Straits during time of conflict. But the problem most pertinent to the Balkans was the belief by the British and French, inherent in the Lausanne Convention, that Balkan defense was at the Straits not the Danube and the need, therefore, for the Balkans to maintain close relations with Turkey to safeguard themselves. But they were cut off from Istanbul by Bulgaria, and unless the Bulgarian issue was resolved, the Balkans were in danger of becoming a captive area from the south.

German remilitarization of the Rhineland in 1936 made apparent to the West and the Balkans alike the enfeebled Balkan position in terms of

defense. Therefore, in June-July 1936, the Lausanne Convention participants met at Montreux and agreed to the remilitarization of the Straits by
Turkey. And, though reaffirming the principle of freedom of passage for
commercial vessels, the Montreux Convention tightened up requirements
for passage of military vessels, and in time of war non-Black Sea powers
were allowed to send only light vessels into the Black Sea while Black Sea
powers could send capital ships of any size into the Mediterranean. Besides
remilitarization of the littoral, Turkey's position was enhanced by the provision that Turkey was allowed to close the Straits in time of war or imminent danger.

While the Montreux Convention increased Turkish control of the Straits,
it did nothing to rectify the major weaknesses of Lausanne threatening to
the Balkans. In fact, it magnified them, for the importance of the Turkish
link was enhanced, but no steps were taken to settle the Bulgarian question which precariously interrupted the Balkans from Turkey, and little
was done to enhance Turkey's very limited ability to fortify the Straits.
Also, Germany and Italy were once again excluded, giving Hitler and Mussolini points of grievance to exploit, while the Russian position was empowered. Finally, the move did nothing to strengthen intra-Balkan relationships, because while the Balkan Entente generally supported the idea
of increased Turkish and therefore Balkan control over the Straits, they
were incensed by Turkey's failure to consult the other members of the
Entente and as a consequence, Turkish hegemony in the area.

Hitler appreciated and exploited both the British emphasis on the Straits
rather than the Balkans, and the weak Turkish position with regard to
fortification, and he even scoffed at the negotiations themselves, rejecting
the British claim that this was a successful example of peacetime revisionism, allowing instead that the Turks would have refortified them in any
event. He confidently told Hungarian Foreign Minister Csáky that it was
unlikely that the Turks would ever advance against Hungary through Rumania, as "the Turks had shown themselves lazy" with regard to fortification and "incredibly little had been done in the years since the Montreux
Convention."[8] Italy meanwhile, simply did not consider Montreux as
binding.

The diminution of Great Power control of the Straits was symbolic
of the times, particularly of the British and French desire to redefine their
interests in the face of the Axis threat. This was synonymous with the Balkan desire to gain greater control over their own affairs even at the price

of weaker defense. For what they hoped, was that in extracting their affairs from those of the Great Powers, they would strengthen their position and gain the possibility of neutrality in the coming struggle, a position which would not have been possible were they tied to the West. This theme was repeated in the Rumanian efforts to gain control of the Danube.

By the Versailles Treaty, the affairs of the Danube were administered by a multinational Commission of the Danube. The emasculation of internationalism and its instrument the League of Nations, and Turkish success at Montreux caused Rumania first in 1936 and then in 1938 to call for unrestricted sovereignty over the mouth of the Danube by replacing the European Commission of the Danube with an "International Commission." In 1936 the Soviet Union encouraged the Rumanian effort to abolish the Commission and suggested increasing the number of countries represented on the new commission, presumably to include her.[9] In 1938 Germany withdrew from the European Danube Commission and then proposed reconstituting it so that it was composed of riparian states only, thus excluding Great Britain, France and Italy. Berlin also proposed a new parallel technical commission formed only with German and Rumanian participation and stated her intent to negotiate unilaterally with each Danube state on the issue. The Balkan states were generally with Rumania in the reconstitution of the Commission as a way to give more power to the sovereign states, but were against the exclusion of Italy, France and Great Britain.[10]

The Rumanian campaign was finally successful on August 8, 1938 at Sinaia when, as a prelude to Munich, the European Commission renounced all powers incompatible with Rumanian sovereignty. The problem, however, was that on March 1, 1939 Germany and Italy were admitted to this Commission with the result that Rumania now found herself vying with Germany for control of the Danube, a contest in which Rumania was certain to lose. Practically speaking, Germany controlled the Upper Danube after Prague (Germany and Hungary divided up the Czech merchant fleet and consummated several agreements regarding division of freight traffic), and so with the Danube half gone to Germany and the other half under serious threat, not only was a basic geographical factor uniting the Balkans disrupted, but the natural link between the Straits and the Danube weakened as well. Surrounding all of this, was the fact that in this scheme of Balkan unity, Great Power interests were once again involved, but this time it was dominated by the Axis rather than the West.

The other Balkan problems, its link with Poland, followed a schismatic course similar to that of the Straits and the Danube. France had pinned her security to Poland through a military alliance in 1921, and then tried to link Poland and herself together with the Balkans by a series of uni-lateral arrangements, for example, alliances between Poland and Czecho-slovakia, Poland and Rumania, France and Rumania, France and Yugo-slavia. But the unilateral nature of the arrangements prevented creation of any collective Balkan defense system which would bring all countries into concerted action. The Poles, for their part, refused entreaties by the Little Entente to join, saying they desired to remain politically separate.[11]

The first crack in the Polish-Danube link came when Hitler and Pilsud-ski signed a pact in January 1934. This was followed by a Franco-Soviet agreement and the subsequent reoccupation of the Rhineland. Under the circumstances of the Polish-German link an the Franco-Soviet link, the Balkans took the position that they would be better to sever the northern connection, which appeared to open up avenues for adversaries on both sides. This position was reinforced given traditional Polish-Hungarian friendship, and was cemented with emotion during the Munich crisis when Poland failed to support Czechoslovakia while taking steps of a revisionist nature, and during Prague when, as Gafencu said, Beck had played a mean trick in consenting to Hungary's total occupation of Ruth-enia without prior consultation.[12]

The split between Poland and the Southeast went even deeper than those events and crises, in the end proving to be the difference between creation of the peace front and its failure. The Ententes, for instance, were from the earliest period in their conception, dedicated to the maintenance of the status quo at any price, while Poland on the other hand, was ready to fight Germany or Russia as she had done many times before. From the Polish point of view connection with the Southeast was of little value; "Rumania is a broken reed," said the Polish Ambassador in the U.S., "her military strength inadequate, her government honeycombed with corrup-tion and incapable of confronting a crisis."[13] Beyond differences in inter-est and style driving them apart, were divisive historical chords, chief among them Catholicism and the absence of Ottoman rule, Orthodoxy and Islam. Anecdotal to this point was the refusal of the Archbishop of Krakow to receive King Carol on June 28, 1937 (as Germany threatened) because of personal disapproval on "religious grounds" of his relationship with his mistress, Madame Lupescu.[14]

* * * * *

Perhaps the following can be said about the basic framework of Balkan federalism in the interwar period. The impetus as it materialized in the Balkan and Little Ententes was nationalistic, not federalistic. In reality, these two groupings were defensive coalitions whereby status quo states were joined together against revisionist states. Hence, it is not surprising that they did not fulfill a purpose often assigned to them, that of providing a Balkan defensive bulwark against Fascist and later Soviet aggression. Second, from the beginning the centripetal movement that there was, was closely connected with the politics of the Great Powers. In effect, France and the Western Powers backed the status quo groupings while Germany and Italy backed the revisionist coalitions, for example, the Rome Protocol States. Finally, the idea of Balkan federalism in some measure belied the realities of Balkan existence in that the affairs and survival of the Balkans were closely aligned with those of Turkey and Poland, and any such schemes must take the affairs of those two states into close account if not into the federation itself. In the case of Turkey, Bulgaria interrupted a solid Balkan grouping between the Straits and the Danube, and in the case of Poland, self-chosen isolation by Warsaw, friendship with Hungary, and a host of other differences, prevented a necessary north-south East European alliance.

On the outside, the increasing disinclination and inability of the West to posture their influence in Balkan affairs on the one hand, and growing Balkan chauvinism on the other, appeared to be nudging a new policy of "the Balkans for the Balkans" along. The Straits were handed over to Turkish control, defense of the Danube was approaching sovereign riparian status, and the Balkan countries were beginning to disengage themselves from Central Europe and Poland. Unfortunately, the reemergence of the Balkans out from under the umbrella of the West was less a sovereign action than a reaction to German movement east. As such, it set a group of states free who had neither the ability to defend themselves individually, nor the inclination to do so collectively. In fear and opportunism, they reacted unilaterally not collectively, and as such, the phrase "the Balkans for the Balkans" came to mean not Balkan unity and liberation from Great Power politics, but disunity and increasing dependence on Germany rather than the West.

The Balkans for the Balkans

In outlining the requirements for Turkish security with regard to the Balkans, a Turkish deputy stated in early 1939; "The Balkans must belong to the Balkan countries, the Balkans must remain aloof from the world struggle as much as possible, and the Balkans should not fall under the domination of any Great Power." He acknowledged, however, that the Balkans constituted economically a part of the German "living space," but that Germany must look to the Balkans not as part of herself, but as partners.[15] A sovereign Balkans, a neutral Balkans, and a free Balkans—these were the elements of the concept which was to dominate the hopes of the Southeast during this period. At the heart of the goal was the idea of a common policy and unity within the nation-state framework, and in the years preceding 1939, the Balkan countries tried to find that common link. But the problems were enormous; sovereignty often implied revisionism against one another, concepts of neutrality differed among them while its advantages were questioned, and the power and will not to be dominated by Great Powers was often lacking. In fact, in trying to handle their own affairs, remarkable disunity rather than unity was displayed often to their own very great dispair and detriment.

For, in moving out from under the West's sphere due to the rise of German strength and the loss of Western protection of their borders, the Balkans settled down into a pattern of competition personified in the Little and Balkan Ententes whereby Greece, Yugoslavia and Rumania were against Bulgaria, and Yugoslavia, Rumania and Czechoslovakia were against Hungary; and whereby the Little Entente representing the Upper Danube was pitted against the interests of the Balkan Entente representing the Lower Danube. With each German inspired crisis—the Rhineland, Anschluss, Munich and Prague, the positions of the Balkan states hardened, and rather than drawing together in the face of isolation and vulnerability to Axis rapaciousness, they grew apart in the pursuit of their own national interests and in the nationally oriented interests of the Little and Balkan Ententes. As such, they became more not less vulnerable to Great Power politics.

A dispatch by U.S. Military Attache in Istanbul, Royden Williamson, on November 16, 1936 wraps in a nutshell the story of the dream versus the realities. He reported that a Turkish publication, *La Republique* praised

the high ideals of the Balkan Entente noting it had "raised them to fratern-
ity and understanding of where their interests lie," and instead of living in
constant envy of a few acres óf ground, "the Balkan states have come to a
feeling of mutual esteem . . . ." The article then hailcd the cordial reception in Sofia of the Yugoslav Prime Minister and subsequently Turkey
seemed to offer her own olive branch to her old enemy of 1912. At the
heart of the euphoria surrounding Balkan Entente consolidation and the
possible entry of Bulgaria into the Pact, stated the article, was "The fundamental idea in the Entente [that] Balkan affairs are the affairs of the Balkan states. Henceforth the great powers shall not make use of any of its
states as instruments." In contrast to this bucolic version, the real story,
reported Williamson, was that Turkey was seeking to keep some Balkan
states like Rumania from tying the Little and Balkan Ententes together in
the face of Hitler's moves in Central Europe, thus involving Turkey. And
he said, the truth about Bulgarian entrance into the Entente was that she
had no thought of doing so without territorial recompense.[16] Both the
dreams and realities of Balkan Federalism were apparent in the events of
1936-1938.

The three major threats to the Balkans in 1936 were growing economic
dependence on Germany, the remilitarization of the Rhineland, and as a
consequence of the former the rearmament of Hungary. A vain attempt at
Balkan collaboration to counter economic strangulation was attempted by
Czech leader Hodža in the so-called Hodža Plan of 1936 which envisioned
economic and political cooperation among the six states bordering on the
Danube (Austria, Hungary, Czechoslovakia, Rumania, Yugoslavia and
Bulgaria), and an extension of the system of commercial treaties between
Czechoslovakia and Austria, and Czechoslovakia and Hungary. In a state-
ment to the press on February 14, 1934, Dr. Hodža said:

> I think we must bring together the economic systems of the Little
> Entente and of the Rome Protocol (Italy, Austria and Hungary). As
> far as they wish to enter the system certain members of the Balkan
> Entente might also be considered.[17]

The plan was brought up for discussion at the Economic Council of the
Little Entente on March 7-8, and though nothing definitive was forthcoming, its deliberation was continued by economic experts. However, the
general fear of Czech industrial overlordship inspired in part by German

propaganda, and the more advantageous links with Germany already established, made the plan generally unpopular among the predominantly agra-
rian Balkan states. Meanwhile the political enmity between Hungary and
Rumania and the basic unwillingness of the Balkans to extend their connections to Central Europe, particularly after Anschluss and the crisis over
Czechoslovakia sealed the fate of any sort of connection between the Lower and Upper Danube states, generally dooming the plan.

Sensing the dangers that remilitarization of the Rhineland held for
them, the Little and Balkan Ententes tried to close ranks. They set up a
Marine Commission, signed aviation agreements, and took steps to create
a Central European postal and telephonic system. The Permanent Coun-
cils of both the Little and Balkan Ententes met in May, and in communiques following these meetings, both Ententes expressed concern for the
gravity of the international situation, firm support for the League of Nations, recognition of the part they themselves played in preserving the
peace of Europe, and they made pledges for further solidarity on the economic front.[18] Above all, the pièce de résistance of their policies was the
maintenance of the status quo, but to that end they were unsuccessful in
taking concrete steps to defend it. At a Little Entente council meeting in
Bratislava in November 1936, efforts were made to convert the Entente
into an alliance of mutual defense against attack from any order, but this
got nowhere due to differences of opinion among the Czechs, Rumanians,
and Yugoslavs, and fears of Habsburg restoration.

Dedication to the status quo caused both Ententes to make statements
with regard to the inviolability of frontiers, and while this was a warning
to the Axis, it also closed the door to rapprochement with Bulgaria and
Hungary. Point two of the Little Entente communique of May 7, 1936
pledged support for the continued independence of Austria and opposition "aux changements de frontière par un révisionnisme malfaisant."[19]
The communique issued by the Balkan Entente of May 6 read:

> La politique de l'Entente Balkanique étant basée sur l'intangibilité
> des frontières actuelles et sur le respect de la sécurité, le Conseil
> permanent a envisagé les moyens les plus efficaces pour en assurer
> la stricte application dans la région de l'Europe où vivent les États
> balkaniques.[20]

The problem of accommodation with Hungary was further aggravated by the sanctioning on November 12, 1936 by the Rome Protocol states of Italy, Hungary, and Austria, of Hungarian remilitarization. The Little Entente issued a communique on the subject two days later, proffering their displeasure and making clear that any such rearmament must be accompanied by a frontier guarantee to be acceptable. In part, the communique read:

> The States of the Little Entente consider it necessary to recall in that connexion that, as long ago as May, 1933, they expressly accepted the principle of equality of rights in armaments, but with the proviso that this principle should be applied on the line of a reciprocal guarantee agreement and that strictly defense guarantees of security should be offered.[21]

Thus, in the face of triple threats of 1936—economic dependence on Germany, remilitarization of the Rhineland and then of Hungary—the Balkans did indeed draw together, but more like a cocoon into a shell than an expanding front of unity. For they disassociated themselves from the Upper Danube politically and economically, and then hardened their position vis-a-vis Hungary. In effect, the Balkans were becoming isolated collectively and individually, as was Hitler's intention.

In 1937, German plans for the extinction of Czechoslovakia moved forward. Basic to the isolation of Prague, was the disruption of the Little Entente, which was to be accomplished by the detachment of Rumania and Yugoslavia. Poland was to be the instrument of the former, Italy and Hungary of the latter. The Polish plan was to break up the Little Entente through alliance with Rumania and then to create a revised group of states composed of Poland, Rumania, Yugoslavia and Bulgaria.[22] At first the plan showed little signs of success. Colonel Beck visited Bucharest in April of 1937, but Rumania, largely due to Poland's friendship with Hungary, refused to abandon Czechoslovakia and if anything, extended her relationships rather than limiting them.

Italy, meanwhile, within a week of the announcement of the Rome-Berlin Axis in November, in an attempt to carve out her own sphere and to draw off Yugoslavia from the Little Entente, extended a hand of friendship to Yugoslavia, signing the Italo-Yugoslav Accords. This offered considerable quid pro quos to Belgrade, including economic concessions, possibilities for a minorities settlement, and security with regard to Albania. Then Hungary began to make moves to improve relations with Yugoslavia, resulting in a Hungaro-Yugoslav Friendship Treaty.

Interpretations varied as to the results for the Little Entente. Having moved to better relations with Bulgaria and Germany as well as Italy and Hungary, the Yugoslavs felt their position had been strengthened all around. Dr. Stoyadinović, therefore, was able to reassure President Beneš during his visit to Belgrade in April that he had no intention of abandoning either the Little Entente or Czechoslovakia, and when the Little Entente Conference opened on August 30, Yugoslav editorial comment was to the effect that Yugoslav policy was closer to the Little Entente than six months ago.[23] On the other hand, when the Permanent Council of the Little Entente met in Belgrade on April 2, the chief object was to induce Yugoslavia to expand its military obligations under the Entente, especially as it concerned Czechoslovakia, but the idea was dropped due to the cool reception by Yugoslavia and the weakening of French influence in Belgrade.[24]

In the face of the German assault on the Little Entente via Italy, Hungary, and Poland, the Entente met many times during 1937—in Belgrade on April 1-2, at Geneva on May 27, on the Danube on June 16, at Sinaia on August 30-31, and at Geneva on September 27. At each meeting the participants pledged support for the League of Nations, fidelity to France, and firm attachment to the Entente.[25] The most important aspect of the meetings centered around hopes that the Balkan and Little Ententes could be strengthened by rapprochement with Hungary, the possibilities of which had been drawn from cautious statements by the Hungarian Prime Minister early in 1937 and later in May by the Foreign Minister.

During the summer, the Little Entente discussed three main points: 1) its recognition of Hungarian rights to equality of armaments; 2) the giving by Hungary of an undertaking of non-aggression to include, if possible, acceptance of frontiers; 3) and the undertaking by the Little Entente states to carry out the provisions of the minorities treaties to which they were bound. After promising negotiations, however, the Little Entente states encountered a number of difficulties. Hungary wished to negotiate individually rather than collectively, and she claimed recognition of her equality as a right and pre-condition, not as a bargaining point.[26] With a highly charged anti-revisionist election imminent in Rumania and Yugoslav agreement, the Little Entente took the position that they could only negotiate as a group, that any recognition of Hungary's rights must be accompanied by a Hungarian non-aggression declaration, and that a minorities agreement, though open to negotiation, could not be part of the Pact.

Though the Little Entente position, based largely on strong anti-revisionism, can in part be blamed for the failure to reach accommodation with Hungary, the Hungarians for their part also gradually saw the advantages of supporing the German position, particularly in regard to Austria and Czechoslovakia. The Italians then changed sides and began to support peace between Hungary and the Little Entente as a bulwark against Germany. And, it is questionable whether or not a Little Entente accommodation with Hungary could have saved Czechoslovakia, for the Little Entente alliances were directed only against Hungary, and as early as 1937 the Little Entente seemed intent on, if anything, expanding its good neighborly relations, not in order to promote a front against Germany, but in order to neutralize itself, and to adopt an "on-the-fence" policy.[27] Point eight of the Little Entente Communique of the April 1-2 meeting read:

> Le Conseil permanent constate que les trois États de la Petite Entente restent opposés à tout conflit idéologique international que conque et refusent de se ranger dans l'un ou l'autre des fronts pourrient se former éventuellement'[28]

Yugoslavia, in her search for security, also turned toward shoring up relations with Bulgaria. The result of this effort was the signing on January 29, 1937 of a Pact of Eternal Friendship. Both the Little and Balkan Ententes supported this effort, which at first appeared to be the long hoped for breakthrough toward bringing Bulgaria into the Balkan Entente. The April 1-2 communique of the Little Entente read:

> C'est dans ce sens [bettering of relations with other powers] quels constatent avec satisfaction les accords de la Yougoslavia avec la Bulgarie et l'Italie, étant convaincu quils contribueront effacement au renforcement de la paix.[29]

A statement by President Metaxas at a banquet in honor of the members of the Permanent Council of the Balkan Entente in Athens read:

Je tiens à souligner que nous avons considéré le Pacte d'amisigné le 24 janvier dernier à Belgrade entre la Yougoslavie et Bulgarie, comme il'annonciateur d'un avenir meilleur non seulement pour ces deux pays mais pour tous les pays balkaniques.[30]

These statements, while valid in terms of the part Bulgarian pacification played in Balkan security, belied the fact that the Bulgaro-Yugoslav pact was made without informing the other Balkan Entente powers, and as such, it rendered the Pact's pledge of "eternal friendship" questionable due to the nature of Balkan Pact obligations.[31] In addition, a rapprochement in Yugoslav-Bulgarian relations simply put additional pressure on other Pact members to square their disputes and claims with Bulgaria on a unilateral basis, while giving Bulgaria a better position to bargain from, and it opened a break in Yugo-Greco and Turkish relations as well as nourishing Hellenic-Turkic animosity against a coalition of South Slavs.[32] As a result of increasing vulnerability to Bulgarian revisionist claims, the Balkan Entente actually hardened its position in respect to frontier questions. President Metaxas stated in his speech honoring the Permanent Council of the Balkan Entente, that the Entente. . . . "à proclamer notre ferme décision d'assurer le respects des traités en vigueur et le maintain de l'order territorial établi dan les Balkans'"[33]

Along with the tendency to protect themselves by bilateral rather than multilateral agreements, the Balkan Entente, as had the Little Entente, found itself unable to transform a political agreement into a military one without which no real protection to themselves could be afforded. In 1936 Rumania proposed a mutual exchange of supplies and officers and standarization of equipment, but Turkey turned a deaf ear, apparently feeling she had much to give and little to gain. This was followed in 1937 with a Turkish statement to the effect that there was no secret miltiary convention among the Balkan Entente, it being only a political understanding based on the principle that all Balkan frontiers were one. According to observers of the time, that declaration in itself, alongside Axis pressures, caused Yugoslavia to better relations with Bulgaria and the Axis, in turn pushing Greco-Turkish cooperation to new heights and leaving Rumania isolated.[34]

Forces for Balkan unity in 1937 were dealt a final blow when on September 14 Great Britain met with Bulgaria, Egypt, France, Greece, Rumania,

Yugoslavia, Turkey and the USSR at Nyon. There she made it clear that her interests were not enough to make a commitment in the Danube.[35] In effect, this spelled the end of British support for the Little Entente and for the unity of the Upper and Lower Danube, though it implied that British interests lay elsewhere, probably at the Straits, and therefore with the Balkan Entente. To that end, the British, like the Germans, supported the Bulgaro-Yugoslav rapprochement, though the British did so for the purpose of forwarding a Balkan Entente-Bulgarian detente, while Germany did so in order to increase pressure on Czechoslovakia and to weaken the unity of the Ententes.

Anschluss in March 1938 thrust Germany forward into the Balkans, establishing a common frontier with Hungary and Yugoslavia and encircling four-fifths of Czechoslovakia. Not only did this alter the position of the small states to Germany, it caused acceptance of revisionism to take a giant step forward. At a Little Entente meeting in May, Stoyadinović made the dangerous statement (since Yugoslavia, like every Balkan state, had large numbers of minorities and were thus open to large-scale revisionism), that since Yugoslavia was formed on the principle of all Slavs being united, they could not oppose the German doctrine,[36] and then the Balkan Entente proceeded to recognize the Ethiopian conquest (in return for Italian adhesion to Montreux). In intra-Balkan politics Anschluss sent the "Jackels looking for pickings," which in the Balkans meant Hungary and Bulgaria. Under such an awesome threat, the Little and Balkan Ententes took concrete steps for the first time to reach a collective agreement with both revisionist states.

At a meeting of the Permanent Council of the Little Entente held at Sinaia on May 5, the states reaffirmed their desire to continue their negotiations with Hungary begun in the preceding year. On August 23 at Bled, the Council announced the results of the summer's negotiations which took the form of a provisional agreement on which a joint communique by the Little Entente and Hungary was issued simultaneously.[37] By this agreement, the states of the Little Entente and Hungary mutually renounced all recourse to force in the settlement of disputes between them, and Hungary's equality of rights as regards armaments was recognized. The communique also stated that there had been preliminary discussions on other questions (minorities), but the text had not been definitely agreed upon, allowing each country to handle minority questions as a domestic matter. Though the Bled agreement attempted to relieve tension in Central

Europe and dissuade Hungary from passing completely into the Axis camp, after the Czech crisis the balance of power was so radically altered in Europe, that the agreement was useless in terms of in any way giving Hungary a choice. Because of this, the right to rearm given to Hungary at Bled without a concommitant pledge to renounce claims of border rectification, hurt rather than helped the Balkan and Little Entente positions.

Meanwhile, the Balkan Entente attempted to shore up its ranks on the other side by coming to some accommodation with Bulgaria. When the Balkan Entente met on July 31, 1938 at Salonika, however, the member states were unable to bring Bulgaria into the Entente. But in order to hopefully secure her friendship, the Balkan Entente renounced the military clauses of the Treaty of Neuilly and the provisions of the Lausanne Convention of July 24, 1923 concerning the frontiers of Thrace in exchange for a pledge of peaceful intent.[38] Though the agreement was hailed as an initial step toward full integration of Bulgaria into the Balkan Entente, Bulgaria, with no promises toward the Balkan Entente, secured equality of rights in the matter of armaments, and the demilitarized zones on each side of the frontiers between Bulgaria and Turkey, and between Bulgaria and Greece and Greece and Turkey in Thrace, were abolished. The Salonika agreement, like the Bled agreement, simply increased the Bulgarian position vis-a-vis revisionism, and in so doing weakened the Balkan Entente without expanding it or altering its role in the direction of providing a better Balkan defense against the Axis. Nor did it do anything on behalf of Balkan neutrality.

The results of Salonika and Bled in terms of Czechoslovakia were soon evident. At the meeting of the Little Entente at Sinaia on May 3-5, Rumania and Yugoslavia reiterated that they would give Czechoslovakia aid only in the event of Hungarian action but not in a German-Czech conflict as she had requested. In the military talks accompanying this meeting, Yugoslavia went so far in her abandonment of Czechoslovakia as to withdraw the offer to commit troops in the event of an attack not just by Germany, but by Hungary (on any one of the three), an obligation which had been at the heart of the Little Entente pact. The extent of Yugoslavia's neutralization, both in terms of Hungary, Germany and the Little Entente is evident in a conversation between Ciano and the Yugoslav minister on April 15, in which Stoyadinović already envisioned the disintegration of Czechoslovakia and asked only that Hungary not create a *casus belli* for him as a member of the moribund Little Entente.[39]

On the other hand, despite the Yugoslavs, the Little Entente refused the Hungarian demand for revisionism against Czechoslovakia in return for neutrality vis-a-vis the other two Little Entente powers, at least presenting a common front to the extent that they did not sanction this kind of rape. Rumanian Foreign Minister Comnen stated that he could not abandon Czechoslovakia, stressing the common interests in view of the growing German danger (to which Kánya replied there was no such danger to Hungary).[40] Such Rumanian allegiance, however, should be seen for what it was, that is the increased danger to Rumania should Hungary gain at Czechoslovakia's expense, a fear that was connected with the belief that due to longstanding Hungarian-Polish friendship, Poland would very likely do nothing on Rumania's behalf should Hungary attack as a result of the dissolution of Czechoslovakia. Such continued Little Entente allegiance to collective action against Hungary was of great advantage to Hitler, as it served to stabilize the disruption he himself had created.

The German reaction to Balkan efforts to close ranks at Salonika and Bled can best be described as confident of their failure. The Germany Minister in Bulgaria, speculating on what Bulgaria would do, wrote on May 31, 1938 that Sofia wished to be free to face the future with as few commitments as possible.[41] All the while, Bulgaria was reacting positively to the Berlin supported Bulgaro-Yugoslav rapprochement which was designed to detach Yugoslavia from the Balkan Entente and so, when at Salonika, Bulgaria failed to join the Entente, Berlin was not surprised. Some mention should be made of Hitler's heated reaction to Bled, however, which was a reaction not to his failure with regard to foreclosing on Balkan solidarity, but to what he considered his failure at Munich.

The communique regarding Hungarian agreement with the Little Entente at Bled was issued on August 23, 1938 at the very moment when Hitler wished pressure on Czechoslovakia to be at its greatest in order to gain Prague's capitulation. In an explosive interview aboard the "Patria" at Kiel on August 23-24 between Hitler and Ribbentrop on the one hand and Hungarian President Imrédy, Foreign Minister Kánya, and Regent Horthy on the other, Hitler advised Budapest that this move had been extremely "ill-timed" because it took considerable pressure off Prague and because it was received abroad as a rift between Hungary and Germany;[42] later he blamed this Hungarian perfidy for the need to reach a negotiated agreement at Munich along nationality rather than territorial lines. The Hungarian statesmen countered that Yugoslavia must remain neutral in order for Hungary to do so, that accommodation with Yugoslavia allowed her to concentrate her troops against Czechoslovakia, and that non-fulfillment of Hungarian revisionist claims against Czechoslovakia freed Hungary from her obligation not to use force. Hitler appeared unimpressed by the Hungarian logic that what was good for Hungary was good for Germany.

In November Prince Paul and King Carol agreed to the termination of the Little Entente,[43] Munich having exploded it by the removal of one of the members. Into this vacuum came Poland and Italy, reviving the idea of a Rome-Budapest-Bucharest-Warsaw Pact which would have solved the awesome Balkan problem of bringing Hungary back into the mainstream of East European politics and providing the necessary link between Poland and the Southeast. Poland, who had been adverse to supporting the Little Entente or its member countries in support of Czechoslovakia, but who was now ever more fearful of an advancing Germany, began to promote the idea of a common Polish-Hungarian frontier, a Rumanian-Hungarian rapprochement, and then cooperation of Yugoslavia, a scheme the Italians also liked in order to keep Germany out of Southeastern Europe. But the scheme was really only a paper musing of Beck's because of the necessity of destroying Czechoslovakia to establish a common frontier, Hitler's resistance to a plan which would have cut Berlin off from the East, fears of Italian hegemony, and the heavy inroads already made in isolating Poland from East and Southeast Europe.[44]

History ponders the responsibility of Bucharest and Belgrade in bringing about the end of a grouping which weakened their position particularly vis-a-vis Hungary but also vis-a-vis Germany. While it can probably be said that the attempts by the Little Entente to close ranks by bringing Hungary in were half-hearted and too late, there were many factors outside their control. Hungary, for instance, rejected the offers, preferring to deal with Hitler, and Poland was unsupportive of Rumanian efforts to come to the aid of Czechoslovakia by allowing the Soviets across her territory and Warsaw refused to rein in Hungary. But even if the Little Entente countries had settled their disputes with Hungary and gained the support of Poland, could Czechoslovakia and the Little Entente have been saved?

It seems unlikely that without support from London and Paris (upon whose action the Soviets said their aid rested), the Little Entente could have survived. It is difficult to imagine, for instance, a Little Entente pledge of support for Czechoslovakia, even backed by Hungary and Poland, as sufficient to deter Germany or move Czechoslovakia into active resistance. Indeed such a statement of resolve might have brought on the very conflict the West was so desperately trying to avoid. It seems more likely that a strong show of resolve by the West in support of the Little Entente would have bolstered the Little Entente in support of it-self, rather than the other way around, for it seemed well recognized at the time that until the West had the means and the will to aid Greece, Turkey, Rumania, and Yugoslavia, not only against Germany, but against Hungary, Bulgaria, and Russia as well, the Balkans were unlikely to con-cede to Bulgaria and Hungary, abandon German defense against the re-visionist states and Russia, or jeopardize the general peace of the area. However, the two were not unconnected in that a unified East European front would have reduced the chances of internecine war, thus giving the West a political weapon to offset their military deficiencies.

The view that the West, not the Little Entente was responsible for the death of Czechoslovakia, was a convenient interpretation for East Euro-pean statesmen as they shifted their policies accordingly into commitment appeasement of Berlin. Rumanian Foreign Minister Gafencu writes *ex post facto* that the damage of Munich had been done in terms of the small countries who now had "to approach Germany directly to obtain from it certain guarantees which the international security system could no longer provide."[45] The Reich was ready to consider these matters but only gave the desired guarantees in exchange for new engagements.

After Munich, the two surviving members of the Little Entente and the other members of the Balkan Entente did what they could to preserve the aura of Balkan unity, but the trend was more toward bilateral agreements than real unity. In November, King Carol of Rumania requested a visit with the Yugoslav Prince Regent to show solidarity, and on February 1, 1939, Gafencu arrived in Belgrade stressing the solidarity of the Danube basin, close Rumanian-Yugoslav ties, and anti-revisionism.[46] In October 1938, the Bulgarian and Yugoslavian Minister Presidents met at Nish, the result of which was a communique reaffirming the Friendship Pact of 1937 and pledging a deepening and widening of economic and political relations. This was followed by a meeting in Sofia from January 23 to February 9, 1939 during which Kiosseivanov made some concessions to Yugoslav

claims in Macedonia (using the formula "legitimate rights" rather than
"minorities,") hoping to gain a more friendly Yugoslav attitude toward
claims to the north (against Rumania) and outside of Macedonia.[47] Meanwhile, Turkey and Greece took steps to solidify their Friendship Pact
resulting in a new Greco-Turkish treaty in 1938 extending the mutual
guarantee of the inviolability of frontiers to the other frontiers of the
two countries.[48]

With the demise of the Little Entente, the formal structure of Balkan
unity fell upon the Balkan Entente, but it soon became clear that it was
already open to the maneuvering of Italy whose coveted Balkan position
had been threatened at Munich. Bloc-counterbloc politics thus got under
way. In early 1939 Ciano was envisaging a Rome-Belgrade-Bucharest bloc
to disrupt the Balkan Entente and upstage Germany south of the Danube.
In Budapest, Ciano urged Hungary to pave the way for rapprochement
with Yugoslavia; in turn Hungary agreed that Ciano should play the role
of "honest broker." Shortly thereafter Ciano went on a hunting expedi-
tion with Stoyadinović in Yugoslavia (January 16-22, 1939), during which
rumors abounded that Italy was attempting to persuade Stoyadinović to
abandon Rumania in preparation for dismemberment (by Hungary and
Bulgaria) in return for guarantees of borders with perhaps "symbolic"
concessions to Hungary. But, after all the fanfare and press died down,
Stoyadinović had refused any loosening of ties with Rumania for the sake
of friendship with Hungary, acknowledging that while Yugoslavia must
tend toward a new Danubian Europe and a broad system of agreements
in the Balkans, it must revise its position without breaking away from the
Balkan Entente. Thus did the traditional groupings hang together precariously as new political forces swirled around challenging and weakening
them.

* * * * *

The Balkans-for-the-Balkans goal had proved elusive as the Axis powers
began to move East, and the revisionism produced by that interruption at
Vienna, Munich and Prague paralyzed any movement for Balkan unity and
disrupted those groupings already in existence, due to fears of Germany,
fears of neighbors, and fears of revisionism. Axis exploitation of border
and minority differences and the legitimization of change in that regard

particularly at Munich, magnified the disputes already so formidable between the Little Entente and Hungary, the Balkan Entente and Bulgaria, Poland and the Balkans and the Upper and Lower Danube. And it created counterblocs, alternative groupings and bilateralism, cutting across both Ententes, causing further disarray and dysfunctionally for unifying forces already in place. Efforts to extend the framework of the Ententes, to include excluded members, and to support existing membership failed as at Salonika, Bled and Munich with the result that the Little Entente was destroyed and the Balkan Entente increasingly open to Great Power maneuvering. As such, the Balkans-for-the Balkans phrase began to mean not freedom to square disputes without interference, or unity as a bulwark against external aggression, or even preservation of existing sovereignties, but neutrality in the face of assaults on fellow Entente members, neutrality in the face of Great Power conflicts, and national survival at the expense of Balkan survival. These preludes to Balkan unity in 1937 and 1938 became the leitmotifs of Balkan collectivism in 1939.

Having left the sphere of the West, the Balkans had been set adrift in the direction of Berlin, a direction which was littered with fabricated factionalism and disunity. While Hitler's policies until 1939 are most easily connected with revisionism rather than status quo and with centrifugal rather than centripetal forces, this was not always so, for he too valued peace in the Balkans and he backed revisionism only to the point of usefulness to him, as often using the Ententes to block the revisionist impulses of Bulgaria and Hungary which he himself had excited. However, the renewed interest of the West in the affairs of the Southeast in 1939 and particularly the Western encirclement policy which began pulling the Balkans back toward the West and toward consolidation and unity as a bulwark against the Axis, caused Hitler to rededicate his efforts to disruption of Balkan unity, dependency on Berlin, and neutrality. The resultant tug-of-war between encirclement and anti-encirclement policies and powers, focused more dramatically in the Balkans than anywhere else in Europe, and it began to draw in other interested parties like the Soviet Union. Therefore, for the Balkans, a policy of isolation was no longer possible. The time that they must choose was well at hand and the choice that was made, if not dramatic, was in a sense crucial.

The Great Powers and Balkan Solidarity

The Balkan dream that their foreign policy could be made independent of the Great Powers was a dream as basic to sovereign freedom as is freedom from military occupation. But, as the Great Power conflict approached, accompanying it was the race on both sides to acquire allies to insure a positive outcome, a race which in its inner parameters focused on the Balkans. While the Balkan countries could not change the basic direction of the policies of the Great Powers to which they were only a pawn in a larger game, their reaction was important and particularly within the framework of the Soviet Union which composed the next ring of defense for both sides.

There were those who from the beginning questioned whether Balkan unity was enough to keep them safe, contending that sovereign states are incapable of disciplined cooperation for a long period and that East Europe was destined to be controlled by the Great Powers. Underscoring this theory was the belief prevalent at the time that the collective power position of these states militarily, economically and politically was not sufficient to give them an adequate defense against the Axis. On the other side were those who argued that disunity could be played upon, ultimately leading to a loss of sovereignty one by one, and that the best hope for survival was to come together and then tie up with the West and the Soviet Union. Even the Gemans believed that disunity was advantageous only to the point where outside intervention (in this case the Soviet Union) was not elicited and that unity and pacification were essential to their plans against Poland and the West. What they objected to was the emerging Western program which sought unity as the first step in the creation of a front against the Axis, a plan which began to evolve in late March and early April, 1939 after the basic decision was made that German expansion must be stopped.

Actually, the framework of the plan was Churchill's. In a speech on May 9, 1938, he referred to "this powerful group of Danubian and Balkan states. . .firmly united with the two great Western democracies," taking into account "the enormous power of Russia." On April 3, 1939 Churchill addressed the House of Commons saying it was no longer possible to speak of a "Danube organization," that stress must be put on the Balkans. In Churchill's view the steps needed to be taken were "full-inclusion of Soviet Russia in our defensive peace bloc," and "the promotion of unity in the Balkans," for if they "allow themselves to be divided, if they depart at all from the simple principle of the Balkans-for-the Balkans people," they could not save themselves or "play a decisive part in averting a general catastrophe." Ten days later, Churchill talked with Rumanian Foreign Minister Gafencu about winning Bulgaria over to the cause of the Entente by cession of South Dobruja. In a speech on April 28 to the people of the United States, he put the final touches on his blueprint (and attempted to woo Washington too) when he emphasized that encirclement of Germany was not to be military or economic, but "a psychological encirclement," to deter Hitler, not to promote aggression.

As the British tried to implement this program, the Axis powers countered it move for move. Their general plan, as outlined by State Secretary Weizsäcker on May 9, was:

> . . . to regulate our relations with the individual States of the Balkan Entente directly. This policy has been successfully pursued in recent conversations with Rumania and Yugoslavia. The present British attempt to make the Balkan Entente the tool of a policy directed against Germany and to draw Bulgaria into this must naturally meet with our opposition.[49]

Key to the British idea of a Balkan collective security system was the strengthening of the Balkan Entente, and this, in turn, revolved around bettering relations with Bulgaria. The Salonika Agreement of July 31, 1938, Kiosseivanov's statement before the Sobranie in July, 1938, the Balkan Entente Council meeting at Ankara in Turkey in 1938 during which the Bulgarian question was given special consideration, and hopeful talks between the Bulgarian and Rumanian Foreign Ministers in March 1939 seemed to reveal Bulgaria's inclination to make common cause with the Balkan Entente. But the onrush of events of early 1939 and particularly the Great Power contest which was beginning to take shape in the East, seemed to sap life from any further ameliatory moves, while the guarantees hardened both sides of the question of revisionism.

Nevertheless, while Gafencu was in London on April 25, Halifax and Chamberlain pressed him into concessions to Bulgaria in order to entice Sofia to join, but Gafencu's attitude was that this could not serve the cause of peace in that revisionist concessions would precipitate widespread revisionism and increased demands, not just by Bulgaria, but Hungary too.

He further argued that it would be of no use to make concessions to Bulgaria if it drove Yugoslavia out of the Entente as it was likely to do in that a border settlement with Rumania and Greece would add pressure on Yugoslavia. Finally, he said, Bulgarian entrance into the Entente might simply strengthen the Axis hand by allowing Bulgaria to play her game, while outside it she was contained by Turkey, Greece, and Rumania.[50]

The Greeks were also against revisionism, particularly after the Bulgarian Prime Minister reiterated that Bulgarian claims did not preclude an outlet to the Aegean. This both the Turks and Greeks opposed (a policy the Bulgarians interpreted as a long range policy of Turkey's to seize western Thrace, which they said would be possible as long as it belonged to Greece, but which would be more difficult if occupied by Bulgaria). Kiosseivanov observed that Western action came too late, that activity toward a democratic front would only accelerate Hitler's preparation for self-sufficiency, and that confidentially he was struck "by how little the French and British Ambassadors understood about the question of Southeast Europe."[51] Seemingly at an impasse, particularly when Gafencu was supported in his view in Paris,[52] London temporarily dropped the idea of bringing Bulgaria into the Entente by means of revisionism.

The idea came up again, however, when the British learned that Bulgaria would pursue a policy of consultation with other Balkan states in order to preserve "collective neutrality" of the area.[53] Grasping at these straws, the British dispatched a trade mission to Bucharest with permission to allow a credit of two to five million pounds. Then they used the good offices of the Turkish Foreign Minister, who was not adverse to territorial concession· in Dobruja (not Thrace), to urge Gafencu to compromise on the Dobruja question in the name of Balkan neutrality if not for collective security reasons. Meanwhile, Saracoglu used the occasion of Kiosseivanov's visit on May 16 (during which the Bulgarian Prime Minister sought assurances against Turkish action in the area unsettling to the peace and dangerous to Bulgaria as a result of the Anglo-Turkish Declaration), to once again nudge Bulgaria toward the Balkan Entente.[54]

But neither side budged, and during Gafencu's trip to Ankara on June 9, the issue of accession to the Entente via revisionism was laid bare. At a diplomatic reception at which Bulgarian Minister Christov was present, British Ambassador Hugh Knatchbull-Hugessen tried to win Bulgaria with Rumanian territorial concessions. At his instigation and with Gafencu's acquiescence, the Turkish Foreign Minister put the question to the Bulgarian Minister of whether or not "she would be satisfied with S. Dobruja," to which, according to Gafencu, Christov responded, "Obviously Bulgaria would not be satisfied with so little." Gafencu then asked if all Bulgarian claims were conceded, would Bulgaria join the Balkan Entente, to which Christov responded that even in that event, Bulgaria would be neutral (a position they also communicated to the Germans).[55]

Fearful of the results of the Bulgarian Prime Minister's visit to Berlin in July, the British made one last try, suggesting to the Rumanian Minister that perhaps a general rapprochement between Rumania and Bulgaria could be worked out rather than concessions of a territorial nature. Tilea replied that, "if the Rumanian Government were convinced that the Bulgarians were genuinely well disposed, something might well be arranged with regard to Dobjuja."[56] But by this time both Turkish and Yugoslav enmity toward Bulgaria had grown, there was a pervasive and growing fear throughout the Balkans that rapprochement with Bulgaria would smack of "encirclement," and the German program, which put considerable arms and economic pressure on Sofia and then made assurances that Germany would not guarantee Rumanian borders as Kiosseivanov feared,[57] foredoomed any hope that there would be concessions on either side.

In June, danger of Balkan unity again threatened the Axis. After Gafencu's second swing through the Balkans, it was rumored that he was planning a defensive pact which would extend the obligations of the Balkan Entente. Italy had already branded this as an "encirclement front" move, and so Axis pressure began in earnest. Efforts were made to promote a counterbloc of Yugoslavia, Hungary and Bulgaria, hinted at in the Bulgarian press and dubbed the "Little Axis." On June 26 Nazi Minister without Portfolio, Dr. Hans Frank, visited Bulgaria and the Bulgarian press gave Frank's appeal for "the neutral bloc" in return for support of Bulgarian and Hungarian revisionist demands against Rumania, Yugoslavia, and Greece, prominent display.[58]

None of these bloc schemes went anywhere, being simply part of the diplomatic interplay attendant to the Great Power tug-of-war for the Balkans. Gafencu's statement of an expanded Balkan Entente was a unilateral statement unbeknownst to other Entente members, while the Little Axis idea was simply another Nazi propaganda play to win Bulgaria and

and Hungary with revisionism while threatening the status quo states. What was significant here was how Balkan national sentiment could and was played upon. Gayda wrote in *Giornal d'Italia* that while refusing to take a "dramatic view" of the attitude of the guaranteed states, Italy was keeping a watchful eye on Balkan developments "with their conflicting interests and the trends toward revisionism for the sake of greater justice and enduring peace."[59]

Besides preventing extension of the Balkan Pact, the Germans were intent on weakening it by pressure on its two weak links, Yugoslavia and Rumania. Yugoslavia they pressured in the direction of leaving the Pact, a policy which had a dual purpose when it was learned from the German Minister in Sofia that Bulgaria would join the Anti-Comintern Pact "if they were covered by Yugoslav denunciation of the Balkan Pact."[60] Meanwhile, the Italians tried to draw Yugoslavia from the Balkan Pact by emphasizing the traditional Yugoslav fear of the Turks and by encouraging Hungaro-Yugoslav rapprochement. The anti-Turkish approach had particular appeal after the Anglo-Turkish Declaration, the Assistant Yugoslav Minister of Foreign Affairs admitting that it was not failure to consult or fear of loss of neutrality which was the basis for Yugoslav opposition to the Declaration, but fear of the Turks "whose three century domination of the Serbs was not recalled with any satisfaction."[61] As far as rapprochement was concerned, both Axis partners pressured Hungary to let Yugoslavia know it renounced all territorial claims and by this means to bring Yugoslavia to Hungary.[62] When indirect pressure failed, Italy resorted to a more direct approach, assuring Belgrade that Italy would send no large force north of Tirana and that she disclaimed interest in the Yugoslav district of Kossovo which had long been an object of Albanian desires. By the opposite means, Ciano threatened, inveighing against the Balkan Entente particularly Turkey as if forcing Yugoslavia to choose between the Axis and Entente, and when that failed, he turned to more radical schemes of breaking up Yugoslavia by paying off Croat insurrectionists.[62]

In many respects Rumania held a key position in German efforts to control the Balkan Entente. Not only was she the basis for revisionist concessions to Bulgaria, but Rumanian Foreign Minister Gafencu was acting President of the Balkan Entente in 1939 and from that position he acted as the leading architect of Balkan unity, making numerous trips throughout the area during this period. Hitler rightly suspected that

Rumania's interest in the Balkan Entente and other Balkan groupings was not to formulate an anti-German front, as was the British and Russian, but rather to provide some reinsurance for Rumania against her enemies, Hungary, Bulgaria, and Russia, should war begin. Since Germany also had an interest in maintaining the Rumanian entity against the same enemies, the Nazis did not encourage Rumanian withdrawal from a Pact which could be of some use to them too, but rather to control the Pact's operation. To this end Berlin attempted to make Rumania dependent on Germany rather than the Pact by pressuring Rumania's most longstanding ally, Yugoslavia, to withdraw and by siding with Rumania against Hungary when necessary.[63]

Though Germany watched efforts to strengthen the Balkan Entente closely, continually following a policy of disruption where possible, it was the Anglo-Turkish Declaration and the threat that via Turkey the Soviet Union and Balkans would be linked to the West, which rattled the East European political section in Berlin. The reasons were obvious. The likelihood of Bulgaria joining the Entente was remote, of Hungarian defection even less so, and the insecure positions of Rumania and Yugoslavia all but paralyzed them. This was not true of Turkey who, having already openly declared for the West, was the crucial psychological as well as military pivot for delivering the Balkans and Russia into Western hands.

This made German Ambassador von Papen intensify efforts to woo Turkey back to a neutral position by removing the Italian threat to Turkey, a strategy which, as we have seen, did not find favor in Berlin because of the desire to keep Italy from going to the British. Then von Papen got the idea to bring Turkey around by inclusion of Italy and Bulgaria in the Balkan Entente. Right before the Anglo-Turkish Declaration, von Papen put the proposal to Ankara, but Saracoglu turned it down on the basis that:

> . . . it had been the entry of Italy into Albania which had necessitated (the) Turkish policy of understanding with (the) Western Powers and that (the) actual admission of Italy into (the) Balkan Entente would be the last straw.[64]

Berlin did not fully support the von Papen idea of weakening the Balkan Entente by accession of Italy, Albania, and Bulgaria anyway. On May

9, State Secretary Weizsäcker wrote that "there will be no question of the accession of Albania now bound to Italy by personal union," and "we have no reason to force Bulgaria into the Balkan Pact against her will."[65] The reasons why they preferred not to disturb the Balkan Entente, according to Cinkar-Marković, were because Germany needed an entity to maintain Southeastern equilibrium and to satisfy Rumania and thus nullify the Polish-Rumanian alliance, and because Hitler needed a bulwark against growing Italian attempts to upstage German influence in the Balkans by creation of an alternative Balkan bloc composed of Rome-Belgrade-Budapest-Sofia, which was supposedly designed to cut across the Balkan Entente, isolate Yugoslavia and detach the Balkans from Turkey.[66] Berlin, therefore, began pouring cold water on the budding Yugoslav-Hungarian friendship nourished by Rome, in order to maintain individual control over the Balkans and Hungary.

Danger of another Balkan bloc scheme surfaced on June 10 when Berlin received reports to the effect that Turkish offices would be used to patch up Hungarian-Rumanian difficulties in order that Rumania would be secured enough to offer South Dobruja to Bulgaria, and that Hungary was participating in the scheme. The idea was in connection with the Yugoslav proposal for an alternative neutral pact composed of Yugoslavia, Bulgaria, Rumania and Hungary with subsequent adherence of Turkey. Csáky told the German Minister that "out of consideration to the Axis," Hungary intended to treat the proposal in a dilatory manner, but that he had instructed his Minister in Ankara to ask for Turkish mediation "which he knows hold no prospects—in Hungarian revisionist claims on Rumania." In rather obscure logic, Csáky claimed that this move would:

> . . .lend support to the Rumanian thesis that Rumanian concessions to Bulgaria would constitute a dangerous precedent in view of Hungary's claims, and thus to prevent Bulgaria's accession to the Balkan Pact and her defection to the Western Powers.[67]

What Hungary really hoped, of course, is that a Bulgarian-Rumanian rapprochement with territorial concessions on the part of Rumania would weaken the Rumanian position vis-a-vis Hungarian revisionist demands.

Berlin showed a certain concern over the Yugoslav initiative. What disturbed Weizsäcker particularly was the Turkish role, for:

> Given Turkey's present attitude toward the Axis Powers, it is scarcely suitable for her to be made the mediator in Balkan affairs not only by Yugoslavia, but now also by Hungary even though Hungarian action is intended as a matter of tactics.[68]

Therefore, he told Erdmannsdorff that due to Turkey's inclusion in the "Encirclement Powers," no position of supremacy in the Balkans could be accorded to Turkey. Berlin's view, he said, was that the "neutral bloc" idea was of interest to Berlin only if it meant the end of the Balkan bloc in its old form, that is "if it would mean Turkey and Greece leaving it."[69] In Weizsäcker's view, this did not appear to be the intent of Yugoslavia and certainly not of Hungary, and it gave the impression of a Hungaro-German schism as well as allowing the possibility that Hungarian efforts would actually promote Balkan rapprochement and possibly even entrance of Bulgaria into the Balkan Entente.

The Germans had to contend not only with British and Italian (and surrogates Turkish and Hungarian) efforts to form favorable Balkan coalitions, but Soviet as well. In early February 1939, Foreign Minister Litvinov dropped the suggestion of a Black Sea Pact at a luncheon given by the Turkish Ambassador for several diplomats. Litvinov greeted the formal gathering of Southeastern states diplomats as "former Balkan Entente" members, indicating that in the Soviet view the Balkan Entente was already dead due to the recent Yugoslav-Italian rapprochement and the threat to Rumanian independence by German encroachments into the Danube. Litvinov, therefore, proposed replacing the Balkan Entente with a Black Sea Pact composed of littoral states of Russia, Bulgaria and Turkey in order to protect their respective interests in the Black Sea area.[70]

The Germans appear to have been curious but not seriously threatened by the idea whose basic weaknesses, Balkan nationalism, antipathy for the Soviet Union, and fear of Germany seemed immediately apparent. Gafencu admitted as much to Potemkin, explaining Rumanian reluctance in terms of fear of providing Germany, and because of advantages accruing from Rumanian and Polish positions as a buffer. To U.S. Minister Gunther, he made apparent another reason, and that was the difficulty of swinging Rumanian public opinion to the point of accepting closer relations with Russia.[71] Shortly after the Black Sea Pact idea became known to the Germans, Rumania made her position clear to Berlin, declaring against it, and then the Balkan Entente itself failed to endorse the idea at a February meeting.

The other threat occurred as a result of Potemkin's swing through the Balkans in late April early May,[72] during which Potemkin tried to grease the wheels of Bulgarian entry into the Balkan Entente, as well as to promote a Russo-Turkish alliance. The Turks for their part hoped to bring about a closer understanding between Rumania and Russia, since the Turks were reluctant to make any gurantees to Rumania until Russian relations with Rumania and Ankara were clarified. On April 28, Potemkin arrived in Ankara having been in Sofia two days earlier. He told the French Ambassador in Ankara on April 30 that the Bulgarian Prime Minister had declared to him that Bulgaria was ready to join the Balkan Entente in return for Southern Dobruja. Then in his conversation with Saracoglu he gave the latter the impression that he thought the Turkish government was not taking a strong enough stand with Rumania in attempts to win Bulgaria to accession with territorial concessions. Finally he promised that Russian influence at Sofia would be used to promote a satisfactory settlement between Bulgaria and Rumania.[73] But, Potemkin was unable to effectuate any sort of Rumanian-Bulgarian rapprochement, for on his return trip to Sofia on May 7, Potemkin was alarmed at Bulgaria's pro-Axis leanings and strident revisionism, and in Bucharest on May 8 Gafencu himself dashed hope of a breakthrough with Bulgaria when he affirmed that Rumania would not give any concessions to Bulgaria until the latter affirmed her solidarity. Meanwhile, the Bulgarian Prime Minister assured Berlin that the Potemkin visit had had little internal effect, Pan Slavism being well under control.

* * * * *

Thus did the Great Powers pull at the hamstrings of the Balkans. For the British, who wished to create an Eastern and Southeastern front, this meant a program aimed at Balkan unification, the first step of which was the wedding of Bulgaria to the Balkan Entente, after which the Entente would be linked with the Anglo-Turkish Declaration and then with Russia. The Germans, wishing a quiescent and benevolent Southeast, found the Anglo-French, Italian and Russian program threatening in its attempts to coalesce a grouping willing and able to challenge Germany hegemony. The

Nazi's, therefore, threatened against Bulgarian adherence to the Entente, attempted to weaken the Balkan Entente internally by pressuring Rumania and Yugoslavia, squelched the idea of any counterblocs, and basically adhered to the dictum that dealing with each country individually would produce the successful divide-and-rule situation they sought. In the second tier of interested powers were Italy and Russia. Italy, desiring to extend her own position in the Balkans at the expense of Britain, Germany, and Russia, advocated an alternative bloc of states south of the Danube under her own tutelage, while Russia, by way of the Black Sea states, offered a similar hegemonic ring.

The Balkan countries reacted evasively to all of the programs and in their own national interest. Fear of Germany and war on their territory, suspicious of Russia, dubious that a diplomatic grouping of states (in the absence of material) could deter Hitler, and most of all clinging to revisionist-anti-revisionist policies which were at the heart of national existence, they presented obstacles enough to put the British plan to rest. On the other hand, to safeguard themselves from becoming Hitler's next object of revisionism or invasion, they dallied with unification ideas, making moves toward Bulgaria, talking with the Russians via Ankara, interesting themselves in Italian counterbloc schemes, and exhibiting strong cohesion within the Balkan Entente.

Out of their individual reactions began to emerge a program of neutrality as the best path to secure themselves from Nazi, Soviet and Balkan revisionism and more important, to exclude them from the approaching Great Power war. While the neutrality was not as benevolent as Hitler wished, unfortunately for the West it served Hitler's cause better than their own which needed an active fighting force, not a group of inert states who were still open to nationalist maneuvering. In effect, the failure of any of the Great Powers to win the Balkans, led to the next step in the game, that is negotiations among the Great Powers themselves and the inclusion of the Soviet Union, the Balkans now becoming the quid pro quos. How the Balkans were neutralized and what they hoped to gain from a policy which obviously had its pitfalls for them, is the final episode in the story of the Balkans and of its backdoor federalism.

The Neutralization of the Balkans

On February 20, 1939 a regular but much publicized conference of the Balkan Entente was held in Bucharest, and while the events which occurred after appeared to shift the Balkans in another direction, the themes dominating that meeting basically set the course of Balkan affairs during the crucial spring and summer of 1939. The first question involved whether or not the Balkan Entente was going to extend its obligations to meet the growing Axis threat. There was much discussion of methods of resisting German and Italian political and economic pressures, and there was general recognition that the Balkan states needed to transform the Entente from a mere arrangement for the presence of the status quo inter se to a genuine Balkan union of defense against outside aggression. In this respect the presence of Cinkar-Marković rather than pro-German Stoyadinović seemed hopeful as did the decision that general staff discussions would take place.

But while the initiative, which was mainly Turkey's, was rhetorically acceptable to all states even Bulgaria, it was qualified by so many conditions and reservations that it ultimately proved stillborn. The Greeks and Turks, therefore, used the occasion to beef up the Greco-Turkish alliance which the Greek press characterized as the bedrock of Greek security, not the Entente. As the *London Times* commented, while there was a common desire in the Balkans to preserve their independence and cooperate, it was hardly enough to "prevent individual states from flying off at a tangent because of the fear of far greater desire for self-preservation," and it noted that the Greco-Turkish alliance was most secure only because it was still relatively removed from the mobile and threatening frontiers of Germany and because the British and French fleets were still the strongest in the Mediterranean. Though Saracoglu went to great lengths to link the Greco-Turkish alliance with the Entente, remarking on February 27 that the "perfect" relationship between the two countries was the "basis of our foreign policy and it is the basis of the Balkan Pact . . .", everyone still wondered if "the foundations would protect the upper walls" and there was speculation that the policy made sense only if Turkey was working on the side of England, since Germany's policy was to divide and conquer while Britain's was to resist by unity.[75]

Like the Greeks and Turks, the Rumanians and Yugoslavs used the occasion to shore up their own bilateral relations particulary after a potentially damaging meeting in January between Yugoslavia and Bulgaria. At a meeting which preceded the opening of the Conference, Gafencu and Stoyadinović agreed on a Four-Point program which included: 1) reiteration of a decision to defend their borders; 2) determination to adopt a "conciliatory" attitude toward all countries of the Danube Basin particularly Hungary and Bulgaria (but not to give up territory); 3) approval of plans to build a highway connecting Trieste with the Black Sea via Zagreb, Belgrade and Bucharest; 4) maintenance of the present Yugoslav-Rumanian alliance. Both, while wanting better relations with Hungary, agreed that Hungarian demands were unacceptable.[76]

The other important factor to come up at the Conference, was the question of entrance of Bulgaria into the Pact. Some hope was expressed along the lines of better relations with Bulgaria due to Salonika (commercial relations were to be opened), but the real problem was laid bare when the Bulgarian representative, who was there as an observer, read a statement which was concerned almost wholly with Bulgarian revisionist aspirations including cession of Dobruja and a corridor to the Aegean. Yugoslavia urged Rumania and Greece to make these concessions, but both were unwilling to make the revisionist sacrifice, and Turkey and Greece were against the corridor idea because it would form a barrier to free military support and might bring Yugoslavia and Bulgaria closer together forming a preponderently Slavic bloc in the Balkans. Greece offered to accord Bulgaria every facility like a free port in Salonika, but this was unacceptable to Sofia.[77]

While the communique issued at the end of the meeting stressed solidarity, it also came out against revisionism, extension of obligations, and Great Power intervention, and it ommitted any reference to prolongation of the Pact (due to expire in the next month) except to intimate a meeting in Belgrade a year hence. While the official view in Balkan capitals was that much had been accomplished, the public was less certain, believing that the Balkan Entente did not go far and "less far now than ever."[78] Evident in the proceedings was the fact that old suspicions and divisions lingered, and that in the face of a recognized German danger, decisions would be made on a national ad hoc basis with as much distance from the Great Powers as possible. The events of March and after only crystallized that position.

This was evident in Balkan replies to the British round-robin letter of March 17, two days after Prague brought on the collapse of Czechoslovakia in which Balkan attitudes toward aid to Rumania were sought.[79] President Metaxas said that he would examine the proposal sympathetically in collaboration with Yugoslavia and Turkey, but that everything depended on Yugoslavia, who if neutral, would make it impossible for Greece and Turkey to guarantee assistance to Rumania. On March 18 an anxious Prince Paul confirmed that nothing but a neutrality that would be "grudgingly benevolent" toward the Axis could be expected in a general war, but he did not exclude giving aid to Rumania if she were attacked by Hungary. Turkey replied on March 19 that she would carry out her obligations under the Balkan Pact only, but if the British were to make proposals of their own, these would be studied in a friendly spirit.

The threat to the Balkans was temporarily lost in the flurry of diplomatic activity surrounding the British guarantee to Poland on March 31, but the invasion of Albania on April 7 renewed it and gave Gafencu's visit to Istanbul on April 8-9 added meaning. At that meeting, in a splendid show of bilateral unity, the two agreed on seven points to strengthen the Balkan position. Point one read:

> The Turkish and Rumanian Governments would make every effort to reinforce the Balkan Entente and to increase its efficacy in action. They would pursue with regard to Bulgaria a benevolent and friendly policy in the spirit of the Salonika agreement.

In the next few points, the two agreed to avoid any unnecessary provocation and to try to "obtain guarantees from the Great Powers," and that if the two were forced to make a choice between the Great Powers:

> . . . it was understood that Rumania and Turkey would act in common and would insist that their allies of the Balkan Entente should join the group which was uniting and organizing itself with the object of creating a common resistance to tendencies directed towards domination which threatened their independence and security.

Pour four provided that if Rumania and Turkey were involved in a war as a result of extension of the Polish-Rumanian alliance or any alliance Turkey might conclude with a third power, that the obligation of assistance under the Balkan Entente would operate against the hostile intervention of any Balkan State. In the other points, Turkey promised "benevolent and friendly neutrality in all questions of ships passing through the Straits if Rumania became involved in war and Turkey was neutral," and both agreed that in any conversations with the Great Powers for the organization of a common resistance, Rumania and Turkey would try to obtain effective military assistance and in any case, to consult each other in all circumstances and if necessary to engage in staff talks.[80]

At first glance this was a comprehensive and hopeful program which Gafencu termed as the first step in the implementation of the British program.[81] Under close scrutiny and in the face of actual circumstances, this bilateral exhibition of friendship made no progress on issues key to solidarity—revisionism, reciprocity, and enlargement of obligations. And it was lacking in authority, for not only was the agreement between only two of the five Balkan Entente members, it was on behalf of the two who were strategically interrupted by Bulgaria.

As it evolved in the late spring and early summer of 1939, the dangerous situation with Bulgaria (with Hungary less so because the Axis had more direct control over her) and the threatened withdrawal of Yugoslavia from the Entente by internal dissolution or external invasion, were situations explosive enough to paralyze the Balkans. As far as the Bulgarians situation was concerned, the Entente intention (unlike London's which was to form a front against the Axis), was to blunt revisionism and safeguard against external threats via Bulgaria. As such, there were two options—to bring Bulgaria into the Entente or to contain her by Entente threat. When the first option failed, a Balkan explosion threatened whereupon the Entente, with Hitler's blessings, exercised the second option forcing neutrality on Bulgaria too.

The Salonika agreement, the Balkan Entente meeting in February and the Saracoglu-Gafencu seven-point program had all expressed a desire to better relations with Bulgaria, but all had lacked reference to territorial claims. British and German involvement in the question, caused Turkey to suggest that Bulgaria be admitted to the Balkan Entente, that there be a general guarantee of frontiers, and that Rumania declare her willingness to consider Dobruja. Under such pressure, the Rumanian position seemed to soften. Officially, Bucharest agreed to study the question, and soon after, Prince Paul of Yugoslavia and King Carol of Rumania make a display of unity, met on Carol's yacht at Turnir Sevein (April 19), at which time they seemed confident that Boris would join the Balkan Entente.

On April 21, members of the Bulgarian Parliament revealed that the Balkan Entente had extended a new invitation to join with strong hints that some Bulgarian aspirations would be met by offers of a portion of South Dobruja, but that the offer had been declined with the insistence of great concessions and the belief that a more generous offer could be made. Meanwhile, Kiosseivanov, in a speech to the Parliament's Foreign Affairs Committee, stressed Bulgarian neutrality and in exact terms spelled out the nature of Bulgarian aims:

> ...7,695 square kilometers of South Dobruja from Rumania, 8,712 from eastern Greece between the Mesta and Maritsa rivers, and 2,566 from western Yugoslavia in the district of Streeumitza . . .

which corresponded to the 1913 borders. In addition Kiosseivanov promised not to conclude secret agreements with Parliament. In all circles, even the opposition, it appeared "there was support for the Bulgarian policy not to accept anything short of full restoration."[82] The Turks, after "a stormy session with the Bulgarian Minister," finally agreed that nothing short of full satisfaction of territorial demands could swing the Bulgarians around. In their view, this was a great nuisance not a great threat in case of Italian or German invasion of the Balkans, because any invader driving to the Straits would have to gain absolute control of Bulgaria and Bulgaria, therefore, would be put on the defensive.[83] This was not the case with Rumania, however, where revisionism more than invasion was the threat.

Undaunted by Bulgarian immutability and revisionist clamor, the Balkan Entente maintained its composure, issuing a statement from Bucharest to the effect that the attitude caused no surprise, but that the Balkan Entente was gratified by Bulgaria's intention to achieve her aims by peaceful means.[84] Unable to bridge the impasse within the Southeastern framework, the Balkan countries involved in this dispute reverted to using the Great Powers to strength their respective positions. The Bulgarians first tried to use the Russian bogey, the press reporting on April 26 that the visit of Soviet Ambassador Potemkin was of utmost importance—all on the very day that it gave publicity to its territorial demands against Rumania and Greece. The implication was not just that Russia backed their claims against Rumania, but that Bulgarian demands could easily become quid pro quo for Soviet adherence to a pact with Britain. More fuel was added to the fire when German industrialists arrived in Sofia, whereupon Bulgarian indignation erupted over a speech by President Metaxas in which he denounced Bulgaria's claims against Greece.[85] On the other side, the British-French decision to go ahead with guarantees to Rumania without concessions, reinforced the Rumanian position and hardened the Bulgarian position.

The intractable verbal positions on the part of both Rumania and Bulgaria at the end of April were transformed into outright action at the beginning of May when Bulgarian demonstrations for return of land held by Greece and Rumania took place during a military parade, the first such display since the Bulgarian military restrictions had been put aside. Then, on May 10, there was a Bulgarian-Rumanian border incident in which 23 Bulgarians were reported shot by Rumanian troops en route to a trial for smuggling salt. (The Rumanians reported it as 20 members of a Macedonian border group caught in a military trap set at the frontier.) The incident took on political overtones when, as a result, Bucharest intensified its colonization of the Dobruja province, and Kiosseivanov for his part, failed to restrain Macedonian Comisadjas' (revolutionaries) renewed activity which he had, for the past years, repressed.

On the heels of the incident, seven Turkish divisions were reported moving to the border causing Kiosseivanov to say that Bulgaria had "no friends." Then, under considerable Nazi economic pressure, the Bulgarian Prime Minister was invited to Berlin. Fearing the worst, he stopped off in Belgrade en route to and from Berlin where the Yugoslavs, themselves feeling semi-isolated as a result of the Balkan drift to the West (Anglo-Turkish Declaration) and suspicious that Turkey resisted revisionism in favor of Bulgaria due to Turkey's desire to claim Thrace for themselves, took on the role of peacemaker, believing that they were and had been for a long time (since Alexander) in the best position to deal with Bulgaria as claims against her were less strong that against Greece and Rumania.[86]

The communiques and press reports concerning the Kiosseivanov-Cinkar-Marković meetings were effusive in espousing a similarity of view and "unanimity" of interest in intra-Balkanic and international relations. In this regard the Yugoslav paper *Vreme* pointed particularly to Kiosseivanov's success in remaining outside all existing dissension which is "why friendship with Bulgaria is so highly quoted everywhere . . . ."[87] The Germans themselves encouraged this dissident rapprochement commenting that it stabilized the situation in the Southeast and that she understood the mutuality of their peace and neutrality policy, a policy which was a disappointment to the peace front. How much this neutrality alignment had to do with German pressure is unknown, but Kiosseivanov who left for Berlin fearing "embarrassing questions," returned safe and wondering "whether it really occurred."[88]

The "brotherly nations having firmly decided never to draw their swords against each other," while a convenience to both sides in diffusing Axis and allied pressure, never turned the key which would unlock the door to Bulgarian entrance into the Balkan Entente—revisionism. In July when the question of a general Dobruja settlement came up again, the Bulgarian Minister said that distrust between the Balkan states was so great, they never could unite, and then even Prince Paul of Yugoslavia came out against territorial concessions to Bulgaria, stating a strong mistrust of Bulgaria and saying that, while he would like to see a Dobruja settlement, he opposed a Bulgarian outlet to the Aegean which would certainly, he said, become "another port of entry to Italy."[89] The idea lost favor on all sides when Bulgaria admitted that cession of South Dobruja would not satisfy Bulgaria and that even if her claims were met, Bulgaria would not enter the Balkan Entente and she would remain neutral.

The failure to bring Bulgaria into the Balkan Entente or at the least to lessen the peril of the frontier disputes, made all the Balkan states more inclined than even to neutrality. But the May 12 Anglo-Turkish Declaration posed an even more serious threat to the continued neutrality of the area for it definitely placed Balkan Entente member Turkey in the allied camp. The shock waves of this were felt particularly in Belgrade where an infuriated Axis and particularly Italy renewed efforts to either detach Yugoslavia from the Balkan Entente or destroy her from within. In response, Yugoslavia began to distinguish between the neutrality policy of the Balkan Entente and Turkey's "new orientation."[90] and to espouse an alternative to the Balkan Entente, the Yugoslav inspired coalition of "neutral bloc" states.

Skittishness about their precarious position, caused Cinkar-Marković to argue that the Anglo-Turkish Declaration had been a violation of the Balkan Pact's provision that members were to be "clearly" and "frankly" informed of negotiations with outside powers relative to the Balkans (whereupon the Turkish Minister pointed out that Yugoslavia had not done this with regard to Albania),[91] and to come out strongly against Article six (providing for consultation between the two countries about the security of the Balkans) because it compromised Yugoslav sovereignty. And he began to warm to the anti-Turkish "neutral" bloc idea (Yugoslavia, Rumania, Bulgaria, and Hungary) which Ciano was promoting, telling the Germans that Yugoslavia found Turkey's shift to the Allies as divergent from the interests of the Balkan states, and that she desired to buttress her policy of neutrality by a rapprochement with "similarly oriented neighboring states."[92]

Then he set out for Italy, causing fear among the other Balkan states that Mussolini would request Belgrade to leave the Balkan Entente, and that under such pressure, Yugoslavia would acquiesce. But no such request was put to him there, and he resisted entreaties to conclude a separate agreement with Hungary which was to be the first step in the formation of the neutral bloc. In this regard, Yugoslavia made it clear that an agreement could be concluded with Hungary only if a similar one were made with Rumania. Yugoslav resistance and Italian reticence apparently were somewhat influenced by Berlin's only lukewarm reception to the neutral bloc idea.

By this time, not just Yugoslavia but also Rumania was feeling adverse pressure due to Article six of the Anglo-Turkish Declaration. Before leaving for Ankara on June 9, Gafencu received threatening messages from both Axis members. Alongside that, she was faced with warming Yugoslav-Bulgarian relations. Therefore, instead of trying to convince Cinkar-Marković that strengthening the Turkish position in the Mediterranean would be advantageous to Rumania and Yugoslavia as he did on a previous occasion, Gafencu agreed to go to bat for the viewpoint that an extension of the Anglo-Turkish Declaration to the Balkans would be inimical to the illusion of Balkan independence.[93]

The Germans seemed delighted at the disturbance the Anglo-Turkish Declaration was having, and so they began to use this to pressure the Balkan Entente toward neutrality realizing that a neutral Balkan Entente could be a powerful weapon in maintaining the Balkan peace they desired. Commenting editorially, the *Volkischer Boebachter* noted that the strict neutrality of the Entente in 1938 had kept them safe, but that this was now jeopardized by the radical change in Turkish policy and that Rumania and Yugoslavia, recognizing the danger, were making determined efforts to maintain their neutrality even if it meant forming a new league.[94]

On June 9 in Ankara, Gafencu made strenuous efforts on behalf of the Balkan Entente and especially Rumania and Yugoslavia, to obtain assurances from both Saracoglu and the British Ambassador that Article six of the Declaration would not be reproduced in the Anglo-Turkish Agreement and that no more form be given to the May 12 Declaration. Both Saracoglu and Knatchbull-Hugessen tried in vain to convince Gafencu that better arrangements for Balkan security would strengthen not weaken the Balkan Entente and that the agreement in no way altered the rights and duties of the Entente. They pointed out that Prince Paul had returned from Rome and Berlin unscathed, and then they assured Gafencu that Clause six would not be included *tel quel,* but there was no promise that the British and Turkish governments would not carry out the intention they had announced in Article six of continuing to consult together on Balkan affairs.[95]

After it was clear that Article six would not be expunged from the Declaration, Gafencu went to work to try to get it omitted from the Franco-Turkish version of the Declaration, arguing that the Balkan Entente needed to agree prior to the commitment on the Turkish pact. Turkey countered that nothing in the Balkan Entente prevented a state from agreeing with other states for their own security nor a need to notify in advance. Nevertheless, Gafencu continued his mission, visiting Athens from June 16-19 in an attempt to establish a common attitude among Greece, Yugoslavia and Rumania against any commitment to an anti-aggression bloc as a result of the Declaration, to show a restored Balkan front following reports of a Yugoslav defection, and to quell Bulgarian territorial aspirations. As a result, in mid-June Metaxas joined Gafencu in the suggestion that the Franco-Turkish Declaration be postponed and on June 20 a similar plea was sent by Yugoslavia to Ankara, Paris and London along with the alternative suggestion that Article six be dropped from the French version.

While there seemed to be an emerging schism between Turkey and the other members of the Balkan Entente over the issue of extension of obligations, this was more apparent than real, for the Turkish interpretation of the agreement was fairly in tune with that of the Balkan Entente whereby the Anglo-Turkish Pact dealt with Mediterranean security and the Balkan Entente with security against Bulgaria. In addition, Turkey consistently adhered to a policy of neutrality and displayed great warmth to Gafencu and support for his efforts on behalf of Balkan solidarity. Likewise, there is considerable evidence that the Yugoslav position on the matter was more rhetorical and for Axis consumption than substantive, for while the Yugoslavs believed the Anglo-Turkish Pact had the potential through Article six of extending the war to the Balkans, they also realized that the key to their survival lay with British control of the Mediterranean which was their only supply route, and that the Anglo-Turkish Pact greatly aided this cause.[96]

Because the need for Allied unity seemed more pressing than Gafencu's fears, the French Declaration was made in an unexpurgated form, but in his address to the Grand National Assembly on June 23, Saracoglu tried to pacify Rumania and Yugoslavia explaining that Article six did not alter the independent character of the Entente and its part as "an independent factor in the service of peace," but that it was intended to show that the Mediterranean was not the limit of the Turkish search for security. While Gafencu's trip had not produced results with regard to the Declaration the warmth and spirit of solidarity which greeted him everywhere was more heartening, and on his return to Bucharest it was reported that he was preparing a defensive pact which would extend the present obligations of the Balkan Entente to go to each other's aid in the event of aggression from any quarter, not just Bulgaria. This and the failure to expurgate Article six brought new wrath down upon Rumania and Yugoslavia from Axis quarters and a consequent return to the theme of neutrality by the Balkan Entente.

Gafencu's efforts at Balkan solidarity exclusive of Bulgaria had the undesirable effect of isolating Sofia to the extent that it threatened to throw Bulgaria from a neutral position into Axis arms. This was as unacceptable in Sofia as it was in Bucharest, and so Kiosseivanov went to confer with Prince Paul and Cinkar-Marković in Belgrade on July 11, where, in a bid for rapprochement, he promised that Bulgaria would not use force to regain territory. The communique issued at the end of the talks emphasized the need for closer economic ties and a "policy of independence and neutrality 'as the best answer' to the interests of Bulgaria and Yugoslavia and of peace in the Balkans."[97] But the easing of tensions between Sofia and Belgrade caused Hungary to resume pressure on Rumania, and the apparent detachment of Yugoslavia from the Entente caused the Axis to resume pressure for outright withdrawal.

Mounting revisionist pressures, Axis threats, and precarious Balkan sovereignties, were further threatened in mid-July by the British approach to

Berlin and by Soviet negotiations carried on simultaneously with the West and Germany, which either way might sacrifice the Balkans. This caused the Balkan Entente and its member states to finalize its neutrality policy all-around. The Rumanians assured the Germans they did not wish to enter into alliance with either the USSR or the Axis "as Rumania would thereby be a bridge between the hostile groups across which war would be conducted."[98] Then the Balkan Entente made it clear they would support Rumania only against Bulgaria not Hungary, and that they would not extend their obligations to Poland. There was left only Entente neutrality vis-a-vis Bulgaria to complete the circle of Balkan neutralization, but that was to come in an oblique way as threats of a Balkan explosion and a Great Power war loomed.

On August 12 as Ciano and Ribbentrop were talking in Salzburg, the Commission of Danzig arrived in Munich and the British and French military missions arrived in Moscow. The stress and strain of all of this along with stepped up militarism which was everywhere present, threatened the Balkans with total disintegration and even war. In Yugoslavia, Croat leader Dr. Maček was waving the seccessionist flag. "If Civil War should open the way to Germany," he said, "all right, let Germany come and make order."[99] The Government, meanwhile, called up four classes of army reservists for maneuvers along the German and Italian borders.

At the same time, King Carol, on Gafencu's urgent communication, returned home ten days early from his "vacation" spent in the Mediterranean discussing with the Turks plans in case of war. Among the "serious developments" reported by Gafencu was the implication that Csáky's visit to Ribbentrop had for Romania.[100] In Istanbul Turkish maneuvers in Thrace were announced following rumors of Bulgarian-Turkish border clashes, a move the Bulgarian Prime Minister believed was for the purpose of forcing Bulgaria into the Balkan Entente, but which Turkey stated was to prevent an Axis threat to march to the Dardanelles.[101] On August 16 in Sofia military maneuvers by Turkey, Rumania, and Greece on all three Bulgarian frontiers were reported, and King Carol, the same day at a Navy Day celebration at Constanza said, "Our frontiers, traced with blood, cannot be altered without risking a world cataclysm."[102] In this tense situation one Yugoslav official pointed out that it was not Balkan arms purchases from Germany (which had been going on for a long time) which was to be feared, but rather an attack by Turkey and Rumania to involve

Bulgaria in a general conflict.[103] Thus were the Balkans, perched atop their failures in bringing Balkan federalism from the shadows into reality and caught in the maelstrom of Great Power politics, poised to become for the second time in the twentieth century, the "Powder Keg" of Europe.

In this very tense situation wherein the oncoming Great Power conflict was mirrored in oncoming conflict with Bulgaria and possibly Hungary, the Balkan Entente countries drew together in a spirit of collective defense. Greece began to fortify her borders calling up 80,000 men, and the visit of Greek Under-Secretary Mavroudis to Turkey, indicated possibilities for Turkish-Greek cooperation beyond benevolent neutrality (the Greeks having said for the first time that they were with the Western Powers). Meanwhile, talks between Rumanian King Carol and Turkish President Inönü paved the way for Turkish-Rumanian cooperation and stiffened the King's attitude to resistance in the belief that Bulgaria no longer offered a serious menace. In fact, the Turkish three-pronged move to alliance with Rumania, Greece and the Soviet Union appeared to make Balkan solidarity tied to the Soviet Union the real possibility Hitler had long feared.[104] And in Yugoslavia, steps were finally taken to consummate a Serbo-Croat agreement adding greatly to Belgrade's internal and external national strength.

In the face of such solidarity, Bulgarian revisionism was capped and this, along with mounting fear of war in the area, caused Bulgaria herself to shift to neutrality by refusing the anti-Comintern and toning down her revisionism. In this respect the Bulgarians feared sudden attack by Rumania and Turkey in view of forestalling any plan of military action which the Axis powers may have had involving Bulgaria on the side of the Axis in a general conflict. Kiosseivanov said that all the Balkan countries more than ever desired neutrality, and that due to the failure of the Anglo-Franco-Russian combination, Italian neutrality, and German aims which were only economic, "war in the Southeast would be avoided." Even on the Dobruja issue, Kiosseivanov mellowed, and while avoiding a direct answer to a settlement of the Dobruja issue, he said that he had recently approached Rumania and that Bulgaria would wait with patience and not "break any glass."[105] Ironically, therefore, at the moment of greatest defeat for the cause of Balkan unity, the realities of where that disunity could end, led the Balkans back to the path of informal unity whereby to a one, the Balkan countries declared their neutrality vis-a-vis themselves and the oncoming Great Power war.

On the other hand, Balkan neutrality had been a key feature in Hitler's plans and as such, Balkan neutralization was as much a victory of Hitler's policies as a self-chosen path of the Balkan countries. And while neutrality served the purposes of the Axis and Balkans better than it did the Western Powers it was not a complete victory for Hitler either, for he needed not just a neutral and quiescent Southeast, but a benevolent, stable, and loyal Southeast, and this he did not get. As such, his own aggressive and divide-and-rule politics, the tempo of which was stepped up due to Western pressures in the opposite direction, created a situation in the Southeast necessitating his going to the Soviets to insure Balkan neutrality and hence Soviet neutrality.

Conclusion

In retrospect, the policy the Balkan Entente was to follow during 1939 was a continuation of the one followed in preceding years and specifically reiterated at the February 20, 1939 meeting. At that time the Entente came out against Bulgarian revisionism, Great Power involvement, and extension of obligations. Adherence to this position was in large measure realized by Balkan answers to the British round-robin letter of March 17 seeking support for Rumania, the April 8-9 Saracoglu-Gafencu meetings, Yugoslav and Rumanian efforts to disassociate the Balkan Entente from the Anglo-Turkish Declaration, and the reticence of Entente members to associate either unilaterally or collectively with the Soviet Union or Poland. Basically, the Balkan Entente had declared itself neutral vis-a-vis the Great Powers, Turkey, and even in reciprocal relations among itself. The one exception was Bulgaria, but in the end they informally did that too.

The wisdom of their position was given credence in the months from April to August when the West and the Axis struggled to win the Balkans to their side. The guarantees sent the first shock waves of Axis protest through the Balkan capitals, but it was the Anglo-Turkish Declaration which, in placing one of the Entente members on the side of the West, threatened the neutrality of the others. Rumania and Yugoslavia particularly were the recipients of both Axis (Hungarian) and Bulgarian pressure, for as Axis efforts to disrupt Balkan unity increased, to a like degree did Bulgarian revisionist pressure increase also. By mid-summer, Balkan unity was threatened with disintegration by a Yugoslavian withdrawal or internal dissolution, creation of an alternative neutral bloc, and Rumanian-Bulgarian border skirmishes all of which could lead to a Balkan war.

In this tense situation the Balkan Entente countries drew together, against Bulgaria, against Balkan involvement in an Anglo-Turkish Pact, and against association with Poland and Russia. This display of interdependence and will to fight against Bulgaria, cooled the situation in the Balkans, for not only did all the Balkan countries, including Bulgaria, wish to avoid a Balkan war, so also did Germany, Italy, Russia and the West. Under close examination what appeared to be the Balkan program was also Hitler's, for while it was he who inspired division, but it was he also who kept the caps on Hungarian and Bulgarian revisionism, discouraged counterblocs, and supporting the continued existence and neutrality of the Balkan Entente.

There are several questions which arise at this point. First, would the Balkans have had to declare their neutrality vis-a-vis the Great Powers and reciprocally had they increased their unity by integrating Bulgaria into the system? As it was, old and past antagonisms and the power of nationalism, in part spawned by the Great Powers, rose their heads to bewitch the intricacies of Balkan reconciliation, and because the Bulgarian and Hungarian dilemmas were never solved, they became the bedevilers of Balkan rapprochement.

Let us suppose the Balkan Entente had been successful in bringing Bulgaria into the act. Would it have declared against the Axis? This seems unlikely for many reasons, chief among them that a declaration for the West would have placed the seat of war in the Balkans, which was above all what the Balkans wished to avoid. History itself supports this idea, for even Bulgaria declared her neutrality at war initiation, and the basic orientation of the Balkan Entente by 1939 was not just anti-Bulgarian, but anti-involvement. The shying away from intra-Balkan commitments was for the same reason.

The other question involves the validity of the concept of Balkan neutrality in so far as it safeguarded national existence. In one sense, the failure of the Balkans to connect themselves with the West via Turkey or even the Soviet Union or to extend their inter-or intra-Balkan relations against the Great Powers, made Balkan neutrality a figment of the imagination, for in reality such a policy was synonymous with the Axis policy which was designed to isolate Poland and provide a secure rear flank against the West. Thus, the Balkan "neutrality" policy was in reality pro-Axis. This was a shrewd perception on the Balkan part with regard to the actual balance of power of the times. For, in effect, the most immediate threat to their national existence was Germany or German-inspired and backed Hungarian or Bulgarian revisionism. Thus, neutrality vis-a-vis Berlin served well the purpose of keeping war from the Balkans, a policy which happened also to be Hitler's.

But such a neutral policy did not insure loyalty to Berlin, for it was in part the product of the West's bulwarking of the Balkans as well as fear of Berlin. Therefore, in the absence of Balkan political adhesion to the Axis Pact, the Nazis needed some reinsurance that neutrality would stick particularly if the power position of the West improved. Well aware of the fickle and self-serving loyalties of the Balkans and unable to imperialize the Southeast and maintain Soviet neutrality too, the Nazis sought a new avenue to Balkan neutrality which led straight to Moscow.

The Soviet Union was another important factor in Balkan neutrality, for any Balkan eruption would very likely place Soviet troops on Balkan soil as well. The unfortunate aspect of Balkan neutrality with regard to Moscow is that, as it provided no bulwark against Germany, it likewise provided no defense for Russia or worse yet, it set the Balkans adrift to be put up for barter. Therefore, Balkan appeasement was an important factor in bringing the Soviets to the Nazi negotiating table and the subsequent realization of the Nazi-Soviet Pact, in turn bringing on the war, but not a Balkan war.

The Soviet factor, and whether or not the Nazi-Soviet Pact was advantageous to the Balkans, will be discussed in the next chapters. Suffice to say here, that the Soviet Union was a crucial issue in the events of April to August, 1939, particularly in the issue of Balkan neutrality (fear of Russia) and in the Western efforts to form a peace front. Yet the Soviet Union need not have assumed the magnitude of importance it did, for no one was really anxious to come to terms with this enigma of Euro-Asian politics, least of all the Germans.

In terms of the Balkans, what brought this about was the simultaneous wooing of Moscow by London and Berlin over the issue of control of Poland and the Balkans. Had the Soviet Union been truly neutral, declaring to neither side, the Balkans would have been safe. Moscow was not, however, having aims and interests of her own in the Balkans which, for the moment, were better served by going with Germany. It is this element of the Pact, its aggressive nature in terms not only of Poland but of the Balkans, which surprised, revolted, and turned World War II into a Balkan tragedy for the West.

CHAPTER IV

THE SOVIET UNION—PRELUDE

During the 1920s and early 1930s, the omnipresent Soviet threat to the Balkans, inherited from Czarist days and reinforced by the Bolshevik Revolution, was temporarily lost in a swirl of collectivist politics, in the rise to power of Germany, and in the realities of Soviet physical weakness. This might have remained the case had not German power and Western enervation set in motion, in Gafencu's words:

> . . .the progressive upheaval predicted by Mr. Churchill which was destined to bring the course of the valley of the Danube all the way to the Black Sea into the orbit of power politics.[1]

The West looked east in order to save itself and tie a ring around Germany, while the Germans took steps in the East to prevent that. The result was that overnight the Soviet Union was elevated to Great Power status, and in this way was ressurrected the Eastern Question, making the Balkans for the second time in the twentieth century the object of a power struggle between Germany, Russia and Britain.

As we have seen, by 1939 German Balkan aims of economic domination and benevolent neutrality, based largely on Balkan fragmentation, had been achieved. The Balkans, the West, and the Soviet Union seemed satisfied with that arrangement until Prague, Albania, and the threat to Poland made it appear that German imperialist aims lacked limitation, and that open-ended appeasement in the East would lead to the destruction of the West. The British decision to make a stand in East Europe threatened Germany, the Balkans and the Soviet Union alike. We have already noted the nature of the Balkan reaction which was to secure its neutrality in the coming conflict between the West, Germany and possibly the Soviet Union by bulwarking the frontiers against border revisionism and by preventing the extension of inter-locking commitments which could bring down on them a Great Power war, a Balkan war, or German wrath. The German reaction was to thwart the formation of an encirclement front by threat and then by overtures to Moscow.

Neither the Balkan program nor the British program had much appeal to the Soviets who, during these five months, from April to August, struck out in a different direction, toward Berlin. Churchill, as well as most Westerners, appears to have emphaszied the need for Soviet security as the motivation behind this move. In his view, the Soviet Union "was to renounce a system of security which no longer inspired it with confidence," and that the Moscow agreement was "the culminating effect of the policy of Munich."[2] Yet, as the following discussion with suggest, there was another side to Soviet Balkan aims and interest which had a great deal to do with a dialectical and internationalist view of world politics and negotiations, and with expansionsism.

Balkan Aims and Interests and the Peace Front

Russian interests in the Balkans are longstanding, and the historical links with the past seem not to have escaped the supposed novelty of the Communist regime. Stalin, the prime architect of Soviet foreign policy of the time, was a man who had never been outside Russia, and so he fashioned a Russo-centric policy which, despite Communist rhetoric, established its roots deep in the past. Stalin, for instance, fully appreciated Ivan the Great's role as "gatherer of Russian lands" and in particular Moscow's aim of gathering in by war and diplomacy the territories which had belonged to Russia before the Tartar conquest, a policy which oriented Russia south in the direction of the Baltic Sea, its littoral, and Constantinople

On July 19, 1934, Stalin, in a letter to fellow Politburo members, took to task Engels' essay of 1890 entitled "The Foreign Policy of Russia" in which Engels coupled Russia's drive for Constantinople with the German annexation of Alsace-Lorraine. Engels, Stalin wrote, had erred in explaining Russia's acquisitive foreign policy more by the pressure of a gang of foreign adventurers than by the need for an outlet to the sea and seaports for enlarged trade and strategic position. In addition, he said, Engels had omitted the imperialist contest and the British role in the coming war.[3] (After the Soviet incorporation of eastern Poland in 1939, the theme reappeared, the Soviet press alluding to the historical antecedents and honoring Stalin as the "gatherer" of Russia.)

The policy of neutrality in order to make gains for Russia also had antecedents in Russian history, particularly in connection with Moscow's refusal to fight Europe's wars. Ivan the Great denied requests of European Christian rulers to join a coalition formed to fight against the Ottoman Turks despite the obvious menace of Turco-Islamic inroads onto Russian territory, while Alexander I at Tilsit pulled Russia out of the war against Napoleon, thereby emerging with hegemony over much of Eastern Europe. While Stalin never referred in specifics to czarist programs, the thoroughly Russian nature of his education suggests that he found his heroes in the Russian past and not the Western experience which had nourished classical Communist ideology.

This became apparent in Stalin's inclination to equate land and territory with power and strength. It was on this basis along with allusions to the past that he claimed Bessarabia. In 1924, according to Christian Rakovsky, Litvinov wished to recognize Rumanian sovereignty over Bessarabia in order to settle the question, and because he viewed as outmoded the view that territory was security. Opposed were Rakovsky, Chicherin, and Stalin who felt it desirable to maintain Bessarabia as a "Soviet irredenta."[4] Empirical evidence suggests that the power Stalin wished to derive from Bessarabia was not just territorial, but tactical, that is as a bargaining weapon and as a way to keep open a link with the West.

In 1932, for instance, when the Rumanians and Soviets were trying to hammer out a non-aggression pact, the Soviets used their claim to obstruct progress in the negotiations, but once the U.S. recognized the Soviet Union (June 16, 1933), the non-aggression pact followed soon after (July 3, 1933). By this pact, the Rumanian Government considered that Russia recognized the Rumanian claim, but the Soviets considered the question in abeyance until 1939 when they needed it again in the negotiations with Germany.[5]

Intrinsically speaking, both offensive and defensive strategic considerations are evident in the Soviet wish to control Bessarabia. The position of this province at the mouth of the Danube could serve as a buffer as well as a base for further advances toward the Balkans and the Straits, and it became particularly valuable in 1939 and in the first days of the war when Germany became dependent on Rumanian oil (which was only 30-50 minutes from the Bessarabian border) and began to use the Danube as the main artery in its supply system. The racial justification for claiming Bessarabia are less apparent, the population being over one-half Rumanian and one-fourth Ukrainian. Regardless, Stalin continually infiltrated the area in the 1930s with arms and propaganda in order to predispose it toward the Soviet Union should a future need or opportunity arise to advance in that direction.

In part, the bid for territory was a bid for power in the international community for only by this route could the Soviets hope to play a part in the respective definiton of spheres without war.[6] This helps to explain Soviet irritation at being excluded from Munich and the paltry diplomatic efforts made in Balkan capitals, for the Soviets believe that their fate would be decided in a larger arena and that the Balkans were not something to be bargained with as the British sought to do, but which were to be bargained for. The other side of the coin was that Balkan fears of Russia were such that relationships that there were followed on the coattails of the Great Powers and were bilateral rather than multilateral in nature.[7]

In the Soviet view, the issue of control of the interim states would be made not by a Balkan decision to go to one side or the other, but by the war which was to be fought by the Great Powers. Since Soviet weakness in the 1930s by in large prohibited any advances of their own or the twisting of the situation in an advantageous direction, the Soviets supported the status quo of the area which, up until 1939, put them in the Western camp and after that in the camp of Germany. In support of this policy, the Soviets pursued friendship with Turkey and opposition to Italy, and they did not support the Balkan Pact because, like Germany, they were wary of any grouping which could be turned against them, preferring a manipulative situation on their borders, and because of the adverse effects it had on Bulgarian relations with neighbors of the Soviet Union.[8] On the other hand, they did not support Bulgaria either. When the Bulgarian Minister stated in 1934 that Bulgaria was ready to place itself in the position of a "client state" of the USSR in return for which the Soviet Union would endeavor to establish closer relations between Turkey and Bulgaria (the purpose of which was to enlist aid in obtaining a Bulgarian outlet to the Aegean), the Soviet Union refused to be a party to it.[9] Any other moves the Soviets made in the direction of the Balkans, like at Montreux or in connection with Czechoslovakia, were always in league with the Great Powers, in support of the status quo, or to their own advantage.

In Stalin's mind, land was power and power was the ability to promote world revolution, so that offense and defense, security and chance, the Russian state and Communist ideology, nationalism and internationalism were always linked instead of being mutually exclusive as was often the West's perception of Stalinist aims. The association between territorial gains and extension of the power of the Soviet Union on the one hand, and the progress of the revolution on the other, led Stalin naturally to look west along his European frontier. In 1921 Stalin wrote that Soviet Russia would be better off in terms of capitalist encirclement if it had "as neighbors one large industrially developed or several Soviet states," and in 1926 he wrote that it would be better if "the present capitalist encirclement is replaced by a socialist encirclement."[10] Though there is some dispute by Stalinologists as to what countries Stalin was talking about,[11] there is little doubt that it would have been useful to have Western influence diminished in the area, and for this reason Stalin supported the Rumanian effort to abolish the international control of the Danube and replace it with her own.

In the Soviet quest for revolutionary, national, and defensive power, strengthening from within seemed constantly frustrated by domestic problems and world isolation. Thus, the Soviets sought another path, that of weakening the other combatants. One aspect of Litvinov's collectivist policy of the 1930s, therefore, was the promotion of disarmament of others and the wedding together of the West to save Russia. Litvinov's speeches continually harped on Hitler's strategy of dividing the opposition and of the need for all to disarm, not of ways to seriously reduce the Soviet or German threats to Europe. In fact, there is some evidence that the Soviets did not want Germany to abandon her designs on Austria at the behest of Britain, France, and Italy, as it might be at the eventual expense of the Soviet Union. Therefore, when collectivism appeared to exhibit its supreme failure at Munich, it was not seen as such in Moscow. If anything, it elevated the power position of the Soviet Union within that framework. Litvinov made such an observation at the time saying:

> Henceforth the USSR has only to watch from the shelters of its frontiers, the establishment of German hegemony over Central and Southeast Europe. And if, by chance the Western Powers finally decide to wish to stop it, they must address themselves to us for . . . we shall have the last word.[12]

And, far from abandoning the policy after Munich, Moscow continued to support it, engaging in talks along these lines with Great Britain and France all during the summer. Though both Hitler and the West interpreted the dismissal of Litvinov as a sign that the Soviet Union had abandoned collectivism, the official reason given at the time was "ill health," and since the war the explanation has been that in threatening times it is necessary to have a person of greater "experience and popularity." Stalin did not damn Litvinov, not just because this was his policy also, but more likely because it was a policy which still might be useful, and because he had become an impediment to another path he wanted to explore.

On the other side of collectivism was the idea that a capitalist conflict could be useful to the Soviet Union, an idea which Lenin originated and Stalin espoused. But in promoting conflict Stalin wanted to be able to pick the time, place, and conditions under which Russia would enter. Addressing the Central Committee on January 19, 1925, Stalin saw a new war was inevitable and that to prepare did not necessarily mean Russia should initiate hostilities. If war comes, he said, we shall not sit with folded hands; "we shall have to make a move, but the move will come last."[13]

How far Stalin was prepared to go in promoting a capitalist war has been debated by those in the field. Some argue that Stalin promoted Hitler's rise to power by failing to support the German Socialists against him, and others contend that, while Stalin did nothing to support Hitler's rise to power, he did nothing to prevent it.[14] Certainly Stalin had read *Mein Kampf* and recognized Hitler's aims in the East. On the other hand, the German Socialists were as unlikely to hand over territory or aggrandize the power of Stalin as were the Nazis. Thus, for Stalin, both the German

Socialists and Nazis were potential catalysts for a capitalist war and at the same time equally unfriendly to Soviet aims. That Nazi militarism may have appeared more threatening than German Socialism may not have bothered Stalin. In view of his assumption that war was inevitable and because struggle was the stuff of the revolutionary, which Stalin was, besides being the only route to a change in the balance of power in the end, it is very likely that German Socialism and the German Nazism had an equal appeal to Stalin and that neither were more to be feared than Capitalism.

In fact, Stalin gave little import to the role of ideology in achieving Soviet aims. Litvinov, who considered himself merely a shuffler of diplomatic documents and presumably speaking for Stalin, said on December 29, 1933, "We have, of course, our opinion of the German regime . . .but we Marxists are the last who can be reproached for permitting our feelings to dictate our policy." And in December, 1937 he told foreign correspondents that the Anti-Comintern Pact "was dust in the eyes of Western Democracies, that ideology are nothing to Fascists," that the West will fall prey first, and that Russia had the Red Army and vast territory, that the Germans read history and that they believed in Bismarck's policy of reinsurance with Russia, not the Kaiser's.[15] On the other hand, Stalin was not adverse to venomously invoking doctrine when it served his purpose.

Likewise it seemed to matter little to Moscow that the Balkan states were basically anti-Communist during the 1930s or that they were detaching themselves from the West and sinking into the Nazi orbit. For going back to Lenin's theories of the role of "Third World" states in Communist revolutionary theory, it was to the Soviet advantage to support all nationalist independence movements, Communist or non-Communist, in order to create an independent block of states along the Soviet periphery which presumably would look to Moscow for protection against any new threat like the German one, and whose isolated independence could later become one of dependence. When the British decided to make a stand in East Europe, the Soviet postion was further enhanced in that, in the inevitable war between Germany and the West should Hitler move east, the Soviet Union's position vis-a-vis both powers was crucial. In this respect, the importance of the capitalist war should not be overlooked, for in the absence of a competitive Soviet power factor, it was war that gave the Russians the chance to advance into the Balkans both at the negotiating table and otherwise, thereby turning defense into offense.

The Soviets, who regarded ideologies as unimportant in their maneuvers (not their goals), were never truly adverse to a linkup with Germany if that proved advantageous. In this respect, the Nazi-Soviet rhetorical combat engaged in during the peace front days was part of a strategy to inspire the capitalist war, not a measure of true enmity. In fact, alliance with Germany looked more attractive as the peace front gained momentum, for the more the Soviets inspired it, the closer war come, necessitating Soviet withdrawal or isolation from it, and assurances that the war would be a capitalist one and not in their direction. This, of course, was the crucial point, for the plan to be successful requied that Western resistance be moved to a point whereby the West required Hitler's first attention. But even if the Soviets were unable at the crucial moment to shift the war West, Stalin had two powerful weapons at his disposal; one was the importance the Soviet Union gained to the West even if they were invaded first (since a German conquest of the Soviet Union would place overwhelming odds against the West), and the other was the territorial and political assets Russia had to defend herself in the long run.

The "peace front" policy the Soviets began to pursue in the 1930s was an extension of the rapprochement policy designed to break out of isolation (and gain status) which was pursued in the 1920s, but now it was spawned by a fear of Germany rather than the West. Behind it lay themes constant to Soviet foreign policy, including neutrality in a capitalist war, impartiality to ideology, collectivist activities with the West in order to deflect the thrust of the Nazi assault and gain Great Power bargaining status, Russo-centrism, isolation, and finally bluff as to the real intent and power of the Soviet Union. In Stalin's speech to the Seventeenth Congress of the Communist Party Soviet Union on January 26, 1934[16] all of these motives are apparent. Stalin began by noting that the world had fallen into an economic crisis and that as a result there had been a tremendous growth in tension in the capitalist world exemplified in the rise of Fascism and the growth of armaments. In view of that, he said, the Soviet Union had adopted a "peace policy," which was based not on weakness but on the growing strength of the Soviet Union. But, he added, this new orientation was "not a question of fascism," (here he noted good relations with Italy) nor of a changed attitude toward Versailles. He said:

> We never have any orientation towards Germany, nor have we any orientation towards Poland and France. Our motivation in the past

and our orientation at the present time is toward the USSR and toward the USSR alone.

He explained that:

If the interests of the USSR demand rapprochement with one country or another which is not interested in disturbing the peace, we
adopt this course without hesitation.

The theme of neutrality in the coming capitalist struggle was under-
scored by Karl Radek, editor of *Izvestia* and member of the Communist
Party Soviet Union. He wrote:

In any given concrete case, such a pact means a guarantee of Soviet
neutrality in conflicts which may arise among the capitalist nations
conceded in exchange for the undertaking by the latter to refrain
from attacking the Soviet Union or intervening in its domestic affairs . . . .[17]

The pacts Radek were referring to followed shortly; January 11, 1934 a
Franco-Soviet Trade Pact was signed, and on May 2, 1935 a Franco-Rus-
sian Pact and May 16 a Russo-Czech Pact. In between, the Soviet Union
joined the League of Nations (September 19, 1934), launched the Popular
Front in July-August 1934 at the Seventh Comintern Congress, and gained
U.S. recognition the same year. That these pacts were not a sign of friendship or jeopardization of Soviet neutrality was noted also in the West where
a French statesman opined that the Franco-Soviet Treaty would not produce assistance to France if there was war (but would serve to prevent the
Soviet Union from assisting Germany).[18]
    Whatever Stalin said about this new "peace policy" in terms of Soviet
neutrality, it was clearly directed against Germany and was so interpreted
by the West. In his speech to the Seventeenth Congress in 1934, Stalin
connected his peace policy with whatever pacts were necessary to secure
the Soviet Union against what he called the new German policy, which was
like the German Kaiser's "who at one time occupied the Ukraine and
marched against Leningrad, after converting the Baltic countries into a
place d'armes for this march."[19] And whatever Stalin said about the

strength of the Soviet Union, the new pacts were clear evidence that the capitalist war was yet on the horizon and that in the interim, Soviet weakness necessitated connecting herself with the West in order to promote resistance and prevent Soviet isolation. The Balkan countries fit nicely into this connection for, as they were in the Western sphere too, resistance not only protected the Soviet border but promoted a capitalist war where the Soviets could benefit most.

Stalin's peace policy was pursued during the next several years with considerable success in terms of the tempo and warmth of dialog carried on with the West. Essentially it was in the hands of Soviet Foreign Minister Litvinov, who in his cosmopolitan, less revolutionary style, in a sense, created the mirage of Soviet "collectivist" foreign policy. But underneath, the policy was a failure as early as 1935 and 1936, in that connection with the West could fulfill the peace policy only if the West strengthened itself and exhibited a willingness to use this strength. Otherwise, the ring around Hitler was only a paper cordon, and connection with the West would result in bringing the Soviet Union into the West's war without commensurate protection or compensation, and rather than Soviet peace and a capitalist war, the Nazi-Soviet war would be the result.

In the face of aggressive Axis policies and Western appeasement,[20] the East European countries also began to appease Hitler, opening the way for German penetration and exposure of the Soviet west flank. Little Entente devotion to the USSR via Czechoslovakia was ruined by a shift in Rumanian policy signaled by the replacement in 1936 of the pro-Soviet Titulescu with the pro-German Antonescu who felt that an alliance with the Soviet Union was too dangerous. This was a blow to the Soviet peace policy, for during the early years of Hitler's rise to power, there was a certain long-distance affection between the Central European powers and the Soviet Union due to the fact that the Soviet Union could act as a brake to German aggression without being the clear threat she was to the states which bordered her directly. Of this link, Austrian Minister Marek said that Vienna's close relationship with Russia had nothing to do with ideology, but of necessity in maintaining the balance of power in Europe and in preventing the materialization of an agreement between the Soviet Union and Germany.[21]

Theoretically, the exposure of East Europe and the weakness of the West should have driven the Soviet Union toward active diplomatic efforts to wed together a cordon of East European states attached to the Soviet Union in a sort of collectivist "peace" pact like the one Stalin had pursued in the West. Yet he seemed little inclined to do so. The obvious reason why such a front did not materialize despite the commonality of interest, was the deep distrust of every East European and Balkan country of the USSR and the knowledge that the USSR could not help economically. In Hungary the resentment over the Bela Kun experiment lingered, and in Rumania Soviet irredentism regarding Bessarabia was suspected. In Yugoslavia the Serbo-Croat antagonism produced a government which feared communist relations with popular front governments more than German aggression, while in Bulgaria the aura of anti-Stamboliskyism remained. In addition, both the Balkan and Little Ententes were dedicated to the status quo, and there was an increasing tendency in all East European capitals once Western strength in East Europe waned, to avoid provoking Hitler's wrath by allying with Moscow.

The less obvious reason was that Stalin wanted the interim states weakened so that the West would come begging, and if they did not, the Soviet Union "had the Red Army and vast territory," while a Soviet stand in East Europe would only lead to premature exhaustion without utilizing Russia's greatest defensive asset, the enormity of the land. Indeed, all of Stalin's activities during these years—the purges, the move of industry east, collective diplomacy—appear directed toward preparation for a defensive war until such time as German and Western exhaustion would allow him freedom to, unimpeded, move west. As late as March 22, 1939 the British evaluation was that there:

> . . .was little likelihood of a collapse of the Soviet regime from internal reasons whether or not the USSR became involved in war, and that, while the defensive power of the Red Army and the Soviet air force was considerable, their value in an offensive war would be much less.[22]

Amidst the failure of Stalin's "peace" policy, that is a strong Western defense system, Stalin in retrospect saw one bright spot. At Yalta he hailed Montreux as a victory,[23] for the Soviets had disliked the principle of parity established in the Lausanne Agreement, expecting instead special consideration for their greater interests at the Straits. At the Montreux Convention held in June-July, 1936, Russian presence as one of the major participants among other things, was significant in the prestige it carried. The Convention went on to modify the provisions for passage through the Straits to Russia's advantage, for while the principle of freedom of passage of commercial vessels was reaffirmed, non-Black Sea powers including Great Britian and France, could send only light vessels into the Black Sea, while Black Sea powers could send capital ships of any size into the Mediterranean.

The Soviets, however, had not obtained everything they wanted, as their proposals allowing the Soviet fleet to exit and attack a hostile fleet in the Mediterranean and then retire to the Black Sea without risk of pursuit, were not accepted. In the fight over egress of Soviet ships, only Great Britain and Japan supported curtailing Soviet exit rights while France and the Balkan Entente supported Soviet rights, particularly Rumania as it increased for Bucharest the possibilities of fulfillment of the Franco-Czech Pact by supply of material via the Straits and Turkey to Rumania and Czechoslovakia.[24]

There was also friction between the Soviet Union and Turkey, whose control over the Straits had been considerably strengthened at Montreaux by permission granted to Turkey to remilitarize the Straits, and by the power given to Turkey to close the Straits in time of war or imminent threat. Hence, Turkish good favor to Moscow was imperative, and yet, Turkey showed signs of fear of the Soviet Union, resulting in a cooling of Turkish-Soviet relations and improvement of those with Great Britain. In addition, she felt stronger than the Ottoman Empire to exploit the bargaining position she obtained by Montreaux and the network of alliances she had built up,[25] making her a pivot point in an embryonic Western security system reaching from the Danube to India, but one with no gains for the Soviet Union.

Thus Stalin's positive statements regarding Montreux at Yalta were decidedly political and do not match what appears to have been the Soviet attitude of the time. Instead, the Soviets seemed disgruntled with the new arrangement which, instead of taking control of the Straits and handing it to the Soviet Union, had abolished a defunct international arrangement and created a new relationship based on sovereign alliances built on self-interest. Litvinov's speech on the visit of Turkish Foreign Minister Aras to Moscow on July 12-17, 1937 and the resultant communique is remarkably guarded.[26] Much more serious for the Soviet Union in light of cooling

Russo-Turkish relations, was th safety of the Straits itself, for if Hitler realized the inability of Turkey to actually defend the Straits, Russia did too.

* * * * *

Thus, in many ways it appeared the "peace front" had failed. The West did not join together in a tough stand against Hitler, rather they appeased him. Disarmament did not take place, rather the armaments race took a great leap forward particularly in the Fascist countries which threatened the Soviet Union on two borders. The withdrawal of Western support for the Balkans economically, militarily, and politically encouraged the gradual shifting of Southeast Europe into the Nazi orbit, exposing the Soviet frontier. Even Turkey's new position as keeper of the Dardanelles threatened the Soviets, for Turkey could not defend the Straits and would not grant the Soviets the right to do so. Actually the peace front worked only if the West grew strong and took to the field in the West, engaging the Nazis, leaving East Europe to the Soviets.

The "failure" of the "peace policy," however, did not place the Soviet Union in the precarious position which Western and Soviet propaganda often portrayed. For one thing, the Soviet Union had never placed itself in the West's collectivist framework, but was simply encouraging a Western diplomatic effort from which it might benefit. Moreover, the withdrawal of the West from Southeast Europe, while it left a vacuum for Hitler to fill, likewise increased the ability of the Soviet Union to exploit the area since only two contestants remained in the struggle for the Balkans—Germany and Russia. If Russia chose not to fight for the Balkans, there would be no war. On the other hand, should the West wish to reintroduce its power or Germany to move in either direction, it is with Moscow that some deal must be struck.

Finally, appeasement for both the West and the Soviet Union could go just so far before national border lines would be reached and war the result. But Russia had a great deal more available retreating area than the West, as history has amply shown. For these obtuse reasons, the Soviets maintained a surprising confidence in their revolutionary triumph and the strength of their defensive position, and this "dark side of the moon" goes a long way toward explaining why Russia's isolation was nothing more than the self-imposed policy she had followed all along, and one which she ultimately turned into triumph.

The Isolation of the Soviet Union

Though the Soviet Union, during the crises of 1938, continued in outward form to follow the patterns of the peace front and to propagandize its virtues, it seemed apparent that it had failed and that the Soviet Union was already searching for a new path to security and opportunity. In the meantime, the bare facts of Moscow's position, that is its growing isolation, itself became a policy earmarked with the leitmotiv of neutrality in the coming conflict, a theme which indirectly signaled Berlin of Moscow's willingness to consider another approach more amenable to the Nazis. Actually neutrality in a capitalist war had been Moscow's policy all along. It was only the changed circumstances, particularly the increasing threat of war, which made it more easily distinguished from the West's wishful interpretation of collectivism and the belief that the Soviets would fight.

Outward signs that a shift was in the wind appeared in the form of untoward treatment of foreigners, purges of the Army and Soviet Foreign Service (Litvinov was one of the few to survive), and deterioration in relations with Turkey and France. In this regard, Stalin made two statements of interest. At the February-March 1937 Plenum session of the Central Committee, he emphasized capitalist encirclement without any distinction between friendly states, democracies, and fascist states as he had done in his January 1934 speech in which he clearly branded the Nazis as aggressors. Then, in the February 14, 1938 *Pravda,* in reply to a letter written by a young Soviet named Ivanov, who had questioned the need for the purges, Stalin emphasized the need to secure the internal socialist victory and thus the Revolution by expulsion of Trotskyites and by the strengthening of arms. Western observers interpreted it as part of a "new policy whereby the Soviet Union, while retaining its basic concept and aim, considered it necessary to make a radical alteration of its policy . . ."[27] and German sources noted that both Potemkin and Litvinov had tried to minimize the impact of Stalin's letter in clear recognition of its import.[28] In effect, declared neutrality in advance of the event, egged Hitler on while appeasing him, in effect encouraging aggression but deflecting it. (The Russians accused the West of the same tactic against Moscow.)

Meanwhile, Litvinov, in his astute style, predicted Anschluss, but like Stalin, maintained a noble aloofness from any obligation, moral or otherwise to the threatened East European countries, noting that Hitler and Mussolini had Chamberlain on the spot and that the latter would have to make some arrangement with the dictators. When Anschluss did occur on March 15, 1938, Litvinov warned the West of the "indubitable menace" which threatened large and small countries, and then he pledged that the Soviet Union was ready to participate in "collective action" to check further aggression, but he failed to suggest that the Soviet Union would take any action of its own.[29] When the West responded, U.S. Ambassador Davies noted a considerable speedup in Soviet prepardness, reporting arms expenditures at approximately 28 percent of the total revenues, with roads and fortifications being built all along the Western frontiers, ruthless hostility to all foreigners, including Germans, and supreme Soviet self-confidence that the Soviet Union could take care of itself.[30]

As the threat to Czechoslovakia loomed, Litvinov took the same tack of berating the West for its inaction, but this time he infused it with an aura of hostility for the West and with innuendos which amounted to Soviet severence of its ties with the West. In a speech on the international situation at an election meeting in Leningrad on June 23, 1938,[31] he said that the League of Nations was "stricken with paralysis," and he implied that the foreign policy of the West was directed against Russia as much as Germany when he said, "The entire diplomacy of the Western powers in the last five years resolves itself into an avoidance of any resistance to Germany's aggressive action . . . ." Then Litvinov answered his own question as to the why of this strange policy of the West, by saying that cooperation with the Soviet Union is essential but, "they fear if they defeat the aggressor states in war," they will "destroy the artificial dam against the labor movement." And for the first time he berated the East Europeans for their collaboration in the plot and the West for offering them as sacrifices, saying:

> European Powers no longer have any allies among the middle and small states of Europe. Some of these states have openly entered the orbit of the aggressors,[32] others, for fear of the latter, are mumbling about neutrality . . . . Their declaration of neutrality is tantamount to saying that they reject the help of the League of Nations, the help of friends . . . .

Litvinov ended his speech of June 23, 1938 by outlining the new direction of the Soviet peace policy which would now be pursued by the strengthening of Soviet defenses, the development of the Soviet economy, annihilation of fifth column and espionage, and the reminding of aggressors of Russian willingness to fight. The shift was noted in German documents by the German Ambassador in Moscow, Schulenburg, who reported the indiscriminate closing of 22 consulates which he attributed to "espionage psychosis" and the tendency "toward isolation."[33]

As the Czech crisis approached, the Soviet Union, for not the first time in history, was closing its doors to the West, disappearing into the vast limitless steppes and the frozen snows of Russia to gather and preserve her strength alone. The mystery surrounding Soviet intentions and technical questions regarding fulfillment of the Soviet-Czech alliance was thereby increased. Repeatedly, Litvinov said that the Soviet Union would live up to its obligations regarding Czechoslovakia, but that the responsibility was France's, and that meant obtaining Polish and Rumanian permission for Soviet troop transit.[34]

Litvinov strove hard during this period to maintain the credibility of the Soviet commitment saying that in the event of Czech rejection of a German-British-French ultimatum and a decision by Prague to fight, though giving the Soviet Union the moral right to renounce the Pact (in that such an ultimatum would include the eventual denunciation of the Soviet-Czech Pact), the Soviet Union would honor the pact as Moscow was "not seeking pretext to evade obligations."[35] And, Potemkin told the Polish Charge in Moscow that if "faced with a Polish act of aggression against Czechoslovakia," Moscow would denounce Article two of the non-aggression pact of 1932 between the USSR and Poland,[36] while recent Soviet historiography even refers to Soviet offers of unilateral aid to Czechoslovakia. (Purportedly Stalin told K. Gottwald that the Soviet Union was ready to give military aid if Czechoslovakia would defend itself and if she asked for Soviet assistance.)[37]

These Soviet statements must be balanced against the situation as it existed at the time which made it appear from many points of view that the Soviet Union would not under any circumstances find herself having to honor her obligations. One reason was the resistance of Rumania, Poland, and Czechoslovakia herself to Soviet aid. Polish interests in Teschen made Warsaw unofficially collaborate with Germany and Hungary for the breakup of Czechoslovakia. And Rumania dragged her feet on the issue of aid to Czechoslovakia, finally agreeing to air transit rights for the Russians but not ground troop passage. The Czechs, meanwhile, turned down proposals of the Red Army for a mixed commission to examine defense plans of both states as the Czech staff did not want to reveal secrets, being unconvinced of Moscow's assertion that it was not in contact with the German General Staff.

Beneš further explained to a session of the Ministerial Council on the eve of acceptance of the Munich agreement, that in the case that only Russia came to Czechoslovakia's assistance, a war of all against Russia would ensue and England would go against her, for the:

> ...West would have believed that we (were) an instrument of Bolshevism in Central Europe; Poland, and Hungary would have considered Soviet assistance an attack against them; the West would have at best wailed and washed its hands of a German-Soviet war.[38]

Also he said, Czechoslovakia would have been responsible for all the consequences, possibly of a Bolshevik Revolution in the whole area of Central Europe against the West's resistance. The view that the West did not want Prague to accept Soviet aid seems to have been prevalent in German circles as well, where the emphasis was on the West's desire to keep the peace and come to some accommodation with Germany.

Though it is uncertain how much the Soviets knew and understood of the Czech, German, Franco-British and East European positions (though as we have seen, Little and Balkan Entente public statements made it fairly clear they would not go to Czechoslovakia's defense), it seems at the same time apparent from Soviet actions that either they counted on not having to go to Czechoslovakia's support or they did not intend to. German and British diplomats in Moscow noted that the Soviet Union showed no signs of preparing herself to defend Czechoslovakia despite her bellicose statements and broad claims of loyalty. And according to recent historiography, on September 30 at 9:30, before Beneš accepted the Munich decision, he called Soviet envoy Sergei Alexandrovsky to enquire of Moscow what its position would be "if Czechoslovakia entered the war against Germany (assuming) that she would have England and France against her . . . ." For unexplained reasons, Alexandrovsky did not advise Moscow of the Beneš inquiry until shortly before noon.[39] (At 12:50, after discussing the situation with his Council, Beneš made known his decision to accept the Munich dictate.)

In analyzing Soviet policy, the obvious conclusion is that the Soviets were prepared to aid Czechoslovakia only if the West did, but, certain that the West would appease at Soviet expense, and that there was sufficient reluctance in East Europe to accept aid, they were certain they would not have to. Already launched on the path toward isolation and neutralization, why then did Litvinov make such a point of honoring Soviet obligations? And why, at the last moment, was unilateral assistance offered? The answer to this question is at the heart of Soviet policy, for despite Stalin's profound distrust of the West, the only way the Soviet Union could be secured and make advancement at the same time was by participation in the agreement at Munich. Through this she would achieve Great Power status, secure against an agreement at her expense, and possibly gain control over the interim states on her border which were, not only her protection, but an entree into European politics and the advancement of the life of the Revolution.

The Soviet response to Munich suggests disgust and intimidation at not being included. *Pravda* stated sardonically on September 21 that the Soviet Union was indifferent to which imperialist "brigand," Germany or Britain, would fall on this or that colony, and Molotov, in a speech on the international situation on November 6, 1938 said, "The four strongest imperialist states of Europe did, without much trouble, defeat little Czechoslovakia."[40] However, rather than weakening her position, Munich strengthened it by raising the ante, for as Litvinov stated, the Soviet Union had no choice but to retire to the wings and watch the establishment of German hegemony over all of Southeast Europe, eventually necessitating a Western call for help.[41] Meanwhile, the Germans had to endeavor to offset or prevent that link and to strengthen their economic ties with the Soviet Union, presumably as a vehicle to establish relations if they had to, and otherwise to secure crucial raw materials and to make the Soviet Union dependent economically.

Falling back upon themselves, the Soviets after Munich again harped on Soviet defense and preparedness to fight, as they had done after Anschluss. Molotov, in his statement on the international situation on November 9 said, "We will not bargain with the Fascists," and "We shall answer any provocative attack on the Soviet Union by the instigation of war."[42] Then he accused the West of giving into the excesses of Fascism because it had a greater fear of the working class than of Nazi imperialism. Meanwhile, the Russian Charge in Berlin let it be known that links with the West were ruptured, saying that the Franco-Soviet treaty must be considered dead.[43]

* * * * *

The isolation spawned by Anschluss and Munich served to expose the Soviet wish for neutrality which had been the underlying feature of collectivism and the "peace policy" whereby others in the West would fight the Soviet war against the Nazis. But whereas collectivism had been self-imposed isolation and neutrality, now the West, East Europe (and the United States who had rejected Soviet intimations of collaboration in the Far East), imposed this from the outside. The real danger for the Soviets was that Western appeasement destroyed hopes of the capitalist war upon which the neutrality policy was founded. Therefore, they could not isolate themselves from a Nazi move in their direction.

The way back for the Soviets was first to strengthen themselves which they did by internal purges, expulsion of foreigners and as a result of the latter exhortations of supreme self-confidence that they could and would unilaterally defend themselves. The other way was to shift sides in the game whereby instead of supporting the West against the Nazis to start the capitalist war, they would support the Nazis against the West. To this end, the Soviets began softening up the propaganda line against the Nazis, which they followed up with an appeasement of their own, offering up the line of states along their borders, accusing them of being collaborators in a plot against the Soviet Union by going into the German orbit and declaring their neutrality. Even if this strategy did not actually effectuate a Nazi turn West, it had the tactical advantage of threatening the West.

Therefore, the Soviets did not completely abandon their collectivist policy either. Rather, they continued to warn that the West must unite, and during the Czech crisis, though certain their offers would never be appreciated, they made statements to the effect that they would honor their commitments and give aid. These offers served many purposes; they absolved the Soviets from guilt, gave impetus to any Western inclination that might be left to come to Czechoslovakia's aid, made a bid for a Soviet place at the Munich negotiating table, and helped to forestall a Nazi-Western deal at Soviet expense while keeping open the possibilities for Soviet gain.

The Czech attitude toward acceptance of Soviet aid presaged that of the Balkans. Prague declined such offers because a bilateral link of that nature would give the West the reason it needed to withdraw support from Czechoslovakia, and because it set up a situation whereby a Nazi-Soviet war might ensue on Czech territory with the resultant destruction of Czechoslovakia. The Balkans were quick to follow suit, discouraging any links with the Soviet Union, bilateral or otherwise, in the fear that such collaboration with Moscow would give Hitler the reason he needed to move east and the Soviets the excuse to "defend" the border states.

As the West disengaged itself from East Europe, the Soviet stake in the area naturally increased, for as the Nazis moved east neither Western nor East European resistance was there to stop them. Ironically, it was this untoward situation which advanced the Soviet bargaining power, for should the West chose to take a stand against Hitler in the East, Soviet help was ever more necessary, while for Hitler, his only apparent opposition in the Balkans now seemed destined to come from Moscow. Therefore, a great deal now hung on the German interpretation of Soviet interest and the German perception of the changes Munich had made on Soviet policy and their own. And it was these charges which prepared the groundwork for Nazi-Soviet rapprochement when Britain opened the door.

From Munich to Prague—The Origins of the Link with Berlin

Schism between Moscow and the West and the consequent plunge of the Soviet Union into isolation was pleasing to Berlin, but apparently not unexpected. For two reasons Berlin seemed at all times confident that the Soviet Union would not act on its connections with the West—one was ideological, the other pragmatic. Ideologically, the Germans appreciated the fact that the Soviet Union would never fight the West's war and indeed welcomed a German-Western conflict from which the Soviets could benefit. From a power position, Germany placed great emphasis on the Japanese threat in the Far East, the feebleness of the Red Army, the weakness of the Russian industrial state and domestic politics, and their isolated political position.

From a strategic point of view, Russian aid to the West depended on Poland or Rumania granting troop passage, which was unlikely, and the Red Army having to force the Carpathians with no place to maneuver. In addition the Germans felt confident of their ability to maneuver in East Europe when, after Munich, the French acknowledged that in case of an uprising fomented by Germany in the Ukraine, the French did not feel bound by treaty to help as the treaty with the Soviets applied only to overt aggression against the Russian frontiers. Thus, while the West can be blamed in its weakness for appeasing Hitler by sacrifices in East Europe, the Soviet Union in its own weakness seems equally guilty. Nor did Moscow do anything to offset German economic penetration into the Balkans or in any way exert herself for the survival of the Balkan states, a green light which Berlin seems clearly to have appreciated.

As early as November 25, 1937 German Ambassador in the Soviet Union, Schulenburg, reported that the Soviet Union was dominated by a fear of Germany, leading to an increase in arms expenditures, a wave of terror, and difficulties in the German-Russian economic negotiations.[44] About the same time the German Foreign Ministry reported that Franco-Soviet relations were paling due to the Russian fear of being drawn into war in the Far East, the purge of the Red Army, and the effects of the anti-Bolshevik propaganda campaign by Germany and Italy whereby Czechoslovakia did not want to appear compromising. By January 1938, Schulenburg was reporting that Soviet isolationist policy which was considerably ascerbating relations with East European neighbors like Czechoslovakia and Turkey, and then he noted the attention given in the Soviet Union to the improved power position of Germany and to its war aims.[45]

Though relations between the Soviet Union and Germany during this period do not reflect any deterioration (except toward isolation which was indiscriminate), the Germans tried to paint such a picture. In a speech before the Reichstag on February 20, 1938[46] Hitler stated that Soviet-German cooperation was impossible, and on March 29 Ribbentrop instructed the German Embassy in France to give publicity to the bad Soviet-German relations, particularly to the incident of a German being tried in Moscow for treason. This tack, of course, put Germany in the role of Balkan defender against Bolshevism, softened up the West, and as Weizsäcker noted, drove France to the conclusion that she had no choice but a pact with the Soviet Union (to the detriment of East Europe). While the Germans were panning Soviet-German friendship, the Soviets were popularizing it which, according to Schulenburg, was to drive the West toward the Soviet Union. But for internal consumption, *Tass* published stories of German "warmongery" in Czechoslovakia and Russia.[47]

Noting the weak Soviet response to Anschluss and Litvinov's benign speech to the League of Nations regarding Abyssinia, the Germans became increasingly certain that the Soviets would do little in regard to Czechoslovakia. On May 30 Schulenburg wrote that the Soviet attitude was increasingly self-serving, and he predicted that due to the strained internal situation and the danger of war on two fronts that "The Soviet Union will intervene only if she herself is attacked, or if it became manifest that the outcome will be favorable to Germany," a position which could always be defended by the lack of a common frontier and uncooperative deportment of intervening powers. To give substance to his view, Schulenburg drew attention to the fact that it was only three days after the Havas telegram from Paris on May 22 concerning the conversation of Bonnet with the Czechs, that the Soviet Union made public its support for Czechoslovakia.[48]

On June 23, 1938, in his speech to the Leningrad constituency, Litvinov defended his policy of collective security and placed the blame on others, particularly the West and East Europe for its failure. In interpreting the speech, Schulenburg found it benign, objective toward German policy, illustrative of a desire to leave open all possibilities, and that East European resistance to Soviet aid had been offered as an excuse rather than the reason the Soviets failed to extend their commitments into Europe. As German Charge Tippelskirch concluded on July 5, the Soviets simply no longer saw the Franco-Soviet and Czech-Soviet pacts as acting in her favor as they did not protect Russia from attack.[49] Schulenburg's feeling that the Soviet Union could no longer count on her border states as a defense barrier or as a benevolent factor in Soviet acts of resistance was substantiated by German reports from Rumania where the Rumanian Minister Petrescu-Comnen denied allegations that Rumania would allow Soviet troop passage, and where the general diplomatic view was that for Rumania to accept British or Russian help would be a disaster. Right before the German assault on Czechoslovakia in September, Schulenburg reassured Berlin that the "attitude of the Soviet Union has not changed" and that Russia would not fight.[50]

Though there was no striking outward transformation in Soviet-German relations from Munich to Prague as some predicted,[51] it was during this period that on both sides the rapprochement idea took shape. By the Munich Pact, one of the aims of German foreign policy had incidentally been achieved, that is the exclusion of the Soviet Union from European politics. In fact, the German Embassy in Moscow only days after Munich

expected Litvinov's dismissal. Soon Schulenburg was actively exploiting
the increased Soviet need for German goods as a result of her isolation
to negotiate a new economic agreement, and on October 26, 1938 he was
thinking of clearing up other outstanding issues between the two governments in order to promote a Nazi-Soviet rapprochement. But he concluded that Soviet policy had undergone no major shift since Munich, and
though they had given up "yesterday's methods," they continued to rely
on themselves and their own armed forces and industrial base.[52] Meanwhile, Berlin still counted on an agreement with Britain and the Japanese
threat as sufficient deterrents to the Soviet Union. Hence, German policy
remained in limbo.

On the Soviet side, it appears that the isolated position of the Soviet
Union was duly recognized, but this did not prompt Soviet desperation.
On the contrary, Litvinov noted the increased powerbroker role which
now fell to the Soviets, a role which the Soviets encouraged by playing
London off against Berlin in order to insure promotion of the capitalist
war. For on the one hand the Soviets sought to emphasize the German
danger to the West, supposedly encouraging the West to look to Moscow
(which could be used as leverage with Berlin as well as reinsurance against
Germany). On the other hand, they attempted to warm up to Germany
and frighten the West by expressing the view that German, Italian, and
Soviet maneuvers were working to weaken British land and air communi-
cations between the Near East and India.[53] Above all the Soviets stressed
their neutrality all around, covering the Czech crisis in a brief and unobtru-
sive manner and remaining quiet during the Polish occupation of Teschen
(where they had at first threatened to denounce the Polish-Soviet Non-
Aggression Pact if Polish troops entered Czechoslovakia).

The trial balloons turned into official policy on March 10, 1939, when
Stalin gave a major address to the Eighteenth Congress of the Communist
Party Soviet Union[54] just prior to the German occupation of Bohemia and
Moravia. Though this speech was later attributed to bring about the Nazi-
Soviet rapprochement,[55] it was surprisingly noncommittal on Moscow's
part, and gave ample opportunity for all concerned to interpret it as he so
chose. For Western consumption Stalin continued to harp on fascist aggression and the Soviet desire for peace, but he also condemned the West
for its nonintervention policy which he branded as giving free rein to war,
and he blamed the Western press, not Germany, for increasing Soviet and

German tension in the Soviet Ukraine. In conclusion, Stalin outlined the major tenets of Soviet policy which were: 1) to continue its emphasis on peace; 2) to be cautious not to be dragged into others' wars; 3) to strengthen the Red Army; and 4) to strengthen the international bond of friendship. Thus, while ambiguous in terms of relations with the West, Germany, and East Europe, this speech was explicit in terms of the Soviet determination to defend herself if her frontiers were violated.

German documents suggest that Berlin had long before this perceived Soviet intent as opportunitistic, and that it was Germany who would pick the time and place of rapprochement. Indeed, the whole course of Soviet-German relations was already reoriented before this speech, as the Germans, in their increasing need for raw materials, stepped up negotiations for an economic pact. In November, 1938, Göring admitted a weakness in the German raw material position, and he demanded that an attempt be made to increase imports from Russia. In the Soviet Union Schulenburg reported economic chaos everywhere, and the consequent Soviet desire for German goods.[56]

Therefore, on December 22, 1938, the Germans proposed a new credit agreement whereby the Germans would export 200 million RM worth of German exports for an equivalent amount of Soviet raw materials over a two year period. The negotiations bogged down temporarily because the Soviets wanted the negotiations to take place in Moscow. Speculating on Soviet motivation, Director of the Economic Department, Wiehl, said:

> The strong desire to have a German delegation come to Moscow can therefore only be interpreted in the sense that the Soviet Government would demonstrate to the outside world the value placed also by the Third Reich on the continuation of economic relations.[57]

The Germans, also concerned about the political implications of the negotiations, considered that their interest in obtaining a favorable credit agreement was "so great that it does not appear expedient to frustrate the negotiations anyway . . . ." They therefore proposed a compromise whereby instead of a delegation, Counselor of Legation Schnurre and a few others would go to Moscow on January 30 from Warsaw, and "would in fact accompany Ambassador Count von der Schulenburg, who was at present in Germany," thus making it look as if Moscow was just another stop on Schnurre's swing.[58]

The reason for this was that Ribbentrop was making preparations for a Polish state visit, which would presumably capstone the anti-Soviet Polish-German combination, and in turn dilute the need for rapprochement with the Soviet Union. But, on the 26th in Warsaw, even before Ribbentrop began his conversation, the *Daily Mail* and several French papers published the startling news that Schnurre was on his way to Moscow to develop a broad Soviet-German economic exchange. Ribbentrop was furious. He wrote:

> At the moment when I want to achieve basic collaboration between Germany and Poland against the Soviet Union, they knife me in the back with this scandalous disruptive report. Schnurre should return to Berlin at once.[59]

Of concern to Ribbentrop in forcing the Polish capitulation, was that news of a Nazi-Soviet link would destroy his program of "softening" up the West, particularly Great Britain where it had the potential of bringing the anti-Bolshevik/anti-German forces together to unseat Chamberlain. And, of course, it made the dissolution of Czechoslovakia necessary.

Schulenburg, for his part, was disappointed, not only because of the meaning the schism had in terms of withholding vital raw materials necessary to Germany, but because of political reasons having to do with the need to have a benign power in the East. In this regard he did not believe Japan was a sufficient deterrent to the Soviet Union. In his memo of February 6, 1939 he said that "from a very good source" he had learned that under no circumstances would Japan let the fisheries issue develop into a conflict, and that Japan was not a sufficient deterrent to Soviet action against Germany. As he praised the sincerity of the Russians in that "the Soviet press did not publish a single word about the affair, expressing the view that it was the Poles who had leaked the information" to the French press.[60]

Apparently Ribbentrop's failure in Poland and Göring's insistence on the need for raw materials kept the economic negotiations alive, but they were suspended again on March 8. The reason given was economic. The Ministry of Economics reported that the German economy was not in a position to make the necessary deliveries, regrettable "in view of Germany's raw material position . . . ."[61] But there were political considerations as well, for this was only a few days before Prague when it was imperative that the Germans present the West with the idea that German intentions were in the East, not the West. The economic affront to Moscow had its repercussions in the Kremlin, in that from here on the Soviets carried on their conversations with the Germans in the most cautious manner, fearing that the discussions were intended only to exact greater concessions from the British.[62]

Despite Schulenburg's persuasion that Soviet policy was opportunistic and there was a need to protect Germany by some concrete agreement with Moscow, Berlin continued to treat the Russians off-handedly. The results of Munich and Prague were at the heart of this confidence for it was believed that links with the West had been destroyed and that a Tripartite Pact with Japan was now possible. Prior to the Czech collapse, Germany had objected to a Tripartite due to its unfavorable reaction in Britain and France and their consequent desire to rearm, but since it was seen in a different light due to the fact that the position of the West and Russia was weak, Chamberlain and Daladier and their pacificism appeared strong, German armaments had been speeded up, and American isolationism increased. As far as the Soviets were concerned, Japan was a concern second to the Nazis but feared particularly should Germany and Japan actually get together. Of this the Germans were well aware, noting in 1938 and 1939 the effort by the Soviets both publically and privately to bring about an aura of Soviet-American cooperation against Japan.[63]

It should be noted at this point, that despite efforts by the West and Germany to isolate and exclude Russia from European affairs, the Soviets never thought in any other terms and fashioned their policies with a global view in mind. Therefore, the Balkan states and Poland, despite their importance on the Soviet frontier, figured into Soviet strategy only as they fit into the big picture, and the Soviets, rather than concentrating on them, directed their efforts toward defining their relationships with the Great Powers, knowing that the small states would fall accordingly. Hence their willingness to claim or sacrifice them. Certainly it appeared after Munich that, with the Little Entente destroyed, the Balkan Entente emasculated, and Balkan countries dancing to Hitler's tune, the benevolent neutrality of the Balkans was an accomplished fact, moving the German frontier to Russia's doorstep. It must also have seemed that pressure on Poland meant that German designs were in the East, Poland being the most facile route into Russia.[64]

To counter this, the Soviets turned the tables on the West using an appeasement of their own, with the hope that giving way in the East would turn the Nazi drive back toward to the West, incidentally bettering Nazi-Soviet relations and pressuring the West in Moscow's direction. The Soviet tactic was the following—to invite a German agreement over the problem by blaming the West not Germany for alleged designs on the Ukraine, and then by strictly defining the Soviet sphere of interest at the frontier, thus abandoning East Europe as had the West. Editorials in *Journal de Moscou* on December 27, 1938 and January 10, 1939, both stated that the West was responsible for the "Ukrainian problem," suggesting that Hitler leave Eastern Europe in peace and go in search of his prey in the West. The articles went on to ask, "How can it be imagined that Hitler would abandon all of a sudden the line of least resistance . . . ?" (meaning the West.)[65] The same theme was repeated by Stalin in his March 10, 1939 speech when he said that the uproar over the Ukraine was meant to arouse the Soviet Union against Germany. In the meantime, the Soviets continued to exhibit confidence in their ability to defend themselves, Litvinov voicing unconcern to foreigners as to the Nazi threat.

Their appeasing tactics seem to have worked, at least with the German diplomatic corps, for a *Pravda* editorial of March 13 referring to the West as provocateurs in a German-Soviet fight, was positively received by members of the German Embassy who expressed satisfaction at the tone of Stalin's reference, and they proffered the opinion to Hitler, that amelioration of the political situation between the Soviet Union and Germany might be developed. The reality, of course, was that Hitler's designs were against Czechoslovakia not the Carpatho-Ukraine, and hence the Soviet appeasement had little effect on Hitler's policy except to note the opportunism with which the Soviet Union approached relations with the West.

The other element in Stalin's appeasement policy, was a strict definition of Soviet interest. Points two and four of Stalin's March 10 speech spoke directly to this question. Point two stated that:

> We stand for peaceful, close, and friendly relations with all the neighboring countries which have common frontiers with the USSR. That is our position; we shall adhere to this position so long as these countries maintain like relations with the Soviet Union, and so long as

they make no attempt to trespass, directly or indirectly, on the integrity and inviolability of the frontiers of the Soviet State.

Point four read:

We are not afraid of the threats of aggressors, and we are ready to deal two blows for every blow delivered by instigators of war who attempt to violate the Soviet borders.[66]

In interpretating this speech, U.S. Charge Kirk said that Stalin came close to saying that he would carry on normal and friendly relations with any country as long as it would not directly threaten the interests of the Soviet Union, and that these countries "were very closely associated with the frontiers of the Soviet Union,"[67] though Stalin was also careful to connect Soviet interest with indirect threats to the Soviet Union which could be inspired by German Fifth Column work in the Balkans.

The veracity of Stalin's comment that Soviet interests stopped at the frontier, seemed substantiated for Berlin on March 13, 1939 when Schulenburg answered instructions of March 8, to investigate the truth of a report printed in the *Daily Express* to the effect that the Soviet Government had informed the Governments of Poland and Rumania that if their western frontiers were attacked, Soviet Russia would employ her forces to oppose such an attack. Schulenburg reported that he could find nothing to substantiate the report and that the Soviet press so far had not taken up the affair, and that at any rate, Rumania and Poland found such aid undesirable.

He speculated however, that it was possible that the Soviet Union had put out the order to "stimulate interest in the Soviet Union in British political circles," and to act as "a diversion in view of Gafencu's visit to Warsaw and of revival of a Polish-Rumanian alliance." In conclusion, wrote Schulenburg:

It is my opinion that it may be a Soviet trial balloon similar to Litvinov's recently published soundings regarding a Black Sea Pact. The object of these experiments is to bring the Soviet Union into international politics.[68]

In the days after Prague, Moscow remained cautious in its reaction, uncertain of whether Hungarian rather than German occupation of the Carpatho-Ukraine meant Hitler had abandoned for the moment his drive East.
Therefore, the Soviet appeasement campaign continued. Voroshilov's
speech to the Party Congress which Stalin had addressed five days earlier,
was covered in Soviet papers on March 16, and it reiterated the theme that
the bourgeois countries were directing German strength against the Soviet
Union, and he accompanied this with detailed accounts of Soviet military
strength, which, he said, should be sufficient to restrain any aggressor. To
further assure Germany of Soviet benevolence, *Tass* stated on March 21
that there had been no collusion on the Soviet part to aid Poland and
Rumania should the Germans threaten them, and that neither Poland nor
Rumania had appealed to the Soviet Union for help or indicated danger.[69]

Meanwhile Litvinov put the official stamp on Soviet kowtowing. In his
"Note to the German Ambassador in Moscow Regarding the Incorporation of Bohemia into the German Reich," Litvinov blamed Czechoslovakia,
not Germany, for the events of March 15, stating that Czechoslovakia
was a seat of unrest and an unviable state which did not correspond to
fact, and that he was unaware of any State Constitution which allowed
it to abolish its state without the peoples' consent as Dr. Hácha had done
on March 15. But he also considered the occupation arbitrary and aggressive, and condemned it as serving to signal Hungarian invasion of Carpatho-
Ukraine and that in view of that action, the Soviet Union could not recognize the act.[70] Reaching to the bottom of the political grabbag, the Soviets
began playing Yugoslavia's dubious game of exploiting Rome-Berlin jeal-
ousies. Soviet press items on Mussolini's speech after Prague, made the
backhanded notation that the Rome-Berlin Axis was still intact despite
German penetration of the Balkans (and then they went on to accuse
London and Paris of being the abettors of aggression).[71]

* * * * *

On April 6, one day prior to the Italian invasion of Albania, which was
to shake the Balkans and bring British power into the area, U.S. Charge
Kirk made a perspicacious analysis of Soviet policy. He said that the isolation of Munich and recent events (here he referred to the fate of Czechoslovakia and Memel, the threat to Danzig, and the German economic

stranglehold on Rumania), had brought the threat of Nazi aggression closer to the Soviet borders, but that the Soviet Union did not necessarily see this as pursuit of a policy of expansion east and that it may be regarded as merely preparatory to action in the West or the Southeast, "which would not necessarily constitute a direct menace to the Union." He noted, however, that Soviet troop movements to the frontiers showed that the Soviet Union did not exclude the possibility, and that Soviet reaction was based on the danger to the Soviet regime of war, the strength of the Soviet Union which could not yet outdo Germany, and fear of a two-front war. These factors, he concluded, led to the Soviet policy not to oppose any country which did not directly threaten the Soviet Union, not to get involved in conflicts for the sake of others, to await developments abroad, to make no commitments which would limit Moscow's scope of action, to promote divergences among nations, to divert or lessen attack on the Soviet Union, and in case of attack, to align herself with others to lessen the danger to their own frontiers.[72]

Thus, the origins of the Nazi-Soviet link began in the wake of Munich, from September, 1938 to April, 1939 on the Soviet side openly expressed as an attitude in Stalin's speech of March 10, and in action by the renewal of economic negotiations between the two countries. At this point the pressure for the opening of such a link was largely on the Soviet side, in that Munich had opened the German path into the Carpatho-Ukraine and had given impetus to a Nazi-Japanese pact. After April, this was reversed in that the Germans needed the pact due to the failure to obtain a commitment from Japan and the threat that Russia might join the West. As the Soviets had predicted, war itself placed the Soviet Union in an empowered position, a position they expertly exploited.

Conclusion

Between 1935 and April, 1939, perhaps the following observations can be made with regard to Soviet policy toward Germany and the Balkans. The Kremlin was appreciative of both the power and ideology of Nazism, and because of the nature of its political and economic situation, was able to protect itself much earlier than the West by solidifying the political position of the Soviet regime and preparing the Soviet defenses. On the other hand, the Soviet Union's best defense was its offense, that is the

promotion of the capitalist war. This was essentially the motivation behind the "peace front" whereby encouraging Western collectivist defenses
while maintaining their own neutrality, they would be exorcised from the
capitalist war during which the enemies would destroy each other and the
Soviets would be enriched. When the Western nations failed to build up
their own defenses and began to appease Hitler, the Soviets disengaged
themselves from the West and began to shift toward the Nazis, encouraging
Hitler to go against the weak link in the West. Essentially, the Nazis were
no more to be feared than the West, and because of their geopolitical
position, the Soviets were always cognizant of the key swing position they
possessed in European politics.

Despite efforts of both the Nazis an the West to relegate the Soviets to
a second-rank power position, the Soviets never thought in terms other
than Great Power status, fashioning their policies in a global perspective.
In this respect, they viewed the future of the border states in terms of
Great Power relationships, attached to one side or the other, not as states
with lives of their own. Even their approach to Bessarabian irredenta suggests more tactical than strategic or ideological interest. They were therefore indifferent to which capitalist power held hegemony in the area, Nazi
or Western, and were concerned with the Nazi movement into the area only
as it reflected Western appeasement. In addition, they believed that greater
gains could be made with less cost (than war) by internal infiltration and
threats of their proximity.

For these reasons, and the antipathy and fear they generated in every
Balkan capital as a result, the Soviets concentrated little effort in the direction of Balkan diplomacy except as it might be directly beneficial to them.
They did not encourage Balkan groupings like the Little and Balkan Ententes because they thereby lost a certain trump in regulating Balkan affairs to their own advantage and because they were under the West's umbrella, but they did support a Black Sea Pact under their own tutelage. In
order to weaken Western influence in the area, they encouraged the Rumanian effort to abolish the International Danube Commission and to
hand the Straits back to Turkey. In regard to the latter, they attempted
to make changes at Montreux to their own advantage. Nor did they make
any effort to offset German economic penetration of the area, not just
because they had nothing to sell and no money to buy, but because they
wished to maintain their own economic as well as military self-sufficiency.

Finally, they were committed to action on behalf of the Balkan and Eastern European states like Czechoslovakia only in league with the West, and
used East European antipathies and fear of the Nazis as a convenient excuse not to act except when the actual Soviet frontier would be violated.

By 1939, Western appeasement had led to a shift from Western to Axis
hegemony in the Southeast. This did not necessarily bode ill for the Soviets who considered both as adversaries and who realized the importance
of their position to both sides. For if the Nazis should move West as blue-
printed in *Mein Kampf,* a neutral rear was ever necessary, while if the
Nazis moved east, the West would likely seek Soviet aid. And even if the
West appeased all the way to the Soviet frontier resulting in a Nazi-Soviet
war, the West could ill afford to allow the Nazis access to the full Soviet
material base. On the other hand, they could do nothing until either side
moved in their direction, and so were faced with the uncertainties of playing a waiting game.

On the German side, the post-Munich period found Berlin confident
that a pact with the Soviets would be unnecessary. There were several
reasons for this—Russia's isolation from the West, confidence that a pact
with Japan could be signed, belief that the West would come to terms
with Hitler as would Poland, the new Soviet policy which divorced Moscow from the West and appeased Hitler, and in the Balkans, complete exposure of the Soviets to Germany as a result of the threatened position of
the Balkan Entente, the threat Berlin posed to the Soviet Ukraine as a
result of German acquisition of the Carpatho-Ukraine, and the increasing
tendency in the Balkan states for self-neutralization and benevolence toward Hitler. The complete irreverence with which the Germans treated the
Soviets was an exhibition of their self-confidence. Economics Minister
Schnurre, on his way to Moscow, suddenly, but with no apologies, turned
back at the border when his trip was exposed to the public.

Not all of the German diplomatic corps exuded the confidence in the
neutralization of Russia that Hitler and Ribbentrop did. Both Ambassador
Schulenburg and Economics Minister Wiehl stressed the need to develop
relations with the Soviet Union. Schulenburg believed that the pact with
Japan was far from secure, and he argued that the Soviets were not isolated from the West, but were playing both sides against each other, Munich
having increased the Soviet bargaining position vis-a-vis the West. Wiehl
argued that Germany needed Soviet raw materials. Both, however, were

voices in the wilderness until Göring's plan to tie down Poland failed. This was the turning point and the beginning of a string of setbacks which turned Berlin toward Moscow to secure the eastern flank and tie down Balkan neutrality.

The Soviets, for their part, had not depended on the West to defend them and had never participated in the peace front in a collaborative sense. Therefore, the demise of collectivism was less serious than the appeasement of the West, which, in accommodating Hitler's drive east, perpetuated the thrust in that direction, virtually bringing Berlin by 1939 to the Soviet frontier. The threat of a Nazi-Japanese link added to the precariousness of the Soviet position. The Soviet Union attempted to counter Western appeasement by itself appeasing, and this led to the seeming reversal of Soviet policy which, instead of emphasizing links with the West and anti-Fascism, emphasized avenues of accord with Germany, the weakness of the West (to turn the war east), good relations with the United States, and aloofness from all capitalist wars.

The Munich period also made clear to the Russians not just the desirability of normalization of relations with Germany, but the possibility of it, since they counted that the West's weakness would cause them to look to Moscow, strengthening the Soviet bargaining position in Berlin to the point that a pact need not be made on German terms. Therefore, the Soviets were careful to leave open the door to the West. Above all, the Soviets maintained a surprising confidence that they could defend themselves and of the importance of their geopolitical position, recognizing that they held the keys to the defense of the Balkans for the West and of their neutralization for Germany. In this respect, the reentrance of Britain into the Balkans was crucial to the development of the Nazi-Soviet Pact whose origins can be found in German insecurity with regard to the neutrality of the East, and the increased bargaining strength resulting from the importance the Soviet position assumed to the West.

Along the way, the Soviets never abandoned their allegiance to ideology, in that peace and war were evaluated only in terms of an ideological goal to which territory and nationality were linked as the repository of strength. Thus could the Soviets advocate peace for the Soviet Union, but war for others, and in so doing, they increased their power to negotiate with the West, and forced the Nazi decision to seek out Russia and not to concede anything in the Balkans.

CHAPTER V

THE SOVIET UNION AND THE BALKANS
APRIL TO AUGUST, 1939
DIALECTICS IN THE EAST

As far as the Soviets were concerned, the immediate six months after Munich were precarious days due to isolation from the West and uncertainty as to the direction of Hitler's next moves, but even in these untoward times Moscow maintained a surprising confidence in her ability to face Germany alone if she had to. The situation was dramatically changed when beginning in late March and then in April the British and French decided to make a stand in the East, for this enabled the Soviets to put into motion the dialectics of pitting the British against the Germans for Soviet favor which culminated in a Pact producing the Capitalist war which the Soviets had long desired.

Historiography of the Nazi-Soviet Non-Aggression Pact has concentrated on Soviet weakness and defensive concerns as the major component in the Pact's culmination.[1] By concentrating on the Balkans, where the Germans had achieved hegemony and wanted pacification, this study brings to light another facet of Soviet motivation which was based on strength, primarily diplomatic, not weakness, for the West's determination to defend East Europe in the Southeast as well as in Poland, strengthened the Soviet position making negotiation with the Germans on a par basis possible. The result was that the Soviet Union made considerable offensive and defensive gains, not only in Poland, but in the Balkans and in her European power position. For, in addition to the strengthening of the Soviet position, that of the Germans deteriorated. Japan refused alliance, the independence of the Balkan position was strengthened at the same time the German need for Balkan neutrality increased, Britain rearmed and refused accommodation, Poland remained stolid, Turkey joined the West, Italy became a liability with regard to Balkan neutrality and loyalty to Nazi aims, and the Germans found themselves competing with the British for Soviet favor.

Meanwhile, the entry of the British into East Europe gave some measure of support to the Soviet frontier, it put a brake on Japan, and it elevated the strategic importance of the Soviet Union. All in all, as a result of the events of April to August, the Soviets bargained from a considerably strengthened position, and this is reflected in the generous terms granted for Moscow's neutrality particularly in Poland, the Baltic and in Bessarabia. Even in the Balkans, where Germany conceded nothing, the Soviet position was enhanced to the degree that the chances of war there were diminished and the Turkish predisposition to grant the Soviets a favorable revisionism of Montreux were increased. So, while it is true the Soviets needed neutrality more as a result of the inevitability of war in their West, so did the Germans need Soviet benevolency and neutrality more, and for this they were willing to pay a price which the West could not and would not match.

The Balkans themselves had a part in this interplay, for while it looked like Poland would offer resistance, it seemed certain the Balkans would not. Since British interests were greater in the Southeast, they were more persistent in its defense and uncompromising in its sacrifice, driving the Germans and Soviets together on the issues of pacification, mutual definition of enemy, and territorial revisionism. The explosive nature of Balkan politics, considerably more fragile once the Great Powers set their contest there, also played a part, for as the chances of war there increased, Balkan, Nazi, Soviet, and Italian interests were more in jeopardy than British and French for whom a second front was useful but not indispensible. Finally, diplomatically, the failure of the Balkans to join together in an encirclement front caused the British to have to go directly to the Soviets which was the crucial element in Hitler's turn toward Moscow and Moscow's key bargaining weapon.

The Guarantees and the Soviet Union

The Soviet reaction to the new direction British policy was taking appears all but schizophrenic. At one moment Moscow was loudly applauding the resistance movement, clamoring for a joint position and exhibiting pain at the slightest rebuff. At the next moment she was desperately trying to disassociate from any collaboration with the West which could in the least rankle Hitler's ire or foreclose on a Nazi-Soviet rapprochement. Underlying this ambivalence were basic uncertainties as to which policy—isolationism, collaboration with the West, or agreement with Hitler—would be most advantageous or which would materialize. For this troika policy, which the Soviets were to pursue in some measure or another up to the signing of the Non-Aggression Pact, hinged somewhat on Hitler's will and his reaction to the West's new determination to stem the tide of Nazi aggression. But it also had its offensive aspects and was designed to confuse the West and threaten Hitler, thereby setting up a dialectical situation whereby both the West and Axis powers were competing for Soviet favor.

Beneath the ambivalence was a basic confidence that Russia could if she had to, defend herself. This in itself gave Stalin an enormous advantage in his initial dealings with the West, and it made it possible for the Soviets to set their own price for participation in the war against Hitler in the East, a price which included negotiation as a Great Power over the heads of the interim states and the requirement that all the interim states be included in any such agreement. The British, in part unaware of Soviet confidence in their defensive position but helpless in the face of the malevolent use Stalin intended to make of these dealings with Hitler, hoped that the Soviets would find similar advantage in a declaration of unilateral support to the frontier states somewhat along the lines of the West. Such was not the case, and so, taking an uncompromising stand, the Soviets withdrew to the wings to await either the West's acceptance of their demands as the price for participation or a Nazi interest in the same desiderate as the price for neutrality.

In their reply to the British inquiry regarding Soviet help to Rumania, the Soviets voiced skepticism that the USSR might help Rumania while Britain's hand was free, but they continued to seek ties with the West by suggesting a Six-Power Conference to include Britain, France, Rumania, Poland, Turkey, and the USSR. This initial bid to participate in the settlement of affairs in East Europe as an interested equal, was rejected by the British, arousing some suspicion and resentment on the Soviet part as well as recognitin that with the West's refusal, an effort must be made not to alienate the Germans. A *Tass* communique of March 21 was careful to note that the USSR had not promised aid to Poland or Rumania and they had suggested a Six-Power conference as it "might have provided the greatest possibilities for the elucidation of the actual situation and for the definition of the position of all its participants," a proposal which had been rejected as "premature."[2] On the West's part there was equal underlying disquiet and suspicion that they were being used to open the road to Berlin. French Foreign Minister Bonnet said that as usual, the Russians have put their feet in the platter knowing that Rumania would never accept a conference in Bucharest with Russia and that it was Litvinov's way of "getting around the question."[3]

From the beginning, the East European states, in this case Rumania, became the nexus around which all Soviet-Western relations revoled. The Soviets made their defense of these states conditional on terms which could and would not be met by the West, and rather than mar the aura of improving Soviet-Western relationships, which was necessary to both sides, the interim states were blamed. The Rumanian reluctance to associate with the USSR noted by Bonnet was followed by a similar Polish rejection of such an association. Shortly after the British rejection of the Soviet Six-Power conference idea, Britain suggested a quick Four-Power statement on the part of Poland, the USSR, France, and Great Britain, but Beck objected because it implied Russo-Polish friendship and would directly threaten his policy of balance between Germany and Russia. Aware of Polish objections, not surprisingly the Soviets then accepted the Four-Power statement idea, obviously aware of the problems involved. To add to the difficulties, they tacked on new criteria besides Great Power status for participation with the West, namely that all the states from the Balkans to the Baltic, must be taken into consideration in any agreement reached.[4]

The British decision to initially refuse the Soviets on both accounts was based on a number of factors, most of which had to do with the desire to link up with the Soviet Union only as a last resort. Among the reasons were suspicion of Russia's intent and her value as an ally in that she seemed unprepared for an offensive war;[5] the emphasis the British placed on Poland rather than the Soviet Union in terms of the fact that she was the key to safeguarding the British blockade plans against Germany and in providing a second front; the belief that if Great Britain linked up with Soviet Russia on European security, she would be cutting her own throat, as this would automatically indispose a large number of other countries who were violently anti-Soviet;[6] and the hope that Soviet Russia could be reached by other means without alienating the East European countries, in that if the Poles could be persuaded to promise help to Rumania and the two states were assured of Anglo-French help, they might not object to attempts by the Western Powers to secure Russian help in some form. Finally, there seemed an apparent need for haste to do something on Poland's behalf as there were sensational reports of German troop movements in the press on March 27,[7] and fear of the results of Beck's interview with Moltke in Warsaw and the Polish Ambassador's interview with Ribbentrop in Berlin on March 26-28.

While the British and French failed to accept the first Soviet offers in toto and concentrated initial moves on the East European states, they recognized the paramount importance of a "friendly Russia," and therefore took care to include the Soviets where possible and to preserve the working relationship with the Soviets which would allow the kind of multilateral rather than bilateral link with Moscow they envisioned as eventually materializing. At the same time, it seemed not unreasonable to believe that the Soviets in their own interest would be willing to join the West and to help Poland if called upon, and that coming to an agreement over the heads of these Eastern states might itself force Hitler to consolidate his power in the Balkans and Poland. Besides, the importance of Russia at the time did not seem so great that East Europe must be sacrificed to Moscow, and sacrifices which the West later seemed willing to make, were occasioned by fears of a Nazi-Soviet pact not by the real value of the Soviet Union.

In the negotiations with Poland which followed on April 4-6, transforming the interim guarantee to a permanent one, London continued to maintain the view that the Soviet factor must ultimately be addressed if a true security system in the East was to evolve. To this end, Chamberlain asked Beck whether Russia would not in fact be the only source from which Poland could hope to replenish her munitions in the event of war, and he said that the British Government should "try to establish such relations as would enable them to expect help from Soviet Russia in case

of war." And in the "Summary of Conclusions" connected with the permanent guarantee, it was noted that while the British appreciated the difficulty of associating the USSR with such collaboration, it was their con-
viction that it was important, nevertheless, to maintain "the best possible
relations with the Soviet Government whose position in this matter could
not be disregarded."[8]

The view that giving "Poland precedence over Russia in order of entry
into a security system" was a crucial factor in losing Russia to Germany,[9]
does not take into account either the early capitulation the alternative
would have been to the Soviet concept of a peace front dominated by the
Great powers, the detrimental effect it would have had on the small powers and Italy, or the proposition that the Soviets did not really want to be
included anyway wishing only to use the British approaches against Germany. Indeed at the time while displaying some uncertainty and a certain
sense of rebuff, the Soviet attitude was not hostile or derisive, for it was
evident that the British commitment without any commensurate Soviet
sacrifice, in some measure protected them too. On March 29 following
Chamberlain's statement to the House of Commons on March 28, Maisky
commented that the proposed guarantees would be a "revolutionary
change in British policy" which "would increase enormously the confidence of other countries and might have a very great effect," and on the
morning of March 31, Maisky agreed to a suggestion that Chamberlain
might refer in a general way to the principles of Russian foreign policy
with which the statement seemed to be in harmony.[10] Likewise, the
Russian press received the guarantee to Poland, though not without
some acrimony, quite positively. *Izvestia* on April 2 commented:

> If France and Britain are honestly determined to resist aggression
> and to stand for collective security, then they can count on the full
> support of the only country that bears no responsibility for Munich
> and unchangingly protects the interest of peace and the independ-
> ence of nations.[11]

While supporting the West, Moscow was careful not to annoy Berlin.
On April 4, *Tass* denied a Havas report published in *Le temps* and *L'Oeuvre*
that Moscow had "undertaken or promised to undertake to supply Poland
in the event of war with war materials and to deny its raw materials market

to Germany," and in an article in *Journal de Moscou* entitled "The Problem of Collective Security," the Soviet Union made it clear that they had assumed no obligations regarding Poland.[12] Thus it appears that, far from being alienated, the Soviets saw the British guarantee to Poland as the fulfillment of the very peace policy which they had been trying to engineer, and it had the added feature at this point of pushing the door open to Berlin while leaving the other options of isolationism or a link with the West intact. The excuse of alienation came later when it was a convenient way to rationalize negotiations with the Germans and then to justify the Pact itself.

Soon after the unilateral guarantee to Poland, Albania was invaded and along with it appeared the threat to Greece and renewed threat to Rumania. During the formulation of the guarantees to these two countries the British again pressed the matter of interlocking obligations with Poland and of the participation of the Soviet Union. The Rumanians, like the Poles, were not anxious to make the choice between Germany and Russia before the war broke out but were more ameliatory than Poland. Cretzianu stated that if war took place, Rumania might not refuse Russian help and might even ask for it, while Gafencu and Saracoglu in their talks on April 8-9 agreed on the need for some connection with the Soviet Union.

While the British went ahead with the Rumanian and Greek guarantees in their unilateral form, they were now contemplating a new approach to Moscow to see whether the Soviet Government would be prepared to give a similar unilateral guarantee to Poland and Rumania, a suggestion which was the basis for the opening of formal Anglo-Franco-Russian negotiations on April 14-May 31, the day after the guarantees were announced. In the meantime, the Soviet reaction to the Greek and Rumanian guarantees once again was guarded but not hostile, threatening linkage with the encirclement front but maintaining enough distance to invite German advances. Soviet press and radio statements expressed gratification that the Soviet collective security policy appeared to be gaining ground, but they said that a mere British guarantee to Greece was insufficient as single guarantees like that to Poland, diverted the tide of aggression but did not check it. What was needed in the Soviet view was a defensive bloc of Turkey, Rumania, and the Soviet Union.[13]

The hopscotch pattern of Soviet policy which nourished very conditional relationships with the West only to the degree that it did not interfere with pacific relations with the Germans, showed up on the economic front as well. On March 22 the British Secretary of Overseas Trade reached Moscow to take up the question of a durable commercial agreement, the Russians having earlier nourished this quasi-political contact by agreeing to the principal British desiderata concerning outstanding Russian debts to Great Britain and that the negotiation should be carried on in London. But within three weeks of Hudson's return to London, Maisky was taking a new line to the effect that the Soviet Government saw no reason for any further discussions of the debt question or on trade. But, in order to use them as a lever against the Germans, the communique issued at the end of Hudson's visit referred to "a friendly exchange of views of international policy" which had shown the "points of contact" between Russian and British "attitudes in the domain of the consolidation of peace," and it expressed the belief that this personal contact would "contribute to the consolidation of Soviet-British relations and to international collaboration with the view to the solution of the problem of peace."[14]

It appears, therefore, that the Soviet sense of rebuff at being left out of the guarantee process must not be taken too seriously, for from the beginning there was ample evidence that it was a fainthearted policy designed as much for Berlin's consumption as Moscow's safety. On balance, the Soviets seem to have gained more than they lost. Advantageous was the fact that British resolve could bulwark them against Japan as well as Germany, and it enhanced the possibilities of a capitalist war without Soviet commitment. And in the likelihood that Hitler should decide to move against Russia, he would have to move through East Europe and the unconditional nature of the guarantees could protect Russia as well as fortify the East Europeans to fight. Then too, the guarantees reduced Hitler's ability to use revisionism to threaten and bludgeon the Balkan states and Poland into submission and perhaps German occupation. This helped to keep Germany at a distance from the Soviet border. Finally, as a projected program of East European defense, for which the guarantees formed the basis, the Soviet Union must certainly be involved, and this anticipated Soviet participation moved the Soviet Union from a position of subservience to Nazi demands should Moscow seek neutrality in Berlin, to that of a bargainer, for a Soviet-Western coalition was certain to threaten Hitler enough that Soviet neutrality would be worth a price. Thus, the guarantees offered protection, future participation, and power for the Soviets.

Next to the gains, the dangers of the guarantees to the Soviets seem remote. Untoward for the Soviets were the facts that the door seemed closed on territorial compensation as a quid pro quo for Soviet participation, that they excluded and isolated the Soviets from European politics (a position they said they wanted), and that they could so busy the British in East Europe, that the Japanese could move in the Far East unhindered.

It was not the guarantees as much as the failure of the guarantees to materialize into the projected "peace front" which the West envisioned as a deterrent and if need be a fighting front against Germany, which opened the Soviet road toward Berlin. For this failure, in which the Balkans played a part, compelled the British to initiate unilaterial discussion with the Soviets, thus achieving one of the Soviet's main aims, status as a Great Power. Because the Balkans feared a Western-Soviet deal at their expense, this reinforced Balkan neutrality and maintenance of ties with Germany, in turn enhancing the possibility of achieving Soviet aims in East Europe through Western concessions, and if this failed, using the negotiations themselves as leverage in Berlin.

The other untoward element with the respect to the stillborn Western peace front, was the fact that revisionist/anti-revisionist rivalries were enhanced as a result, and this too drove the Balkans toward a neutral position in the coming war, destroyed any defensive value the Balkans and East Europe might have had for the Soviets, and destabilized the area, thus devaluing the whole Western program for the USSR. Therefore, they were anxious to see if protection, neutrality, and gain could not be obtained elsewhere. The other side of the coin, of course, is that once the West had guaranteed Poland, Greece, and Rumania, they were anxious to bring the Soviet Union into the "encirclement front." This in turn led to the beginning of Berlin's interest in tying down Soviet neutrality, and for the Soviets, it was the shift in Hitler's policy around which their policy revolved.

* * * * *

In order for the British to have successfully concluded their policy of a peace front, it has been suggested that the West should have negotiated with the Soviets first rather than guaranteeing the East European states, and by this route brought the East European states and the Soviet Union together against Germany. It seems unlikely this would have achieved the purpose, for the fear of a Western-Soviet deal might have driven these small states into Germany's arms, and it would have resulted in the very thing the bilateral Western-Soviet discussions did, enhancement of the Soviet position in Berlin. Besides, as soon will be shown, the aims of both sides in negotiations were decidely different, making the outcome of any such discussion whether held before or after Balkan discussions, much the same.

The more subtle suggestion has been that the British should have withheld the guarantees until the Balkans had made sufficient adjustments in their borders, for instance in making concessions to revisionist Bulgaria and Hungary, that they could have come together in a united East European front making Soviet participation unnecessary or at least multilateral in form. While a more potent argument, it must be recognized that Balkan interest in participating in a Great Power war was only as it helped or hindered their concept of national survival, their receptivity to the guarantees being more a matter of anti-revisionism than anti-Germanism, and if the British had forced this upon them, the West would have been a threat equal to if not greater than either Germany or the Soviet Union. In pushing for revisionism, the West might have gained Bulgarian and Hungarian friendship, but she surely would have alienated the other Balkan states and Poland and lost what she set out to achieve, a second front in East Europe. In addition, the threat of such a front might have pushed Hitler to consolidate his power or set off an uncontrollable wave of revisionism and war.

In other words, the British did what they could under the circumstances, with the hope that at least for the anti-revisionist Balkan states, British support would bulwark them against a Nazi, Balkan, or Soviet onslaught, the results of which might have simply imbued Germany with greater power, driven the Soviets to a neutrality deal with Berlin, and ultimately weakened the Western position. As it was, there was hope that some countries in the East would hold out until the West could rally its strength, and that the Soviets had not dissimilar aims in wishing to deter Germany until such time as their defenses had matured.

The Soviet Need to Negotiate–Berlin and London

As has already been discussed, failure to wed what was left of East Europe, that is Poland and the Balkans together, drove the British to the unsavory task of negotiating with the Soviets, an unpleasantry which was somewhat shared by the Soviets who did not wish to pledge to fight for aims in the Balkans which were not theirs in order to protect themselves. What drove them to this position was the fact that neutrality could not be obtained by political isolation, and despite confidence that war in the East enhanced their importance to both sides, the West had not yet shown a propensity to give in to Soviet demands nor had the Germans come knocking at their door. The net result was that some reinsurance was needed, for a Nazi-Western deal was as pertinent to the Soviets as a Nazi-Soviet deal was to the West.

The realities of Soviet isolation, making contact with London essential, were everywhere evident. The U.S. had rebuffed the Soviet overture in 1938 and 1939 for the sale of ships and exchange of information and then excused itself from active participation by failing to revoke the neutrality legislation. The Chinese were immobilized, locking the Soviets into the Japanese conflict with a threatened tripartite alliance and a two-front war to haunt them. To the south, the Saadabad Pact, which bound Turkey with Afghanistan, Persia and Iraq against Soviet expansionism, was secure. To the north, the Baltic States continually refused Russian "help," leaving the Baltic and North Seas open to aggressors. Poland, during the discussion of a Four Power Pact, had refused to abandon her balancing act between Berlin and Moscow.

In the Balkans, the situation was equally discouraging. Rumania, ever skeptical of Moscow (popularly phrased, "if ever the Russians get in, they would never get out"), would never agree to the terms necessary to Russian defense which meant acquisition of Bessarabia if not more. Relations between the two countries had sunk so low that since the departure of Ostrowsky in February, there had been no Russian Minister in Bucharest,[15] and so fearful was Bucharest of German wrath if there was the least deviation from neutrality, that when Potemkin crossed the border on April 24 en route to Ankara, no official contact was made.[16] Even the sentimental and Slavic attachment of Bulgaria to Russia was not enough to overcome Bulgaria's basic fear of Russia, which was based on the Bulgarian assessment that Russia would not fight in a European war, and after captialist destruction, would occupy all of East Europe.[17] Meanwhile the Balkan Entente had rejected the Soviet inspired Black Sea pact, pitting the Balkans as a whole against the USSR. In order to keep links open with the West, there seemed only the hope now that some favorable arrangement could be made with Turkey, or that the projected British-East European peace front would materialize with some degree of Soviet association.

Seemingly for these two reasons, the sounding out of the Turks and giving momentum to the British peace front, Potemkin was dispatched by Ltivinov to Ankara on April 29-May 5, and then on his return to Sofia, on May 7, Bucharest on May 8, and Warsaw on May 9-10, and after that, it was expected that he would go to Geneva to see Halifax. As the Anglo-Turkish negotiations for a mutual assistance pact were in full swing when Potemkin arrived in Ankara, Potemkin was also very likely eager to learn if the terms for such an agreement would be detrimentaal to the Soviets.

According to Saracoglu, the talks were carried on in a friendly manner, and the Russians were satisfied that the direction of the Anglo-Turkish talks had not altered Montreux and were not detrimental to Soviet interests. Saracoglu's conclusion was that Russia would be no obstacle to the encirclement front, and that a Russo-Turkish agreement could be arranged after a Turkish agreement with the West. Potemkin, he said, had applauded Turkey's understanding with Great Britain, had given assurances that Turkey could count on material support from Russia, and had pledged to do all he could to strengthen the Balkan Entente.[18] But on May 15, an article in *Izvestia* welcoming the Anglo-Turkish Declaration of May 12 as "one of the links to prevent extensive aggression" took occasion to emphasize the closeness of Russo-Turkish relations rather than the British effort.[19]

Whatever outward portrayal of optimism Potemkin may have displayed that the encirclement front was in a state of rapid evolution, must have been dimmed by what he learned about the provisions of the future Mutual Assistance Pact which did not link Turkey with the Balkans and thus with encirclement. Likewise, while the agreement did not sacrifice Turkish sovereignty at the Straits, leaving the possibilities for a Soviet-Turkish pact open, it must have been clear to Potemkin that the Turks were unlikely, in view of their recent leanings toward the British (which offered protection against not only the Germans but the Soviets as well), to concede to the Soviets the only kinds of demands (control over the Straits) which would give to them some measure of gain and protection.[20] In addition, Saracoglu had refused promises of aid to Russia if Moscow came to Rumania's defense against Germany on the grounds of uncertainty about Bulgaria's attitude.

What Potemkin learned on the rest of his trip must have been even more disquieting. While doing what he could to promote the British encirclement program, it was obvious everywhere that there would be no formation of an interlocking Balkan and East European front. In Sofia, Potemkin was alarmed at the pro-Axis leanings of Bulgaria, and to offset this he tried to urge their leaders to steer a course more friendly to the Balkan Entente. But the clamor for the return of lost provinces he heard and Kiosseivanov's own position in this regard, made him conclude that it would be difficult to organize solid resistance in the Balkans and to bring Bulgaria toward the Balkan Entente as long as this continued.[21] In Bucharest on May 8, the impossibility of Balkan rapprochement must have become obvious when Gafencu affirmed that Rumania would not give any concessions to Bulgaria until the latter had affirmed her solidarity. More heartening was Gafencu's statement that he was willing to extend the Polish-Rumanian alliance to include countries other than the Soviet Union. But in Warsaw, Beck dashed these hopes by refusing any such extension wishing not to antagonize Berlin.

Despite what Potemkin learned, he displayed a great deal of optimism reporting to Gafencu that "the resistance front was crystallizing everywhere," and that his travels indicated that in the Balkans there was "a desire for union in view of Hitler's threats." And, according to Gafencu, Potemkin believed in the happy outcome of negotiations between Moscow and the West saying, it was understood everywhere that in one form or another, collaboration with the USSR was necessary and that Russia would continue a policy of "cooperation" with the democracies and opposition to German expansionism.[22] The Turks reinforced this view, saying that it had been on Inönü's suggestion that Potemkin had visited Warsaw and Bucharest and that everywhere he had been received, he had given hopeful expressions of the possibilities of cooperation.[23] Even in Warsaw Potemkin stressed to Beck reinvigoration of the Polish-Soviet Non-Aggression Pact and he suggested broadening the scope of commercial agreement.[24]

Whether this optimism was for Berlin's consumption or because he really believed the Soviet Union could reach an agreement with the West fortifying the East European and Balkan countries enough that they would abandon their neutrality, settle their disputes and form a peace front, is unclear. Despite Turkish optimism, there were those at the time who saw sinister motivation in the Potemkin visit. French statesman Leger saw it as preparation for accommodation with Hitler in that Potemkin's friendly embrace strengthened Turkish opposition to signing a pact with Great Britain and France until a guarantee from the West could be obtained for the Soviet Union.[25] And Gafencu said (in retrospect) that the whole purpose of the Potemkin trip was to sooth Balkan and Western fears of Soviet aggression in order to prevent the Balkans from turning to the West and from strengthening their own defense system while intimating that agreement with the West was possible. The policy, said Gafencu had excellent success particularly in Poland, but that everywhere it created an illusion and a false hope cherished all over the Balkans that Balkan unity could be achieved after a Soviet agreement with the West. If, Gafencu wrote:

> ...the states bordering on the Soviet Union could have grasped a little of what was actually going on beyond their Eastern frontier, they might perhaps have avoided more than one political error and many deadly shocks.

Gafencu does not blame Potemkin for outright duplicity, recognizing instead that carriers of Russian policy, once beyond the border, often gave official views "a turn of mind" which more than once led to "the wrong impression."[26]

Actually, one suspects that Potemkin was sincerely carrying out one facet of Soviet foreign policy as he seemed bent on a program using Soviet influence to try to influence Bulgaria to limit its demands to Dobruja, noting to Gafencu how difficult it would be to organize solid Balkan resistance as long as Bulgaria clamored for lost territories. He even alluded to revision of Soviet claims to Bessarabia when he told Gafencu that the Soviet Union would soon give "proof" of its wish for a general entente.[27] The problem, of course, was that the Western oriented foreign policy of the Kremlin was not the only direction in which the Soviets were moving. Stalin's March 10 speech had alluded to another which was followed up on April 17 by a feeler toward Berlin, and while the latter was not common knowledge, the dismissal of Litvinov on May 3 was an outright and open gesture. While Potemkin was in Ankara, it was announced that Litvinov, for health reasons, would be replaced by Molotov. Along the remainder of Potemkin's route, he assured the Balkan countries that the shift meant no change in Soviet policy. The Turks were even optimistic, hinting that Litvinov had failed to go along with Turkish suggestions and that the resignation cleared the way for closer relations with the democracies as Potemkin would likely be the next Commissar of Foreign Affairs.[28] Indeed, in outward form, there were no immediate changes until Potemkin was called back before he could go on to Geneva to meet Halifax.

While Litvinov later said he suggested his own retirement, Astakhov's accounting at the time was to the effect that it had been brewing for six months, he and Molotov being no longer in accord, and that Stalin, "while esteeming him, did not like him."[29] Whatever the personal element involved, Stalin did not denigrate Litvinov's policies which were also obviously his own. But because Litvinov was a Jew, and because he symbolized collective security, his dismissal could not help but intimate a Soviet shift which would be more receptive to any Nazi initiative that might come its way, indeed it invited it. In terms of the Soviet image abroad, the shift signified that the Soviet Union considered itself as "arrived," and was preparing to deal with the Great Powers on a par basis instead of in the casual foreign way in which Litvinov was treated. And whatever was intended by the moves, the Germans partook it as a gesture in their direction. Hitler later said that "Litvinov's dismissal was decisive,"[30] and the move at the time resulted in concrete actions on Hitler's part. On May 6 Hitler asked for a briefing on the Soviet position, and on the same day, Ciano talked to Ribbentrop in an attempt to secure Italian interests vis-a-vis the Soviet Union particularly in the Balkans.

The West rather than analyzing the effect Litvinov's removal would have on German policy, concentrated on the effect it would have on their own negotiations, and in this regard there seemed to be two theories. One was that the change augured well for the British-French-Soviet negotiations as it eliminated any frictions of the past and removed the Litvinov idea of the indivisibility of security and peace, therefore making it easier for the Soviet Union to accept the British idea that the Soviet Union give unilateral assurances to the states from the Baltic to the Black Sea guaranteeing them against aggression. The other theory, significantly, came from the countries adjacent to Russia who believed that the Soviet Union was dedicated to peace for economic and ideological reasons, and that the Soviet Union was disgusted with appeasement and believed Hitler would understand a "bold military alliance of a concrete character," a policy to which Litvinov had been unable to convert the West, necessitating a tough, new negotiator with the full expectation that the Soviets would raise the ante.[31]

The Soviets for their part, still very uncertain that the Nazi link would materialize, needed to maintain a strong and active negotiating position with the West as well as putting out feelers to Berlin, and so they removed Litvinov without damning him. The most important historical result of the Litvinov removal is the way the Nazi interpreted it, rather than the Soviet motivation which appears multifaceted. Nazi receptivity makes Soviet timing appear ingenious when, in fact, this was but another of a long list of Soviet invitations for rapprochement which had previously left Berlin unmoved. Suddenly, Nazi needs immortalized it.

The Soviet need to pursue paths both to London and Berlin was enhanced in May due to the Italians. Well aware after Albania that the Italians were capable of upsetting Geman plans to neutralize the Balkans, the Soviets were concerned after the signing of the Pact of Steel on May 22, that the West would not be able to woo Italy away from Germany, that the Axis partners had come to some agreement over spheres and action in the Southeast, and that a green light had been given to Italian (and her surrogates') presence there which, much hated, could destabilize the area. The increasing propensity of Hungary (backed by Italy) and Bulgaria to advance their own revisionism in the Balkans was already well in evidence.

Once again, the Soviets founds their best route to Berlin through London and support for encirclement. On May 31 Molotov gave a speech in which he labeled the Pact of Steel as "a treaty basically of an aggressive character," but he went on to threaten the West and appease Hitler by noting the absence of any Anti-Comintern features in the Pact.[32] By this time too, the Soviets were very likely aware that more than anything else, British encirclement and Western enticements of Russia into the enemy camp, had driven the Axis partners together, and that this would very likely cause Germany to prevail on Italy in the matter of the status quo of the Balkans and a pact with the Soviets. During the Milan conversations on May 6-7 leading up to the Pact of Steel, advance publicity from Italian sources gave the world to understand that an alliance between Germany and Italy was only suggested as a possibility in the event that Great Britain and the USSR came to an understanding.   But in a memo drawn up for Ciano's conversations with Ribbentrop, Mussolini agreed to approach Russia but only "to prevent Russia from adhering to the bloc . . . but no further policy of that kind, being the antithesis of the present position . . . ."[33] (Later, of course, Mussolini supported the Pact for his own reasons, that is as reinsurance against both Soviet and Nazi entrance into Rome's claimed Balkan sphere in event of war.)

*   *   *   *   *

Thus, for the Soviet Union, the Italian-German interplay suggested two things—one led them to London, the other to Berlin. The tying of the Axis knot increased the threat to the Soviet southwestern frontier and the danger that an Axis war would be prosecuted in that direction. Therefore, both as protection and as reinsurance against being left alone to face the Steel Pact partners, the Soviet Union found it advantageous to enter into discussions with the West. On the other hand, Italian official statements during the Steel Pact negotiations and the very fact that Germany sought them, seemed to indicate that Germany feared the impact of the British encirclement drive and particularly the adhesion of the Soviet Union to this Pact. It must have occurred to Moscow, therefore, that Germany would pay a price for Soviet neutrality and that the more ardently the Soviets entered into discussions with the West, the more generous German terms might become and the more amenable Mussolini would be to go along.

The Soviet need to negotiate on both sides displays all the characteristics of classic Communist dialectics, for in playing London off against Berlin a new synthesis more advantageous to the Soviets was produced. In a more subtle dialectical sense was the dichotomy that in each untoward Soviet circumstance, there was an opposite and fruitful gain. For instance, the fracturing of Balkan unity witnessed by Potemkin, the Turkish turn to London rather than Moscow, and the Italian challenge to Balkan stability drove the Soviets to seek reinsurance against Fascist aggression and a Balkan explosion in the Southeast. But at the same time, these unfavorable circumstances threatened Germany's control of the Balkans, so that what was so harmful to the Soviets, opened the road to Soviet security and gain in Berlin. The Soviet negotiations with the West, in other words, made possible a new direction and Litvinov's dismissal was the symbol of the new thesis-antithesis which for the first time foreshadowed a synthesis which rested on the mutual interest of the Nazis and Soviets in the temporary pacification of the Balkans. The fact was, the Soviets had to negotiate on both sides in order to produce the kind of neutrality they needed.

Viewed in this light, the British program was a huge success in breaking down Germany, but it was a failure in the power it gave the Soviet Union. Viewed in this light, also, the British instinct not to negotiate with the Soviet Union would have served them well. On the other hand, the failure to weld the Balkans together made the threat of Soviet alliance with the Germans the only pawn Moscow held. Amidst such fears of Germany and isolation, and in the face of divergent aims and interests, the Anglo-Franco Soviet negotiations were begun. At issue was the fate of Poland, the Baltic states, and the Balkans. The Soviet Union had arrived—through the backdoor and now that they had, offensive aims took over.

The Anglo-French-Soviet Talks and the Balkans

Once the British and French had guaranteed Poland and two of the Balkan states, the West's relationship with the Soviet Union naturally involved those states, for even if the nature of any trilateral alliance was strictly among the three against Germany, the likelihood of war in East Europe was self-evident. And even if the war was not in the East, the only way the Soviet Union could reach Germany in order to aid the West was by crossing the interim states. The other factor was that any collective Balkan action hinged on the relationship the West established with Russian since Turkey, at its nexus, had made it clear that unless an alliance was signed between France, England, the Soviet Union, and Turkey, Turkey would not give military assistance to Rumania. Untoward in this situation was the fact that all nations, but particularly Poland and Rumania, were bitterly set against any deal with Russia. Therefore, the conditions under which the Soviet Union would fight, were of paramount importance, and they all involved the interim states.

However Soviet interests are defined—neutrality, "peace," defense, security, balance of power, achievement of Great Power status, or ideological gain, they in some way or another boil down to the question of who controlled the Balkans, Poland, and the Straits? For in the situation as it evolved in 1939 there was no such thing as neutrality, for whatever the Soviets did, they helped one side or the other. This was well illustrated in the Nazi-Soviet and Anglo-Franco-Soviet negotiations where both the Nazis and Allies competed less for Soviet favor than to prevent Moscow from going into the enemy camp. The argument that the Germans could offer neutrality.[34] while the West would only offer participation in the West's war, does not hold up if one examines the Allied-Soviet negotiations in which London asked at the least for benevolency and at the most for aid of a highly circumscribed nature, and if one considers the fight to be only against Germany. For, in fact, what the Germans were offering was aid in the war against the West in the form of benevolency,which was no more than the West was seeking in their negotiations. Essentially, once the British began negotiating for Soviet aid against Germany and the Germans began negotiating for non-aggression, the Capitalist war the Soviets had long sought was a certainty, and therefore, protected and fortified, the question for the Soviets was a price tag, a price the Soviets had already placed on the Balkans and Poland.

Therefore, the basic issue at the heart of the Anglo-French-Soviet negotiations and the German-Soviet negotiations for the Soviets was control over the border states (for the Germans it was Soviet neutrality and for the West Soviet benevolency), and it is fair to say that these Soviet aims in the Balkans and elsewhere were well understood and appreciated in the West, Berlin, and the Balkans, but that in 1939 the West was unwilling to sacrifice those interests. Balkan statements to the effect that they too wished to avoid involvement with the Soviet Union afterward became the scapegoat for the West's refusal to hand over to Moscow control of the Soviet frontier states, but they were only part of the West's interests and were not even the basis of the Balkan objection which, while fearful of the nature of Soviet interests in their direction, of Bolshevization and of Britain's giving in to Russian territorial demands in exchange for an eastern front,[35] were primarily centered around fears that if the Soviet Union and Britain linked up, this would antagonize Hitler, leading to occupation, and a Balkan war. (The exception here was Turkey who, less fearful of war and Germany, advanced the idea that once Britain and Russian came to an agreement, Turkey could too.)

Furthermore, there is considerable evidence to suggest that Soviet emphasis on defensive concerns, insecurity, suspicion, peace, and neutrality was a tactic used by the Soviets in the negotiations in order to make gains in East Europe or to stall the outcome in favor of a deal with Germany, and that they felt increasingly secure after the guarantees and the tempo of German interest increased. On March 16, 1939, and several times after, Soviet Commissar for Defense Marshal Voroshilov, gave a detailed account of Soviet military strength to deter it,[36] and on June 2 Soviet Ambassador to the U.S., Oumansky, stated that the Soviet Union had not budged regarding their demands as to the Anglo-French-Russian front, as there was still "considerable elbow room for Germany in Europe without bringing Germany to the frontiers of the USSR."[37] Even the Hungarian press noted that in the British-Russian pourparlers, Russia had the advantage because a defense pact was not of urgency to her and thus she was not eager to make concessions.[38]

There were other such observations at the time, U.S. Ambassador in the Soviet Union, Steinhardt, reporting a considerable Soviet feeling of security in Europe based on the fact that Germany could not attack Russia without invading Rumania or Poland or both, and in that case Moscow felt assured of Anglo-French military assistance.[39] Henderson offered another explanation opining that the breakdown in Polish-German relations in March and the British guarantees had changed the whole picture, for now the Soviet Union no longer feared a Four-Power European settlement and thus had no need of collective security.

> If it does not come to terms with Great Britain it will do so only on a basis which will give it what amounts to hegemony over East Europe and which will render it impossible for at least many years to become a united Europe.

He concluded by noting that the Soviet Union was dominated by an aggressive spirit, a desire to include additional peoples and territories in her sphere, and the wish to take advantage of the situation whereby both belligerents would be exhausted.[40]

Perhaps the best argument on behalf of the idea that the basis of Soviet interest in negotiations with the West was as a lever against Germany with control of the interim states as the offsetting sacrifice, is the record of the negotiations themselves, for one by one all the security and neutrality problems on a trilateral basis were solved by the agreements worked out with regard to reciprocity, definitions of aggression, and military arrangements, all except the question of those dealing with the interim states, and here both the British and Soviets refused to budge. The original dialog between the Soviet Union and the West, broken off in March and April because of the Polish and Rumanian refusal to be a party to any international arrangement to which the USSR was a member, was reopened in mid-April by Britain and France on a trilateral basis due to their inability to convert the guarantees to a reciprocal system and to the growing danger that the Soviet Union would be neutral or seek alliance with Germany. The Soviets, for their part, had nothing to lose.

On April 14, the French suggested a tripartite agreement encompassing a guarantee of mutual assistance if either the USSR or the Western Powers should become involved in war with Germany on account of help given to Poland or Rumania.[41] But the British, who were less concerned than the French about a direct German attack against them and therefore did not want direct reciprocity, suggested only that the USSR should make a unilateral declaration that Russian assistance would be available, if desired, to any European neighbor of the Soviet Union which resisted aggression.[42] Both suggestions, however, made Poland and the Balkans the focus of the reciprocal agreements. The difference between the French and British proposals was considered a terrible blunder by some who thought that it weakened the Western position, because it alluded to a schism in the allied ranks, and because the British position could fortify the Poles against a Polish-Rumanian rapprochement, thus preventing realization of the encirclement front.[43]

While the Soviets preferred the French suggestion guaranteeing them aid,[44] they responded on April 17 with a counterproposal which was supposedly to combine the British and French proposals, but in reality was a statement of very broad Soviet interests underscoring Stalin's belief that only force, not a diplomatic lineup of Great Britain, France and the Soviet Union, would stop Hitler,[45] and that the heart of any agreement revolved around the decisions made in regard to Poland and the Balkans. The Russians proposed a Three-Power Pact valid for five to ten years accompanied by a military convention to provide for assistance of a military nature not only in Europe, but to "all East European countries between the Baltic and Black Seas and bordering on the USSR in case of aggression against these States." They also wanted Britain to state publicly that their guarantee of Poland came into play only in case of aggression by Germany, and that the Polish-Rumanian alliance should be declared to be operative in the case of aggression against Poland and Rumania or else revoked altogether (as it was directed presently only against the USSR).[46]

The Soviet proposals were exactly what the West had tried to avoid. A declaration shifting the thrust of the Polish-Rumanian alliance away from Russia towards Germany would place these two countries in an anti-German camp, and the Soviet formula for assistance by omitting the British phrase "if desired," raised the dreaded prospect of Russian military occupation, a threat which was given some credence in late March and early April by the Soviet offers of "help" to Estonia and Latvia and later to Finland, which considerably compromised the territorial intergrity and independence of these small states. And they continued to question the real value of Soviet aid in wartime,[47] while attending to the mood of Poland and Rumania, which remained loyal to the statement made by the Rumanian Ambassador to Bonnet in March duplicating those of the Polish Ambassador that:

> In time of peace we cannot make any agreement whatsoever to permit Russian troops to enter our territory or to receive assistance in the form of munitions, guns, tanks or airplanes from the Soviet Union; but in time of war, we would be ready to take help from the Devil himself.[48]

In effect, what the British wanted was the benevolent neutrality of the Soviet Union, not the active participation.

The Soviets, if judged by statements made by Litvinov, Molotov, Maisky, Suritz, and the Russian press,[49] aggrandized Soviet participation, particularly in the East. They emphasized that because of their geographical position, the new commitments they were being asked to undertake would expose them to direct attack from Germany and that, in any case, they would bear the brunt of the direct aid given to East Europe. They remembered Munich and cited the possibility that Poland and Rumania would offer no resistance, therefore they wanted the guarantee system to be extended to all the states on their frontier with the right to intervene in those states even if intervention was not requested or desired. And they wanted complete reciprocity between themselves and the Western Powers with a military convention to define the exact nature of the help.

For the next three weeks, from April 17 to the British proposal of May 8, discussions between the British and French tired to come to terms with the Russian proposals. Bonnet suggested that if either France or the Soviet Union were drawn into war on account of promises to Poland or Rumania, that aid would go, not to those countries, but to the Soviet Union or France. This was agreed to by Rumania and Poland, but the Soviets wanted Poland and Rumania named in the agreement and as this was unacceptable to Warsaw and Bucharest, Bonnet offered a countertext not naming these states but stating all states of East Europe and the Balkans.[50]

Circumstances then pushed the British toward compromise, not on the issue of unrestricted Soviet aid to East Europe, but on the issue of Soviet-British reciprocity. There were fears that Potemkin had been sent to Ankara to strengthen opposition to the Turkish signing of a pact with the British and French until the Soviet Union was guaranteed. Then it was reported that Litvinov's removal was occasioned by the proposals which Halifax had made on April 14, Stalin being enraged at begin relegated to a third-rate power, and that Stalin would now withdraw into isolation and then proceed to make large-scale economic agreements with Germany.[51]

On May 8, after consultation with Paris, Warsaw, and Bucharest, the British made a revised proposal to Molotov which was designed to convince Moscow that the Russians were not being asked to go it alone against Germany. It provided for a unilateral declaration undertaking:

> . . . that in the event of Great Britain and France being involved in hostilities in fulfillment of these obligations (to Poland and Rumania), the assistance of the Soviet Union would be immediately available if desired, and would be afforded in such a manner and in such terms as might be agreed.[52]

Once again, Britain was pressing, not for a large Soviet undertaking (necessitating a quid pro quo) as Moscow liked to portray, but rather a kind of benevolent neutrality or participation of a highly circumscribed character.[53]

As might be expected, on May 9- a *Tass* communique questioned the nonreciprocal nature of the British proposal, and a May 11 *Izvestia* article showed the emphasis the Soviet Union now attached to full and unconditional reciprocity including Poland and the Balkans. It read, in part:

These three Powers, bound by a pact of mutual assistance on the principle of reciprocity, should guarantee the other States of Eastern and Central Europe which are threatened by aggression. . . . Great Britain says nothing about the aid which the USSR should naturally receive . . .should it be involved in hostilities owing to the fulfillment of the obligations it may assume in guaranteeing any of the States of Eastern Europe.[54]

On May 15, the Soviets formally rejected the British proposal and then stipulated the three indispensible conditions for Soviet participation— a tripartite pact of mutual assistance, Finland, Estonia and Latvia must be included in the guarantee system as well as Poland and Rumania, and there must be a military convention to determine the terms of assistance to each of the guaranteed states which were essentially the same conditions (elaborated upon) as the Soviets had stated on April 17.

The reason for Soviet obstinancy was variously interpreted in the West. The French were apt to emphasize British tactics and Soviet defensive concerns. At one point Leger told Bullitt that the Soviet Government had explained privately that they were very uncertain of the Rumanian situation which might be reversed in one night by the assassination of the King of Rumania and along with it, the possibilty that Rumania would not resist a German attack whereupon German troops would cross Rumania to attack the Soviet Union. Therefore, "the Soviet Union desired to be confident of British support no matter what might be the future action of the Rumanian Government."[55] But others stressed the increased Soviet sense of security, on the one hand as a result of the guarantees and Anglo-Turkish Declaration, and on the other as a result of the German Ambassador's interview with Molotov in which the latter said that economic relations must be put on a political basis.[56] Meanwhile, according to leger, the Pact of Steel impressed both Maisky and Halifax, and while he inferred toward compromise, the impression may have been different on both—for the British to come to terms with the Soviets and for the Soviets to come to terms with Berlin.[57]

At any rate, the British decided to give in on the reciprocity issue, in part because Halifax had decided after a conference with the Russians in Geneva, that if there was to be any deal, it would have to be on their terms and in part because the advantages seemed to outweigh the disadvantages. In this regard the disadvantages of not giving in were increasingly seen as leading to a Nazi-Soviet Pact, the isolation of Russia, and a war between Germany and the West leaving the Soviet Union in a position to dominate Europe rather than what had been the original intent of entering into discussions with the Russians which was to deter Hitler.[58]

As the threat of such a Nazi-Soviet pact increased, the British tended to upgrade the nature of Soviet participation, but they did so within a framework which made it unlikely by covering the reciprocity in the East European states (where it was most likely to occur) with conditions, by putting it under the cloak of the League of Nations anti-aggression formulas, and by bringing in Turkey, Poland and all the rest of the countries. On May 25 the British and French offered their new proposals, which gave in on the issue of reciprocity but included a proviso that Russian assistance should be only if requested, and it included the clause "without prejudice to the rights and position of other powers" (Article V).[59] When the British had inquired of the Polish and Rumanian attitudes, Rumania said it was delighted to have a guarantee from the Soviet Union provided Rumania was not to be specified, and it would have no objection to the British guarantee of the Soviet Union. According to Halifax, Poland gave the same answer.[60]

Since Molotov received a copy of the draft before formal presentation, he had a chance to study it, and upon formal receipt on May 27 (seated on a dias in the Kremlin with Seeds and Payart at his feet), he voiced immediate objections. He said that reference to the League of Nations was a means to delay help to the Soviet Union that provisions for concerted action were too vauge, and that Article V, which was intended to preserve the rights of the small guaranteed states, was designed to safeguard the rights of an aggressor. "What need was there to protect the small states, since intervention would be in their own interest," he asked? Seeds bluntly replied that the Western Powers recognized the right of small states "to limit even friendly intervention in such matters as . . . passage of troops."[61] Then Molotov switched emphasis and said that the real issue was the guarantees to the Baltic states. and later in a speech before the Third Session of the Supreme Soviet USSR on May 31, while acknowledging the progress made on the issue of trilateral reciprocity, he lent emphasis to Soviet demands regarding East Europe and a military convention, and the Soviet belief that neutrality would be better than fighting the West's war without compensation.[62]

In conclusion, Molotov hinted that economic discussions with Berlin might be resumed, which was probably intended not only as a sounding to Berlin, but as a gesture of threat and/or encouragement to the West to accept the Soviet counterproposals which were handed to Seeds and Naggiar on June 1.[63] The Soviet proposal stated that the conditions bringing the tripartite into action were direct aggression against any of the signatories, agression against Belgium, Greece, Turkey, Rumania, Poland, Latvia, Estonia and Finland, and assistance to any European state which asked for it. Article V required a joint armistice and peace, and the Soviets demanded elimination of any reference to the League and that the political agreement would come into force only upon signature of a military convention. The vast Soviet participation envisioned by Molotov raised suspicion in the West as to the real interests of the Soviets and rendered the frequent opinion that Stalin was determined to obtain the highest bid possible.[64]

Among other things, the French found the proposals unacceptable because:

> France and England could certainly not consent to giving the Soviet Union support for an extension of Bolshevism in Eastern Europe and that acceptance of the Soviet proposal would mean consent to the establishment of a Soviet protectorate over the states named in the note.[65]

On June 7 in a statement to the House of Commons, Chamberlain noted similar difficulties, particularly with regard to the position of certain states "which do not want to receive a guarantee on the grounds that it would compromise the strict neutrality which they wish to preserve."[66] Nikonov, speaking for the contemporary Soviet view, says that this British-French position regarding the buffer states was the key stumbling block to negotiation.[67]

By this time, the British and French were becoming irked at the slow pace of negotiations, and so they tried to speed them up by sending a special envoy, Strang, to the Soviet Union on June 12 with more power to negotiate.[68] The numerous conversations which took place on June 14-August 4 were marred on both sides by suspicion, frustration, and dissatisfaction. The British and French were constantly misled by the Russian habit of emphasizing one point to which the West made concessions, only to find a new point emphasized. The Russians, for their part, complained of delay and procrastination. On June 29, 1939, Politboro member Andrey A. Zhdanov, in a signed article to *Pravda,* stated that England and France had "no wish for an equal treaty with the USSR" in view of the fact that it took the West only a short time to reach agreement with Turkey,[69] a statement which must be balanced against Astakhov's admission in mid-June to the Bulgarian Minister in Berlin, that the Russians had deliberately been carrying on negotiations in a dilatory manner.[70]

The growing strength of the Soviet negotiating position is evident by the fact that during the entire course of the negotiations carried on for almost two months by Strang, the British were put in the position of trying to accommodate themselves to the Soviet demands originally made in April. This was noted in the German press which, commenting on the Molotov-Strang communique, pointed with satisfaction to the upper hand now held by Russia.[71] And in the Balkans, where there was a tendency to take at face value Soviet statements that they could defend themselves, the growing power of the Soviet position did not go unnoticed.[72]

On June 6 the British made a new proposal for a tripartite pact which attempted to satisfy Soviet demands that all the frontier states must be included in such a pact while bowing to the wishes to these states that they not be named specifically and not receive Soviet aid unless requested.[73] On June 16 Molotov rejected this formula due among other things to the fact that, in not mentioning the name of the "European Power" (which was meant to be Germany), it could have been the USSR whereby the West would have had to defend Poland against the USSR and vice-versa.[74] Molotov then said on June 16 that he thought it best to postpone the question as not being ripe for agreement and for the three powers to conclude a pact of mutual assistance in case of direct aggression. The West did not like this type of pact because it did not take into account obligations to Poland and Rumania, but they kept it in mind as a last resort. Molotov withdrew his proposal on June 22, since the West had not at once accepted it, and reverted to his proposals of June 2 adding the Baltic states but refusing aid to the Netherlands and Switzerland.[75]

Soviet emphasis on the Baltic states now began in earnest, and whether this was for Berlin's consumption[76] or a sincere effort on the Soviet part to gain quid pro quos where the British might be more apt to make concessions, in not known. At any rate, they pressed for Soviet guarantees arguing

that the people (as distinct from the government) really wanted guarantees, that the West had imposed guarantees on Greece and Rumania under
the same conditions the Soviets wished them imposed on the Baltic states,
that due to the weakness of these small states, they must be defended by
the Great Powers, and that the security of the Soviet Union could only
be obtained by such guarantees.[77] Latvia and Estonia, in response, accepted German offers of non-aggression pacts at the end of June. These
German gains in the Baltic and the lack of activity with Berlin apparently
led Molotov on July 3 to agree to Naggier's suggestion of June 21 that the
names of the states should not be included in the text of an agreement,
but in a secret agreement. But then there was a dispute over which states
were to be included, the Russians arguing that the obligations already
undertaken were so heavy they could not extend themselves to Switzerland and the Netherlands unless they were given something in return. They
suggested that this might be Turkey and Poland concluding mutual assistance pacts with the USSR.[78] To this the Turkish Government was willing,
but knowing it was a waste of time with Poland, the British fell back on
the idea of consultation in case of an attack on or threat to a state not
named in the agreement.[79]

Soon a dispute arose over the definition of a much used phrase in the
negotiations "indirect aggression." The British thought of it in terms of a
German attack on the interim states, as opposed to an attack on France
or Great Britain or Russia. The Soviets, however, wanted indirect aggression included not only of this kind, but of the kind utilizing "new" techniques used by the Nazis to gain control of Austria, Czechoslovakia, and
Memel without firing a shot, and so Molotov proposed that "an internal
coup d'etat or reversal of policy in the interests of the aggressor" be the
accepted definition. The negative reaction of the British caused Molotov
to advance a new definition on July 9; "use by a European Power of the
territory of one of the states mentioned for purposes of aggression against
that state or against one of the three contracting parties." The British
liked this no better (the French were disposed to accept the formula),
and here they refused to budge, stating that they could not be a party to
any arrangement placing them in a position of becoming accessories "to
interference in the internal affairs of other states."[80]

By July 23 a deadlock had been reached over the entire issue of the
second plank in the Soviet program, a system of guarantees along her

border, and three days previous the British had abandoned their idea of a direct tripartite, which had been the first plank in the Soviet program, when Strang advised that the Russians would insist that it be accompanied by the third plank of their program, a military convention.[81] The British and French then decided if they remained firm on the question of not allowing Soviet intervention in the interim states, they could give way on the question of a military convention being signed simultaneously with a political agreement.[82] Important in pressing the British and French toward compromise were the reports that the French had been receiving from Berlin and Moscow since the end of June that the Russo-German trade talks were about to be or had been resumed.

When Seeds proceeded to tell Molotov on July 23 that the British Government accepted in principle, simultaneous signatures of a political and military agreement based on a direct tripartite pact but not the Soviet definition of indirect aggression, Molotov seemed satisfied. What made him so amenable is unclear. It could have been either that he was glad to be getting down to what the Soviets considered the important questions, or because concrete Anglo-Soviet discussions could induce Germany to raise the terms of their offers during the Soviet-German economic discussions which had resumed on July 22. At any rate, the impasse over the definition of indirect aggression put a temporary end to political negotiations causing Strang's recall to London on August 4, but the Russians did not call off the military mission and so it arrived in Moscow on August 12.

Like the political negotiations, the military talks were pregnant with suspicions and delays. Soviet delays were probably not unconnected with the stepped up tempo of the Soviet-German economic negotiations and then the discussion of political questions between Schnurre and Astakhov on July 26, so that it is possible the Soviets wished to develop and feel out this connection a little more before involving themselves so heavily with the British. In this regard a *Pravda* article of July 27 entitled "Germany Would Lose," U.S. Minister Grummon interpreted either as an indication of the greater security of the USSR and thus the increased reluctance to sign a pact with Great Britain and France, or as added reason for Berlin to come to terms.[83] British footdragging was due to fear of leaking military information prior to a political agreement, and to hopes that, by keeping the talks going, other Russian action could be sidetracked long enough to prevent Hitler from putting his plans into action.[84]

At the first three meetings on August 12-13,[85] Voroshilov made it clear
he was interested in plans not principles and he asked pertinent questions
like how many British troops could reinforce the French Army and what
troops were available if war was in the immediate future. Then at the
fourth meeting on August 14 Voroshilov asked the "cardinal" question.
Could the Red Army move across northern Poland and "in particular the
Vilno Salient across Galicia in order to make contact with the enemy?
Will Soviet troops be allowed to cross Rumanian territory?" The British
and French insisted that these were political questions and that the Soviet
Union must ask Rumania and Poland as they were sovereign states, but
Voroshilov insisted it was the British and French responsibility to consult
Poland and Rumania, and without a solution to that problem, it was useless to continue "an enterprise so obviously doomed to failure." The contemporary Soviet view of this as expressed by Nikonov,[86] is that this
thinking exhibited deliberate unwillingness to have an effective military
alliance with the USSR and revealed the real aim of the West which was
to intimate to Hitler that the Soviet Union had no allies, that she was
isolated and hence, Hitler could attack.

The next day, August 15, Voroshilov presented plans for military collaboration should war break out, but on August 16 he rejected a suggestion that a document be drawn up based on his plan, saying it was useless to continue the conversation until a favorable reply on troop passage
had been received. However, he went on to fix a date for the next meeting
so as not to give rise to reports that the conference had broken down. At
this meeting on August 21, Voroshilov made a statement to the effect that
the conference should be adjourned for a "longer period" due to the fact
that he was much occupied with autumn maneuvers, but if answers to his
"cardinal questions" were received, the conference could be convened
immediately. On the same day, August 21, in the afternoon, Stalin accepted the proposal that Ribbentrop should come to Moscow immediately
and on August 22 the Russian press announced that Ribbentrop was coming to Moscow to conclude a Pact of Non-Aggression.

During the eight day period from August 14 when Voroshilov had presented his "cardinal questions" until August 22, the British and French
tried to induce the Polish Government to retract their refusal to allow Soviet troops to enter Poland. The Polish Ambassador in Paris, Lukawiewicz,
when apprised of the situation remarked, "What would you say if you

were asked to have Alsace-Lorraine guarded by the Germans?" And Beck, even in the face of the French persuasion that the negotiations might fail without Poland's consent, and that it involved Rumania and Turkey as well, argued that if Poland acquiesced, the Germans would immediately be informed (the Russians would take care to advise them) and war would be inevitable. While he agreed that his views might change if war came and his back was to the wall, they were too strong to avoid a breakdown of negotiations.[87] News of the Non-Aggression Pact prompted the British to make a fresh demarche in Warsaw on August 23. Beck, now argued that the Russians had made right of entry a *sine quo non,* knowing it would not be granted, thus giving them an excuse to break off the negotiations, but he agreed to common action under certain circumstances. It was too late, however, for on August 25, two days after the signing of the Nazi-Soviet Pact, Voroshilov said it made no sense to continue the discussions.

After the Nazi-Soviet Pact, Beck asked that negotiations for an Anglo-Polish mutual assistance pact be speeded up with the hope that it would deter Hitler. On August 28 it was signed, and for the first time Poland extended her obligations to cover Belgium, Holland, Lithuania, Latvia and Estonia. But, even at this late date, under pressure of war with Germany and a possible German-Soviet deal, there was no provision with regard to Rumania except to put on record the unilateral obligations of both parties. While the Poles were probably correct in their view that the Balkan ability to help them was negligible, their reluctance to go south was a crucial element in the failure to obtain East European security, for that was a major plank of both the British and Soviet security systems, and it gave the Soviets the opportunity to ask for more and the Southeastern states another reason to maintain their neutrality.

Conclusion

Poland has received the major brunt of the blame in history for the failure of the Anglo-French-Soviet talks, particularly from the point of view that in not giving in to Soviet demands, Soviet security was placed in jeopardy.[88] Contrary to such views, it appears from this study that as Churchill observed, if indeed the Russian problem was security, the world was not Britain's to divvy up, and if they did, it would lead straight to war as if Moscow was given a free hand in East Europe, "tomorrow we would be

unable to protect what does belong to us."[89] And while much attention
has been given to Poland in the Anglo-Soviet talks, the Balkans were as
important if not more so, for from the beginning, the Soviets made, as a
condition for reciprocity, unconditional Soviet aid along the whole range
of their frontier, and they never really budged from that position. Likewise, the British were as careful to protect these states as they were Poland,
and their interests were greater there.

Nor was the problem even one of security for the Russians, for they
felt confident of their defensive position and would take an offensive
position in East Europe only if they were given some control from the
Baltic to the Black seas. In fact, the British were asking a great deal less
of the Russians, making a chimera of the argument that, for giving more
they must get more. In the final analysis, the Nazis and the West asked
for about the same thing—benevolent neutrality, but the Nazis were willing
to give more for that, and that the real issue for the Soviets was territory,
which gave them offensive security and fulfilled national and ideological
goals is evident in the record of the Anglo-French-Soviet negotiations.

In the negotiations with the West, the Soviet program was at odds on
every count with the aims of the West who wished neither to directly ally
themselves with the Soviet Union, aid in her defense, or enrich Soviet
power by any protection they might offer her by territorial aggrandizment
with East European or Balkan possessions. It is interesting that they gave
way on every issue, the tripartite and a military convention, all except
that of control of the interim states, which was at the heart of what they
were trying to defend not just against Germany, but against the Soviet
Union as well. In this sense, a second front was of secondary importance,
for they could have had it if they had given in to the Soviets on the issue
of the interim states. In essence, the Anglo-Franco-Soviet talks were as
clearly aimed at defining Soviet-Western aims and spheres in the Balkans
and Poland as were the Nazi-Soviet talks. And to have extended the Soviet
sphere would have been as antithetical to Western interests as it was to have
allowed a similar extension by the Germans. Any compromise that there
was on Britain's part, was due to fear of a Nazi-Soviet pact, hence the last
minute pressure on Poland to allow Soviet troop passage.

The question arises then, with such disparate interests, why were the
negotiations carried on at all? It would appear that at first, both the West
and the Soviets clearly wished it as a deterrent to Hitler. As the summer

wore on, however, the Soviets had another motive too, for as the Germans showed signs of interest in an agreement with Russia, the Soviets became certain that Hitler had decided on war and that deterrence was no longer an option, but now the negotiations gave them the necessary bargaining tool to pressure the Germans into, not only agreement, but possibly a price for agreement. This was an option closed to the West who, though they wished some sort of agreement with Russia, made it clear by the guarantees that unlike Munich, Poland, Rumania and Greece could not be bargained for. The German-Western battle lines were drawn in March and April, and this gave the USSR a key swing position. American sources particularly, point to the dual Soviet aim of bargaining power and deterrence, but not agreement in discussions with the West.[90]

In this regard, it was crucial for the Soviets to maintain a strong negotiating position with the West, for it was only through this that a dialectical situation pitting London against Berlin could be activated. The guarantees and Franco-British search for an East European front put the thesis-antithesis process into motion, for immediately the Soviet Union became important to the West, it threatened Germany, and the more ardently the Soviet-Western courtship was pursued, the more moved was Germany to approach Moscow and to be generous, in turn upping the ante for the British. What gave the Soviets the power to manipulate the dialectical framework to their advantage, was their lack of dependence on either side, afforded by a unique geopolitical positioning, sheer size, and myopic Communist idealism.

If the Soviet and Western positions were clearly drawn with respect to the Balkans and Poland, what of these states themselves? What was their position and contribution in the contest between the West and Germany for Soviet favor which ended in failure for the West? From the foregoing discussion it seems evident that, though the Poles and Rumanians were reluctant to be associated with the Soviet Union or to allow any Soviet infringement on their sovereignties, it was the divergence of British and Soviet aims in the Balkans and Poland which capped the negotiations' defeat. On every question, debate came back to the interim states, the Soviets wanting unconditional rights of intervention, the British denying them that. The Polish and Rumanian anti-Soviet behavior was a sidelight. At the basis of Polish and Rumanian reticence was a fear of provoking Germany. Hence, the Rumanians (and Poles) allowed that they would accept a Soviet guarantee, but wished only that they not be named, and they made it clear that, while they would accept no Soviet aid before war began, after, their position would be completely different. Likewise, they were reluctant to extend the provisions of the Rumanian-Polish agreement to include Germany, and as reinsurance against Soviet perfidy, they were unwilling to abrogate it. The British position was not unlike this, for while they wanted a limited association with the Soviet Union in order to deter Hitler and keep the Soviets from linking up with the Nazis, they did not want a fighting front in which the Soviets could make gains.

A more potent argument in prosecuting the guilt of Rumania and Poland than their reluctance to accept unconditional Soviet assistance, is that these small states, in shying away from intra-Balkan and Balkan-Polish reciprocity and declaring their neutrality, prevented the creation of a Western-backed Eastern front, which in turn created the need of the West to seek out Russia or at least to do so from a position unsupported by the interim states themselves. In doing this, the Soviets were not only given the tool they needed to negotiate with the Germans on a basis allowing them gains which the West could not or would not match, but it created the reason itself for such negotiations. In particular, the threat of a Balkan front would have made Hitler think twice about Poland. On the other hand, the weakness of the Balkan states and Poland and the inability of the West at that point to supply the necessary weaponry and troops, made them reticent to in any way provoke Germany or invite Moscow, though their major fears and stillborn rapprochement centered around war and the tangle of national antipathies which that could unravel. Hence the unrelenting attachment to neutrality and unilateralism.

Is there anything, then, which would have made the Soviets go to the side of the West? One suspects only a stronger Germany with an attack on the USSR in mind, or an earlier German alliance with Japan, both of which would have made the Soviets choose the West as the side to help and to accept the determination of the framework within which the Soviets would operate in East Europe. One suspects, that given the German alternative, even if the West had given the Soviets an unrestricted hand in the interim states, the Soviets would not have gone over to the West, first, because in not being the West's to give, precious Soviet military exposure would have been necessary, and second, because the German quid pro quos had the effect, not just of enriching Soviet power, but diminishing that of Germany.

And so, it seems, history is written with a certain inevitability, an obscure logic, and a dispensible but necessary tragedy. For one doubts, given the basic power positions of the time that history would have been different even if the West and the Soviet Union had reached agreement. For given Soviet aims and her power position, Hitler would have gotten Poland, the Soviet Union with or without its definition of indirect aggression and right of troop transfer would have been unable to prosecute an offensive war in the East, and the Balkans would have found their most advantageous position in neutrality and then with Germany. For it was Hitler who made history in 1939, and nowhere is this more evident than the creation of the Nazi-Soviet Non-Aggression Pact, for while the receptivity was in Moscow, the genesis of this was in Hitler's hands completely. It was the Nazi quest for neutrality, not the Soviet, which gave Moscow the ability to exploit the situation, choose sides, and accrue benefits.

CHAPTER VI

THE NAZI-SOVIET NON-AGGRESSION PACT
DETENTE IN THE BALKANS

The unsettled position in the East due to Franco-British activity, caused Germany to seek assurances of Soviet neutrality, and for this they were willing to allow the Soviet Union to temporarily assume some power position there. In seeking out the Soviet Union for this role, Hitler most likely regarded the Soviet Union as the weaker choice[1] with the idea that the Russian aggrandizement would be short-lived and that they could eventually be overwhelmed. But there were other reasons too, and these included the isolated position of Russia and the animosity felt by the East European states toward the Soviet Union, which could help to throw these small states back into the arms of Germany. In the meantime, a British-Soviet link would have been forestalled. The Pact, in not turning over territory except in Poland, implied that Germany needed the Soviet Union as a partner in neutralizing the Balkans and that the Soviets had a not dissimilar interest. For while German attention was in Poland and indeed until France was defeated and Germany could once again turn East, the German policy was for status quo in the Balkans and even more so once the war began, while the Soviets had been given time and a war which would weaken both their Balkan enemies.

The surprise with which popular sentiment greeted the Pact was due to several factors: first, the rapidity with which the Pact was achieved, particularly amidst the ongoing Soviet talks with the West; second, the ideological about-face it seemed to signal to a world conditioned to belligerent Bolshevik-Nazi rhetoric; and third, the false hopes harbored by many that such a pact would never materialize. Contrary to popular opinion, there were many who understood the advantages for the Communists of neutrality in a capitalist war, and that in their choice of sides, the Soviets too were counting on Germany being the weaker participant, enhancing the possibilities of an exhaustive war for the capitalist combatants.

Surprise that there was in the formulation of this Pact is, perhaps, better placed in the German camp than the Soviet one (though the idea can be found in *Mein Kampf*), for the Soviets, in linking themselves with the West during the 1930s, had already demonstrated their pragmatic capacity. But for Hitler, whose independent bellicosity had given the world the impression that he operated from a position of power and ideological purity, the Pact signalled a blatant weakness in the Nazi position and a betrayal of Nazism. The German need to secure their rear, brings to the fore one of the ironies of history, for it was the pressure of the British resistance particularly in the East which occasioned this need. Hence, the very success of the British program occasioned its greatest failure, for in threatening to deter Hitler, it promoted him to seek out a new ally.

Nowhere did the British program have more impact than in the Balkans, for while Poland had always followed a policy of neutrality, the British program turned the Balkan states from helpless puppets into states of independent will, questionable Nazi loyalty, and fickle neutrality. The increased danger of war was commensurate with the German need to satellitize the Balkans, and so Hitler sought a new source of pressure to bring them back into the fold. This Pact, which was completely devoid of sentiment and imbued with a sense of morality which was distasteful to the West, was not a tragedy for the Balkans in the sense that it betrayed them to Russia or made them again a puppet of Germany, for ironically, it produced a standoff in the area (even in regard to Italy), and it achieved for the Balkans what even the British program could not. It preserved their neutrality and kept the war from their land which would unleash what was feared most in the Balkans, the Pandora's box of wholesale revisionism. The tragedy came before the Pact, when the Soviet Union was elevated to a power position sufficient to reawaken the Eastern Question, and it came after when war did come to the Balkan lands ending in a Soviet victory.

The only way the course of history ultimately could have been altered, is if the power position and will of the West would have been sufficient to defeat both the Soviet Union and Germany. In 1939 it was not.

The Nazi-Soviet Negotiations

The lengthy and arduous Anglo-French-Soviet negotiations were matched by equally faltering Nazi-Soviet pourparlers, largely due to Stalin's expert use of dialectics, secretiveness, bluff, and dilatory tactics in which he successfully played London off against Berlin. Despite this, German documents suggest that Hitler never seriously questioned whether Stalin would agree to a pact or not. It was assumed he would. Nor did Hitler have any qualms about doing so himself, even amidst ferocious anti-Bolshevik Nazi propaganda and sentiment. However, his habit of taking one problem at a time and of isolating a particular victim, did not necessitate its serious consideration until Polish obstinance, Western resolve and Japanese and Spanish unilateralism[2] proved a deadly combination, driving him to take precautions alien to his swaggering self-confidence. And even then, it was not a precaution against Soviet action, as much as a countermove to prevent Soviet alliance with the West or benevolent neutrality, and to stabilize the Balkan situation, for as Ribbentrop told the Bulgarians in mid-July, Germany was indifferent as to whether or not Russia signed an agreement with the West, as they were convinced that owing to Russia's internal situation, Russia would not go to war.[3]

Hitler's confidence that the Soviets would dance to his fiddle and that he had the Russian situation well in hand, was evident as early as April 11 when, in his Directive to the Supreme Commanders of the Wehrmacht in preparation for "Operation While" against Danzig, he said, "intervention by Russia is not expected." On August 8, he told Csáky that "Bolshevism might put on a nationalist helmet,"[4] and on August 12-13 at Obersalzburg he told Ciano that Russia would not be willing to pull the chestnuts out of the fire for the Western Powers and that Stalin's position would be endangered as much by a "victorious Red Army as a defeated one." And, he added, the price would not be great, as Russia was at most interested in enlarging her access to the Baltic a little, and Germany had no objection to that.[5] To the German generals on August 14, Hitler noted that the Soviet Union well understood the need to destroy Poland, and that the Ukraine was not a problem because promise of delimitation of spheres was clearly in the Soviet interest.[6]

If Hitler was so confident in the Soviet desire for neutrality and the limited nature of Soviet territorial interests, why did he find it necessary to pin down the USSR by means of a pact and particularly a pact generous in its quid pro quo, when it was at the risk of losing possible anti-Bolshevik allies, alienating the German people, and further perplexing the Italians, possibly even spurring them on to further action in the Balkans to protect their interests there? In his letter to Mussolini on August 25, 1939, he listed some of his reasons—the general situation of world politics, the necessity of securing a clear statement of position from the Japanese Cabinet, the fact that relations with Poland had grown worse due to England, and the favorable attitude of Russia which had been evident since the departure of Litvinov.

Then Hitler singled out the need for reinsurance against Russia and the pacification of the Balkans when he said that "through these arrangements the favorable attitude of Russia in case of any conflict is assured," and then he underlined his statement that *"the possibility of the entry of Rumania into such a conflict no longer exists."* In the next paragraph he wrote:

> Even Turkey under these circumstances can only envision a revision of her previous position. But I repeat once more, *that Rumania is no longer in a situation to take part in a conflict against the Axis.* [The underlining was Hitler's.] [7]

In the same vein, to his Commanders he noted the need to insure Balkan neutrality in the absence of occupation, for Italy was weak and therefore "operations were not feasible in the future."[8]

Reinsurance against Russia and pacification of the Balkans were not unconnected in Hitler's mind, and both were the direct result of British and French policy. In a speech on July 19, 1940 justifying the Pact in the fact of the Soviet takeover of Bessarabia, Hitler said:

> The Russo-German relations are definitely regulated. The main reason for this regulation was that, supported by small powers, England and France uninterruptedly charged Germany with plans of conquest

that were wholly beyond any interest of Germany. It was stated that
Germany would occupy the Ukraine, that Rumania was threatened,
and finally they even feared Turkey.

Under these conditions I thought it proper to reach a sober understanding of interests with Russia in order to determine once and for
all what Germany believed it should regard as its area of interests for
the future, and what Russia, on the other hand, regarded as important for existence. . . .[9]

Hitler's policy was, in effect, the divide-and-rule principle used so effectively to regulate Balkan policy before, this time by the way of Russia
rather than Hungary and Bulgaria, both of which were too volatile, unstable and unreliable to secure Rumanian neutrality. By this route too,
he hoped to negate Turkish perfidy and turn Ankara away from the West
back to a more neutral position. Others concurred in Hitler's assessment
of the effect such a pact would have on the Balkans. The German Ambassador in Rome, Mackensen, telegraphed Ribbentrop on August 25 expressing his view that:

Consideration for Bessarabia would paralyze Rumania's freedom of
movement in favor of Poland in the case of conflict. Thus Rumania
would be left to the Hungarians.[10]

And he agreed "that Turkey would not have to revise its attitude." Mussolini, in his letter to Hitler on August 25, wrote similarly, to the effect
that "The Moscow treaty muzzles Rumania and can alter the position of
Turkey. . . ."[11] That the Soviet Union had a similar interest was implicit
in Hitler's reasoning.

Hitler was actively supported in his approach to Russia by the German
diplomatic and military corps who for their own reasons wanted rapprochement. The diplomats wished to avoid German isolation and the military
to avoid a two-front war, both of which had been so costly to Germany
in the past. The dean of the German diplomatic corps in Moscow, von
Schulenburg, was of this old school which believed in *Realpolitik* and
Bismarckian diplomacy, and so he played down Communism and played
up the Soviet lack of strength and fear of Germany, certain that the Soviets did not want involvement and that Litvinov's policy of collective

security was only to stiffen Western resistance.[12] Meanwhile German economic ministers were emphasizing the German need for raw materials from the Soviet Union, and more important the danger of a Franco-Soviet alliance which would keep Germany away from Soviet raw materials and manpower.

Until Munich impetus for contact with Russia had come largely from the German diplomatic corps and one can only speculate that had Hitler followed his diplomats' rather than his own instincts and concluded a non-agression pact in late 1938 or early 1939 when the low point of Anglo-French resistance was reached, the terms of the Pact would have been less costly. As it was, Hitler's attention turned to Russia only when the object was Poland. The rapprochement idea was speeded up after Munich not necessarily to reach agreement, but in order to make Poland submit, and was possible due to Soviet isolation and the seeming security of the Chamberlain-Daladier appeasement governments. In October, 1938 the Germans and Soviets agreed to restrain press and propaganda attacks against each other, and by the end of the year Germany, due largely to a raw materials weakness, had taken the initiative in expanding the Russo-German trade mission, a move which had been met with an encouraging response on the Russian side in order to press Poland and the West to their side.[13] Meanwhile, on the diplomatic front there were signs of rapprochement too. At a January 12, 1939 reception of the Diplomatic Corps, Hitler paused and talked for quite awhile with Soviet Ambassador in Berlin, Merekalov, an encounter which was commented on by his Russian colleagues in Berlin and mentioned by Potemkin to Grzybowsky.[14] And a week later *Pravda* reprinted items from the London *News Chronicle* reporting a coming rapprochement.

The Germans planned that after political negotiations were successfully concluded in Poland, Schnurre would then go on to Moscow for purely economic negotiations (since a Polish-German agreement would neutralize Russia). In the German scheme to tie Germany and Poland together, the Germans planned to pay Poland off with the Soviet Ukraine. "We are interested," said Ribbentrop to Beck, "in the Soviet Russian Ukraine only to the extent that we inflict damage on Russia everywhere we could, just as she did on us." He went on to say that:

I could well imagine that in the course of an agreement . . . we may
very well be moved to regard the Ukrainian question as covered by
a special Polish perogative and support Polish aims in every way in
dealing with the question.[15]

The Russians seemed well aware of the point of Ribbentrop's Warsaw visit,
for Litvinov warned the Poles to expedite their own negotiations with the
USSR in order to forestall German intrigue. The Poles for their part continued to try to maintain a policy of balance by declining both the German and Russian proposals, at the same time forestalling a Nazi-Soviet
deal at their expense by leaking the story of Schnurre's visit to Moscow.[16]

Unfortunately, while Polish policy momentarily stalled a Nazi-Soviet
rapprochement, its failure to accommodate itself to Hitler made a Nazi
approach to the Soviets all the more necessary. The Soviets obviously
understood this and so they showed no rebuff at the Schnurre snub. Thus,
by the end of February, the economic negotiations were begun anew with
Mikoyan agreeing to deliver raw materials to the full extent. But the Russians asked also for a larger credit, and by early March the economic negotiations foundered over the basic incompatibility of political and economic
interests whereby Russia needed raw materials for her own economic and
military development and wished not to enrich the power of Germany,
while Germany needed her own material and was likewise reluctant to
see Russia's power increased by German supplies. Despite the fact that
the economic negotiations lacked real substance for political reasons, the
Russians, as was their habit, continued to use the economic link with the
Germans to further political aims. Stalin in his March 10 speech referred
to the development of economic relations hoping thereby to threaten the
West and keep the door open to Berlin. Likewise, the Germans for political reasons decided to put them off, for with Czechoslovakia in mind,
they needed to soften up the West.

Though the German diplomatic corps in early April tended to believe
that the Soviets distrusted the West and protected by the guarantees
meant to "remain neutral in a capitalist war and thereby increase its own
strength vis-a-vis Nazism,"[17] the opening of direct Soviet-Western discussions on April 15 posed a potential threat to Nazi designs for a neutral
Russia and for Balkan pacification. More important it bulwarked the Soviets into a number of cautious advances to the Germans from which they

could easily withdraw or use against the West, and it enabled the Soviets to make claims as to territorial interests. In mid-April the Ambassador of the Soviet Union in Berlin, Merekalov, made a demarche stating that in case of aggression against Finland, Estonia, Latvia or Lithuania, the USSR would intervene, which was a careful identification of interests conflicting with neither German nor allied interests or spheres.

Then on April 17 he called on Weizsäcker. His excuse was to inquire with regard to delivery of Russian orders from Skoda, but in the conversation he went on to discuss German-Soviet relations, noting that ideological differences do not affect relations between countries, for example between Italy and the Soviet Union, and the same was possible with Germany.[18]

On May 3 Litvinov was replaced and a concrete move on Germany's part followed. Schnurre told Soviet Charge Astakhov on May 5 that Soviet contracts with Skoda would be fulfilled and that Astakhov's request that economic negotiations be resumed, would be examined. When he asked if Molotov's appointment would result in any shift in policy, Astakhov's reply that Molotov was not a specialist in foreign affairs, Schnurre wrote, had significance.[19]

A few day after this visit, Schnurre and German Counsellor of the German Embassy in Moscow, Hilger, were summoned to Hitler to give an account of the situation in Russia. According to Hilger, Hitler quizzed him as to whether or not a Soviet-German link was possible and then he asked Hilger to assess how things looked in Russia. Hilger was evasive and pondering, answering to the effect that Bolshevism was dangerous but could be neutralized by political and economic ties, that the strength of the Soviet Union had increased but that the purges had weakened her, and that Stalin was erecting a new state on patriotism not Communism. Hitler's reaction to Hilger's recital was that the German diplomat had fallen prey to Communist propaganda, but that if he was right, then there was a need to take measures to dilute her strength.[20] Apparently Hitler's confidence in Soviet real and diplomatic weakness was slowly being eroded away, and therefore, that a pact to neutralize her and prevent her from going to the West would be necessary.

On the heels of this conversation, the Anglo-Turkish Declaration was signed and so Ribbentrop, who was presumably reflecting Hitler's views, instructed Schulenburg to use extreme caution, but to feel out Molotov on a Schnurre visit. In his instructions, Ribbentrop told Schulenburg to show no concern over the Ango-French-Soviet negotiations.[21] On May 20 Schulenburg wired the results of his interview, reporting that Molotov had stated that:

> The Soviet Government could only agree to resumption of the nego-
> tiations (economic) if the necessary 'political basis' for them had
> been constructed.[22]

On the basis of this reply, State Secretary Weizsäcker, fearful that the pro-posal would be used by the Kremlin to exert pressure on England and France, instructed Schulenburg to sit tight to see if the Soviets would speak more freely. On the other hand, he stated, "we sooner or later must take some action," and he noted how difficult it was to learn anything about the English-French-Soviet negotiations.[23]

In the next week, pressure on the German side for negotiations with Russia increased due to Hitler's May 23 announcement of an attack on Poland at the earliest date and Chamberlain's May 24 statement in Parlia-ment to the effect that Anglo-Russian negotiations had produced agree-ment on essentials. At the same time, the signing of the Pact of Steel on May 22 gave them some leverage. But there was debate over how to ap-proach the Soviets. Ribbentrop advocated a forthright carrot and stick approach, offering threats of German power and Western perfidy along-side concessions along the lines of assurances of peaceful aims, quid pro quos and promotion of a Japanese-Russian rapprochement, but Weiz-säcker urged caution, a course Hitler adopted because of doubts that conciliation with Japan was possible.[24] It was decided to use Hilger's return to the Soviet Union to resume economic negotiations as a starting point for discussions of political nature but even this seemed too forward, so the plan was scrapped and replaced with the idea of talking with Soviet Charge Astakhov in Berlin, using the Soviet request for maintenance of a trade delegation in Prague as a pretext for political clarification. The agenda was to include as a prerequisite, Soviet recision of a foreign policy which included world revolution and ascertainment of whether the stage of negotiations with the West allowed the Soviets to negotiate with Ger-many, for above all, the Germans wanted to obtain information prior to embarking on a course which would simply deliver the Soviets to the West.[24]

According to Weizsäcker, Astakhov "pricked up his ears," when he was told that Germany did not wish the matter to follow the course of January whereby the German trade negotiations were cancelled. But, he warned, that since this is true, Soviet Trade Delegation hopes in Prague were affected by Soviet relations with Great Britain. Astakhov was noncommittal in his answer to this. Weizsäcker then went a step further and tried to dispel Soviet fears of German anti-Soviet designs by saying that normalization in relations with Poland had been obstructed by Beck, and that the "German policy toward the Ukraine was refuted by the German conduct in the case of the Carpatho-Ukraine, but this also produced no comment.[25] The Soviet answer to both the British and French proposal of May 27 and the German feeler of May 30 came by way of Molotov's May 31 speech to the Supreme Soviet, in which he conceded that while progress had been made in negotiations with the West, no agreement had been reached covering guarantees of a reciprocal nature to all countries bordering on the Soviet Union, and that in the meantime, trade negotiations with Germany were not out of the question.[26]

On June 9 the Soviet Union agreed to Schnurre's visit under certain conditions. The lack of prompt and positive response on Stalin's part seems to have frustrated Hitler, and the knowledge that the Soviets could no longer be intimidated and were negotiating from a position of considerable strength, must have harmed his ego. Therefore, at the end June, a Memo from Berghof stated that Hitler had decided that in view of the Russian answer of June 9, Germany was not interested in the resumption of economic discussions. And Weizsäcker believed that enough had been done for the moment, perhaps hoping to call the Soviets' bluff.[27]

From mid-June until mid-July when the Soviets were thick in negotiation with the West, the German diplomats tried to ascertain Russian motivation and price. They noted the *Pravda* statements regarding the importance of the Baltic states to Soviet security, and they learned from a conversation between Bulgarian Foreign Minister Dragonov and Soviet Charge Astakhov, that if Germany declared she would not attack the Soviet Union, that Moscow would conclude a non-aggression pact with Germany and probably refrain from concluding a treaty with Britain. And they were certain that Astakhov had correctly reported home Weizsäcker's statements of May 31 regarding the German wish for rapprochement and that the Soviet Union had to make a choice. But they were also aware that the

Soviets were playing a political game and that they were presently "riding a high horse" due to the negotiations with the West.[28] The opposing Soviet contention that the Germans were playing a political game, German Charge Tippelskirch interpreted as reflecting the Soviet's true opinion as well as being a matter of tactics.[29]

Finally, in mid-July when it appeared the British and French were not going to give on the issue of the interim states, Mikoyan ordered his Soviet trade representative in Berlin, Barbarin, to tell Schnurre that he could sign an economic treaty in Berlin and that points of discussion could be cleared up. Weizsäcker immediately instructed Schnurre to act in a "forthright manner" in the economic negotiations, and with respect to the political negotiations, he empowered Schulenburg to pick up the political threads, and if approached by the Japanese, to downplay Japanese-Soviet differences.[30] From here on things moved rapidly on both the political and economic front. (On July 23 the British agreed to simultaneous signature of a military and political tripartite pact.) On July 26 at a dinner party in Berlin given by Schnurre for Astakhov, the conversation passed quickly to political discussions and the bargaining point of mutual accommodation in East Europe. Schnurre outlined three stages in which negotiations might transpire: 1) reestablishment of collaboration in the economic field, 2) normalization and increased political negotiations, and 3) reestablishment of good political relations along the lines of the Berlin Treaty[31] or a new arrangement.

Astakhov answered that negotiations must be slow and gradual, as a reversal of German belligerency was hard to believe. He mentioned as menacing to the Soviet Union, German relations with Japan, Munich, and the free hand gained in East Europe, and that Germany

> . . . regarded the Baltic states and Finland, as well as Rumania, as our sphere of interest, which had completed the Soviet Government's feeling of being menaced.[32]

Schnurre countered that German aims were in a different direction, against Great Britain and Poland, not the Soviet Union, and that the true German intent in Finland and the Baltic countries was shown by the non-aggression pacts, and that friendship with Japan was not directed against the Soviet Union. Furthermore, said Schnurre, good relations with Germany were barred by the Soviet relations with Great Britain and that the Soviet Union must choose. Then he asked:

> What could Britain offer Russia? At best participation in a European war and the hostility of Germany, hardly a desirable end for Russia. What could Germany offer against this—neutrality and keeping out of a possible European conflict. And if Moscow wished, a German-Russian undertaking on mutual interest which, just as in former times, would work out to the advantage of both countries.[33]

Schnurre's conclusion regarding the conversation was that the Soviets had not yet decided what to do, hoping to deter important decisions with both the British and French. By this time, anxiety in Berlin was begining to show. Schnurre, in a secret addendum to Schulenburg, noted that "Politically the problem of Russia is, being dealt with here with *extreme urgency,*" and that Ribbentrop and Hitler had daily conversations on the subject hoping to obtain results as soon as possible, both on the negative side ("disturbing British negotiations") and on the positive side ("an understanding with us").[34]

Therefore, on August 2, 1939 Ribbentrop himself received Astakhov, at which time he hinted at the possibility of an agreement with Russia on the fate of Poland, and then he made a sweeping statement to the effect that "from the Baltic to the Black Sea there was no problem which could not be solved to our mutual satisfaction." This was obviously a bribe, for when Astakhov several times attempted to pin him down to more concrete terms, Ribbentrop gave him to understand that that could be done only when there was a fundamental remoulding of relations, the basis of which was noninterference in internal affairs and abandonment of a policy directed against German vital interests (presumably negotiations with the English and French). On the same day Schulenburg had his interview with Molotov in Moscow which turned into a sparring match over the good intent of both parties, and produced no results.[35]

Rumors of British concessions to the Soviets[36] and the pressure of the coming Nazi move on Poland, cause more anxiety in Berlin, and so Schulenburg was ordered to refute rumored arguments that after defeating Poland the Germans might offer the Western powers "a separate peace to obtain a free hand in the East," and to threaten that if Russia chose the side of Britain, she would face Germany alone as in 1914. In Berlin Schnurre arranged another interview with Astakhov (August 10) wherein he asked the Russian how he viewed the Polish question and then urged Russia to come to an agreement with Germany. To Schnurre's disgust, on August 12, the same day the Anglo-French military mission arrived in Moscow, Astakhov suggested that discussions should be undertaken in degrees.[37]

This was not the word from Moscow, however, for on the same day as Hitler and Ribbentrop were at Obersalzburg telling a shocked Ciano about their Polish plans, they received word that the Russians had agreed to a German being sent to Moscow for political negotiations. Ribbentrop immediately instructed Schulenburg to arrange an interview with Molotov for August 15, and at that time to make haste toward a speedy clarification of Russo-German relations. But at the scheduled interview (the day after Voroshilov had put the "cardinal" question to the English and French), the Soviet Foreign Minister treated the trip in a dilatory fashion though he went on to inquire as to the German views on a non-aggression pact, joint guarantee of the Baltic, and whether Germany was prepared to influence Japan toward better Russo-Japanese relations. Ribbentrop hastily instructed Schulenburg to answer Molotov's three questions in the affirmative (there was no offsetting demand to the effect that Russia forego a pact with the West), and to state that speedy clarification was desirable due to the seriousness of events.[38]

At eight p.m. on August 17 Schulenburg told Molotov that Germany was ready to grant the Soviet requests but Molotov again stalled, reading a reply to the effect that before Ribbentrop came, the trade and credit agreement would have to be signed, that a non-aggression pact with a special protocol defining interests would have to be concluded, that a Ribbentrop visit would have to be thoroughly prepared, and that he disliked publicity. Then he suggested that both governments prepare drafts of non-aggression pacts.[39] On August 19 full agreement was reached in Berlin on the text of a Credit and Economic Agreement, giving to the Soviets additional orders to the amount of 200 million RM in exchange for raw materials for Germany and including a Confidential Trade Protocol with provisions for arbitration, visiting of factories, and so forth, but the Soviets delayed signing the treaty until the next day under pretext of waiting instructions from Moscow.

On the same day, August 19 (two days after the Russians had adjourned the military conference with the West *sine die* until the West cleared the "cardinal" question), Schulenburg had two interviews with Molotov, the first one producing no results. Schulenburg was called back later, presumably at Stalin's intervention, wherein Molotov stated that Ribbentrop could come to Moscow on August 26 and 27, and he then proceeded to present a Soviet draft of a Non-Aggression Pact. The next day, August 20, Hitler, in a telegram to be given to Stalin at once, accepted the Soviet draft of a non-aggression pact, and stated that the question of a supplementary protocol could be quickly clarified when the ministers conversed. Hitler then proposed that Ribbentrop be received no later than August 23, a request which Stalin agreed to on August 21 (the day Voroshilov adjourned the Anglo-French negotiations with the statement they could be readjourned any time if a positive answer was forthcoming).[40]

Hitler gave Ribbentrop full powers to negotiate a treaty and "all related questions," and to sign any agreements resulting from the negotiations. He flew from Berlin to Moscow arriving at 1 p.m., on August 23. He met with Stalin and Molotov at the Kremlin in the afternoon and, during a three-hour discussion agreed to a non-aggression pact with a secret supplementary protocol defining spheres. The Germans were evidently prepared to give way to any obstacle which presented itself in favor of the Soviet Union, acquiescing in the Soviet text of the accompanying communique which played up the Soviet Union as a peacemaker and initiator of the proposals,[41] and accepting the Soviet draft proposal for a treaty almost in toto.[42] The only controversy that came up was whether Hitler would agree that the two Baltic ports of Libau and Windau would be in the Soviet sphere. Hitler immediately complied, and then further consented to a change of phrase in the preamble concerning friendly Soviet-German relations which Stalin did not see how he could so suddenly present to the public "after they had been covered with pails of manure by the Nazi Government for six years."[43]

During the night of August 23-24 Ribbentrop, Stalin and Molotov met again and, according to German documents,[44] in a banquet style atmosphere, discussed a wide range of questions including Russo-Japanese relations, animosity felt toward Great Britain by all three statesmen, and France which Stalin considered strong but Ribbentrop considered weak. During the conversations, Stalin showed a particular concern over Italian aspirations in the Balkan area. He asked whether Italy's aims extended beyond Albania, the annexation of which seemed to him of "no particular value to Italy." "Had Italy aspirations for Greek territory?" he asked.

Ribbentrop replied to the effect that Albania was important to Italy for strategic reasons. Moreover, Mussolini was a strong man who "could not be intimidated," and Il Duce had welcomed the Nazi-Soviet rapprochement. Stalin's line of questioning seems to have implied that he believed Germany had granted the Italians some interest in the Balkans, and that there was some reinsurance against Germany in this for Moscow as long as Hitler could control Italy and maintain Balkan pacification and neutrality, in effect making the Non-Aggression Pact possible without a division of spheres there. On the other hand, Ribbentrop's response suggests also that if Stalin's query was in search of a sphere there, the Germans meant to hold firm in their support of the surrogate Italians which provided some shield for the Germans in the Southeast as well. Finally, Stalin asked what Ribbentrop thought about Turkey. Ribbentrop replied that Turkey had been one of the first to join the encirclement front despite German efforts. Stalin and Molotov offered that the Soviet Union "had also had unfortunate experiences with the vacillating policy of the Turks," and then everyone agreed that it was basically England's fault for pouring money into Turkey to encourage propaganda against Germany.

Many toasts were drunk during the nocturnal meeting, Molotov and Stalin drinking repeatedly to the new era of Russo-German relations and to the German nation. At one point, Molotov raised his glass to Stalin and remarked that it had been Stalin, "through his speech of March 10, which had been well understood in Germany," who had introduced a reversal of political relations. At about midnight the Non-Aggression Pact and Secret Protocol were signed, and at 1 p.m. on August 24 Ribbentrop phoned the news to Hitler. On August 24 at 1:30 p.m., Ribbentrop left Moscow after having in less than 24 hours, done what the British never did accomplish in months of negotiations.

* * * * *

Authors disagree in their analysis as to who was the major protagonist in the Pact's culmination and as to the inevitability of the link.[45] Certainly the preceding discussion serves to emphasize the importance of British policy particularly as it related to control of the interim states.

In the first place, both sides considered an agreement only if an agreement with Great Britain was not forthcoming; for the Germans that meant British acquiescence in their plans against Poland, and for the Soviets it meant British agreement to a Soviet sphere in the Balkans and East Europe as the price for benevolency in the West's war, and it was the failure of the British to give in on the territorial issues that brought the Fascist and Communist competitors in the East together. Second, the Anglo-Soviet negotiations process provided a tactical threat with regard to raising and lowering the price for agreement as well as a strategic threat, in that agreement with Great Britain would have altered the balance of power to the disadvantage of the other. Basically it was the Anglo-Soviet negotiations and Hitler's aims in Poland which set the pace of the negotiations, first securing Russia to make initial advances to the Nazis, and then pushing the Nazis toward an agreement with Moscow. Even the Pact itself was not intended as a final quest by the Nazis and Soviets but rather as another pressure on Britain to make her submit to the original demand. That it did not, was the Pact's failure for both, making them dependent on uncertain intentions of an unreliable relationship and the working out of the specifics in regard to Poland, Turkey and the Southeast in general.

The Pact was neither spontaneous, inevitable, nor a natural symbiosis of interests, but was a product of an evolutionary development whereby Anglo-Soviet talks combined with Hitler's aims against Poland gave the Soviets the power to negotiate a treaty with some safeguards and other opportunities. But it was not foolproof, and despite rhetoric both then and now that mutual suspicions prevented an Anglo-Franco-Soviet Pact, both the Nazis and the Soviets signed a pact which was underwritten with suspicions at least equal to if not greater than those espoused by their opposite. In fact, the Nazis were more willing than the West to appreciate the dialectics of a capitalist war and its relationship to the progress of Communism, while the Soviets in their quest to secure their borders, indicated their belief that, sooner or later, the heartland theory must be fulfilled. No sooner than the ink was dry on this treaty than both sides began to solidify their positions, the Soviets distributing Communist leaflets in Bessarabia and Germany speeding up armament deliveries to Rumania in order that Rumania would be better equipped to resist Russian aggression.

In the process of working out this treaty, it became clear that in the absence of a treaty with Britain and in the presence of war, certain short-term interests of both parties could be well served by such an arrangement. Important among them was the stabilization of the interim state bloc, for any alteration in borders particularly in the volatile Balkan area could have set off a certain chain reaction, a Balkan explosion and a Nazi-Soviet war, which was above all what this Pact was trying to avoid. With the Soviets on one side and the Nazis on the other, the area was largely im-mobilized and so in turn was Italy. Beyond that, a stable area insured to Germany a steady source of supplies and a one-front war, and to the Soviets a capitalist war away from their borders and time to arm and maneuver. As it turned out, the fluid part of the treaty, Bessarabia, was the nexus around which the carefully set domino patter began to unfold.

The Nature of the Pact in the Balkans

In terms of the Balkans, the title of the Pact, "non-aggression," is in-complete in that it was also a pact of mutual interest and war, whereby the mutual need for pacification of the area led to a fragile detente with regard to spheres while promoting war elsewhere. Neither the Soviet Un-ion nor Germany wished to open a front there, nor did either wish to see British power there. Presumably, Hitler's belief that the Pact would stop Balkan slippage to the West and bring them toward Germany, was in the Soviet interest as well. Hence the linkup between the mutual interest and non-aggression factors of the Pact, which was the basis for detente.

The Pact which the two parties signed at midnight of August 23-24 pro-vided that the two parties would undertake not only to refrain from any aggressive action against each other (Article I), but also to refrain from supporting any third power with which the other party might be at war (Article II), and from participating in any grouping of Powers aimed directly against the other power (Article IV). Analysts of the treaty note both then and now, that this treaty omitted two provisions which had been included in every other non-aggression pact the Soviets had hereto-fore signed—first, that it would not enter into force until being ratified rather than signed, and second, that it would become inoperative if one of the parties attacked a third country. In this sense, the treaty was not a non-aggression pact but an aggression pact of mutual interest, for it allowed Germany to attack Poland without Soviet interference and it fit nicely into Communist ideology theory that the Capitalists should fight it out while the Soviet Union remained neutral.

If the Balkans are fit into this framework, it would theoretically mean that the Germans would be allowed to fight it out with the British there with all the blessings of Soviet neutrality. However, since the treaty also provided, in Article III, that consulation would take place in matters of mutual interest, there was some implication that such action could not be taken without Soviet consent, and perhaps even with some territorial revision.[46] Certainly the Soviet expression of political interest in Bessarabia agreed to by the Germans meant that, at least in that territory, mutual interest must be respected.

In the Secret Additonal Protocol to the Treaty, the Baltic states and Finland were awarded to the Soviet Union and a line of demarcation was to be drawn across Poland. The Balkan states were treated in the following way:

> With regard to South-Eastern Europe, the Soviet side emphasizes its interest in Bessarabia. The German side declares complete political *desinteressement* in these territories.

In effect the treaty was vague with regard to the Bessarabian irredenta implying Soviet rights and acknowledging Soviet political interest and possibly cession at a later date (presumably to be determined by Hitler). At the same time there is the implication that Hitler maintained his economic rights in Bessarabia (the Danube) as well as political and economic rights to the rest of the Balkans. However, the very silence of the treaty in regard to the Balkans illustrates the great sensitivity and complexity of the area to both sides, both because of its internal structure and because it involved the interests of Britain and Italy as well. On the other hand, the obscure nature of the agreement in this area for the moment served both parties well, for it implied the maintenance of peace in the area where an overt definition of spheres would have led to irreconciliable conflicts of interest.

From the German side, the basis for this detente was both military and political. The Soviets had already expressed and the Germans had accepted, a negotiable German interest in all the states along her frontier. Hitler's generosity regarding the Baltic states was based on the belief that Soviet control of those areas could make Poland play into his hands and that there was little danger if the Soviets controlled these states.[47] Based on Hitler's statements to his commanders, it is unlikely that Hitler would have gone any further than he did in signing away the Balkans due to his need to control the Danube, his need for Rumanian oil, and his need to maintain the exclusion of the West and war from the area, which in the wake of the guarantees, could only be accomplished by pressuring the Balkans themselves into neutrality by using the Russian bogey and by neutralizing the Soviet Union itself. On the other hand, Hitler was in a hurry to get the Pact signed and at the moment was above all playing counterpoint to the British and French in their negotiations with the Soviets. So it is very likely that Ribbentrop's statement to Wolcott in Berlin in early December to the effect that Germany had accepted from Russia conditions similar to those offered by Russia to Britain, for example, "a free hand in the Baltic and practically a free hand in the Balkans"[48] was an accurate reflection of exactly what Hitler was willing to give to Russia temporarily in order to keep the British out.

The need for exclusion of the British was emphasized when Weizsäcker informed the Embassy in the Soviet Union on August 23 (while Ribbentrop was deep in conversation with the Soviets) that Hitler wished to put on record that East European problems were to be regarded as belonging "exclusively to the spheres of interest of Germany and the USSR."[49] Though this could have been directed against the Italians, it seems unlikely that this was the case in view of the fact that Hitler considered himself the stronger partner and the Pact of Steel formally, if not otherwise, bound the two countries to concordant action. More likely, it was an answer to a report by the German Press Department that the Soviet authorities on the same day (August 23) had stated that the Non-Aggression Pact with Germany was not incompatible with continuation of the Anglo-French military negotiations and conclusion of a Three Power Pact,[50] (a point that Molotov had in fact made to the French Ambassador in a conversation on August 22, though he also reiterated that such an alliance could not be accomplished as long as Poland refused Soviet military assistance).[51] It is conceivable that the Soviets hoped to conclude a pact with the West and also to gain protection and right to the rest of the East European frontier, which was a concession that the West might now make as she faced the conclusion of a Nazi-Soviet Pact. Hitler, in his statement, put on record that any third power in the Balkans and by the treaty collusion thereof, would violate the treaty.

The magnanimity Hitler displayed toward the Soviets in the treaty, particularly with regard to Bessarabia, was based on his view of German strength which he believed was sufficient to control the Soviets and Italians, and hence to direct the affairs of the Southeast and to counter the British there. The U.S. Military Attache in Yugoslavia reported in December 1939 that the Germans had informed him that if England and France made any move to assist Rumania if Russia attacked, that Germany would immediately attack and through Hungary, and thus the Balkan phase of the war is on, which the allies would avoid until Italy was disposed of.[52] And the German Military Attache in Bucharest said:

> The Russians will not occupy Bessarabia as long as Germany is strong enough. However, should we suffer a serious setback, or have all of our forces engaged, Russia might take advantage of a rare opportunity which may not occur for a long time. As it is now, it will not even come to a showdown between Russia and Germany in this matter.[53]

That the Germans depended on strength and not an agreement to control the Soviets is evident in offers to furnish Turkey and Rumania with supplies to reinforce the Soviet frontier.[54]

In June, 1940 when Germany had its back turned to Russia, was heavily engaged in the West, and most in need of Balkan pacification (at the very moment it was waning), the Soviets, believing they had the Germans over a barrel,[55] proceeded to unilaterally fulfill their interpretation of claims to Bessarabia at the risk of war and destabilization of the Southeast, whereupon Hitler berated Ribbentrop for his carelessness in frameworking the respective Nazi-Soviet spheres in the Balkans. (In a speech for public consumption on July 19 he said that "Germany did not make a move outside of its area of interest nor did Russia.") In his reply to Hitler dated June 24, 1940, Ribbentrop gave the following explanation for the last clause of the Secret Protocol.

> I stated orally our disinterestedness in the Bessarabian question. However, in order not to put down explicitly in *written form* the recognition of the Russian claim to Bessarabia because of the possibility of indiscretion with which we had to count in view of the

then still very vague German-Russian relationship, I chose a formulation of a *general nature* for the Protocol. This was done in such a
way that when the Southeastern European problems were discussed,
I declared very generally that Germany was politically disinterested
in 'these areas,' i.e., in the Southeast of Europe. The economic interest of Germany in these Southeastern European territories was
duly stressed by me.

Ribbentrop went on to say that the provisions were "in accordance with
the general instructions given by the Führer for Southeastern Europe,"
which went "as far as Constantinople and the Straits" if necessary.[56]

There is little doubt that Ribbentrop took some liberties with Hitler's
instructions, for there is no written record of those Ribbentrop referred
to,[57] and in a speech before his Commanders on August 22, he intimated
that he had the Balkan situation under control even without the Soviets,
saying Yugoslavia was tied down by Albania and infected with the "fatal
germs of decay because of her internal situation," that Rumania was vulnerable and open to attack by Bulgaria and Hungary, and that Turkey
had no leadership. If blockaded, Hitler said, "we can use the Danube."[58]
On the other hand, Ribbentrop was probably quite right in suggesting
that the vague nature of the treaty with regard to the Southeast and the
Bessarabian concession was, perhaps, the only way a treaty could have
been signed due to the basically conflicting interests in the area and the
need to emphasize the commonality of interest in pacification rather than
points of conflict. And there is no doubt that Hitler was pressed in his
negotiations with the Soviets in 1939, that his territorial liberalism was
based on the most optimistic predictions of Nazi strength and Soviet
weakness and timidity, that he found the treaty acceptable at the time,
and that while aware of the necessity to control the East, he was apt to
forget the vague and future trade-offs he had made in the area to Italy in
the Pact of Steel and to the Soviet Union in the Non-Aggression Pact.

Nazi statements in the immediate aftermath of the treaty exuded
triumph. The German press labeled it a blow to encirclement, and Hitler
considered his victory so great that, on the morning of the 25th, he rang
up his press bureau for news of the Cabinet crisis in London and Paris
which would lead to a new round of appeasement by the English and
French, and Polish capitulation. "Now," he declared, "I have the world

in my pocket."[59] On the same day, he wrote a letter to Mussolini in which he emphasized the muzzling of Rumania and the neutralization of Turkey.[60] What was not mentioned, however, was how the Pact muzzled Italy as well, for the Italians were unlikely to move unless the Balkans were threatened by England, France or Russia which the Pact also made unlikely.

Among the German military and diplomatic corps there was a certain amount of victorious rhetoric to the effect that the Pact was an instrument of peace which would cause the West to counsel Poland into compromise, but smouldering underneath was the feeling that agreement with the Kremlin had been an act of desperation, disastrous and damaging in the long run in the power it gave Russia.[61] With this in mind, Weizsäcker emphasized in his instructions to missions abroad that the act was needed to ward off a Soviet pact with the West, and that it was not an expression of friendship for the Soviet Union or capitulation, but rather of control in the East.[62] For Balkan consumption, von Papen also emphasized the peaceful results of the Pact particularly as it related to Italy and the Soviet Union, but wishing to predetermine British guilt and to hang the threat of Italian action over Balkan heads should they deviate in the least from the field of neutrals, von Papen said that Italy would not move unless and until Great Britain and France moved.[63]

Thus, for the Germans it was hoped that the Pact would do three things in the Balkans: 1) frighten Britain into further appeasement in East Europe particularly in Poland and very likely in the other guaranteed states as well; 2) push particularly Rumania but also Turkey and the rest of the Balkans away from the West into either a pro-German or neutral position; and 3) provide a more secure Balkan status quo, including the immobilization of the Soviet Union and Italy in the area. This third point was reiterated by the Germans to the Italians all through the summer of 1940 "for fear of playing into the hands of the USSR even more than having to divert forces from the campaign against Great Britain and Egypt,"[64] and to the Soviets to limit their revisionism to Bessarabia. In the meantime, it seemed that the price they had paid had not been too great.

The Russian public, meanwhile, awoke one day to find that their most dreaded enemy was now a friend, but if the fiercely patriotic but politically docile Russians had any reaction, it must have been that there were distinct advantages to such a Pact—Russia would be saved from war without sacrifice, and as it turned out with great gain, for it recovered for

Russia much of the territory she had lost in her early revolutionary weakness and land which for every Russian was considered part of the national heritage. That there might be some need to convince the populace of that was evident in Molotov's speech of August 31[65] to a special session of the Supreme Soviet opened in Moscow on August 28 to ratify the Pact (at the same time it ordered a new conscription law reducing the age of callup and lengthening the period of service). Molotov developed the line of argument already apparent in the Soviet press, that the Anglo-Franco-Soviet discussions were doomed to failure because of "Western dilatoriness" and an "inserious attitude," occasioned by Anglo-French fears that the ". . . conclusion of a serious pact of mutual assistance with the USSR might strengthen . . . the Soviet Union which it turns out is not in their interests." Then he remineded those who questioned his policy that relations between countries were not regulated by "ideologies, but by external relations" which were now "good-neighborly" with Germany, and that by this Pact:

> . . . the field of war in Europe is reduced and, even if it does not prove possible entirely to avoid war in Europe, the extent of such hostilities will now be restricted.

Toward the end of the speech Molotov gave a classical exposé of the Communist and Soviet viewpoint.[66]

> Do these gentlemen really find difficulty in understanding the meaning of the Soviet-German Non-Aggression Pact on the strength of which the USSR is not obliged to allow herself to be dragged into war either on the side of England against Germany or on the side of Germany against England? Is it really difficult to understand that the USSR is following, and will continue to follow, its own independent policy, the aim of which is to further the interest of the people of the USSR and those interests only? (prolonged applause). If these gentlemen desire to fight let them fight each other without the Soviet Union (laughter and applause).

Upon conclusion of this speech, by an unanimous show of hands, the Supreme Council of the USSR ratified the Pact. On September 3, when Great

Britain and France finally declared war on Germany, this momentous act was not mentioned in the Soviet press, and when the foreign press finally asked for the Government's attitude, the official response was to refer it to Molotov's August 31 speech, a speech which openly acknowledged that the Nazi-Soviet Pact meant war.[67] However, in an interview with the Polish Ambassador immediately after the war had begun, Molotov gave a different version of Soviet motivation which emphasized defensive concerns, for he expressed surprise that England and France had actually declared war on Germany. Then in late November Stalin denied an alleged statement reported by Havas that on August 19 in a speech to the Politboro he had said that "the war must continue as long as possible in order to exhaust the belligerents," though the facts suggested otherwise, the Soviets haveing assured Poland of economic assistance in order to bulwark them to fight.[68]

As far as territorial gains are concerned, the Soviets never admitted to the possibility though the vehemence of their denials suggests just the opposite.[69] On the other hand, it must be recognized that territorial issues were secondary to the Soviets who believed that these would come once the European power balance was altered in their favor. In this respect, Molotov's emphasis on dialectics in his August 31 speech must be taken at face value, as must Stalin's defense of his "peace policy" two years later in which he cited eighteen more months of peace and a chance to rearm, but not territorial gain. In part this helps to explain the limited dialog concerning Balkan spheres in the Nazi-Soviet negotiations (while making a chimera of Soviet emphasis on them in the Anglo-French-Soviets talks), and it makes understandable two Balkan gains the Soviets did hope to make by the Pact—Turkish concessions at the Straits and a negotiable Balkan Bessarabian position.

* * * * *

In conclusion, the nature of this non-aggression pact in terms of the Balkans seems to have been one of mutual interest based on non-aggression and Balkan pacification. The question of spheres, therefore, did not emerge, though it lurked below the surface should the Balkan status quo in any way be altered. This arrangement had considerable advantages to both sides as long as peace was maintained; for both it excluded the West, it caught the Balkans up in Nazi-Soviet pincers, it gave to the Soviets a bargaining position, and to the Germans a continuing flow of raw materials. In formulating this arrangement, it can be said that both sides went about as far as they could go in compromising their territorial interests, for the Germans did not give into the Soviet expression of interest in Rumania, and the Soviets did not give up their interest in Bessarabia for gains in Poland and the Baltic.

The problem with the Pact, however, is that it did not exclude German action in the Balkans or Soviet action in Bessarabia, and once the peace of the area was disrupted, the question of spheres had to be addressed. By the terms of the treaty, consultation on problems of mutual interest was provided for, and very likely Stalin hoped that the time bought to rearm while Germany exhausted herself fighting, would allow him a viable Balkan bargaining position should it come to that, particularly because once the war in the West was begun, status quo of the Balkan area was ever more important to Hitler and hence more open to concession. The invasion of Russia, of course, changed all that, but the prelude to that invasion found the Soviets talking with the Italians over a division of Balkan spheres, while Hitler tried to exchange with Stalin a Balkan sphere for a sphere in Near Asia, all of which goes to illustrate the incompatibility of Nazi-Soviet Balkan interests and the chimera of a pact which avoided pertinent questions and made some obtuse division between political and economic interests. However, at the time it was a unique attempt at detente obviously acceptable to both, and its basic framework served the greater Soviet purpose of a Capitalist war and the German purpose of a neutral rear.

Balkan Reaction to the Pact

France particularly was shocked and despondent upon receiving news of the Nazi-Soviet Pact. As Daladier put it, the Pact placed France in a tragic situation, for their whole diplomatic framework was in shambles, and Poland, without the aid of Russia, could not last more than two months. Then the brunt of Germany would be on France, and while French soldiers were being slaughtered, Gemany would swallow up one after another—Poland, Rumania, Hungary, Bulgaria, Greece and Turkey.[70] Equally pessimistic were predictions that the Non-Aggression Pact was really an alliance whereby the Soviet Union would dominate Asia and Germany, Europe, thereby effecting an end to the Balkans.[71] While most statesmen agreed that the Pact gave Hitler a green light in his Polish venture, some regarded it as a defeat for Hitler who, in negotiating with the Russians, had acknowledged this power factor in the East, had handed over territory, and in effect vastly increased Russian power and allowed them to "purchase an opportunistic policy out of developing conflicts in East Europe."[72]

Certainly suspicious were the Italians who suspected that Hitler had traded the Balkan sphere for Soviet neutrality or even if not that, had vastly increased the power of the Soviets in the Southeast thus diminishing their chances of a cost-free acquisition in that area. The Italian Foreign Minister, therefore, immediately informed the Soviet Charge that Italy retained freedom of action in spite of the German and Italian alliance,[73] and then Ciano began thinking in terms of exploiting the German "master blow" by readying Italy "to gain something in Croatia and Dalmatia."[74] However, when Polish and British capitulation failed to materialize, the Italians, considering themselves unprepared, saw the wisdom of not committing Italy in any large way, though Hitler reinforced the idea saying the Nazi-Soviet Pact would safeguard against the hostile intentions of the East European states particularly Turkey and Rumania, thus preserving the area for later exploitation.[75]

In the Balkans, reactions to the Pact were quite benign largely because they had not wanted an eastern front anyway and, because understanding competitive Nazi-Soviet interests in the area, they believed the non-aggression features of the Pact protected Balkan neutrality and diluted the Italian threat.[76] This was not the case with Turkey, however, where it was suspected that once Hitler had polished off Poland, Italy would show her colors and join the Führer, and where close connections with the allied front would cause pressure from Russia. In fact, Saracoglu was completely disheartened, viewing it as an absolute surprise and a "*coup de theatre* unprecedented in history." He said the text left no possibility of continuation of Russian negotiations with Great Britain and France, and he viewed the impact as moral not material for the Balkans, because while Poland and Rumania had never wanted Soviet aid, they had hoped for Russian neutrality which now seemed as uncertain as Turkish hopes for an agreement with Moscow.[77] But, for the other Balkan countries, who had never wanted a Pact with the Soviet Union and who had felt the weight of Soviet power even before the Pact, it was just "another scrap of paper" and what mattered was its "future application and how much horse trading preceded it."[78]

In Rumania, for instance, the King expressed no surprise at the Pact nor were there any signs of Cabinet reshuffling or public outcry. In fact, Rumania's neutrality seemed assured (to Berlin's satisfaction), as Rumania would remain neutral unless attacked by Hungary or Bulgaria, while relations with Turkey were governed by the Balkan Entente and therefore she would not join any combination in the Mediterranean. Indeed there seemed distinct benefits in the Pact. Not only was there no longer the possibility that "German-Russian differences would one day be settled on Rumanian territory," but with increased Nazi-Soviet trade, demands on Rumania and pressure for *Drang nach Ukraine* would decrease.[79] More important, Hungarian neutrality seemed assured by Italian neutrality,[80] while prospects for better Hungaro-Rumanian relations took a positive turn due to the weakened position of Budapest with regard to Yugoslavia (whose position vis-a-vis Italy had been strengthened), Germany (the passage of German troops across Hungary appeared imminent), Russia (who might penetrate Rumania and thus be on the Hungarian border), and Rumania herself (on the one hand Bucharest moved troops to the border and on the other offered a non-aggression pact, all with German blessings). The only concern the Rumanians seemd to voice was with regard to Bessarabia and the possibility, as Gafencu told Fabricius, of a Soviet-German agreement there.

If the Rumanains were passive upon news of the Pact, the Yugoslavs were visibly encouraged that their position had been strenghtened by the Pact, primarily because it seemed to assure Italy's neutrality, and it negated the possibility that, for Italy's help, Germany might pay off Rome with Serbian Yugoslavia. In addition, Belgrade believed the Pact would serve merely to increase the hatred against Germany in Europe, and so the Yugoslavs became increasingly confident vis-a-vis Berlin. This was outwardly evident in the appointment of French General Milan Nedić to head the military, in rapid mobilization and deployment along the northern frontier, in the granting of oil concessions to Standard Oil of New Jersey, and in the cessation of wheat and grain shipments to Germany resulting from Berlin's failure to deliver Skoda armaments according to contract. Internally, Yugoslavia was buoyed by the fact that the day before the signing of the Nazi-Soviet Pact, the long sought after Serbian agreement (*Sparazum*) with the Yugoslavian Croats was signed giving them considerable autonomy, and in so doing diluting the strength of the pro-German separatist movement. The Pact also tended to disarm Slavic and Communist sentiment to the Government's advantage, thereby swinging the pro-Russian Serbian Army behind the pro-German crown and thus more toward neutrality.[81] This policy they tried to urge on the Balkan Entente and Bulgaria which was, of course, greatly to Germany's liking. German Charge Heine reported that the Nazi-Soviet Pact had been a bombshell there, and that it was regarded as marking the collapse of the encirclement policy "justifying Yugoslavia's foreign policy to all the world," especially to Turkey "whose whole foreign policy was now left suspended in the air."[82]

The Greeks, with an eye on Italy and anxious over whether or not Great Britain and France would declare war on the USSR, adopted a wait-and-see policy after the Nazi-Soviet Pact was announced, refusing any editorial comment. As time went on and the Italians made no move, the Greeks became more certain that Italian-German interests clashed in the Balkans and that since the Pact, the Italians, uncertain on which side more benefits would accrue, had adopted a foreign policy which was "dictated by developments." Therefore, Metaxas said that Greece was modeling her foreign policy on Turkey's (and hence Britain's), namely that Greece was outside the present conflict and hence felt no need to declare or provoke a quarrel with the Reich. This specious neutrality had widespread acceptance internally, there being less anti-Marxist criticism in Greece, and it was in accordance with that of Yugoslavia and concordant with the Balkan view that the Nazi-Soviet conflict of interests in the Balkans would prevent any early extension of the war to Rumania or the Dardanelles.[83]

For the revisionist state of Hungary, the major reason for satisfaction with the Pact was the deterrent effect on Rumania. This placed her in a stronger position by which to impose her revisionist claims, while securing neutrality which had been threatened by Rumania's drift toward the "encirclement powers." However, both hopes soon began to fade. Right after the Pact, Hungary offered to enter the war on the side of Germany in return for Transylvania, and for added leverage in Berlin, Budapest threatened friendship with Poland and neutrality. Hitler, who above all wanted to maintain the Balkan status quo and to proceed against Poland with Hungary's quasi-help, was furious, and so he threatened to depose Horthy and Teleki, he stopped delivery of certain war material, and then he presented Budapest with an ultimatum to the effect that while desiring no armed assistance from Hungary, Berlin expected Budapest to make a declaration of neutrality (which was certainly a compromise in that he desired Hungarian neutrality vis-a-vis Rumania but complicity against Poland).[84]

Berlin tried again in early September to shift Hungarian neutrality to complicity, calling Csáky to Berlin to discuss a Hungarian move into the Subcarpathian Ukraine to cut off the Polish Southern army, but after seeking Mussolini's counsel, Horthy and Teleki (who were steadfast in the maintenance of independence) held firm even in the face of German bribes in the form of acquisition of Halicz. This caused the Germans to call on the Russians to enter the war as quickly as possible whereupon they quickly moved south toward the Hungarian border. The German refusal to support Hungarian revisionism against Rumania, and Berlin's pressure for Hungarian participation in Germany's war, caused the Hungarians to begin to wonder if Germany had not paid a high price for the Nazi-Soviet Pact including a free hand to the Soviets in Rumania, placing Hungary in a dangerous position if Russia claimed Bessarabia.[85] Then too, there was the realization that Germany had traded in Hungarian pressure in the Balkans for Soviet, thus diminishing any leverage Hungary had had with Germany. Soon thereafter, Hungarian leaders began to reorient their foreign policy toward Rome.

The Bulgarians were pleased with the Pact because on the one hand, in destroying the encirclement front, it preserved Balkan neutrality, and on the other because, in the short run, it relieved them of a delicate international situation whereby they would have been forced to take sides with Russia and Germany against the allies which, it was viewed, would get them nowhere. To the Germans the Bulgarians emphasized pleasure in the fact that the Pact sealed the fate of the British-Russian combination, relieved pressure on them to join the Balkan Pact, doomed a British campaign based on Salonika with efforts to involve the other Balkan countries as in the last war, and added pressure on Turkey to revise her policy.[86]

For non-German ears, the Bulgarians voiced satisfaction with the Pact because, being held hostage to the Germans by economics and revisionism, they found in the Pact liberation from German tutelage by means of Russia. They reiterated to anyone who would listen, that they would not go with Germany, and now that the political challenge to Germany in the Balkans had been dissipated, that Germany herself had "no territorial, but only economic aspirations in the Balkan states." Alongside this, however, was the open acknowledgement that Russian power had been vastly increased in the Balkans, though they preferred to view the danger as minimal, believing the Soviet Union did not want territory but neutrality, having gotten from the Pact "ideological satisfaction." Underneath this attitude were some political considerations whereby the Slavs were the sentimental favorite and whereby favorable revisionism would take place by peaceful settlement, and Turkey drawn off, if the British could be kept out.[87]

But, no sooner had Bulgaria settled back into self-satisfied neutrality, than Soviet and German actions began to challenge their benign view of the Nazi-Soviet Pact. In early September, Germans were evacuated daily from Turkey to Bulgaria and soon the Germans began to reorganize Bulgarian aviation, making clear that Bulgarian neutrality was based more on the relationship with Germany than Russia, and that Bulgaria was becoming more satellized, not less. In the meantime, Soviet revolutionary activity increased as did bids for Soviet favor in exchange for revisionist support.

On the heels of the Nazi-Soviet Pact, Hitler seemed supremely confident that the Turkish need for arms which the West could not supply and the pressure of the Soviets at the Dardanelles[88] would alter the Turkish course. Von Papen told Saracoglu on August 24 that by the Pact "the future blockade of the Axis powers by the British was impossible, and [that] the balance of power in the European situation had been tilted in favor of the Axis Powers," and therefore that Turkey must return to neutrality.[89] The Turks, however, did not believe that the Pact had brought Russia to Germany's side, and although not certain, Saracoglu speculated that while the Pact partitioned Poland, Germany had not given Russia a free hand regarding Turkey. Hence, the opportunity remained to Turkey to come to an agreement with the Soviet Union, the latter having assured Turkey of friendly relations despite the Nazi-Soviet Pact and then extending an invitation to the Minister of Foreign Affairs to come to Moscow.[90]

In addition, Turkey was protected against Bulgaria by her Balkan friends, Rumania, Greece and Yugoslavia, and she did not believe Bulgaria would throw in her lot with Germany anyway. Playing a shrewd game with regard to Italy, Saracoglu continued to emphasize to the Germans that it

was the threat of Italy that drove her to Britain's side (and here he believed that Italy's neutrality was temporary and tactical), and therefore, that
if, in a war with Poland, Britain and France attacked Germany and Italy
joined in, in pursuit of her own vital interest, she could not avoid fulfilling her obligations. Saracoglu proceeded to reject the German economic
proposals, and President Inönü on August 27 told Papen that she would
fulfill her obligations to the Balkan Pact and then he alluded to continuing contact with Great Britain.[91]

For this reason, as well as Italy's under the table support of Hungary
in the realignment of the Balkans, on August 28 Hitler declined Mussolini's offers of help saying, "I do not expect or need Italy's military support,"[92] a stand which belied the political situation whereby Italy's outward support was vital in forcing Britian's hand in Poland. Italy's neutrality was a victory for Turkey and the other Balkan states, and while it is
true Hitler also wished Italy's neutrality in order to maintain the Balkan
status quo, prevent a full Turkish alliance with the West, or unsettle Russia, it was an unpleasant trade-off, for the fear of Italy was key to the
pacification of Yugoslavia in particular and to the Balkan Entente in general. The Greek Premier noted in this regard that Italian neutrality aided
Hitler in that it barred invasion of Germany from the South, at the same
time sparing her the probable necessity of going to Italy's assistance, but
he also pointed out that it was favorable also to the allies who saw the
possibility of wooing Italy as well as keeping the communication lanes
open in the Mediterranean.[93]

Certainly in terms of Greece, Italian neutrality and particularly British
reaction to it, had far-reaching consequences, for the Greeks began to
model their attitude on Turkey who in declaring neutrality was following the British plan to accept Italian neutrality at face value and to exploit
it if possible. When Metaxas was asked in mid-September if Greece would
renew the Greco-German clearing agreement, he answered, "Not without
England's consent . . . we shall do nothing, nothing that would run counter
to her interests in the slightest." This had a ripple effect on Yugoslavia
who, now certain of the neutrality of the Greeks and Turkey, could begin to
believe in the reality of Italian neutrality (having been given substance to
their idea that Italian-German interests in the Balkans clashed), and thus
move toward the allies. The allaying of Greco-Yugoslav suspicions was of
no small consequence in the Balkan ability to exert itself against the Axis,

for as U.S. Charge Eliot noted, Yugoslav military roads to the Greek frontier to prevent Italian seizure of Salonika had heretofore been suspected as for more selfish aims whereby Yugoslavia would join the Axis to secure Salonika.[94]

* * * * *

It appears, therefore, that in his quest to maintain control in the Southeast, Hitler had, as he had intended, knocked out the British by outmaneuvering them with Russia, but that in the process he had half lost Italy (Hungary and Bulgaria) and with that, much of the leverage he held against the Balkan slippage to the West. This was appreciated in the area even before the announcement of Italian neutrality, for while there was some fear a Nazi-Soviet Pact might have been made at their expense, the more prevalent reaction was relief because it prevented the Balkans from becoming the seat of a Nazi-Soviet war. And in using Russia rather than Italy in the East, it prevented Italy from attacking, thus achieving and securing the Balkan aim of neutrality desired by revisionist and anti-revisionist alike. On the other hand, their neutrality was based on German desire and power to delimit the war, on Soviet and Italian ambition, and on the extent of benevolency required of them short of occupation.

As it turned out, it was Soviet ambition which soon shook the foundations of Balkan neutrality and laid bare the reality that it was not Nazi-Soviet competition that could keep them safe, but Nazi power and interests. No sooner was the ink dry on the Nazi-Soviet Pact than detente began to give way to Cold War, and cooperation in the Balkans to competition. For ironically, once the war the Pact had begun was set in motion, Nazi-Soviet Balkan interests began to diverge; for the Germans Balkan pacification became more important and for the Soviets less, causing satellization by both to begin moving on a collision course.

Detente or Cold War—Cooperation or Competition

Any security the Balkans might have felt as a result of the Pact was soon shattered by the Soviet invasion of Poland on September 17 and the subsequent signing of the Treaty of Boundary and Friendship dividing Poland, laying bare Soviet aggressive intentions and renewing the prospect of a Nazi-Soviet war and a division of spheres. While various Soviet statements were designed to emphasize the defensive character of moves,[95] everywhere in the Balkans there were uncertainties as to the meaning and the effect it might have on Italy and Turkey, with the Germans themselves adding to the obfuscation. The German Ambassador in Moscow told the Greek Minister that the invasion was not in accord with any agreement, but in Rumania the German Air Attache (Gerstenburg) said that German and Russian action had previously been mutually agreed upon whereby Russia had promised not to molest the Baltic states or Rumania. Meanwhile, an official German source in Yugoslavia said that the Germans permitted Russia to occupy two-thirds of Poland as it allowed an economy in German divisions needed to occupy Poland, it rendered British claims of war arms to restore Poland more difficult, and it whetted Russian desires for conquest.[96]

As with the Non-Aggression Pact, most Balkan statesmen tended to believe like Prince Paul of Yugoslavia that the settlement dividing Poland was not a Pact of Friendship, for if Germany and Russia were really in collusion, it would be the end of Europe. The Bulgarian Prime Minister concurred, saying the Russians invaded Poland to keep Germany from coming East (the Ukraine). In interpreting the Soviet initiative as unilateral rather than collaborative, both Yugoslavia and Bulgaria saw advantages for the Balkans in terms of blunting German influence, neutralizing Italy and therefore Hungary too, and in safeguarding Rumania (due to a Soviet guarantee and troops on the border).[97] But in Rumania there was outright fear of the Russians and that Germany would give in, though Bucharest was temporarily assuaged when Molotov assured Gafencu that the Soviet Union would not invade.[98] Like the Balkan countries, Italy seemed uncertain and anxious over the Soviet move, and while not ready to believe Italy had been betrayed, Ciano admitted to not knowing where close German-Russian association would lead, and the new Italian Minister to London, Bastianini, predicted Russian entry into the Balkans which he saw as a greater danger to Italy than the British-German struggle and was the reason for Italian neutrality.[99] Ankara, on the other hand, feared that the British and French might declare war on the USSR, jeopardizing their neutrality.

The initial Balkan reaction to the Russian move into Poland, while displaying uncertainty, was not hysterical, for Nazi-Soviet competition seemed to signal the end of German hegemony while German strength and interests gave them some safety against Russia. Soon, however, a number of Russian actions began to threaten those presumptions, among them open backing by the USSR of Bulgarian revisionism and Bolshevization, Soviet efforts to realize a mutual assistance pact with Turkey, and as a consequence of the former, increased Soviet pressure on Rumania.

Soon after the Non-Aggression Pact, Russian Deputy Markov stated that Russia approved of Bulgarian territorial claims on Rumania and that Soviet help would be forthcoming, as "it is the opinion of Comrade Stalin that Bulgaria should have justice."[100] By October reports began appearing to the effect that the Soviet were negotiating with the Bulgarians for a form of joint action against Rumania whereby when the Russians took Bessarabia, the Bulgarians would take Dobruja, a deal the Turkish Ambassaor to the Soviet Union believed the Russians would consummate before the Soviet-Turkish conversations in order to pressure Ankara,[101] and which others viewed as intended to bring about Bulgarian signature of a Black Sea Pact under Russian leadership. Along with revisionist activity went Bolshevization, the Rumanians reporting that they had intercepted Bolshevik propaganda to Communist cells in Bulgaria stating that the Soviet Union had temporarily agreed with Germany in order to view the rapid downfall of capitalism and that German imperialism would be of a brief nature. The Bulgarian Prime Minister played down this activity stating that there had always been Communist activity and offering the information that no approach had been made by the Russians affecting the international situation,[102] but the facts were soon to speak otherwise.

More threatening to the Balkans was the impending visit of the Turkish Foreign Minister to Moscow (in response to a pressured invitation) where, it was feared, the Turks would be forced by Russia or in collusion with Germany to make an agreement unfavorable to the Balkans. This became of particular concern because of the arrival of Ribbentrop in Moscow on September 25 to discuss the settlement of Poland and it was feared other outstanding issues as well, possibly involving Rumania and Turkey.

The Rumanians were particularly apprehensive because it appeared that Russia now had the upper hand as Hitler did not want to fight on two fronts. In their view, Hungary's Ruthenian frontier and Rumania's Bukovina, both with Ukrainian minorities, no longer seemed safe as Russia was on each frontier, and at the time the Bessarabian Deputy reported that manifestos were circulating to the effect that the Bolsheviks would enter and "come to the aid of their brethren in Bessarabia before the end of the

month." Thus, the result of the Moscow trip, which could mean the end
of Turkey and hence Rumania's strongest ally on whom they were dependent for receiving aid from the allies, was "awaited breathlessly."[103]
(Typical of the divergence of Balkan views, was the Yugoslav reaction
which was hopeful that Soviet pressure could steer Turkey away from
the allies and thereby insure Turkish and Italian [therefore Hungarian]
neutrality.)[104]

Above all the Turks were affected, and while they said it would not
alter their ongoing negotiations for a military alliance with the British and
French, on September 21 they finally stated that they would not sign the
agreement until after the trip to Moscow. Meanwhile the Turkish Ambassador tried to assuage the Rumanians, telling them that the purpose of
the talks, according to the Russians, was to discuss formation of a Balkan
union to comprise eventually, if possible, Hungary and Bulgaria and to be
formed with or without Turkish cooperation, preferably with. It was further hoped in Ankara, that Italy, "appalled" by the "opening of the
sluices to Bolshevik hordes," would also support and approve the pact.
The project provided for token cession of Dobruja on the part of Rumania to Bulgaria, but what the Russians would demand was unclear.
The Rumanians were skeptical that such a plan would materialize, noting
that Bulgaria was further now than ever from cession of Dobruja because
of Russian backing and voicing surprise that Russia would sign something
analogous to the Anglo-Franco-Turkish Pact for certainly Moscow would
do nothing to impede the West's power to destroy itself. The Greeks
were fearful that as a result of such a pact, Turkey would be induced
not to sign with Great Britain and France.[105]

As it turned out, the negotiations had little to do with any sort of
Turko-Soviet agreement or Soviet-Balkan coalition, and a great deal to do
with the securing of the Soviet Union against Germany and Britain and
in advancing Soviet territory, with the result that Turkish skepticism of
Soviet motives turned into outright fear. Unbeknownst to the other Balkan states, Saracoglu had had under consideration for some time, Soviet
proposals put to them by the Soviet Ambassador, Mr. Terentiev, on September 4 for a mutual assistance pact analogous and supplementary to an
agreement between Turkey, France and Britain which would become operative in the event of actual or threatened attack on the territories of
either party in the region of the Balkans or Black Sea. Subsequent

negotiations had been carried on with extreme secrecy but with the know-ledge and approval of the British and French.[106]

On September 22 Saracoglu left for Moscow presumably to complete the negotiations and sign the treaty. Though it was believed that the Sov-iets were pursuing a policy independent of Germany and prompted by a desire to bar Germany from the Balkans, it was also suspected that Soviet discussion regarding "mutual assistance" might be tactical only, that is to drive a hard bargain with the Gemans during the Friendship and Boundary Treaty over Poland which indeed it turned out to be (pushing the Soviet border to Rumania). For soon after the Germans left, Stalin put the real Soviet demands to Saracoglu (October 1) which, according to the Turkish Foreign Minister, were preemptory and not in line with former proposals. They were to the effect that Turkey should agree 1) not to participate under any circumstances in hostilities against Russia, and 2) should not make any commitment with respect to the Balkan region more far-reach-ing than the promise of consultation already included in the Anglo-Franco-Turkish Declaration. The Soviet Government also demanded closing of the Straits to foreign war vessels and contraband.[107]

To the former demands, Saracoglu replied that Turkey must be free to carry out the spirit and letter of her obligations to her Western allies, and to the latter that Turkey could not discuss unilaterally modification of the international regime of the Straits as formulated at Montreux. Ap-parently, either Saracoglu's firm stand or the Soviet desire to prolong the negotiations in order to keep the Turks from signing the Tripartite Pact, caused the Soviets to tone down their proposals into a form he felt he could refer to his Government. For two weeks the Turks attempted to build on the apparent Soviet acceptance of Montreux by working out a formula (agreed to by the British and French) providing only for consul-tation in the event of Ankara's going to the aid of Greece and Rumania, and whereby both the Russo-Turkish Pact and the Tripartite would be-come inoperative if Turkey was involved in hostilities with Germany.

Upon being informed of these concessions, however, the Soviet Govern-ment demanded further conditions, similar to demands made twice before but withdrawn, and in addition, the Soviet Government raised the issue of Rumania with the aim of getting assurances of Turkish neutrality not only in the event of the Soviet seizure of Bessarabia, but in the event of the Bulgarian seizure of Dobruja, after which hypothetical situations involving the impairment of Turkish commitments by Britain were raised. Saracoglu said that in the draft the Soviets submitted orally, there was contained clauses which not only precluded a German-Soviet conflict, but considerably weakened Turkish freedom of action at the Dardanelles. Saracoglu's reply was to the effect that Turkey would not go to Rumania's aid in event of Soviet seizure of Bessarabia as it was not covered by the Balkan Entente, but that she would not commit herself in advance to action in the Dardanelles and she would go to Rumania's aid if Bulgaria attacked.[108]

As a result of the impasse, Saracoglu was ordered to return to Ankara on October 17, and a statement was issued to the Soviets to the effect that Turkey could not accept the proposals because they were incompatible with obligations to Great Britain and France, because the guarantees offered to Turkey did not correspond to her obligations, and because Soviet demands were not in conformity with Turkish Straits policy. But in press and public statements, the Turks emphasized continuing friendly relations with Russia, while the Soviets published a communique to the effect that there was a mere pause and that the negotiations would be resumed shortly.[109]

Saracoglu was obviously angered by the whole episode including the fact that he had expected to stay a week in Moscow and had in fact stayed 23 days more, many of which were spent cooling his heels while Ribbentrop was in town, and then he was strung along by proposals and rejections thereafter. Therefore, before he even reached home, he ordered that the Turkish economic demands of the British and French be modified and that the military convention be signed (October 19). In publicizing the Pact, Ankara emphasized that the Pact was not directed against any state and that the object was to keep peace in the Mediterranean and in Turkey's zone of neutrality; but Molotov, in a speech on October 31, expressed the opinion that the Pact was provocative and neglectful of Russian interests.[110]

It is salient at this point to analyze the effect the Nazis had on the Turko-Soviet negotiations. Obviously, the Soviets initially believed that the Pact with Germany did not bar them from carrying on talks with the Turks and that Nazi-Soviet collusion could pressure Turkey in a favorable direction, while the Germans hoped Soviet pressure could turn the Turks away from the West and the Soviets seemed to be cooperating. In early

September, Molotov told Schulenburg that the Soviet Government was putting considerable pressure on Turkey in the sense desired by Germany. But when it soon became known that Ankara and Moscow were talking about a mutual assistance pact applicable to the Straits and Balkans with a restrictive clause disallowing assistance directed against England and France, the Germans objected to the exemption unless a similar one involving Germany, Italy, and Bulgaria was included, and by September 21 they were inclined to think that such a treaty was not in their interests at all.[111]

Ribbentrop, therefore, instructed Schulenburg to tell Stalin that a Turkish-Soviet alliance would only strengthen Anakara's ties with the West to Moscow's ultimate detriment at the Straits, and that it was in the German and Soviet best interest to get Turkey to abandon her plans for an alliance with England and France, which could be accomplished by making conclusion of a Turko-Soviet mutual assistance pact conditional on renunciation of a pact with England and France. Schulenburg reported on September 22 Molotov's noncommittal reply, which was to the effect the Soviet Union was not in principle disinclined to conclude a new treaty with Turkey and, in so doing it would naturally "take full account of the spirit and letter of the German-Soviet Non-Aggerssion Pact."[112]

While it would appear that the Soviets wanted to reach an agreement with Turkey giving Russia preferential treatment at the Straits, protecting her against both Germany and the West, and that the Soviets were also thinking of using the Turkish approach to gain leverage against Germany in the rearrangement of Poland, U.S. Minister in Rumania, Gunther, offered another explanation, to the effect the Soviets desired to throw some weight back behind the West taken from it by the Nazi-Soviet Pact. Too much pressure on Turkey would turn her away from the West to Germany, ring the Soviet Union in both the North and South with Nazis, and weight the equation too much on Germany's side, causing the war to be a short one and upsetting plans to penetrate an exhausted Europe. Therefore, it was in the Soviet interest to keep Turkey with the West and therefore the Soviet border free from Nazi control with the lingering threat of Russia should the West become too powerful.[113]

Reports that Russia wanted a non-aggression pact with Turkey and then rumors of a mutual assistance pact (along with other outstanding issues involving Poland), made Ribbentrop suddenly depart for Moscow on September 25, and in a statement before his departure, Ribbentrop warned that Germany and Russia would never again allow outside interference in East European questions, causing speculation that in addition to matters affecting Poland, "Ribbentrop and Stalin will work out with the acquiescence of Turkey a scheme for neutralization of the Balkans and Black Sea area." The Rumanians particularly[114] were frantic that a Soviet invasion was imminent, especially since in the case of the Russian invasion of Bessarabia, the Balkan Pact did not apply as Bessarabia was not considered part of the Balkans. In fact, reported U.S. Charge Kirk, there was an inclination in Soviet circles in Berlin "to speak with some assurance as to Soviet claims to Bessarabia which they intimate may fall to Russia as easily as did Polish territory," though in German circles the cooperative aspect of Ribbentrop's trip was less apparent than the German need to restrain the Soviets.[115]

In the resultant Treaty of Boundary and Friendship signed on September 28, 1939, the absence of any reference to the Balkans meant that as far as the Soviet Union and Germany were concerned, the basis for Balkan detente established in the Non-Aggression Pact remained the same, and that there were both competitive and complementary forces at work. For while both the Russians and Germans were using the negotiations against the Turks, the Soviets wished only to force Ankara into a more concessive position in their behalf with or without the British (recognizing that the latter connection could yet be useful and was necessary for balance against the Nazis), while the Germans wished to use them to destroy the Turko-British connection completely, throwing Ankara back into Axis arms as well as adding an element of control over the Soviets.

During the negotiations for the Friendship Treaty and then during the Turko-Soviet negotiations, the Germans maintained direct pressure on the Turks and Russians to thwart the Tripartite pact. Hitler received the new Turkish Ambassador, R. Husrev-Yerede on September 27, at which time he told him that good political relations were advisable and that Germany offered rich prospects especially economic.[116] Meanwhile, Schulenburg was instructed to emphasize to Molotov that if the USSR concluded an assistance pact with Turkey, obligations to give assistance against Germany must be expressly and publicly excluded; otherwise confidence in the Nazi-Soviet Pact would be shaken. Molotov answered only to the effect that the Soviet Government aimed to secure full neutrality of Turkey and that in any event, the Nazi-Soviet Pact would be taken into account. By October 12, Germany was confident a pact between the Soviet Union and Turkey to their advantage was near, but on October 17 Molotov told Schulenburg that the negotiations had netted no results,[117] and on October 19 Turkey signed mutual assistance pacts with Great Britain and France. The Germans recognized the defeat that it was to have Turkey sign on with the West, but they also recognized some positive aspects for as one German official put it, Turkey's position was now more precarious and the Soviet attitude to Bessarabia would be more cautious.[118]

As we have seen, in the negotiations with the Turks, the Soviets were loyal to the Germans to the extent that they pressed the German case for exemptions in the pact as regards to Germany, but Moscow did not honor the German request to make signing of the pact contingent on Turkish renunciation of the pact with the West. The see-saw negotiating pattern of the Soviets suggests that their amelioratory position prior to the signing of the Boundary and Friendship Treaty was intended as a ploy against the Germans, and that after the favorable conclusion of the Treaty, to nudge the Turks along into submission to their demands regarding the Dardanelles and Turkish acquiescence in their plans against Rumania, but the stolid stand of the Turks must have convinced them that without Turkish acquiescence on these two points, a mutual assistance pact would be of little value. In this respect, the German request to the Soviets to use the negotiations to gain a more favorable Turkish position to the Nazis, was of secondary interest, and while the Germans tried to paint the picture that Soviet-Turkish negotiations had failed due to Soviet loyalty to Germany, it seems rather, as with the rest of the Balkans, the Soviets' first aim was to keep the war going between the capitalist countries while maintaining Balkan neutrality, and that within that framework, to make any advances possible.

But their inability to make a deal advantageous to them was a defeat, and as the U.S. Minister (Steinhardt) speculated, this was not without bearing on the general line of Soviet policy particularly in its relations with Germany and may have spurred them on to take unilateral action in their own defense in Bessarabia.[119] The Rumanians were acutely aware of this and hence were alarmed at the breakdown in negotiations, but the Bulgarian view was just the opposite, that Russia was hesitating about Bessarabia due to fear Turkey might open the Straits particularly after Bulgaria declined to take joint action with the Soviet Union against Rumania. The Greeks, meanwhile, were pleased by the tenacity of her Turkish ally under pressure of Soviet demands.[120]

The Balkan countries, relieved that the Turks had submitted to neither Soviet nor German pressure, were dismayed that the Turks had abandoned strict neutrality and gone to the West's side. The Rumanian reaction was extremely negative despite the fact that many felt that as a result of the Anglo-Franco-Turkish mutual assistance pacts, any Soviet advance into Bessarabia would be made with great caution. Minister in Rumania, Gunther, reported on October 23 that there was "no echo here of the jubilation in the allied countries over the pact," which was considered "a barrier against German aggression in southeastern Europe." Instead, the belief was prevalent that "Russia presents a much greater danger to this part of the world than does Germany," and that the Franco-British-Turkish treaties made it clear Turkey "will not defend Rumania except indirectly in the case Bulgaria also attacks," and that the British guarantee might apply against Germany but not Russia. The view from Bucharest was that "Russian aggression is just a question of whether and when," and in the end, said Gafencu, "Russia would be the victor in a long war."[121]

More immediately, Rumania saw a Russian move into Bessarabia as the trigger moving Hungary backed by Italy into Transylvania. By October 25 widespread organizations in Transylvania to assist Hungary if there were hostilities with Rumania were in evidence, and with Hungarian complicity. Rumania began to see only Germany in Russia's and Hungary's way, and so the view was coming around that Rumania's only real safeguard was Germany. The Minister of the National Economy then confirmed that Germany was purposely speeding up delivery of arms to Rumania in order to better equip her to resist Russian aggression. But the Rumanians were also convinced that Germany would find it expedient to give way on the matter of Bessarabia as she had in relinquishing the Rumanain-Polish border to Russia, not only to maintain the status quo but to encourage Russia in order to show the world the need for peace, at the same time feeling strong enough to prevent Russia from occupying any more and, counting on Italy to hold Hungary in check and to send airplanes and accessories as in Spain.[122] But by December, it was fairly well agreed in Rumania, that the only real deterrent to the Russian advance on Bessarabia was the British and French fleet being sent into the

Black Sea, so that it was not surprising that in early December the Soviets sent a trial balloon by way of an article in the Russian press concerning Bessarbia in which a Russo-Rumanian mutual assistance pact was suggested.[123] Then toward the end of December the Soviet Commissar of Foreign Affairs made a speech in which he blasted possible British-French action, saying "They propose to defend the integrity of Rumania and Poland. Why only their integrity?" His answer was the same diatribe. "Because they believed that these aggressions . . . would hit us . . . . Why not the integrity of the Black Sea and Baltic states . . . we are left to defend these alone. We can do it."[124]

Other signs of growing Soviet influence in the Balkans also began to appear in the Balkans during the fall. The Hungarian Legation in Moscow and the Soviet Legation in Bucharest were reopened as Russian troops moved to the Hungarian border. Viewing the growing Russian presence with alarm was Italy. When the Soviets invaded Poland in September, the *Observatore Romano* devoted its whole issue to it and condemned Moscow for stabbing Poland in the back, and Rome became extremely vocal in claiming the Southeast. When storm clouds began to appear in Nazi-Soviet relations (in mid-October Germany made a decision to build a Siegfried Line along the German-Russian border), the Italians took an even more strident position, the Italian press editorializing that as Italy faced and defeated Bolshevism in Spain, she would do so anywhere there was an intrusion into the Italian sphere. In December the Fascist Grand Council said that anything that would happen in the Danube Basin was of definite interest to Italy, and an article in *Gazzetta Del Poppolo* of Turin told Russia in plain terms, hands off the Balkans and soon after anti-Russian demonstrations were "permitted, if not encouraged" by the Government.[125]

The Yugoslavs, who initially had seen little threat to Soviet influence and even found it helpful in providing a counterweight to Germany and Italy, in bringing Slav-Teuton sentiment together internally, and in keeping Gemany out of the Black Sea and Balkans, soon found that the growing Bolshevik element began to threaten internal stability there too, by adding a new dimension in the field of foreign affairs, that is between those who were pro-German, pro-Italian and pro-Soviet. Reports of Communist propaganda, violent speeches and demonstrations against the allies, and shootings and beatings suggest that both the Nazis and the

Communists were endeavoring to weaken Yugoslav resistance to external aggression.[126]

Bulgaria too began to feel threatened, fully expecting Russia to soon take Bessarabia with Nazi acquiescence and then hand them Dobruja, and so Sofia dug even more deeply into a policy of neutrality which meant for the moment accepting her boundaries. In mid-October as reports of Communist influence in the country grew, Kiosseivanov made Cabinet changes allowing him more control over foreign affairs (so as not to have to receive Dobruja, at the hands of the Russians, for instance), and then in early November, shaken by the establishment of a puppet Finnish Communist state, with British good offices, Turkish-Bulgarian troop reductions were made, and soon the Prime Minister warmed toward the Balkan bloc idea hoping the Italians could offset the Russian influence.

But rather than advocating resistance to Russia, Bulgarian sentiment led to appeasement all around, the Prime Minister espousing the view that Finland should have made more concessions, that the West should appease Hitler to stop Russia, and on the home front that Bulgaria would allow Russian troops to pass if Rumania resisted a Russian takeover of Bessarabia. Kiosseivanov said the Russian Minister had assured him that the Soviets had no intention of spreading propaganda because Russia wanted a strong Bulgaria and if Bolshevised she would become weak therefore provoking an attack by Bulgaria's neighbors and Italy who could not afford a Bolshevized Russia, but the Prime Minister hardly could have been reassured as the results of the December election came in, whereby two of four opposition deputies were Communist.[127]

The Greek view of the new presence of Russia in the Southeast was skewed by their continued perception that Italy was the main threat. In this regard, Mavroudis believed that Italy was deliberately endeavoring to create war in the north (Rumania) in order to keep Germany and Russia away from the Dardanelles, and to this end Italy was maneuvering as well as she could, warning Germany not to come too close to the Adriatic, withdrawing support from the neutral bloc because she wanted to disassociate from a country she now considered doomed (Rumania), and encouraging Hungary to take action against Transylvania which was certain to happen if Russia attacked Bessarabia.[128] The Greek view that the real threat to the Balkans was Italo-Hungarian exploitation of a Russian move on Bessarabia was close to fact in Hungary, where in mid-

December, Teleki had maps and papers prepared illustrating the approximately one-half of Transylvania Hungary expected Rumania to cede.[129]

The Turkish view of the new presence of Russia in the Balkans was to the effect that the Soviet Union had resorted to czarist imperialism having the Straits as the main goal, but because she was not morally or materially ready to fight for it, she would opportunistically cooperate with Germany and act as a jackal feeding where bolder beasts had killed.[130] Behind this hard-nosed pragmatic view, the Turks had a malingering belief and disappointment that the Russians had violated a friendship which had begun in the days when both countries were international pariahs fighting against intervention, and that they had violated the 1929 Treaty of Non-Aggression (providing for consultation in advance of other political agreements) which the Turks believed they had been faithful to, making the Soviets privy to all negotiations with the British and French.

Hungary was more hostile to the Bolsheviks than even the Rumanians and she particularly feared in October that the Turks would give in to Russia, exposing Hungary to Russian domination which they saw growing in the Balkans as a result of the changes in the Bulgarian Government. But instead of leaning to the German side as the Rumanians were inclined to do, Budapest turned to Italy, which had the added advantage of replacing now defunct German support for revisionism with Italian, which was necessary, according to the Hungarian Foreign Minister, because Germany had given Rumania a guarantee against Hungary in exchange for one of the largest oil fields of Rumania. Soon Budapest began to envisage herself as the dominant force in the Balkans backed by Italy, a part the Italians were glad to play, promising to send Italian troops through Yugoslavia to Hungary if the Soviet Union attacked Hungary.[131]

The Soviet invasion of Finland finally convinced just about everyone in the Balkans that what they had seen protecting them in the Nazi-Soviet Pact, a truce over competitive Nazi-Soviet aims in the Southeast, was over, and, therefore, that neutrality for them was a dead issue, bringing the Balkan pot once again to a boil. Along with that, the idea of a Balkan-Danubian bloc died hard, bedeviled as it was once again by the Axis desire to keep the Balkan countries at loggerheads, by intra-Balkan suspicions, fears, disparate aims and interests, and by bloc-counter-bloc politics. While the origin of the neutral bloc idea (which began to be discussed everywhere in the Balkans by mid-October) is obscure, it was generally believed that the idea originated in Rome and that Rumania latched on to it as a result of her precarious position, particularly her fear of a Russian attack.

Apparently, the Rumanian Ambassador in Greece, Mr. Djuvara, had laid before the Greek Government in mid-November proposals for a neutral bloc in Southeast Europe including Italy, Bulgaria and Hungary, and in so doing he emphasized its neutrality rather than mutual assistance. The Greeks were reserved in their reply saying that they must consult first with Turkey and that in any case the reactions of the Great Powers would be decisive. They did express some favor if Italy was involved thus forcing Italian neutrality, and if territorial concessions to Bulgaria were not involved. They offered the suggestion, however, that the Balkan Entente was a better nucleus involving Bulgaria and Italy, and in this respect Mavroudis believed that the Rumanian proposals had not been sufficiently studied before being hastily "passed around on a platter" and were due to the "panic" which had set in in Bucharest that once Russia had finished off Finland, they would fall on Bessarabia.[132]

The Bulgarians voiced several objections to the idea. Minister Papov said that since all the Balkan states were unanimous in their desire to maintain neutrality and were disposed to wait until after the war to settle their disputes, that a bloc would serve no useful purpose and might involve them in difficulties with the Great Powers. In addition, the general view was that it was aimed primarily at Russia and to a lesser extent Germany and therefore, not neutral, and that its origins were in Rumania and Italy backed by Great Britain through Turkey, and its failure, therefore, would be in Bulgaria's favor. The Bulgarians also objected to the way it was presented to Bulgaria whereby the members of the Balkan Entente came to agreement and then presented it to Bulgaria on a take it or leave it basis. The Prime Minister believed that the bloc would cause Rumania to resist the Russian conquest of Bessarabia, in turn causing Russia to overrun the whole Black Sea coast which the Russians were now fortifying.[133]

The favorable reaction in Hungary to the neutral bloc idea probably had more to do with turning everyone against it, Balkan and Great Powers alike, than anything else. Vornle admitted on October 9 that while Hungary had not been approached to join the neutral bloc envisaged by recent Rome radio announcements and given prominence in other capitals,

Hungary welcomed the move by Italy. What Hungary really seemed to welcome, however, was not a neutral bloc, but the part Hungary would play in the rearrangement of the Balkans to her own advantage with Italy's blessings. To this end Hungary first went to work to weaken Rumania. After a frontier incident involving Hungarian minorities in Transylvania, in which many Roman Catholic priests were reportedly involved, Csáky made a pugilistic speech to Parliament (November 21) toward Rumania (characterized by Csáky to U.S. Minister Montgomery as a "periodic pleasantry" enchanged between the two countries). When pressed as to why Italy would encourage Hungary to make trouble with Rumania resulting in the weakening of Rumania in the face of Russian aggression, Eckhardt replied that both Hungary and Rumania now had a common frontier with the Soviets and if Soviet troops took Bessarabia, it would not be a catastrophe, but if she invaded Hungary it would be a tragedy for the world, Hungary being civilized and Roman Catholic.[134]

Clearly the Hungarians believed such a Soviet invasion would be "impossible without all-out war," and that in the interim they should make whatever arrangements they could in the Balkans to their advantage. After the attacks on Rumania, Budapest began to soften up Yugoslavia, first by talks under the guise of a neutral bloc regarding normalization in relations and later in discussions between Maček and Eckhardt, by outright demands (return of Szebedka where 14% of the population was Slav, Baranya, and preferential tariffs). Eckhardt went on to say that Italy recognized that a Balkan bloc was impossible at the present time and therefore desired the union of certain Catholic peoples, for example the Hungarians, Croats and Slovenes in order to stop Russian penetration and that Maček himself believed and backed the breaking away of Slovenia and Croatia and then the union of Serbs and Bulgars.[135]

As far as the Great Powers were concerned, France expressed complete accord at Bucharest with the bloc idea, but in Ankara advised the Turks to go slow. (The indecisiveness was apparently due to a struggle within the Quai D'Orsay between those who believed an agreement with Russia was still possible and those who were concerned with the effects of such a neutral pact on promoting friendship with Italy or the Soviet Union.) Britain, on the other hand, was leery of any pact including Turkey which was not aimed at mutual assistance and instead urged Turkey to work out some sort of agreement with Italy in order to form a neutral bloc. The

Germans, who were habitually interested in blocs only as it served their purposes, were in this case only lukewarm, being interested only as it tended to reinforce Turkish neutrality, though the Italians believed the Germans were against it because of its anti-Soviet character and the fear that if the Russians entered the Balkans, Italy and Hungary would team up. Significantly, Russia was not approached except by Rumania and then Molotov never replied to the note.[136]

Apparently, the plan lost favor with Italy too. Beneath Italy's rejection was the desire not to once again be a stooge for Germany in Balkan pacification (in German circles it was asserted that Italy was acting for Germany thus reinforcing the neutrality of the Balkans, creating a firm front against Russia, and isolating Turkey),[137] the desire to maintain liberty of action as long as possible, and because it might involve the Balkans in Great Power politics at an unpropitious time for Italy. In an address to the Chamber, Ciano said that Italy is a "Balkan power who wishes to see order and peace" and that she did not "see the formation of a bloc as necessary." The Italian retreat on the Balkan bloc idea coincided with the Duce's decision in late December that a Balkan bloc would be counterproductive and more particularly that the Italian stand against Russia would be in Hungary at the Carpathians (not Bessarabia). This decision was based, of course, on their view that Germany would let Bessarabia go and on the increasing hostility in Italy to Russia, not Germany.[138] And, much to the dismay of the Hungarians, who had traded in Germany for Italy only to find as had Yugoslavia that playing Axis powers off against each other was futile, Rome cautioned Csáky against aggression against Rumania, prompting a heightened sense of militarism in Hungary.

The reception of the idea in the Balkans while guarded, seemed to indicate some sort of desire for unity in the Balkans not within but against Germany, and even more against Russian aggression following what the Turkish Ambassador in Greece had called "Hitler's unloosing of the Russian serpent." As the neutral pact idea lost steam, the Balkan countries again fell back on the Balkan Entente as a forum for discussion and coalition, hoping to graft neutrality to it. The four Ministers of Foreign Affairs met in Belgrade on February 2-4, 1940 and again there were discussions of reciprocity of military assistance and concessions to Bulgaria, but nothing definitive was arrived at. Gafencu apparently even proposed that the four states engage themselves individually to defend in common any infringement of territory of one of the member states, but Metaxas objected proposing instead a defense of the national independence of any one of the other states by collective action of the other members. Cinkar-Marković remained wedded to the theme of neutrality for Yugoslavia and avoidance of military alliances. Regarding Bulgaria, Saracoglu obtained from Gafencu assurances that the Triangle of Silistria in Dobruja would be returned to Bulgaria after the war provided Bulgaria remained neutral, and Metaxas said he was willing to grant Bulgaria a free port on the Aegean and free passage across Greek territory to it, but he refused to cede any territory.[139] Thus the Entente was stalemated once again on the key issues dividing and fragmenting the Balkans.

* * * * *

While Western diplomats reeled under the blow the Nazi-Soviet Pact believing it meant the end of the Balkans by division, neutralization, or alliance with Germany against Russia (it did spell the end of hopes of an alliance with the West), such as not the initial perception in the Balkans. Despite the keen appreciation in Balkan capitals of Soviet predatory aims in their direction, the Balkans breathed a sigh of relief because the Pact, in their view, warded off the possibilities of a Nazi-Soviet war or Italian invasion and thus large-scale revisionism, and preserved the neutrality of the area which they had long sought as the best hope for their survival. Positive results of the pacification seemed immediately evident in intra-Balkan relations, both Hungary and Bulgaria toning down their revisionism mostly at the behest of Hitler who having secured the area, was above all interested in maintenance of the status quo.

This aura of confidence was short-lived however, for the Soviet invasion of Poland, pressure on the Turks, and Soviet encouragement to Bulgaria renewed fears that the Balkans would become the seat of a Nazi-Soviet war, a Balkan war, or a division of territory between the two, any of which spelled the end to national survival. There was renewed optimism, therefore, when Nazi-Soviet differences were patched up by the Treaty of Boundary and Friendship, which among other things confined territorial division to Poland. This apparent Nazi-Soviet collaboration threatened peril for the Turks, however, because it was feared that the pressure of both powers would cause Turkey to sign a treaty with Russia giving

Moscow favorable treatment at the Straits and to Berlin relinquishment of Turkish ties with the West. In such a case, the Balkans would be the complete hostage of the powers to either side, as the only hope of allied support to the Balkans was through the Straits, Turkey and Greece.

During the Russo-Turkish negotiations, which for a period were carried on simultaneously in Moscow with the Nazi-German Boundary and Friendship Treaty negotiations, the Soviets again played a dialectical game whereby they used the threat of Russo-Turkish negotiations against the Germans to exact favorable terms regarding Poland, and then the threat of a Nazi-Soviet combination against the Turks to obtain favorable terms at the Straits. The Turks, however, fearful and suspicious, did just the opposite signing the Tripartite with Great Britain and the French. During the Turko-Soviet negotiations, like during the Nazi-Soviet negotiations, the Soviets collaborated with the Germans only to the extent that it helped them, thus displaying once again that Nazi-Soviet interests were both competitive and complementary in Southeast Europe, and that their aim above all was to keep the capitalist war going which now meant not enriching German power too much by forcing Turkey toward the Axis. The Tripartite Pact was not greeted with the enthusiasm one might have expected in the Balkans because, as with the Anglo-Franco-Turkish Declaration, it was feared that Turkish straying from strict neutrality would be detrimental, though it was recognized particularly in Rumania and Greece that Turkish independence was crucial in keeping their route open to the West.

Whether interpreted as a blessing or a curse in the Balkans, one fact was clear all over the Balkans after the Nazi-Soviet Pact, the Boundary and Friendship Treaty and the invasions of Poland and Finland, and that was how enormously Soviet power had advanced in the area. The Rumanians particularly were frantic for they possessed interests immediate to both sides—Bessarabia for the Russians and oil for the Germans—as well as being the focus of Bulgarian and Hungarian revisionist aspirations easily fueled by both powers, and in the case of Bessarabia, unprotected by the Balkan Entente. Equally disturbed by an advancing Soviet sphere was Italy, and so soon there was circulated by Rumania and backed by Italy, another scheme for Balkan collectivism dubbed the "neutral bloc" which envisaged a Balkan bloc including Bulgaria and Italy but not Hungary, and dedicated to neutrality rather than mutual assistance. The plan, like other Balkan unification attempts was stalemated by Hungarian exploitation of

Italian backing, by friction between revisionist and status quo states and those dedicated to strict neutrality and those for qualified neutrality, by fears of Italian hegemony, and by the negative reactions of the Great Powers. Therefore, the Balkan countries fell back once again on the Balkan Entente whose attempts in early 1940 to form a united Balkan front, neutral or otherwise, failed.

The threat of the Soviets, not only as a result of the Pact but because of the very existence of the Pact, above all else, showed German vulnerability and Soviet strength. There was disagreement in the Balkans over how this new strength could be utilized, Yugoslavia for instance seeing it as a weapon of survival against both Axis powers, and Bulgaria as a weapon against Rumania. What this foreshadowed, of course, was the new decision the Balkans faced, Russia or Germany. Even worse was the realization that there had to be a choice, and that no longer was the option of "the Balkans for the Balkans" provided them by the British. A new contest was under way, and only an equivalency of power between the USSR and Germany, not moral principle, could save them now.

Conclusion

Hitler seemed at all times confident that he could have a pact with the Soviet Union if he wanted one. Because it was Hitler's habit to concentrate on one victim at a time, it was not until Poland failed to submit, that the need for the neutralization of the Soviet Union through a pact became apparent to Hitler, though long before this, the German military had advocated such a pact to avoid a two-front war and the diplomats to prevent isolation. In rapid succession Prague, Albania, the guarantees, and the Anglo-Soviet talks, threatened to disturb the peace of the Balkans and bring Soviet interests into play against Germany. Hence, to bring the Balkans back to a neutral position and to prevent a Soviet alliance with the West, Hitler moved toward Moscow. Meanwhile, these same events strengthened the Soviet Union's defensive position, increased her desire for a German expression of neutrality and most important of all, gave the Soviet Union a concession-free negotiating position vis-a-vis the Germans.

The negotiations, which began through an economic medium, soon turned into negotiations against the West with the stakes set by Moscow. The Soviets never budged from their original demand that for neutrality vis-a-vis Germany, their interests from the Baltic to the Black Sea must be considered. The Germans were quite willing to give the Soviets the Baltic states, part of Poland, and Bessarabia, but not Rumania or the Balkans, Rumania primarily because of the Danube and the need for oil, and the Balkans because of their need for raw materials, because of the danger that any division over spheres in this area would turn it once again into the powder keg of Europe, and because of the need to keep Italy on their side.

What to do about the Balkans was a very delicate issue, for both the Germans and Soviets had interests there, and the least revisionism was equal to a Balkan explosion and a runaway war. However, since for both powers pacification of the area was the overriding concern, a detente based on an acceptance of the Balkan status quo was arrived at. Since Bessarabia was not considered part of the Balkans (by the Balkan Entente for instance), and because German power seemed overwhelming, this very vague concession to the Soviets seemed safe. For the Soviets it was a gain in terms of the promise of Bessarabia and in terms of the fact that the Pact provided for consultation in concerns of mutual interests, to which any alteration in the area now applied. The Germans, meanwhile, got continued claim to Balkan material, maintained political control of the area, and secured their rear while the Soviets hoped that the Pact itself would pressure the allies into an agreement with concessions in the Southeast denied them by the Germans.

Despite the fact that the Nazi-Soviet Pact had the potential of crushing the Balkans from both sides, the shrewd Balkan statesmen, whose estimations were based on the familiarity of long years of border history, banked on mutual Nazi-Soviet claims and competitive rather than complementary interests to prevent any such extermination of the interim states, and they were genuinely happy that the non-aggression features of the Pact prevented a Nazi-Soviet war in the Balkans. And, the Pact warded off another threat, that of Italian action. Hence King Carol's comment that nothing had substantially changed. Soviet action against Poland, revisionist statements on Bulgaria's behalf, and negotiations with Turkey, however, made the Balkans once again fearful that precipitous Soviet action would bring on a Nazi-Soviet war on their territory. However, the limited nature of the Soviet action which was directed for the moment against Poland only, the failure of the Soviets to gain concessions from the Turks at the Straits, and the failure of the Anglo and Franco-Turkish Mutual Assistance Pact to extend itself to the Balkans, preserved a little longer the precarious national existence of these small interim states. In the meantime, they scurried about once again trying to form some sor of neutral Balkan bloc, but the idea was scuttled again by intra-Balkan antipathies and Great Power politics.

But detente was already in trouble once the Germans had their backs turned to the Soviets and were using up some of their strength, particularly in the Southeast where the Germans needed the status quo more and the Soviets less and where delimitation of any revisionism was extremely difficult. By the end of 1939 the future of the Southeast was already apparent whereby German acquiescence in a Soviet move against Bessarabia would cause a wave of revisionism and finally the entrance of Italy into the war.

EPILOGUE

By December 1939, some Balkan observers were predicting the end of 🐾 detente and the clash of Nazi-Soviet interests in the Balkans whose nexus would be focused in Rumania. As U.S. Military Attache J. P. Ratay wrote, as long as the war lasted, status quo of the Balkans was of the greatest concern to Germany and increasingly less so to the Soviets who would like to see war on general principle because:

> The States here could not go through a war without revolutions following, and some Slav and one or two non-Slavic countries would be in line to join Russia as Soviet Republics. The way for Russia to the Mediterranean would then be open.[1]

Ratay further speculated that Russia could start a war with the attack on Rumania, which if limited to Bessarabia the Germans might pressure Rumania into ceding (the Rumanians not being fighters like the Serbs or Bulgarians), though the question remained as to whether or not in making concessions, Germany could hold in check Hungary and the rest of Southeastern Europe. Ratay concluded that Germany would strive to avoid a showdown as long as possible, attempt to interest Russia in the Near East and Asia thus not using up vital resources which Germany needed, and that Italy would play along until things were more definite.

At Ratay predicted, Stalin soon began to claim his due and to advance his more secret aims. In late 1939 an article in "Revue Internationale" referred to Soviet intentions in Rumania and in March 1940, Molotov

254

made a speech in which he openly referred to the Soviet wish to get Bessarabia back. In June 1940, exploiting the situation whereby Germany
had her back turned to Russia and was heavily engaged in the West, whereby the possibility of delimiting the war in the Balkans was waning (for also
taking advantage of German preoccupation, in May, Hungary mobilized,
Italy entered the war, and Russian troops moved into the Baltic and toward the Rumanian frontier), and whereby Germany's economic and
strategic interests were most in need of pacification, the newly arrived
Russian Minister to Rumania, Larentiev, delivered a 24-hour ultimatum
to Bucharest demanding the return of Bessarabia and cession of northern
Bukovina (no one seemed certain what that meant).

The King, the Council, and the German and Italian ministers confer-
red all day over the matter and at 7:30 p.m. German Colonel Gerstenburg
told Ratay that:

> The present predicament serves the Rumanians right. They should
> have returned the British guarantee long ago. Now they come run-
> ning to us for help. . . . The negotiations will take place between
> Rumania and Russia, and Berlin will exercise the necessary pressure
> on Russia to keep her from becoming unreasonable. She will get out
> of this that part of Bukovina which is inhabited by Ukrainians. . . .
> Russia will not get Bessarabia. We must take care of our interests
> there which are the mouth of the Danube and 80,000 Germans.

He added that from the military standpoint, "The Russians are putting on
a big bluff. . . ." and that troops on the frontier were "purely a military
demonstration to help along negotiations. . . . I assure you, there will be
no bombing attacks or air invasions of Rumania. For that, Rumania is
entirely too valuable."[2]

In the meantime Rumania had sought out the Balkan Entente members
who in turn counseled her to settle the dispute, giving Rumania another
reason for a peaceful solution. But the Germans, having given a green light
to a conference to settle the matter confident they could dominate, were
outsmarted by the Soviets. The Rumanians in Bucharest were informed
that the Russians would accept the Rumanian proposal to negotiate, but
there was much difficulty in getting the message to the Rumanian Minister
in Moscow, the Russians obviously hoping that the ultimatum time would

expire. In Moscow, when the Rumanian Minister, having received his instructions in the nick of time, proposed negotiations, he was cut short and asked if "it was unconditional acceptance of the ultimatum or not." Caught off guard, he said yes, whereupon immediately a note was handed to him demanding evacuation of Bukovina in two days and Bessarabia in four.

On June 28, the U.S. Attache in Bucharest reported officials of the German Legation in bad humor, and he reported Colonel Gerstenburg as saying, "Yes, the Russians double-crossed us in more than one way. But we will straighten this out and do it soon," and on June 29 Dr. Neubacher, Economics Minister and great friend of Hitler said:

> In this matter the Russians as well as the British put one over on us ...as long as Russia sticks to the terms of this agreement, we shall do nothing. However if Russia endangers our economic interests there, we shall move fast. The Russians are very close to our oil fields, only 30-50 minutes. We may have to establish a nest for our eagles here. We have now large forces free or almost free. We do not need them for England.

Neubacher ended by saying, "Russia has made a big mistake. Hitler is offended and he never forgets."[3] In Berlin the General Staff admitted that the Russian move was not to their liking—"uns nicht angenehm" though it would not be a decisive factor in the war and should have come eight weeks earlier for success.[4]

Another spokesman admitted that the Bessarabian concession might cause Hungary and Bulgaria to also want parts of Rumania, though this was well understood. Events confirmed his misgivings. On June 19 there was rioting outside the German Embassy in Bulgaria for the return of Dobruja and shortly thereafter Hungary began to show fears that Germany would placate Russia at Hungarian expense. Germany and Italy counseled Hungary to patience, but it was clear now that for the Balkans to be restabilized and for German interests to be protected, the Germans must move in, a move now welcomed in Rumania due to strengthened anti-Soviet sentiment and fear of her Balkan neighbors. On July 1 Rumania renounced the British-French guarantee, on July 3 the last Rumanian soldier left the ceded territory amidst a National Day of Mourning, on July 4, a new pro-German Cabinet was installed.

On July 10, Ciano, Csáky and Teleki met without Rumanian presence to do surgery on the rest of Rumania, and when their demands got out of hand, Hitler stepped in and ordered negotiations. The loss of Bessarabia meant nothing compared to what the loss of Transylvania would mean to Rumania, and on this issue the overwhelming weight of Rumanian public opinion was for resistance. This mood and the fact that King Carol could threaten to blow up the oil fields, gave him a not untenable position when he sat down to negotiate.

The decisive factor in their capitulation was the Soviet Union, particularly the Soviet Ambassador's menacing references to a frontier incident which might mean intervention. This was Moscow's way of serving notice to Germany and her allies that the Soviet Union was still interested in the country the Axis powers were carving up without consultation provided for in the Nazi-Soviet Pact. Scared, the Rumanians signed the Second Vienna Awards, giving half of Transylvania to Hungary and a small part of south Dobruja to Bulgaria, hoping to prevent just a little longer a Nazi-Soviet war or total occupation. For the Germans it was a sop to Hungary (and Italy), and an attempt to maintain the status quo of the area, for all the petroleum and natural gas had been carefully left with Rumania, giving Hungary no resources with which to industrialize nor did any part of the Danube pass out of German control.[5]

The dismemberment of Rumania led directly to two other confrontations involving claims to the same Rumanian territory by the Nazis and Russians. Immediately after the Awards, Germany guaranteed what was left of Rumania, which could only have been meant against the Soviet Union, and on September 12, a conference including Germany, Yugoslavia, Hungary, Slovakia, Rumania, Bulgaria and Italy was held in Vienna under German leadership to supplant the European Danube Commission with a Commission in which German influence was predominant. The conference carefully avoided a discussion of the river flowing below Braila bordering on the newly acquired Russian territory, which remained under the European Danube Commission control on which Russia had never been represented. The USSR subsequently announced interest in the matter and insisted that the Danube Delta be administered by the USSR, who was not a riparian nation, and Rumania alone. That same month German troops arrived in Rumania to train, the excuse being to protect the oil fields from British sabotage, but the net effect, which everyone was aware of, was that the non-aggression features of the pact were dependent on the Balkan status quo which was fast being disturbed by the conflicting interests of both parties.

The Italians, of course, felt that the German penetration of the Balkans was a betrayal of their sphere too, and so, eager for glory and fearful that Hitler would leave him out in the cold or restrain him, Mussolini launched an attack on Greece at the end of October 1940. As a consequence, the Italian position in Albania was weakened, making it appear that Britain would gain a foothold there and then extend her influence into Southeast Europe. So Rumania was not enough. Now Bulgaria and Yugoslavia had to permit German troops, and this too angered Moscow.

On Molotov's visit to Berlin in November 1940, Hitler tried to retrieve the threatened situation with the Soviets by offering to Moscow the prospect (since it was not yet his to give) of a sphere in Asia to include the Straits, the Persian Gulf and the shores of the Indian Ocean, in exchange for the Balkans. But Molotov brought the issue back to the Balkans, demanding that Germany and Italy recognize that now Bulgaria lay in the security zone of the Russian Black Sea boundaries, and that the Axis accept the necessity of a mutual security pact between the USSR and Bulgaria (synonymous to the Soviets moving their troops into Bulgaria). Hitler did not assent, and deciding the Nazi-Soviet Pact had lost its value, he decided on December 18, 1940 to invade the Soviet Union.

The struggle for Bulgaria took the form of Germany pressing Bulgaria to adhere to the Axis, while the Russians made statements to the effect that entrance of foreign troops into Bulgaria would activate Turkish action, thus opening the Straits to the British. Boris, like Carol, seemed to believe that ultimately Germany or Russia would dominate Southeast Europe (Britain was discounted as unlikely by both). He was of German descent and feared Communism, and he knew he would get back an outlet to the Aegean if Germany attacked Greece, and so, on March 1, 1941, he signed the Axis Pact, having received word a few days earlier that Germany was sending troops into Bulgaria to keep Bulgaria from Greece, and that Berlin had no intention of attacking Turkey.

Meanwhile, Yugoslavia tried to maintain neutrality in a precarious new act, balancing the Soviet Union off against Germany (just as she had earlier tried between Italy and Germany). In the spring of 1940, she renewed relations with the USSR, and after twenty years of enmity, a trade and military delegation went to Moscow. Relations with Bulgaria improved as a result. At the same time, Belgrade maintained a rigid neutrality, refusing a German offer to seize Salonika while the Greeks were fighting against Albania, and refusing a secret Turkish offer of an alliance which, if accepted, might have kept Bulgaria from yielding to Hitler. Then Prince Paul signed a Pact of Eternal Friendship with Hungary, but in the end all his efforts failed.

On March 25, 1941, Yugoslavia yielded to the Axis Pact, for it seemed she could not defend her frontiers and there was the hope, that as a member of the Axis Pact, Germany would guarantee the Yugoslav borders and not ask for troop passage. Besides, Russia was very far away. Paul's action, however, prompted a surprise coup on March 26, removing him from office. *Pravda* congratulated this bold action, which brought Moscow back to Belgrade. Shortly thereafter, a Soviet-Yugoslav Friendship Pact of practically no value to Belgrade was signed. Yugoslavia too succumbed to the Axis onslaught.

In May, Germany defeated the Greeks and the conquest of the Balkans was complete. As a result of the Soviets' own perfidy, the Germans moved toward the Russian frontier. The Soviet reaction was to try to appease Hitler, for example, expelling the Yugoslav Embassy, but the next stage of the war—Russian isolation and then invasion—was already on. Now the Soviet Union had to ally herself with the West or be defeated, or so it seemed. By the time the Soviet Union joined the West, however, the Russian war had been won, and so the original question set down in the summer of 1939, the price of Soviet participation in a war outside her borders was again posed, but with one important distinction. The war for the Balkans was now one of liberation not defense, and so, not only was the contribution asked of the Soviets greater, but the price tag was higher, the British need greater, and the Balkan voice weaker. And so, the prophecy that the Balkans would go to Germany or to the Soviets, but not the West, was fulfilled, as was the Balkan dictum that neutrality, in whosoever's sphere would mean not freedom, but national survival.

CONCLUSION

In Hitler's long-range theoretical planning, the importance of the Balkans was seen in terms of their position on the road to German settlement of Russia, as they might figure in the isolation of Poland, and as they related to the need to neutralize Germany's rear during the initial thrust against France. In actuality, as events progressed and the German program evolved, the economic value became increasingly important, though this was frequently overemphasized or ignored the basic presumption underlying the economic assault which was political. That is, as the Heartland theory dictated, it was at all times assumed that the Balkans fell within the German strategic and political sphere, which in turn made it possible to exploit the economic advantage without costly occupation. Since the Balkans were potentially as explosive a powder keg to Hitler as they had been prior to World War I, rather than risk any alteration of the status quo, benevolent Balkan neutrality was the aim most amicable to German interests in that it prevented a Balkan eruption involving the Soviet Union, Italy and Britain. Therefore, neutralization, economic satellization and Balkanization were the main foreign policies pursued by Germany in the Southeast.

The period from the Rhineland to Prague saw Germany's shadow spread out all over the Balkans, fulfilling Hitler's vision of a fragmented and paralyzed enclave of small states subservient to Berlin. This was accomplished by carefully orchestrating revisionist-status quo antagonisms in the Balkans by stalemating French action in the East, and by forging an alliance with Italy isolating the Balkans. With the dissolution of Czecho-slovakia, the Little Entente was destroyed and two of the Balkan Entente's key members, Rumania and Yugoslavia, were immobilized. With that, schemes of Balkan unity, strongly entreatied against by Hitler, were no longer an option in the Balkan defense scheme against the Nazis, while Balkan economic dependence took a giant leap forward. The one un-certainty in Germany's Balkan position was Turkey, but Hitler played this down, believing that Turkey would ultimately come to the Axis side because Ankara feared Russia more than Germany, because of Italian pressure, and because an accommodation with Great Britain isolating Turkey could be forged. With Britain out of the picture and Turkey on the German side, Hitler fancied that his main enemy in the Balkans was Rus-sia and, therefore, he concentrated on the Danube not the Straits as the key to control of the Balkans and the route to control of the heartland.

Prague and its aftermath completed the circle of Balkan subduel. The grant of the Carpatho-Ukraine to Hungary for collaboration in the dis-solution of Czechoslovakia bought Budapest's subservience, and the grant of Teschen to Poland put the final touches on the division of East Europe north and south. The changes in territory whetted Bulgaria's appetites, increasing the indirect pressures on intra-Balkan territorial disagreements, and the tendency of all the Balkans to look to German will for protection and relief. Meanwhile, the Soviet Union quietly moved the line of her de-fenses back to her borders, achieving for the Nazis what they wanted in the East—Balkan vassalage and a neutralized Soviet Union, making Polish submission all but inevitable.

Hitler's move to dissolve Czechoslovakia on March 15, 1939 ended allied appeasement and led to the jockeying for position in East Europe that eventually led to war at the end of August. The allies countered the German-Rumanian economic agreement with a guarantee to Poland; after Italy moved against Albania, the allies guaranteed Rumania and Greece and then tied down Turkey; this the Axis opposed with the Pact of Steel and German anti-encirclement. The final posturing came in the effort by both sides to win Russia and when the allies lost, the scales tipped to the German side particularly in East Europe, and the war began.

The reentrance of Britain into the affairs of the Balkans changed every-thing. Suddenly Balkan loyalties were questionable, the prospects of an unpredicted Italian move increased, and most of all, the groundwork for the reassertion of Soviet interests was laid. The major aim of German policy now was to prevent encirclement, an aim which was carried out by the destruction of intra-Balkan and Balkan-Polish unity, by stalemating a Soviet agreement with the West, and by gaining control over Italy. With regard to the former, threats of unleashing revisionist Bulgaria and Hungary (and its reverse, promises of territory to the revisionist nations), cessation of arms sales, overtures to the Soviet Union, and the Pact of Steel were used. Of these tactics, threats of revisionism was definitely the most persuasive, but it had its limitations even for Hitler, for it was a Pandora's Box in the Balkans which, once opened, was difficult if not impossible to control. With regard to the Soviets, the opening of negotiations between Berlin and Moscow with promises of neutrality and territory, it was hoped, would prevent Moscow from going to the side of the West as well as threaten the Balkans back toward neutrality. Meanwhile, the Moscow connection and the Pact of Steel, it was hoped, would control Italy but keep her at Germany's side.

During the spring and summer of 1939, the desire of the Balkan countries as stated at the February meeting of the Balkan Entente to maintain the status quo and to be neutral, was severely tested by the pressures placed on them by the Great Powers to take sides, and by the increased chances of a Balkan conflict brought on by the heightened tempo and pitch of the revisionist-status quo antagonisms which this interference and the threat of war elicited. Pulling from one side toward unity and defense against the Axis were the British and French. Pulling the other way for disunity and benevolent neutrality toward them were the Axis powers. Meanwhile, the Soviet Union faintheartedly interjected the idea of a Balkan defense ring under Soviet hegemony and when this failed, Moscow sat on the fence, threatening the Balkans from either side.

The tug-of-war carried on by the Great Powers all but exploded the Balkan peace which they (and the Nazis) had sought. Balkan Entente reconciliation with Bulgaria became impossible, Rumanian resistance to concessions in Dobruja stiffened, and Yugoslavia and Greece, against whom Bulgaria also had claims, were put on alert. In June and July there were incidents along the Bulgarian-Rumanian border, and it was feared that Yugoslavia would leave the Entente or disintegrate from within. Then as war approached in late August, troops all over the Balkans moved to the frontiers.

During these highly explosive few months, the Balkan states, by now terribly disunified, torn, and fractured by the competitive interests of the Great Powers in their territories and by their own disparate desires and divergent concepts of their own best interests, made attempts to maintain the Balkan peace by reiterating their policy of neutrality vis-a-vis the Great Powers and each other. While admittedly for self-serving purposes and of limited duration, this was, nonetheless, a display of an informal nature of the commonality of interests which the Southeastern states recognized they had. But it must also be recognized that neutrality was Hitler's policy also and probably would not have met with the success it did if unsupported by Berlin.

The overriding fear everywhere in the Balkans of war and therefore their desire to be neutral, caused the Balkan countries to greet the Nazi-Soviet Pact with quiet relief, for the non-aggression features of the Pact diminished the possibilities of a Nazi-Soviet war and a Nazi-Western war on their territories. At the same time, it stabilized their internal disputes and put pressure on Turkey to remain neutral. Meanwhile, they counted on the competitive rather than the complementary interests of the Nazis and Soviets to prevent a division of Balkan territory, a supposition which was challenged when the Soviets marched in to take half of Poland, increased Communist internal activity in the border states, supported Bulgarian revisionism, pressured Turkey for concessions at the Straits, and then invaded Finland. Recognition of growing Soviet power caused the Balkan governments to move again toward Berlin, but it aggravated internal stability and revisionist pressures in the countries and it paved the way for direct Nazi-Soviet confrontation at the nexus of Southeastern spheres in Bessarabia.

The British guarantee system had been meant to be a first step in the creation of an East European defense system including the Balkans, Poland, Turkey, and the Soviet Union, which was to act as a deterrent to war rather than an alliance in war. The question of whether or not a Balkan combination as a first step in that defense ring could have prevented a Nazi-Soviet Pact and war is an intriguing one, but unrelated to the realities of Balkan national interests. It was quite easy for the Western powers, who decided in 1939 that they valued freedom above peace, to have thought that such a grouping would save the area from the countries the West considered its greatest enemies, Germany and the Soviet Union.

However, the realities were that the small states of Southeast Europe have always existed under someone's umbrella, that their greatest enemies were each other and war, and that they had not the strength to collectively defend themselves against anyone. Neutrality, thus, served the Balkan purpose best, hence the reluctance of the Balkans to join together with the West, Poland or the Soviet Union against Germany. In the long run, the only better alternative was the Balkans as a Western battlefield against both Germany and the Soviet Union, a choice which was not viable due to the West's weakness, and may not even have been desirable, as the destruction such a war would have wrought even if the West had been victorious, would very likely have led to internal revolution and large-scale revisionism.

Therefore, rather than joining together in battle, the Balkans neutralized themselves, hoping that there would be a more propitious time in the future to advance their claims or secure their borders, and while Balkan neutrality did not serve the aims of the West, it seemed in the Balkans' best interest. Even today, the wisdom of that policy should not be denigrated, for while under the Soviet umbrella, Balkan nation statism has survived with a strength and vitality which is refreshing to the West and unnerving in other capitals. This would not have been true if the Germans or Soviets had occupied the area, which is the importance of the guarantees and the redeeming feature of the failure of the Anglo-Franco-Soviet talks. For the guarantees made necessary negotiation by all parties within the established nation-state framework, and they bulwarked the Soviets in their negotiations with the Nazis to the point that Hitler could not outright imperialize the Southeast. By the same token, successful Anglo-Franco-Soviet talks would have opened the way to Soviet troops, while their failure set up the framework for the Nazi-Soviet competition necessary to prevent encroachment by either power or Italy on the Southeast. Therefore, Balkan neutrality brought national survival, which even in its most rapacious form, appears to be the wish and desire of these peoples, and to the extent that there has been national survival, there has been freedom too.

Among other things the failure of the Balkan program led the British to open negotiations with the Russians on a bilateral basis. In these negotiations the British asked very little of the Soviets, wanting only a statement of support for the threatened states in the East and a highly circumscribed participation if it came to that. They did so out of the desire to keep the Soviet Union out of East Europe, because they believed the Soviets could and would offer them little concrete aid, and because the negotiations were in part tactical, that is, to keep the Soviet Union from going to the other side. The Soviets, for their part, constantly tried to broaden the scope of their involvement, making demands along the lines of military and political participation in all the states along their Western frontier irrespective of East European wishes. The breakdown of the negotiations came basically because the British would not cede territory in the East and because for the Soviets the negotiations were also tactical, designed to push the Germans into agreement.

The argument that the Germans offered neutrality and the West war does not hold up under close scrutiny, for the Britsh were asking not for participation but benevolency, while there is little evidence to support the idea that the Nazis would have invaded the Soviet Union if Moscow had declared on the side of the West, or that the Soviets would have fought for Poland or any of the Southeastern states, having declared that their defensive interests stopped at their borders. Nor is it quite accurate to accuse Soviet suspicions of the West for the breakdown of the Anglo-Franco-Soviet negotiations, for there were equal if not graver suspicions between the Nazis and Soviets. And to blame the Eastern states for failure to grant troop passage is surely misrepresenting their cause and that of the West, as well as missing sight of the issues involved, for Rumania and Poland readily accepted the need to do so once war began, and at issue for the West was the essence of their program which was meant as a deterrence rather than a wartime alliance, the defense of East Europe being directed against Moscow as well as Berlin.

The real issue for the Soviets went beyond the immediate concerns of the negotiations, deep into the heart of Russian history and Soviet ideology. With a global perspective and a long range view, their major aim was to start a capitalist war from which they could benefit ideologically and territorially. Because of Russian weakness, the means to this end was exploitation of the current conflicts in European and Asian politics as had so often been the case in the past when, due to a unique geographical position, major gains for Russia had been made by all means short of war. Their tactics were dialectical, whereby negotiations were used to gain leverage, to drive the opposing forces into combat, and to maintain at all times a balance between the opposing forces. Thus did Stalin throw his weight with Germany against the West in late August, only to reverse himself later in negotiations with the Turks.

Such interests and tactics were evident long before they were focused in East Europe in 1939. During the late 1930s Stalin did little to prevent the Fascist rise to power and later he joined the West in a "peace front" in order to goad the West into opposing the Axis powers, fueling the embers of conflict but turning it West. During this period, interest in the border states was seen only as it affected the broader pattern of struggle, Stalin at all times viewing these states as belonging to one or another of the Great Powers. War without Soviet participation was seen as advantageous in the border states where it was recognized that there particularly, none could go through a war without revolution, and that even in the most untoward circumstances whereby Germany came eastward, the Nazis would have to come through the border states first.

The theory was not always one hundred percent successful, as for instance during the Munich period when selective neutrality became imposed isolation and a Nazi-Soviet rather than a capitalist war seemed imminent with little leverage left to Moscow except a supreme confidence in her ability to defend herself if it came to that. At this time, Hitler, who was well aware of the real point of the "peace policy" (which was to draw the West into action against Germany leaving the East to Russia) was certain he had Soviet neutrality well in hand without a pact, as well as a free reign in the Balkans and Poland. But the reentrance of Britain into the affairs of the Balkans and Poland destroyed Nazi confidence in both Soviet and Balkan neutrality, it stalemated alliance with Japan, and it regained a negotiating position for the Soviet Union in European politics. The "peace front" once again became a "war front" and neutrality in the capitalist war but not isolation, was on the verge of reality. At stake were the interim states, particularly the Balkans where British interests and Nazi needs were paramount.

In this respect the self-neutralization policy of the Balkans had little effect on the Soviets who believed that the interim states were to be negotiated not with but for. Therefore, as far as the Soviets were concerned, the importance of the Balkan policy was as it affected the British and the Nazis who, because of the failure on both sides to draw the Balkans more tightly to them, increased the importance of the Soviets to both. Likewise for the British, the Balkans being but one phase of encirclement, and it was recognized from the beginning that regardless of what the Balkans did, the Soviets must be approached. On the other hand, the Balkan failure to unify and to commit itself, definitely was a factor, in that Balkan neutralization made it more necessary for the British to seek out Russia, more necessary and possible for Russia to gain some protection along her frontier, and more necessary for the Nazis to approach the Soviets.

The bulwarking of the Balkans against Germany and the threat that the Soviet Union would form a deadly union with the West, particularly the latter, forced the pace of Nazi-Soviet negotiations, which picked up considerable speed as the assault on Poland neared and the threat that the Soviets would go with the West to prevent that increased. The tremendous leverage which the Soviets now possessed, allowed them to claim interest in all the states from the Baltic to the Straits bordering on the Soviet Union. The Germans were willing to cede the Baltic states to Russia because they controlled the Baltic Sea and because of the increased pressure on Poland which would result from the concession. As far as Poland was concerned, the Nazis promised revisionism in exchange for Soviet action, though the extent of Polish territory ceded appears to have gone beyond what had been envisioned due to the failure of Italy and Hungary to take concordant action.

As far as the Southeast was concerned, one of the main reasons behind the Pact was Hitler's desire to exchange precarious Italian pressure on the Balkans for Soviet, but by the same token he wanted to cede nothing due to the need to secure his rear, the need to maintain access to raw materials particularly Rumanian oil, the need to keep Italy at the Nazi side and to control the Danube, and the necessity to maintain control over Balkan revisionism. The Soviets accepted this because they believed the pressure of the Pact would lead to Turkish concessions at the Straits and possibly a Pact with Britain with concessions in the Southeast.

The partial Bessarabian concession acknowledging Soviet political interest but not economic, appears to have been made under pressure to get the Pact signed and to surround Poland and pressure Rumania. Implicit was the belief that Nazi power could force the issue in a favorable direction should the Soviets move, and that it was a safe concession in terms of Balkan politics as the Balkan Entente did not apply there. But it later became the German albatross unleashing a Balkan revisionist wave and unraveling Southeastern neutrality. The general silence in the Pact regarding the Southeast must have been due to the recognition on both sides that due to basically competitive interests, no acceptable arrangement could be reached at that time, and that there was an overriding advantage to both to get the Pact signed as is.

The Balkan detente which was arrived at on the part of the Germans and the Russians was based on the two contradictory themes of all detentes—conflicting interest and mutual need. The conflicting interest involved the competitive aims both had to control the Balkan area, and the mutual need was for its temporary pacification and the exclusion of a third power. The agreement worked out, whereby non-aggression was pledged and a discussion of Balkan interests avoided, was unrealistic in ultimate fulfillment, but quite possible as long as both held the sanctity of the region's pacification above all. In the meantime both benefited from the two year competitive moratorium which stabilized the Balkan area and destroyed the encirclement front, and both saw it as a green light for a war from which both could benefit—the Nazis in the cheap victory it gave them in the war against Poland and France, and the Soviets in delimitation of the capitalist war which they sought as an advancement of their own power.

No sooner was the ink dry on the treaty than the Nazi-Soviet contest in the East began. In rapid succession the Soviets got part of Poland, pressured Turkey (for revisionism at the Straits) without regard to Nazi wishes, pressed themselves on the Baltic states, invaded Finland, supported Bulgarian revisionism, and increased the tempo of Bolshevization in the interim states. The Nazis moved quickly to build the Siegfried Line in the East by moving arms to Bulgaria and Rumania, and in negotiations for the Boundary and Friendship Treaty and Russo-Turkish negotiations to stave off Soviet advances and direct Soviet pressures in a favorable direction. Meanwhile, Italy moved to remind the Soviets of the Italian sphere in the Southeast and to create a Balkan bloc attached to Italy to protect against both Germany and Russia. In the Balkans, growing Soviet power and the precariousness of their neutrality were everywhere recognized. Once again there were vain attempts at Balkan unity, but they failed due to Great Power maneuvering and revisionist appetites among their ranks. By late 1939, a Soviet move in Bessarabia was expected sooner or later, and around that expectation every small country jockeyed for its own position.

While the Nazi-Soviet Pact forced the British and French out of East Europe and set up the situation leading to first German and now Soviet domination, it is likely that even without a Pact the result would have been the same—the extinction of Poland, the forced neutrality of the Soviet Union, the submission of the Balkans to Germany, and the World War begun in the East. If instead, the British had paid for a Soviet alliance with East Europe and the Balkans, given the Soviet interest and ability with Western aid to prosecute an offensive war in the East, the result would have been the Sovietization rather than the German satellization of the Balkans. Nationhood would have been lost either way—in the first instance to Germany and in the latter to Russia.

The Balkans were not lost to the West because of the Nazi-Soviet Pact. Rather, they were lost because the power, not the will of the West to defend them against both Germany and the Soviet Union was lacking, and because, given that circumstance, the national hope of survival for the Balkans rested in the benevolent neutrality toward the power which most immediately threatened it. Underlying this was the force of nationalism which, for Great and Small Powers alike, has been the most potent political force of the Twentieth Century. Great states have not been able to replace it in the Balkans with Empires and the small Balkan states have not abandoned it to unity. The Nazi-Soviet Pact, in placing Balkan neutrality above Balkan empire, bowed to the force of Balkan nationalism which could have destroyed the aims of both and led to a Nazi-Soviet war.

The lessons for the present are pregnant ones. If it is true that Small States are pawns on the international chessboard, it is equally true that they must be played with great skill by the Great Powers to whom they are important. This attention in itself pays homage to their importance, as does the lesson that, by choice, Small States may find their best hope of survival by becoming vassals rather than belligerents, to the powerful not the weak. And unity among the ranks of the pawns has not yet found its place on the political chessboard, making Balkan and other small state federalisms a dream not soon to be fulfilled.

NOTES

Notes to Preface

1. Henryk Batowski, "Proposal for a Second Front in the Balkans in September, 1939," *Balkan Studies,* Vol. 9, No. 2, p. 344.

2. Robert Lee Wolff, *The Balkans in Our Time,* (New York: W.W. Norton Co., 1967).

Notes to Chapter I

1. Adolf Hitler, *Mein Kampf,* (New York, Reynal and Hitchcock, 1940, 1st edition), p. 140.

2. *Survey of International Affairs 1939-1946,* (London: Royal Institute of International Affairs, Oxford University Press, 1958), Vol. I, p. 328. Hereafter cited as *S.I.A.*

3. Hitler, *Mein Kampf,* pp. 641, 654, 656, 658.

4. Ibid., pp. 658, 660.

5. Ibid., pp. 147-148.

6. Hohenthal to War Department, July 22, 1940, File 2657-230/5, U.S. National Archives, *Records of the War Department, General and Special Staffs,* Record Group 165. Hereafter cited as *Rec. W.D.*

7. For an excellent delineation of the technicalities of the trade offensive, see "Germany's Trade Offensive," *The Economist,* November 5, 1938, pp. 262-267.

8. Harry N. Howard, "The Balkans After Munich," *World Affairs,* June 1939, p. 79. Allowed by Chamberlain, November 1, 1938.

9. Ibid.

10. *Foreign Relations of the U.S.-General,* 1939, (Washington, D.C.: U.S. Printing Office, 1939), Vol. I, p. 11. Hereafter cited as *D.US.F.P.*

11. Laird Archer, *Balkan Journal,* (New York: W.W. Norton and Co., 1944), pp. 92-93. Also see Bulgarian Minister Draganov's comment that stories in Sofia regarding the German intent to make an economic colony of the Balkans and also the Reich's attempt to force their way into domestic politics caused bad feelings. *Documents on German Foreign Policy 1918-1945,* Series D, (Washington, D.C.: Department of State, 1949), Vol. V, p. 279. Hereafter cited as *D.Ger.F.P.*

12. *D.Ger. F.P.,* V, pp. 334-35.

13. Ibid., p. 218.

14. Ibid., p. 390.

15. Ibid., p. 233.

16. The Soviets, unlike the Balkan countries, did not allow themselves to become hostages to Germany through economic agreements. In the economic agreement accompanying the Nazi-Soviet Pact, it was Russia not Germany who was awarded the credit, and periodic clearing was agreed upon limiting German purchase only to what could be paid for.

17. *D.US.F.P.,* II, p. 875.

18. *D.Ger.F.P.,* I, pp. 368-69.

19. Ibid., p. 102.

20. April 11-14, 1935, France, Great Britain, and Italy met at Stresa, the main purpose of which was to find common ground against growing German power as exemplified in German rearmament and th consequent threat to Austria. Included in the Joint Resolution concluding the Conference as well as in the Franco-Italian Pact of January 7, 1935 and the Anglo-French communique of February 3, 1935 preceding the conference, were plans for a general reconciliation of Balkan disagreements including proposals for a Danubian Pact and release from disarmament chapters of the St. Germain, Trianon, and Neuilly Peace Treaties for Austria, Hungary and Bulgaria. The Joint Resolution can be found in *S.I.A.,* I, 1935, pp. 159-61.

21. Soviet power and the threat it posed to the Balkans increased enormously as a result of the Pacts of Mutual Assistance with France and Czechoslovakia signed in 1935. Not only did they signify the inability of France to defend East Europe alone, but in order to fulfill their provisions, Soviet troops would have had to cross Balkan territory.

22.	This was evident, for instance, by the dropping of M. Titulescu from the Romanian Cabinet in August 1936. He had been a supporter of the League and collective security with France. His proposal of a pact with the USSR was the "straw which broke the camel's back" so to speak, as the policy of "balance" and non-entanglement gained favor.

23.	*D.Ger.F.P.*, V, pp. 222-23.

24.	Ibid., p. 216.

25.	Ibid., pp. 214-15. The Goga telegram is quoted in full.

26.	Ibid., pp. 202, 220.

27.	For an excellent study of this see Betty Jo Winchester, "Hungary and the Austrian Anschluss," *East European Quarterly*, Vol. X, No. 4, (Winter, 1975), pp. 409-425.

28.	*D.Ger.F.P.*, I, p. 378.

29.	Ibid., pp. 373, 436. The Germans established a Central European Institute in Vienna to direct the intellectual, economic and political goals of the new order, providing the Nazis with enormous knowledge about the intricacies of Balkan politics. An excellent study of this Institute can be found in Leszek A. Kosinski, "Secret German War-Sources for Population Study of East-Central Europe and the Soviet Union," *East European Quarterly*, Vol. X, No. 1, (Spring 1976), pp. 23-34.

30.	*D.Ger.F.P.*, II, No. 74, cf. V, p. 265.

31.	Ibid., V, p. 261.

32.	Ibid., II, pp. 97-108. This was the German Minister in Czechoslovakia, Eisenlohr's assessment.

33.	Ibid., p. 102.

34.	Ibid., V, p. 287.

35.	Norman H. Baynes, *The Speeches of Adolph Hitler,* (Oxford: Royal Institute of International Affairs, 1942), II, p. 1376, and *D.Ger. F.P.*, II, pp. 239, 351, 363.

36.	*D.Ger.F.P.*, II, p. 107.

37.	Ibid., p. 231. In this regard rumors were constant that the Rumanians would grant such rights in return for renunciation by Moscow of Bessarabian claims. German intelligence never turned up evidence to substantiate these rumors, hence a certain Nazi confidence that Rumania would never allow Soviet troops to pass.

38.	Ibid., V., pp. 196, 273, 284-95, 298; II, p. 448.

39.	Ibid., p. 748.

40. Ibid., p. 954.

41. Ibid., p. 401.

42. Ibid., V, p. 296; II, p. 583.

43. Ibid., pp. 401, 611.

44. Ibid., p. 816.

45. Ibid., p. 863.

46. September 12, 1938 the German Minister in Yugoslavia reported that Yugoslavia was a saturated nation and "would likely remain neutral should the conflict be localized." Ibid., V, p. 748. The German Minister in Bulgaria, Rümelin, reported that Bulgaria had agreed with Stoyadinović on May 21 that the outcome would be much like Austria. Ibid., p. 570. German Ambassador in the Soviet Union, Schulenburg, reported on August 26 that the very bellicosity of Litvinov's statements and the Russian press conveyed to him that the Soviet Union would do as little as possible so that at the end of the war "she would have her army intact." Ibid., p. 631.

47. Hibbard to Secretary of State, No. 915, September 19, 1938, File 760 F.62, U.S. National Archives, *General Records of the Department of State*, Record Group 59. Hereafter cited as *G.R.D.S.*

48. Bullitt to Secretary of State, No. 1064, September 25, 1938, ibid.

49. Moffat to State Department, No. 1011, September 16, 1938, ibid.

50. Travers to Secretary of State, No. 850, September 16, 1938, ibid.

51. Kirk to Secretary of State, No. 966, September 21, 1938, ibid. U.S. National Archives, *Post Files*, Record Group 84. Hereafter cited as *P.F.*

52. *D.Ger.F.P.*, V, pp. 707, 711.

53. Ibid., pp. 730-32.

54. Ibid., IV, pp. 99-100. Updated, December 11, 1938, pp. 185-86.

55. Gordon A. Craig and Felix Gilbert, editors, *The Diplomats 1919-1939*, Vol. II, (New York: Atheneum, 1965), p. 603.

56. *D.Ger.F.P.*, p. 341.

57. Ibid., p. 341.

58. Ibid., p. 56.

59. Ibid., p. 31.

60. For an excellent study of this point, see Henry Delfiner, *Vienna Broadcasts to Slovakia, 1938-1939. A Case Study in Subversion,* East European Quarterly, Monograph No. VIII, (Boulder, 1976).

61. *D.Ger.F.P.*, IV, p. 421.

62.   Lane to Secretary of State, No. 517, p. 3, March 18, 1939, File 508, *P.F.*, Record Group 84.

63.   Hibbard to Secretary of State, No. 815, March 27, 1939, ibid.

64.   Stalin's speech of March 10, 1939 referred to the unlikelihood of the "gnat." Joseph Stalin, *Problems of Leninism,* (Moscow: Foreign Languages Publishing House, 1953), pp. 603-4. Hitler told Bauchetsch on March 25, 1939 that he no longer entertained immediate plans for establishing a Ukrainian state. Cf., *S.I.A.*, I, p. 289.

65.   Villaret to the War Department, No. 4679, January 23, 1939, U.S. National Archives, *Rec.W.D.*, Record Group 165. The attaches predicted that Rumania would be carved up as follows: the Banat to Hungary, southern Dobruja to Bulgaria, a new German satellite Ukraine including Bessarabia, northern Moldavia, and all of Bukovina, with Transylvania to be settled by plebiscite.

66.   *D.Ger.F.P.*, V, pp. 302-3. Reported by German Minister in Hungary Erdmannsdorff as stated by Hungarian Foreign Minister de Kánya in an interview in *Volkischer Boebachter,* August 27, 1938,8. Extracts are printed in *Documents on International Affairs,* 1938, (Oxford: Royal Institute of International Affairs, 1939), Vol. I, pp. 274-75. Hereafter cited as *D.I.A.*

67.   Ibid., pp. 338-40. One concrete result produced by this interview was a trade agreement signed on December 10, 1938 which the Germans assessed in terms of a 28-45 percent trade increase in the coming year and an expression of willingness by the Rumanians to collaborate in a comprehensive economic program with Germany. In this regard German Economic Policy Department Director, Clodius, noted that the benefits of such a program were exaggerated in view of the fact that Germany had one-half of Rumania's trade already, but that the fall of the Rumanian regime would be damaging to Germany and so an economic agreement should be signed for political reasons. Ibid., p. 394.

68.   Ibid., pp. 334-35, 352, 360.

69.   Ibid., pp. 316-18.

70.   Ibid., p. 350.

71.   Ibid., pp. 385-86.

72.   *The Soviet Slav Herald* of Belgrade, October 1, 1938, cf., H.Howard, "The Balkans After Munich," p. 79.

Notes to Chapter II

1939

1. American Consul at Geneva, Bucknell, *D.US.F.P.*, I, pp. 2-6. / ✓

2. Horthy told U.S. Minister Montgomery that Hitler would take no actions which might provoke war and that by "intrigue and economic penetration" Hitler would make gains. Montgomery to Secretary of State, No. 651, March 21, 1939, File 740.00, U.S. National Archives, *G.R.D.S.*, Record Group 59.

3. As told by German military officers to American attache in Germany, Gilbert. *D.US.F.P.*, I, pp. 10-11.

4. Gunther to Secretary of State, No. 679, March 24, 1939, File 740.00, ibid.

5. *Documents on British Foreign Policy 1919-1939*, Third Series, (1938-39) 9 volumes, (London, HMSO, 1947-55), No. 297. Hereafter cited as *D.Bri.F.P.*, cf. *S.I.D.*, X, p. 60. Information in other embassies suggest that Tilea's talk of an ultimatum could have been easily believed. The U.S. Minister in Iran reported on March 28, 1939 that the Iranian Foreign Minister and the Turkish Ambassador had received information to the effect that Rumania had secretly promised Germany free access to a Black Sea port and that the German military mission had virtual control of the Rumanian Army. Engert to Secretary of State, No. 48, March 28, 1939, File 871.20, U.S. National Archives, *G.R.D.S.*, Record Group 59.

6. Paul D. Quinlan, "The Tilea Affair—A Further Inquiry." Presented to the New England Historical Association. In this paper, Mr. Quinlan concludes that the British actually accepted Tilea's interpretation that an ultimatum had been presented by the Reich in Bucharest and that British actions were influenced by it, though the British had information to the contrary available to them. According to U.S. Minister Lane, the British Minister had an audience with Prince Paul in which Paul informed him that on information from Germany, there had been no ultimatum by Germany and Paul opined that Tilea had either exceeded his authority or misunderstood his directions. Lane to Secretary of State, No. 541, April 3, 1939, File 508, U.S. National Archives, *P.F.*, Record Group 84.

7. *D.Bri.F.P.*, IV, Nos. 298, 367, 390.

8. Ibid., No. 403.

9. The British rejected the proposal on the basis that a conference that might fail would be dangerous, but beneath that was fear and anti-

pathy for the Soviet Union, the hope that a front could be formed necessitating little collaboration with the Soviets, and the recognition that too much contact with the Soviets could hurt their chances for a sound relationship with East Europe.

10. Montgomery to Secretary of State, No. 148, March 28, 1939, File 762.64, U.S. National Archives, *G.R.D.S.*, Record Group 59.

11. When the Bulgarian Prime Minister sounded out the Turks on the depth of their commitment to Rumania should Bulgaria move into Dobruja, the Turks held firm to their commitments via the Balkan Pact. MacMurray to Secretary of State, No. 20, March 27, 1939, File 508, U.S. National Archives, *P.F.*, Record Group 84.

12. Grigoire Gafencu, *The Last Days of Europe* (New Haven: Yale University Press, 1948), pp. 68-9.

13. *D.Ger.F.P.*, VI, p. 521.

14. Ibid., p. 164.

15. *D.US.F.P.*, I, p. 75.

16. Atherton to Secretary of State, No. 640, March 24, 1939, File 770.00, U.S. National Archives, *G.R.D.S.*, Record Group 59.

17. Complete text in House of Commons Debates, 5th Series, Vol. 345, Column 2415. Relevant parts Appendix I.

18. *D.US.F.P.*, I, p. 100.

19. *Hitler's Speeches,* II, pp. 1590-1602. Also *D.Ger.F.P.*, XI, p. 228.

20. G. Ciano, *L'Europa verso la catastrofe* (Milan: Mondadori, 1948). English translation, *Ciano's Diplomatic Papers,* ed. Malcolm Muggeridge, trans. Stuart Hood (London: Oldhams Press, 1948), pp. 203-5.

21. *D.Ger.F.P.*, VI, pp. 617-20. The "Cavallero Memorandum."

22. Ciano, *Dairio 1939-42,* 2 vols., 4th ed. (Milan: Rizzoli, 1947). English version, *Diaries, 1939 (43),* ed. Malcolm Muggeridge, trans. Stuart Hood (London: Oldhams Press, 1948).

23. Ciano, *Diplomatic Papers,* pp. 270-2.

24. Lane to Secretary of State, No. 565, May 4, 1939, File 508, and Wilson to Secretary of State, No. 1056, March 28, 1939, File 508, U.S. National Archives, *P.F.*, Record Group 84.

25. Ciano, *Diaries,* February 6-7, 1939 entries.

26. Ibid., March 14-15, 1939 entries; *D.Ger.F.P.*, IV, pp. 247-48.

27. Ciano, *Diplomatic Papers,* pp. 277-78. Also *D.Ger.F.P.*, VI, pp. 48-49, and No. 52, 55.

28. *D.Ger.F.P.*, VI, pp. 187-8.

29. Lane to Secretary of State, No. 62, April 6, 1939, File 508, U.S. National Archives, *P.F.*, Record Group 84.

30. *D.Ger.F.P.*, VI, p. 202, cf. fn. 5, unprinted document No. 116/66204.

31. Ibid., p. 194 and 209. Also G. Ciano, *Diplomatic Papers*, pp. 283-86.

32. Ibid., p. 544.

33. *D.US.F.P.*, II, p. 390, and Lane to Secretary of State, No. 70, April 9, 1939, File 508, *P.F.*, Record Group 84.

34. Lane to Secretary of State, No. 66, April 8, 1939, File 508, U.S. National Archives, *P.F.*, Record Group 84.

35. Millard to Secretary of State, No. 455, April 8, 1939, File 765.74, U.S. National Archives, *G.R.D.S.*, Record Group 59.

36. Brent to MacMurray, Memo of Conversation with Bati, No. 322, April 9, 1939, File 508, U.S. National Archives, *P.F.*, Record Group 84.

37. *D.US.F.P.*, II, p. 382.

38. Bullitt to Secretary of State, No. 474, April 7, 1939, File 765.75, and U.S. State Department, No. 503, April 7, 1939, File 765.75, Millard to Secretary of State, No. 842, April 15, 1939, File 740.00, U.S. National Archives, *G.R.D.S.*, Record Group 59; and Phillips to Secretary of State, No. 179, May 1, 1939, and Kirk to Secretary of State, No. 756, April 19, 1939, No. 778, April 12, 1939, File 508, U.S. National Archives, *P.F.*, Record Group 84.

39. Captain McEwen, House of Commons, April 13, 1939, *H.C. Debates*, 5th Series, Vol. 346, Col. 9; *H.L. Debates*, 5th Series, Vol. 112, Col. 606-7. Cf. *S.I.A.*, X, p. 246.

40. *D.Bri.F.P.*, V, pp. 406-25. Cf. *S.I.A.*, X, p. 73.

41. *The Greek White Book: Diplomatic Documents Relating to Italy's Aggression Against Greece* (Washington, D.C.: American Council on Republic Affairs, 1943), p. 5.

42. *D.Bri.F.P.*, IV, No. 534 and V, No. 44. Cf. *S.I.A.*, X, pp. 107 and 109.

43. Appendix II. Complete text of Chamberlain's speech can be found in *House of Commons Debates*, 5th Series, Vol. 346, Col. 13.

44. The Rumanian Minister's guarded public statement can be found in *The Times*, April 15, 1939 to the effect that Rumania wished to develop good relations with all countries and to protect her frontiers.

45.   MacVeagh to Secretary of State, No. 2966, File 508 and No. 1084, File 868.00, U.S. National Archives, *P.F.*, Record Group 84.

46.   *D.Ger.F.P.*, VI, pp. 228, 305.

47.   *D.US.F.P.*, I, p. 174.

48.   Ibid., pp. 131-33 for the full text of Roosevelt's message. For the reactions see Millard to Secretary of State No. 1285, April 18, 1939; Gunther to Secretary of State, No. 1287, April 19, 1939; Montgomery to Secretary of State, No. 1297, April 22, 1939; Lane to Secretary of State, No. 1298, April 19, 1939; File 740.00, U.S. National Archives, *G.R.D.S.*, Record Group 59.

49.   *D.Ger.F.P.*, VI, pp. 309-10 summarizes results. April 17, No. 110, Belgrade; April 17, No. 124, Budapest; April 18, No. 121, Ankara; April 18, No. 44, Sofia; April 19, No. 35, Athens; April 18, No. 195, Bucharest. Only Bucharest answered somewhat evasively, noting that only the Reich government itself was in a position to know whether a threat might arise. Also descriptive entry No. 1026, April 16, 1939, File 740.00, U.S. National Archvies, *G.R.D.S.*, Record Group 59.

50.   MacVeagh to Secretary of State, No. 1220, Kirk to Secretary of State, No. 1222, Lane to Secretary of State, No. 1224, April 29, 1939, Millard to Secretary of State, No. 1240, April 30, 1939, U.S. National Archives, *G.R.D.S.*, Record Group 59. Also MacMurray to Secretary of State, No. 64, April 30, 1939 and No. 1043, May 12, 1939, File 508, U.S. National Archives, *P.F.*, Record Group 84.

51.   In June 1939, for instance, King Carol made an incognito trip to Istanbul for three days and only by accident met Ataturk. When Carol asked for Turkey's resistance to possible German expansion in the Balkans, Ataturk evasively concentrated on improved functioning of the Turko-Rumanian Clearing Agreement. MacMurray to Secretary of State, No. 138, June 22, 1939 and No. 139, June 29, 1939, File 871.001, ibid.

52.   *D.Ger.F.P.*, VI, p. 545.

53.   Ibid., pp. 32-3, 84.

54.   *D.Bri.F.P.*, IV, No. 472,590, V, No. 25. Cf. *S.I.A.*, X, pp. 113-4. *D.Ger.F.P.*, IV, pp. 188-89.

55.   *D.Ger.F.P.*, VI, pp. 276-7 and Kirk to Secretary of State, May 1, 1939, File 508, U.S. National Archives, *P.F.*, Record Group 84.

56.   Memo of Conversation Saracoglu and MacMurray, MacMurray to Secretary of State, May 3, 1939, File 508, U.S. National Archives, *P.F.*, Record Group 84.

57. G. Gafencu, *Last Days of Europe,* p. 121.

58. *D.Ger.F.P.,* VI, pp. 355-56, 365.

59. Ibid., VI, pp. 356, fn. 9.

60. MacMurray to Secretary of State, No. 70, May 10, 1939, File 508, U.S. National Archives, *P.F.,* Record Group 84.

61. *D.Bri.F.P.,* V, No. 217. Cf. *S.I.A.,* X, p. 118. The four stages were 1) issuance of a joint declaration recording the intent of both to enter into a permanent agreement of mutual assistance; 2) negotiations of understanding to cover the interim period; 3) meeting of Anglo-Turkish military, economic and financial experts; and 4) negotiations of a treaty.

62. Ibid., Nos. 219, 286, 310. Cf. *S.I.A.,* X, p. 119.

63. Ibid., No. 506.

64. Appendix III.

65. *D.Ger.F.P.,* VI, pp. 408-9, 430, 437, 544-46. Von Papen wrote to Berlin that Italy should reduce its troops in Albania to reassure the Turks, and on May 5 he suggested bringing Albania and Bulgaria into the Balkan Pact (bargaining for the latter with territorial concessions from Rumania) to upstage British encirclement and buy time against Anglo-Turkish decisions. The German Undersecretary ordered the telegram not to be sent to Ribbentrop in Rome where Pact of Steel negotiations were under way.

66. MacMurray to Secretary of State, May 15, 1939, File 508, U.S. National Archives, *P.F.,* Record Group 84.

67. Ibid. Saracoglu said that in Greece it was genuinely welcomed more than would appear from comments; in Yugoslavia it was received with relief although pressed by the Axis, statements were made against it; and in Bulgaria it was received as a grievous disappointment and a setback to Axis policy.

68. MacVeagh to Secretary of State, No. 3063, May 26, 1939, ibid. One Greek observer noted that the official statement "set a new high for vapid and non-committal remarks," while MacVeagh noted that the public was cheered by British resolve and dilution of the Italian threat.

69. When Anglo-Turkish negotiations had begun, the Turks had wanted to keep the French out because of their desire for secrecy, while the British had preferred bilateral Anglo-Turkish/Franco-Turkish negotiations in order not to give rise to charges of encirclement while at the same time hoping thereby to preserve an aura of harmony. The Turks finally agreed to tripartite negotiations on May 8, but they became indignant

over the question of the cession of Hatay, the negotiations for which were ongoing. The British Government, fearing delays would facilitate German intrigue (due to von Papen's arrival and his attempts to frustrate the Balkan Entente) went ahead with publication on May 12. *D.Bri.F.P.*, V, Nos. 219, 291, 287. Cf. *S.I.A.*, X, p. 117.

70.   *D.Ger.F.P.*, VI, pp. 416, 544-46, 581, 633, 650.

71.   MacMurray to Secretary of State, No. 1175, August 4, 1939, File 508, U.S. National Archives, *P.F.*, Record Group 84.

72.   *D.Ger.F.P.*, VI, p. 846.

73.   Fn. 66.

74.   G. Gafencu, *Last Days of Europe*, p. 166.

75.   *Documents on International Affairs 1939-1946*, Volumes I-III, (London: Oxford University Press for Royal Institute of International Affairs, 1951), I, pp. 171-72. Hereafter cited as *D.I.A.*, trans from *I.M.T. Nuremburg, XXI,* 1569-2818. Also *D.Ger.F.P.*, VI, "Cavallero Memorandum," pp. 618-20.

76.   Ibid., p. 164, cf. Toscano, *Patti d'Acciacio*, pp. 143-4.

77.   For an excellent study of Ciano's foreign policies and the tension between Mussolini and Ciano, and Germany and Italy, see Gordon A. Craig and Felix Gilbert, editors, *The Diplomats 1919-1939*, Vol. II (New York: Atheneum, 1965). Generally, Gilbert believes the Ciano-Ribbentrop animosity was a personal one and that Ciano could not go against Mussolini's pro-German stand. Also, L. B. Namier, *Europe in Decay*, (New York: Mac-Millan, 1950) for the conflicts between Ciano and Attolico.

78.   G. Gafencu, *Last Days of Europe*, pp. 166-168.

79.   *D.Ger.F.P.*, VI, p. 228.

80.   Biddle to Secretary of State, No. 1743, June 16, 1939, File 740. 00, U.S. National Archives, *G.R.D.S.*, Record Group 59.

81.   Lane to Secretary of State, No. 566 May 4, 1939, File 508, U.S. National Archives, *P.F.*, Record Group 84.

82.   Ibid., No. 182, July 6, 1939. Also Gunther to Secretary of State, No. 2115, August 22, 1939, File 740.00, U.S. National Archives, *G.R.D.S.*, Record Group 59.

83.   Montgomery to Secretary of State, No. 122, May 5, 1939, and No. 125, May 17, 1939, File 764.71, and No. 1348, May 5, 1939, File 740.00, U.S. National Archives, *G.R.D.S.*, Record Group 59.

84.   *D.Ger.F.P.*, VI, No. 712, VII, No. 175.

85. Ibid., No. 533.

86. Ibid., Nos. 500 and 508. The Germans had made similar attempts a few months earlier without result.

87. Ibid., pp. 857-8.

88. Ibid., Nos. 656, 673, 728.

89. Reily to War Department, No. B-53, April 18, 1939, File 2069/ 156/5-9, U.S. National Archives, *Rec. W.D.,* Record Group 165.

90. *D.Ger.F.P.,* VII, No. 168.

91. Ibid., pp. 485-87; VI, No. 497, pp. 485-87, 959.

92. Ibid., VI, Nos. 227, 234. Also Bullitt to Secretary of State, No. 101, April 25, 1939, File 762.71, U.S. National Archives, *G.R.D.S.,* Record Group 59.

93. Ibid., Nos. 625 and 627.

94. Ibid., VII, Nos. 361, 386, 486.

95. Ciano, *Diaries,* May 21, 1939 entry.

96. *D.Ger.F.P.,* VI, No. 271. Also Lane to Secretary of State, No. 118, May 3, 1939, File 508, U.S. National Archives, *P.F.,* Record Group 84.

97. Ibid., No. 262, pp. 635-37; 927, 944-45. Also Lane to Secretary of State, No. 117, May 2, 1939, File 508, U.S. National Archives, *P.F.,* Record Group 84.

98. *D.Ger.F.P.,* VII, p. 42, No. 532.

99. By attempting to gain control of the wireless communication system and by issuing a credit of 5 million pounds to equip the Greek army.

100. *D.Ger.F.P.,* VI, pp. 752-3.

101. Ciano, *Diplomatic Papers,* p. 285. There is no evidence that the plan for deposition of the King was further enacted upon.

102. *D.Ger.F.P.,* VII, Nos. 393 and 488.

103. Ciano, *Diaries,* May 21, 1939 entry.

104. *D.Ger.F.P.,* VII, No. 45, 247. Also MacMurray to Secretary of State, No. 1175, August 4, 1939, File 508, U.S. National Archives, *P.F.,* Record Group 84.

105. MacMurray to Secretary of State, No. 105, File 508, U.S. National Archives, *P.F.,* Record Group 84.

106. *D.Ger.F.P.,* VII, No. 247.

Notes to Chapter III

1. G. Gafencu, *Last Days of Europe*, p. 107.

2. Douglas Dakin, "The Diplomacy of the Great Powers and the Balkan States 1908-1914," *Balkan Studies*, Vol. 3, 1962, pp. 327-74.

3. For a thorough discussion of these rivalries see Robert Lee Wolff, *The Balkans in Our Time* (New York: W.W. Norton and Co., 1967), pp. 143-89.

4. For a thorough discussion of the formation of the Balkan Entente see Theodore I. Geshkoff, *Balkan Union* (New York: Columbia University Press, 1940). The text of the Pact can be found in Appendix IV.

5. Whitley to War Department, No. 345-51, November 24, 1933, File 2657-154/6, U.S. National Archives, *Rec.W.D.*, Record Group 165.

6. Barnes to Secretary of State, No. 834, February 18, 1934, File 740. 0011, U.S. National Archives, *P.F.*, Record Group 84 and MacVeagh to Secretary of State, No. 393, November 1, 1934, File 770.00, U.S. National Archives, *G.R.D.S.*, Record Group 59.

7. The rules applied to the Dardanelles, the Bosporus, and the Sea of Marmora. Text of the Lausanne Convention of 1923 can be found in *British Blue Book, Cmd., 1929, and of the Montreux Convention of 1936 in British White Paper*, Cmd., 1249.

8. *D.Ger.F.P.*, VI, p. 1099. In this connection Hitler also often talked of the weak Turkish leadership since Kemal's death. Ibid., V, p. 202, 558.

9. Henderson to Secretary of State, No. 137, October 13, 1936, File 870.811, U.S. National Archives, *G.R.D.S.*, Record Group 59.

10. Harrison to Secretary of State, No. 135, August 8, 1936, Lane to Secretary of State, No. 149, July 16, 1938, and Carr to Secretary of State, No. 154, August 12, 1938, ibid.

11. George to Secretary of State, No. 200, August 25, 1931, File 770. 00, ibid.

12. Gunther to Secretary of State, No. 258, March 19, 1939, File 760F. 65, ibid.

13. Welles, State Department, No. 651, October 10, 1938, File 871.00, ibid.

14. Biddle to Secretary of State, No. 126, June 28, 1937, File 871.001, ibid.

15.   MacMurray to Secretary of State, No. 1085, May 30, 1939, File 508, U.S. National Archives, *P.F.*, Record Group 84.

16.   Williamson to War Department, No. 6706, November 16, 1936, File 2657-T-441/2, and No. 6709, November 8, 1936, File 2657-V-118/19, U.S. National Archives, *Rec.W.D.*, Record Group 165.

17.   *D.I.A.*, 1936, pp. 356-63.

18.   Ibid., pp. 349-54.

19.   Ibid., p. 349.

20.   Ibid., p. 354.

21.   Ibid., p. 310.

22.   Biddle to Secretary of State, No. 481, July 15, 1937, File 770.00, U.S. National Archives, *G.R.D.S.*, Record Group 59.

23.   Reed to Secretary of State, No. 483, August 26, 1937, ibid.

24.   Phillips to Secretary of State, No. 468, April 16, 1937, and Wilson to Secretary of State, No. 458, April 3, 1937, ibid. The Italians concluded that the Entente was broken and dismembered and that Czechoslovakia, therefore, was in the Axis sphere.

25.   The communiques from these meetings can be found in *D.I.A.*, 1937, pp. 340-6.

26.   From *Pester Lloyd,* September 19, 1937, Travers to Secretary of State, No. 482, September 2, 1937, File 770.00, U.S. National Archives, *G.R.D.S.*, Record Group 59. Foreign Minister Kánya said in this regard, "It is inconceivable that the road to rapprochement may be profitably prepared by negotiations as long as minority questions remain unsettled."

27.   Statement by Davila. Hall to Secretary of State, No. 505, ibid.

28.   *D.I.A.*, 1937, p. 341.

29.   Ibid., p. 342.

30.   Ibid., p. 347.

31.   Former Rumanian Prime Minister Iorga said as much. Wilson to Secretary of State, No. 64, February 15, 1937, File 760H, U.S. National Archives, *G.R.D.S.*, Record Group 59.

32.   MacVeagh to Secretary of State, No. 508, January 24, 1938, File 770.00, ibid.

33.   Ibid.

34.   The occasion of the Turkish statement was the 17th Anniversary commemoration of the Republic to which Turkey had invited all the military staffs of the Balkan and Saadabad Pacts, whereupon Bulgaria expressed

concern, causing the statement. Williamson to War Department, August 25, 1937, File 2044/352/3 and August 26, 1937, File 265-331, U.S. National Archives, *Rec.W.D.*, Record Group 165.

35. *British White Papers,* Cmd. 5568, 1937. Also *D.Ger.F.P.,* V, p. 184. At issue were measures to be taken by Britain, if any, against an unidentified submarine in connection with the Spanish Civil War.

36. Lane to Secretary of State, No. 524, May 10, 1938, File 770.00, U.S. National Archives, *G.R.D.S.,* Record Group 59.

37. For the Joint Communiques issued at Bled, see Appendix VI.

38. For the Salonika Agreement see Appendix V.

39. Elizabeth Wiskemann, *The Rome-Berlin Axis,* (New York: Oxford University Press, 1949), p. 121. The same pacifist spirit was communicated by Prince Paul to Berlin. Lane to Secretary of State, No. 85, September 18, 1938, File 760H.00, U.S. National Archives, *G.R.D.S.,* Record Group 59.

40. *D.Ger.F.P.,* II, No. 219, p. 298 (August 18, 1938 as conveyed by the German Minister in Rumania to Ribbentrop).

41. Ibid., p. 427.

42. Ibid., Nos. 367, 383, 390, 392, 402. The quotation is from No. 383.

43. Ibid., V, p. 387. Ribbentrop subsequently instructed all missions abroad that the expression "Little Entente" was no longer to be used.

44. Beck also apparently toyed with the idea of a Scandanavian bloc. As far as a common Polish-Hungarian frontier was concerned, Hitler did not allow this until March 1939 (by the grant of Ruthenia to Hungary), but by then it was useless because Germany controlled all of Czechoslovakia and thus all but surrounded Poland and Hungary.

45. G. Gafencu, *Last Days of Europe,* p. 88.

46. The communique can be found in *D.I.A.,* 1939, I, p. 297. It was reported in *D.Ger.F.P.,* V, No. 240, p. 325.

47. Millard to Secretary of State, No. 214, February 15, 1939, File 711, U.S. National Archives, *P.F.,* Record Group 84.

48. MacMurray to Secretary of State, No. 740, June 4, 1938, File 767.68, U.S. National Archives, *G.R.D.S.,* Record Group 59.

49. *D.Ger.F.P.,* VI, p. 457.

50. *D.Bri.F.P.,* V, No. 385. Cf. *S.I.A.,* X, p. 125.

51. *D.US.F.P.,* 1939, I, March 24, 1939, p. 99.

52. The French policy differed only in emphasis, that is the belief that less attention should be paid to the small states and their revisionist questions, and more to Russia in order to bring about a collective security system.

53. May 11 interview between Bulgarian Minister Montchilov and Halifax. *D.Bri.F.P.*, V, No. 495, p. 530. Cf. *S.I.A.*, X, p. 127. Also Millard to Secretary of State, No. 95, April 21, 1939, File 770.00, U.S. National Archives, *G.R.D.S.*, Record Group 59.

54. MacMurray to Secretary of State, No. 1623, May 16, 1939 and Millard to Secretary of State, No. 1621, May 19, 1939, File 740.00, U.S. National Archives, *G.R.D.S.*, Record Group 59. Also *D.Bri.F.P.*, VI, No. 13.

55. *D.Bri.F.P.*, VI, no. 65, cf. *S.I.A.*, X, p. 130. *D.Ger.F.P.*, V, p. 415.

56. *D.Bri.F.P.*, VI, No. 534, p. 583. Cf. *S.I.A.*, X, p. 129.

57. *D.Ger.F.P.*, VI, p. 76.

58. *New York Times*, June 13, 1939, 10.6, and June 26, 1939, 3.1.

59. Reed to Secretary of State, No. 292, August 11, 1939, File 508, U.S. National Archives, *P.F.*, Record Group 84.

60. *D.Ger.F.P.*, VI, p. 698; V, p. 884.

61. Lane to Secretary of State, No. 163, June 13, 1939, File 508, U.S. National Archives, *P.F.*, Record Group 84. For Ciano's policies in this regard, *Diaries*, May 10 and June 28, 1939 entries.

62. *D.Ger.F.P.*, VI, No. 256. Also G. Ciano, *Diaries*, March 20-21, May 31, 1939 entries.

63. *D.Ger.F.P.*, VII, p. 200. Examples of the latter abound, but a few are that Hitler refused to sanction Hungarian organizations on the Nazi model set up among the Hungarian minorities in Rumania, or Hungarian occupation of Rumanian villages and railroads in the Carpatho-Ukraine.

64. *D.Ger.F.P.*, VI, pp. 418-19.

65. Ibid., p. 457.

66. Lane to Secretary of State, No. 188, May 3 and No. 566, May 4, 1939, File 508, U.S. National Archives, *P.F.*, Record Group 84.

67. *D.Ger.F.P.*, VI, No. 503, p. 692.

68. Ibid., No. 510, pp. 707-8.

69. Ibid., VII, p. 82.

70. *New York Times*, February 9, 1939, 1.5.

71. Gunther to Secretary of State, No. 894, May 15, 1939, File 508, U.S. National Archives, *P.F.*, Record Group 84.

72.   Potemkin went to Bucharest on April 15, to Sofia on April 26, to Ankara on April 28-May 5, to Sofia on May 7, to Bucharest on May 8, to Warsaw on May 10. On May 3 while he was in Ankara, Litvinov was replaced by Molotov. See Chapter V.

73.   MacMurray to Secretary of State, No. 23, April 24, 1939, File 767.71, U.S. National Archives, *G.R.D.S.*, Record Group 59. Also *D.Bri. F.P.*, No. 322. Cf. *S.I.A.*, X, p. 118, fn. 5.

74.   *D.Ger.F.P.*, V, pp. 416, 456.

75.   MacVeagh to Secretary of State, No. 2824, March 2, 1939, File 508, U.S. National Archives, *P.F.*, Record Group 84.

76.   *New York Times,* February 3, 1939, 4.5.

77.   MacMurray to Secretary of State, February 28, 1939, and Mac-Veagh to Secretary of State, No. 2824, March 2, 1939, File 508, U.S. National Archives, *P.F.*, Record Group 84.

78.   MacVeagh to Secretary of State, No. 2824, March 2, 1939, File 508, U.S. National Archives, *P.F.*, Record Group 84.

79.   *D.Bri.F.P.*, No. 390. Cf. *S.I.A.*, X, p. 72. For answers see *D.Bri. F.P.*, IV, Nos. 400, 403, 406-7, 420, 423-5.

80.   Ibid., V, No. 278. Cf. *S.I.A.*, X, pp. 114-5, 122-3.

81.   G. Gafencu, *Last Days of Europe,* pp. 107, 121-2.

82.   *New York Times,* April 21, 1939, 3.6.

83.   MacMurray to Secretary of State, No. 85, June 14, 1939, File 508, U.S. National Archives, *P.F.*, Record Group 84.

84.   *New York Times,* April 23, 1939, 31.1.

85.   Ibid., April 27, 1939, 6.1, April 29, 1939, 8.8.

86.   Joyce to Secretary of State, No. 654, July 17, 1939, File 508, U.S. National Archives, *P.F.*, Record Group 84.

87.   Ibid., and Kirk to Secretary of State, No. 650, July 14, 1939, ibid.

88.   Millard to Secretary of State, No. 44, July 15, 1939, ibid.

89.   *D.Bri.F.P.*, VI, No. 393. Cf. *S.I.A.*, p. 128.

90.   The Yugoslav paper *Politika* July 2, 1939 used this expression.

91.   Lane to Secretary of State, No. 144, May 22, 1939, and No. 146, May 23, 1939, File 508, U.S. National Archives, *P.F.*, Record Group 84.

92.   *D.Bri.F.P.*, VI, p. 839.

93.   *D.Bri.F.P.*, VI, Nos. 602, 618, 626, 633. Cf. *S.I.A.*, X, p. 133. Also Hibbard to Secretary of State, No. 1120, May 27, 1939, File 508, U.S. National Archives, *P.F.*, Record Group 84.

94.   Kirk to Secretary of State, No. 413, May 24, 1939, No. 421, May 27, 1939, No. 451, June 6, 1939, and Lane to Secretary of State, No. 152, June 4, 1939, ibid.

95.   MacMurray to Secretary of State, No. 25, June 12, 1939, and No. 1122, June 27, 1939, File 767.71, U.S. National Archives, *G.R.D.S.*, Record Group 59. Also *D.Bri.F.P.*, V, Nos. 52, 148, 618, 626, 633. Cf. *S.I.A.*, X, pp. 133-4.

96.   Tell-tale in this regard was the visit of pro-ally Egyptian Minister of Foreign Affairs to Belgrade on July 7 (on a return visit from Turkey) during which there were toasts on both sides to good relations, ties with the Muslim people, etc. Joyce to Secretary of State, No. 658, July 22, 1939, File 508, U.S. National Achives, *P.F.*, Record Group 84.

97.   *New York Times,* July 8, 1939, 4.2, and Lane to Secretary of State, No. 1858, July 4, 1939, File 740.00, U.S. National Archives, *G.R. D.S.*, Record Group 59.

98.   *D.US.F.P.,* 1939, I, p. 121.

99.   *New York Times,* August 2, 1939, 18.4.

100.   Ibid., August 12, 1939, 31.6, and Gunther to Secretary of State, No. 2058, August 15, 1939, and Biddle to Secretary of State, No. 2063, August 16, 1939, File 740.00, U.S. National Archives, *G.R.D.S.*, Record Group 59.

101.   Ibid., August 12, 1939, 31.6, and Atherton to Secretary of State, No. 2022, August 15, 1939, File 740.00, U.S. National Archives, *G.R.D.S.*, Record Group 59.

102.   Ibid., August 16, 1939, 7.3.4.

103.   Lane to Secretary of State, No. 38, August 25, 1939, File 740.00, U.S. National Archives, *G.R.D.S.*, Record Group 59.

104.   Gunther to Secretary of State, No. 2103, August 22, 1939, and MacMurray to Secretary of State, No. 2100, August 22, 1939, ibid. For a discussion of the Turko-Soviet talks, see Chapter VI.

105.   Millard to Secretary of State, No. 51, September 1, 1939, and Lane to Secretary of State, No. 219, August 25, 1939, File 508, U.S. National Archives, *P.F.*, Record Group 84.

Notes to Chapter IV

1.   G. Gafencu, *Last Days of Europe,* p. 105.

2.   Ibid.

3.   J. V. Stalin, *Sochineniia,* ed. by Robert H. McNeal, 3 volumes (Stanford: Hoover Institute Foreign Languages Publications, 1967), I, (14): 2-10. Cf. Robert C. Tucker, "The Emergence of Stalin's Foreign Policy," *Slavic Review,* December 1977, Vol. 36, No. 44, p. 564.

4.   Louis Fischer, *Men and Politics,* (New York: Buell, Sloan and Pearce, 1941), p. 35. Cf. C. Craig and F. Gilbert, *Diplomats,* p. 365.

5.   Brodie to Secretary of State, No. 172, October 18, 1932, File 871A-014, and Bullitt to Secretary of State, No. 27, June 14, 1935, File 871.014, U.S. National Archives, *G.R.D.S.,* Record Group 59.

6.   For an excellent study of the presumption that at issue in the Russian quest for the Straits and Balkans was the bid for Great Power status, see Robert H. Johnson, *Tradition Versus Revolution: Russia and the Balkans, 1917,* (Boulder, Colorado: East European Quarterly Monograph, No. XXVIII, 1977).

7.   The Little and Balkan Ententes, for instance, both followed the policy of letting each member state recognize Russia in accordance with its special interests. By 1939 Yugoslavia was the only Balkan state which had not recognized the Soviet Union, largely for internal political reasons.

8.   Apparently, fear of a Slavic bloc did indeed have a positive impact on getting the Balkan Entente signed. According to a certain group in Bulgaria, the Pact provided the necessary delay in resumption of relations with Russia by Bulgaria and Yugoslavia. The fear was that if Bulgaria and Yugoslavia reached a rapprochement, it could be considered a *casus belli* by the other Entente powers and without Russia to draw them off, the full impact would be brought to bear on Bulgaria. Barnes to Secretary of State, No. 834, February 15, 1934, File 740.0011, U.S. National Archives, *P.F.,* Record Group 84.

9.   Bullitt to Secretary of State, No. 33, October 2, 1934, File 761. 74. Also Wiley to Secretary of State, No. 8, March 16, 1935, and Barnes to Secretary of State, No. 7, February 15, 1934, File 761.70, U.S. National Archives, *G.R.D.S.,* Record Group 59.

10.   J. V. Stalin, "The Party Before and After Taking Power," and "On the Social Democratic Deviation in Our Party," *Sochineniia,* 13 vols. (Moscow: Foreign Languages Publishing House, 1946-52), 5:109 and 8: 263, respectively. Cf. R. Tucker, "Emergence of Stalin's Foreign Policy," p. 570.

11. Professor Tucker believes that if Stalin had been thinking in terms other than East Europe, he would not have used the term "border states." The view that Stalin was not referring to aims in East Europe is held by Teddy J. Uldrich, "Stalin and Nazi Germany," *Slavic Review,* December 1977, p. 602. Tucker's response can be found in the same issue, p. 607.

12. Robert Coulondre, *De Staline à Hitler* (Paris, Hachette, 1959), p. 171. Cf. G. Craig and F. Gilbert, *Diplomats,* p. 363.

13. J. V. Stalin, *Sochineniia,* 7:12-14. Cf. R. Tucker, "Emergence of Stalin's Foreign Policy," p. 575.

14. The former view is David Dallin's, the latter is Philip G. Gillette's. R. Tucker, "Emergence of Stalin's Foreign Policy," p. 584.

15. G. Craig and F. Gilbert, *Diplomats,* pp. 353, 358.

16. J. V. Stalin, *Works,* VI, XIII (Moscow: Foreign Languages Publishing House, 1955), excerpts, pp. 383-412.

17. Karl Radek, *Podgotovka borby za novyi peredel mira* (Moscow 1934), a collection of his articles of 1933. Cf. R. Tucker, "Emergence of Stalin's Foreign Policy," p. 586.

18. Chautemps to Bullitt, Bullitt to Secretary of State, No. 196, September 20, 1936, File 751.6111, U.S. National Archives, *G.R.D.S.,* Record Group 59.

19. See fn. 16.

20. On October 2, 1935 Italy invaded Ethiopia; on March 7, 1936 Germany reoccupied the Rhineland; on July 18, 1936 the Spanish Civil War started; on October 25, 1936 the Rome-Berlin Axis was created; on November 27, 1936 the German-Japanese Anti-Comintern Pact was created.

21. *D.Ger.F.P.,* II, p. 64.

22. *D.Bri.F.P.,* IV, No. 498, cf. *S.I.A.,* X, p. 85-6.

23. V. P. Potemkin, *Istoria Diplomatii,* III (*History of Diplomacy*), (Moscow: Government Publication, 1945), p. 571.

24. Text of the Montreux Convention, *D.I.A.,* 1936, p. 648. For analysis of the convention activities see *S.I.A.,* 1936, and Routh, *Actes de Conference de Montreux,* p. 619. For the Rumanian view and Titelescu's speech, Harrison to Secretary of State, No. 110, July 13, 1936, File 761. 71/112, U.S. National Archives, *P.F.,* Record Group 84.

25. Balkan Pact, February 9, 1934; Middle East Pact, July 8, 1937; Pact of Friendship with France, July 4, 1938.

26. *D.I.A*, 1937, pp. 432-35.

27. *D.US.F.P.,-SU*, I, p. 520 (Charge Harrison).

28. *D.Ger.F.P.*, I, p. 235.

29. *Manchester Guardian*, March 18, 1939, and *Mirovoe Khoziaistvo*, 1938, 4, p. 144. Cf. *Soviet Documents in Foreign Policy*, 1933-41, III, edited by Jane Degras (New York: Oxford University Press, 1953), p. 277. Hereafter cited as *D.Sov.F.P.*

30. *D.US.F.P.-SU.*, I, p. 547.

31. *Journal de Moscou*, July 5, 1938. Cf. *D.Sov.F.P.*, III, pp. 282-94.

32. Here he was referring to Hungary who had joined the Anti-Comintern, an act a *Tass* communique equated with loss of independence and justified the closing of the Soviet consulate. Montgomery to Secretary of State, No. 40, February 4, 1939, Kirk to Secretary of State, No. 43, February 4, 1939, and No. 48, February 2, 1939, File 761.64, U.S. National Archives, *G.R.D.S.*, Record Group 59.

33. *D.Ger.F.P.*, I, p. 903.

34. Speech to the League of Nations Assembly, September 21, 1938, *League of Nations Official Journal*, 183, p. 175. Cf. *D.Sov.F.P.*, III, pp. 299-303, and Speech by Litvinov to the League of Nations Assembly on the Soviet-Czech Pact, September 23, 1938, *League of Nations Official Journal Supplement*, 189, p. 34.

35. *D.Sov.F.P.*, III, p. 305.

36. *Izvestia*, September 26, 1938. Cf. *D.Sov.F.P.*, III, p. 305.

37. *Diplomaticheskii Slovar* (1950), II, p. 198.

38. Joseph Korbel, *Twentieth Century Czechoslovakia* (New York: Columbia University Press, 1977), p. 137. The Germans were somewhat responsible for this view, the Czechs having fallen for the anti-Bolshevik propaganda campaign sponsored by Italy and Germany. See fn. 66.

39. Ibid., p. 138. The problem of the telegram is also discussed in Barry Mendel Cohen, "Moscow at Munich: Did the Soviet Union offer Unilateral Aid to Czechoslovakia?" *East European Quarterly*, Vol. XII, No. 3 (Fall 1978), p. 347. Sir John Wheeler-Bennett, *Munich: Prologue to Tragedy* (London: MacMillan, 1964), pp. 126-7. Edward Beneš, *Memoirs of Dr. Edward Beneš* (Boston: Houghton Mifflin, 1954), p. 42, and *New Documents on the History of Munich* (Prague: Orbis, 1958), p. 103.

40. *Pravda*, September 21, and November 9, 1938.

41. R. Coulondre, *De Staline à Hitler*, p. 171. Cf. G. Craig and F. Gilbert, *Diplomats*, p. 363.

42. *D.Sov.F.P.,* III, pp. 309-10.

43. Wilson to Secretary of State, No. 215, September 22, 1938, File 751.6111, U.S. National Archives, *G.R.D.S.,* Record Group 59.

44. *D.Ger.F.P.,* I, p. 898. The German-Russian Economic Agreement of October 12, 1925 formed the contractual basis for trade. In 1935 there was a credit agreement and in 1936 a clearing agreement updating the original. The Soviets wanted in 1937 a 200 RM credit over a long period of time payable only in goods of their choice, thus preventing Russia from falling into the same pit as the Balkans whereby huge credits were accumulated in Berlin.

45. Ibid., II, p. 99. In early February *Pravda* noted the appointment of Ribbentrop and shifts in the military which served to speed up German preparation for the "great war."

46. *D.Ger.F.P.,* I, pp. 916, 920 and V, p. 919.

47. Ibid., II, p. 363. On May 26 *Izvestia* correspondent Alexandrov stated that only because nobody doubted the loyalty of the Soviet Union "did Hitler postpone his risky plans." On May 30 *Krasnaya Zvezda* said the Red Army and treaty with France was a check on German fascism, and only on June 3 did *Pravda* state that "The attitude of the Soviet Union, which is faithful to all its obligations, has never raised doubt among the Czech people."

49. *D.Ger.F.P.,* I, p. 920, and II, p. 467.

50. Ibid., II, pp. 363, 571, 926, 948.

51. Coulondre predicted Munich would throw the Soviet Union into the arms of Germany. R. Coulondre, *De Staline à Hitler,* pp. 160-71.

52. Ibid., IV, pp. 602-8.

53. Kirk to Secretary of State, No. 171, October 20, 1938, File 760F.62, and No. 211, October 1, 1938, File 762.00, U.S. National Archives, *G.R.D.S.,* Record Group 59.

54. *Leninism* (1940 ed.), p. 620 and *Voprosy Leninizma* (11th ed.), p. 565. Extracts in *D. Sov.F.P.,* III, pp. 315-22.

55. At the signing of the Nazi-Soviet Pact five months later, Molotov raised his glass to Stalin and remarked that it was Stalin's speech in March, much misunderstood by the Germans, which had brought about a reversal of political relations. And when Ribbentrop then remarked that Hitler had interpreted it as a wish for better relations, Stalin replied, "That was my intention," *Nazi-Soviet Relations 1939-1941, Documents from the*

Archives of the German Foreign Office, Edited by Raymond J. Sontag and James S. Beddie (Washington, D.C., U.S. Department of State, 1938), Publication 3023, p. 76. Hereafter cited as *Nazi-Soviet Relations*. This statement must be measured against Hitler's statement to Mussolini on August 25, 1939, in which he said that readiness of the part of the Kremlin to negotiate was evident since the dismissal of Litvinov which did not come until a few months later. Ibid., p. 80. Also emphasizing the noncommittal nature of the speech is American historian Isaac Deutscher. Isaac Deutscher, *Stalin–A Political Biography* (London: Oxford University Press, 1949), pp. 429-30. L. B. Namier agrees but minimizes the latter.

56.   *D.Ger.F.P.*, IV, p. 608.

57.   Ibid., p. 621.

58.   Ibid.

59.   Peter Kleist, *Zwischen Stalin und Hitler* (Bonn, 1950), pp. 34-35. Cf. G. Craig and F. Gilbert, *Diplomats,* p. 488. Also *D.Ger.F.P.*, IV, p. 622.

60.   *D.Ger.F.P.*, IV, p. 623.

61.   Ibid., pp. 630-31.

62.   Ibid., pp. 476, 609, 623.

63.   Ibid., p. 516. After April and the West's determined stand, the Japanese became reluctant to enter a Pact with the Axis for fear of provoking Great Britain and France, forcing Germany to seek another avenue for neutralizing Russia. The negative reply from Tokyo was received on April 14, 1939. For the Soviet effort to engage the U.S., see *D.US.F.P.-SU,* p. 551, 592-4, 592.

64.   Hitler, of course, was using the Carpatho-Ukraine both as "a nucleus for further developments in the East," and to provide a pawn in the dissolution of Czechoslovakia, *D.Ger.F.P.*, IV, pp. 40-7, 49.

65.   *D.US.F.P.-SU.*, pp. 731-2.

66.   *D.US.F.P.*, III, p. 318.

67.   *D.US.F.P.-SU.*, p. 750.

68.   *D.Ger.F.P.*, IV, pp. 631-32.

69.   *D.US.F.P.-SU.*, pp. 745-46.

70.   *Mirovoe Khoziastvo*, 1939, 4, p. 189. Cf. *D.Sov.F.P.*, III, pp. 322-3.

71.   Kirk to Secretary of State, No. 131, March 27, 1939, File 765.00, U.S. National Archives, *G.R.D.S.,* Record Group 59.

72.   *D.US.F.P.-SU.*, pp. 750-53.

Notes to Chapter V

1. See for instance M. Beloff (*Foreign Policy of the Soviet Union,* II, p. 225), who says that the vast speeding up of the "disintegration of the political structure and the intermediate zone between Germany and the USSR" followed by the British guarantee which made war inevitable, caused the Soviets to set their course on an agreement with Germany. He concludes, as does this study in a somewhat different framework, that Soviet diplomacy caused war. See also F.L. Schuman, *Night Over Europe,* (New York: A. A. Knoff, 1944), pp. 114-122, who says the Soviets were not convinced after the Hungarian annexation of the Carpatho-Ukraine that the Germans were not going to attack the Soviet Union.

2. Text *Izvestia,* March 22, 1939, and *New York Times,* March 22, 1939. Cf. *D.I.A.,* 1939, I, p. 115.

3. *D.US.F.P.,* 1939, I, p. 79. A similar sentiment was expressed by Litvinov himself when he told Seeds on March 21 that he did not think Poland would sign a declaration of this kind. *D.Bri.F.P.,* No. 461, cf. *S.I.A.,* X, p. 84.

4. *D.Bri. F.P.,* IV, No. 49. Cf. *S.I.A.,* X, p. 84.

5. Ibid., No. 498, Cf. *S.I.A.,* X, pp. 85-6, fn. 5. This was an exhaustive report by Colonel Sword, the British military attache in Warsaw.

6. Ibid., No. 509. Cf. *S.I.A.,* X, p. 88, fn. 5. This sentiment was communicated from the Earl of Perth, British Ambassador in Rome, on March 24, reporting the Hungarian Ambassador's opinion in which Perth agreed, certainly in terms of Italy and perhaps Spain and Yugoslavia too.

7. A *News Chronicle* correspondent expelled from Germany told Halifx that from various sources he had learned Poland would be the next victim. Ibid., No. 556, fn. 1. Cf. *S.I.A.,* X, p.91.And the American Ambassador in London told the Foreign Office his colleague in Warsaw had information that Ribbentrop, having earned credit with Hitler by the Memel coup, was now pressing for action against Poland. Ibid., No. 571. Cf. *S.I.A.,* X, p. 91.

8. Ibid., No. 2, p. 13, and V, No. 16. Cf. *S.I.A.,* X, pp. 99, 101.

9. See V. M. Toynbee, for instance, *S.I.A.,* X, p. 80.

10. *D.Bri.F.P.,* V, No. 4; IV, No. 589. Cf. *S.I.A.,* X, p. 93.

11. Ibid., IV, No. 593. Cf. *S.I.A.,* X, p. 431, fn. 1.

12. *D.Sov.F.P.,* III, p. 328, and Kirk to Secretary of State, No. 1300,

April 13, 1939, File 740.00, U.S. National Archives, *G.R.D.S.*, Record Group 59.

13.   A view expressed by Maisky to Halifax on April 1, 1939. M. Beloff, *Foreign Policy of Soviet Russia*, II, p. 233.

14.   *D.Bri.F.P.*, V, No. 175, and IV, No. 593. Cf. *S.I.A.*, X, pp. 430-31, fn. 1, 4.

15.   Only Charge Butenko remained, but he soon after disappeared alledgedly by Rumanian assassination, but later he showed up in Italy where he said he feared persecution and the terrible conditions in Russia. During Potemkin's visit on April 24, he seemed eager for contact with Rumania and so Gafencu promised a new minister.

16.   The Soviet Legation intimated that Rumania might be put in a delicate position if official contact was made (which could as well have been to protect the budding Nazi-Soviet relationship). Gunther to Secretary of State, No. 19, May 12, 1939, File 874.014, U.S. National Archives, *G.R.D.S.*, Record Group 59.

17.   Bulgarian Minister to Moffat, U.S. State Department, No. 731, March 29, 1939, File 740.00, U.S. National Archives, *G.R.D.S.*, Record Group 59.

18.   *D.Bri.F.P.*, V, No. 379. Cf. *S.I.A.*, X, p. 118. Also Memo of Conversation Saracoglu and U.S. Ambassador MacMurray, May 3, 1939, as well as other reports, File 710-718, *P.F.*, Record Group 84.

19.   *Turkish State Papers, B.I.N.*, XVI, p. 525. Cf. M. Beloff, *Foreign Policy of Soviet Russia*, II, p. 245. Also Grummon to Secretary of State, May 15, 1939, No. 248, U.S. National Archives, *P.F.*, Record Group 84.

20.   These demands were put to Ankara after the Nazi-Soviet Pact on September 25-October 18, 1939 and were similar to those made at Montreux, that is closure of the Straits to foreign warships but open to Soviet exit in time of war. Presumably, the Pact and war added pressure on Turkey to capitulate to Soviet wishes, whereas in the spring of 1939 the Soviet Union saw no hope of revision of Montreux through alliance with Britain's peace front, as neither Britain nor Turkey would have need of revising Montreux with Russia on their side.

21.   Atherton to Secretary of State, No. 626, May 23, 1939, File 770.00, U.S. National Archives, *G.R.D.S.*, Record Group 59. Also G. Gafencu, *Last Days of Europe*, p. 184.

22.   Gunther to Secretary of State, No. 1453, May 12, 1939. File 740.00, ibid. Also, G. Gafencu, *Last Days of Europe*, p. 158.

23. MacMurray to Secretary of State, No. 74, May 15, 1939, File 508, U.S. National Archives, *P.F.*, Record Group 84.

24. Biddle to Secretary of State, No. 74, May 15, 1939, ibid.

25. *D.US.F.P.*, 1939, I, pp. 244-45.

26. G. Gafencu, *Last Days of Europe*, p. 184 and Gunther to Secretary of State, No. 106, May 12, 1939, File 761.71/143, U.S. National Archives, *P.F.*, Record Group 84.

27. Ibid., p. 186.

28. MacMurray to Secretary of State, No. 74, May 15, 1939, File 508, U.S. National Archives, *P.F.*, Record Group 84.

29. G. Bonnet, *Fin d'Europe* (Paris: Hachette, 1946), p. 184. Cf. G. Craig and F. Gilbert, *Diplomats*, p. 374.

30. *D.I.A.*, 1939, I, p. 466.

31. *D.US.F.P.-SU.*, I, pp. 760-1.

32. Ibid., III, p. 334.

33. *New Chronicle*, May 4, 1939. Cf. *S.I.A.*, X, p. 266. And Toscano, *Patti d'Assiaio*, pp. 143-4. Cf. *D.I.A.*, 1939, I, p. 164.

34. Some views, in brief, regarding Soviet interests served by going with Germany; M. Beloff, *The Foreign Policy of Soviet Russia*, believes that the Soviets wanted neutrality, that only the Germans offered them that, and that the negotiations with the West were to exact a higher price; A. Rossi, *The Russo-German Alliance*, G.L. Weinberg, *Germany and the Soviet Union*, L. B. Namier, *Europe in Decay*, all emphasize defensive interests and the desire to stay out of war as the reason for going with the Nazis and that negotiations with the West were as reinsurance; G. Hilger and A.G. Meyer, *Incompatible Allies* argue that Soviet-Geman relations rested on equality of power enhancing their bargaining position, whereas vis-a-vis the West it was less and hence they could obtain less; R. Tucker, "The Emergence of Stalin's Foreign Policy" says the arrangement with Germany accommodated both an aggressive ideological quest and national security; W. Churchill, *The Gathering Storm*, emphasizes the failure of the West to dispel Soviet fears and mistrust as the reason for going with Hitler; I. Deutscher, *Stalin* argues that Soviet xenophobia toward the West could have been dispelled only by bowing to Stalin's desire to push the war as far West as possible; G. Bonnet, *Fin d'une Europe* and G. Gafencu, *Last Days of Europe*, as well as Molotov's August 25, 1939 statement blames Poland for the West's failure to come to an agreement with Stalin; Hitler

himself said the Soviets wanted above all else neutrality; finally, contemporary Soviet historiography (Leo Kinshevich, *U.S. History and Historiography—Post War Soviet Writings*, A.D. Nikonov, *Origins of World War II*) asserts that the Soviets wanted "peace" and neutrality and to preserve defensive interests, and the treacherous desire of the West including the U.S. to utilize the Soviet Union as a pawn against Hitler, turned them toward Germany.

35.   Lane to Secretary of State, No. 212, no date and No. 596, May 26, 1939, File 508, U.S. National Archives, *P.F.*, Record Group 84. The classic statement in this regard by the Yugoslav Minister on August 23, was "The Russians are the same whether they are friends or enemies."

36.   *D.US.F.P.-SU.*, p. 769.

37.   Ibid., p. 769.

38.   Montgomery to Secretary of State, No. 776, June 29, 1939, File 741.61, U.S. National Archives, *G.R.D.S.*, Record Group 59.

39.   *D.US.F.P.-SU.*, pp. 775-79.

40.   Ibid., p. 773.

41.   Text in G. Bonnet, *Fin d'une Europe*, p. 180. A. D. Nikonov, *Origins of World War II*, (Moscow: Publishing House of the USSR Academy of Sciences, 1955), pp. 73-74 quotes from a version of this French communication in the archives of the USSR in which there is no mention of Great Britain. Thus, he concludes that French were suggesting a bilateral not a tripartite agreement.

42.   Halifax to Maisky, *D.Bri.F.P.*, IV, Nos. 170-182, and Seeds to Litvinov, Nos. 166 and 176. Cf. *S.I.A.*, X, p. 438.

43.   Bullitt to Secretary of State, No. 946, April 18, 1939, File 740. 00, U.S. National Archives, *G.R.D.S.*, Record Group 59, or *D.US.F.P.*, I, p. 237.

44.   Grummon to Secretary of State, No. 1442, May 12, 1939, ibid.

45.   L. B. Namier, *Europe in Decay*, p. 242. Namier quotes Stalin as telling Hitler that "We formed the impression that the British and French governments were not resolved to go to war if Poland was attacked, but that they hoped a diplomatic lineup of Britain, France and Russia would deter Hitler. We were sure it would not." (Perhaps it could be said, Stalin made certain it would not.)

46.   *D.Bri.F.P.*, V, No. 201. Cf. *S.I.A.*, X, p. 439.

47.   *D.US.F.P.*, 1939, I, p. 113. This conclusion was reached on the

basis of Colonel Sword's assessment of March 22, 1939 (*D.Bri.F.P.*, IV, No. 498) in which he concludes that the usefulness of the Red Army in an offensive war was much less than in a defensive war, a tendency in certain circles (Bonnet) to overrate Poland's strength and value as an ally, (a view not supported by Noel and Colonel Sword), and the belief that Russia could be counted on for nothing due to internal conditions and unreliability, and therefore, that a price of territory was completely out of the question.

48.   Ibid., p. 80.

49.   *D.Bri.F.P.*, V, Nos. 316, 344, 350-51, 401, 421, 433, 494, 520, 530, 581, 589, 648, 657, 665, 670. Cf. *S.I.A.*, X, pp. 441-2. Also G. Bonnet, *Fin d'une Europe*, pp. 178-86.

50.   *D.US.F.P.*, 1939, I, pp. 239-41. Gafencu told Bullitt on April 28 that he would accept the guarantees if Rumania was not named. Ibid., p. 175.

51.   Ibid., pp. 247-48.

52.   *D.Bri.F.P.*, V, No. 397. Cf. *S.I.A.*, X, p. 444.

53.   That even Western history has been amply imbued with the Soviet version is one of the ironies of the scholarship of the period, though it has served well the need on both sides to rationalize the Nazi-Soviet Pact.

54.   *Izvestia*, May 11, 1939. Cf. M. Beloff, *Foreign Policy of Soviet Russia*, II, p. 244.

55.   *D.US.F.P.*, 1939, I, p. 255.

56.   Ibid., pp. 258-59.

57.   Bullitt to Secretary of State, No. 1582, May 23, 1939, File 740. 00, U.S. National Archives, *G.R.D.S.*, Record Group 59.

58.   Kennedy to Secretary of State, No. 1590, May 24, 1939, and Grummon to Secretary of State, No. 1591, May 24, 1939, ibid. Also *D.Bri.F.P.*, V, No. 389. Cf. *S.I.A.*, X, p. 447.

59.   Appendix VII.

60.   *D.US.F.P.*, 1939, I, pp. 261-62.

61.   *D.Bri.F.P.*, V, No. 657, p. 710. Cf. *S.I.A.*, X, p. 450.

62.   *New York Times*, June 1, 1939. Cf. *D. Sov.F.P.*, III, pp. 413-17.

63.   *D.Bri.F.P.*, V, No. 697. Cf. *S.I.A.*, X, p. 451.

64.   Bullitt to Secretary of State, No. 1644, June 1, 1939, and Grummon to Secretary of State, No. 1655, June 2, 1939, File 740.00, U.S. National Archives, *G.R.D.S.*, Record Group 59.

65. *D.US.F.P.*, 1939, I, p. 268.

66. *H.C. Debates*, 5th Series, Vol. 348, Col. 400-2. Cf. *S.I.A.*, X, p. 452.

67. A. D. Nikonov, *Origins of World War II*, p. 78.

68. The British were well aware that an envoy of Strang's rank might antagonize the Russians, but they believed that with negotiations so uncertain, the higher the envoy, the more resounding the failure, and the Soviet Union might be more amenable if the West did not appear too anxious. *D.US.F.P.*, 1939, I, p. 273, and *D.Bri.F.P.*, V, No. 719. Bonnet on June 7 concurred (no. 74). Cf. *S.I.A.*, X, p. 453. If the Russians resented the appointment as Molotov's *post facto* remark to Schulenburg on August 17 suggests, there appeared no noticeable shift in policy. Churchill himself believed it probably made no difference, and the feeling prevalent at the time was that now that the Soviet Union had a purely Russian government, they were reverting to the policy of long ago, namely ". . .to keep the rest of Europe at arms length upon the ground that Russia was practically invulnerable so long as she remained in a defensive position. . .and did not link her own destinies with those of other European powers." *D.US.F.P.*, 1939, I, p. 274.

69. *D.Sov.F.P.*, III, p. 418.

70. *D.Ger.F.P.*, No. 529, p. 474.

71. Kirk to Secretary of State, No. 1761, June 17, 1939, File 740.00, U.S. National Archives, *G.R.D.S.*, Record Group 59.

72. Montgomery to Secretary of State, No. 776, June 29, 1939, File 741.61, ibid. Strang himself noted his disadvantage which was due in his view to the secured position of the Soviet Union, the fact that the negotiations were in Moscow, and easily exploitable Anglo-French differences. *D.Bri.F.P.*, VI, No. 122 and 376. Cf. *S.I.A.*, X, pp. 455-56.

73. Ibid., No. 35, Annex 2. Cf. *S.I.A.*, X, p. 458. The more general formula included all the states to the East and some in the West, but unnamed; it provided for intervention by the three powers both in case of aggression against a state which asked for assistance and in case of action by a ". . .European power which the three parties considered to threaten the independence or neutrality of another European state in such a way as to constitute a menace to the security of the country concerned."

74. Ibid., Nos. 69, 73, 99, 113. Cf. *S.I.A.*, X, pp. 457-9.

75. Ibid., No. 80, p. 146.

76. It was one of the first German concessions. At the time, the

German Ambassador in the Soviet Union saw it as a blackmailing maneuver against the British and an expression of the Soviet Union's "unchanged mistrust." *D.Ger.F.P.,* VI, No. 582.

77. Articles in *Pravda* June 12 and 29 referred to this question. Grummon to Secretary of State, No. 1904, June 20, 1939, File 740.00, U.S. National Archives, *G.R.D.S.,* Record Group 59.

78. *D.Bri.F.P.,* V, Nos. 206-7, 225-6, 281, 300. Cf. *S.I.A.,* X, p. 464.

79. Ibid., Nos. 252-3, 300, 329, 338.

80. Ibid., No. 378. For a general discussion Nos. 279, 357, 378. Cf. *S.I.A.,* X, p. 464. In this the British were particularly attentive to the U.S. sentiment where there was pervasive sympathy for small states and particularly Finland who had paid her post-war debt.

81. On July 9 Molotov said the Soviet Government was unanimous that a political and military agreement should be initiated simultaneously and that immediately after an announcement could be made. Ibid., No. 381. Cf. *S.I.A.,* X, p. 470. Molotov stuck to this point, rejecting on July 17 the British offer to begin staff talks if Molotov abandoned the idea of simultaneous signature. Ibid., No. 329. Cf. *S.I.A.,* X, p. 471.

82. The French, as opposed to the British had thought it was better to accept the Russian definition of indirect aggression but refuse simultaneous signature, as they saw that the consent of Poland and Rumania was needed and they feared if a political agreement was not signed first, nothing would be accomplished before German-Soviet talks reached a critical stage. British interests were more concerned with safeguarding East Europe, while French were with obtaining Soviet aid. In deference to the French, Seeds, on July 15 accepted Molotov's offer that staff talks should begin at once if Molotov abandoned the idea of simultaneous signature and accepted the British formula for indirect aggression. Molotov rejected this on July 17. Ibid., Nos. 298, 329, 381. Cf. *S.I.A.,* X, p. 471.

83. Grummon to Secretary of State, No. 1954, July 27, 1939, File 740.00, U.S National Archives, *G.R.D.S.,* Record Group 59.

84. *D.Bri.F.P.,* VI, No. 647. Cf. *S.I.A.,* X, p. 482.

85. Minutes of these meetings can be found in *D.Bri.F.P.,* VII, Appendices.

86. A. D. Nikonov, *Origins of World War II,* pp. 84-85.

87. *D.Bri.F.P.,* VI, No. 90, p. 87. Cf. *S.I.A.,* X, p. 171. Beck also argued that the Russians were materially incapable of keeping their com-

mitments and that the political structure of E. Galicia would not survive the entrance of Russian troops.

88.   On the Soviet side, an August 27 *Izvestia* interview with Voroshilov, Molotov's farewell address to the English and French Ambassadors, and to some extent present historiography. Obviously the Russians in not blaming England and France, wanted to preserve something of that link for the future if need be. Gafencu asserts that to compensate for Soviet mistrust, a new factor was necessary, Polish support, and "This they did not get." (*Last Days of Europe*, pp. 218, 319-20.) Even Western historiography lends such a view. Henry L. Roberts in his biography of Beck says the one-sided nature of the conditions laid down by the Polish Ambassador in a conversation with Molotov in May, doomed them from the beginning. (G. Craig and F. Gilbert, *Diplomats*, p. 609.) These were 1) not to accept a Soviet guarantee; 2) nor a mutual guarantee; 3) nor collective negotiations; 4) making their attitude conditional on the results of the Anglo-French-Soviet negotiations; 5) holding off bilateral discussions until the Anglo-Franco-Soviet discussions were concluded. *Polish White Book*, p. 298.

89.   G. Gafencu, *Last Days of Europe*, p. 227.

90.   In this regard, U.S. Ambassador in the Soviet Union, Steinhardt, reported that the Moscow press, having reported the Anglo-French-Soviet conversations without comment all summer, suddenly published an official denial of an August 11, *Volkischer Boebachter* news report alleging U.S.-Soviet cooperation, leaked by the Soviets to the Germans to bring pressure on them. Steinhardt to Secretary of State, No. 832, August 14, 1939, File 741.61, U.S. National Archives, *G.R.D.S.*, Record Group 59.

Notes to Chapter VI

1.   There is some difference of opinion as to how strong Hitler regarded the Russians. In Lord Londonderry's book, *Ourselves and Germany*, Hitler is said to have made a statement to the effect that he respected the military strength of the Soviet Union. On the other hand, authors like Edward Crankshaw say that Hitler had inside information regarding the Soviet weakness (presumably from Rapallo) which was confirmed by the Russo-Finnish War. On May 17, 1939, U.S. Charge Grummon reported that the German assistant military attache in Moscow was asked by the

German War Ministry if there was any reason to believe the Soviet Union was stronger in a military sense and in a better position to undertake offensive action than in September of 1938, to which he answered in the negative. (*D.US.F.P.-SU.,* p. 314.) The disparity in opinion can in part be explained by the difference in the Soviet defensive and offensive positions (the former being strong and the latter being weak), and in Hitler's bravado public statements and his private sentiments. Obviously he believed the Soviets were strong enough, particularly in league with the West, that they needed concrete neutralization even at a price. On the other hand, he rightly suspected that they wished neutrality because of offensive weakness and ideological goals.

2.   In mid-May Goering went to Madrid hoping to induce Franco to join the Axis, but he was not successful, and then in mid-July Ciano went to Spain at which time Spain refused bases to Italy thus pressuring the latter to neutrality.

3.   Millard to Secretary of State, No. 778, July 15, 1939 and No. 823, July 17, 1939, File 741.61, U.S. National Archives, *G.R.D.S.,* Record Group 59.

4.   *D.Ger.F.P.,* VI, pp. 223, 576, 1099.

5.   Ciano, *Europa,* pp. 283-6. Cf. *D.I.A.,* 1939, I, p. 180.

6.   *D.Ger.F.P.,* VII, pp. 552-56 (General Halder's Notebook).

7.   *Nazi-Soviet Relations,* pp. 80-1.

8.   Fn. 6.

9.   Hohenthal to War Department, M.I.D. Report, July 22, 1940, File 2657-230/5, U.S. National Archives, *Rec.W.D.,* Record Group 165.

10.   *D.I.A.,* 1939, I, pp. 186-7.

11.   Ibid., p. 188.

12.   For an enlightening sketch of the personality of Schulenburg and the policies of the diplomatic corps, see G. Craig and F. Gilbert, *Diplomats,* pp. 477-536. For examples of his attitude, see *D.Ger.F.P.,* I, pp. 610, 626, 630, 898, 920, and 928.

13.   The Soviets were well aware of German economic needs and exploited them both economically and politically. Litvinov said in a speech on June 23, 1938 that "The present aggressor absolutely needs quick successes in a war as a result of their domestic weakness and lack of resources. . . ." *D.Ger.F.P.,* I, No. 627, p. 923.

14.   Ibid., V, Nos. 490-1, 493, 495.

15.   Ibid., No. 120, pp. 159-60.

16.   Ibid., IV, No. 487, p. 623. See Chapter V, p. 194, fn. 77.

17.   *D.Ger.F.P.*, VI, No. 161, p. 196. A view also held by Bullitt.

18.   Ibid., No. 215, p. 166.

19.   Ibid., No. 332, p. 429.

20.   G. Hilger and A. Meyer, *Incompatible Allies*, pp. 290-91.

21.   *D.Ger.F.P.*, VI, p. 420. There is no German record of Ribbentrop's instructions to Schulenburg though Italian Ambassador to the Soviet Union, Rosso, reported on May 24 what Schulenburg told him of Ribbentrop's instructions. This can be found in Mario Toscano, *Origins of the Pact of Steel*. There are records of Weizsäcker's instructions which were along the same lines. Ibid., No. 414, p. 527 and No. 442, p. 593. Also in *D.US.F.P.*, 1939, I, May 20, 1939 (U.S. Charge Grumman.) His source was a "member of the German Embassay."

22.   Ibid., No. 424, p. 558. Also *Nazi-Soviet Relations*, pp. 5-9.

23.   Ibid., No. 414, p. 547; No. 424, p. 558; No. 437, p. 586; No. 437, p. 586.

24.   Ibid., No. 437, p. 586; No. 441, p. 589; No. 446, p. 597.

25.   Ibid., No. 451, p. 604.

26.   *D.Sov.F.P.*, III, p. 332.

27.   *D.Ger.F.P.*, VI, No. 583, p. 810; No. 661, p. 910.

28.   Ibid., No. 520, p. 717; No. 529, p. 728; No. 540, p. 741.

29.   At one point, Molotov told Schulenburg that a non-aggression pact was in the German interest not the Soviet, and besides, the Soviet Union could not be sure of its duration as the Polish example illustrated. Ibid., No. 677, p. 928; No. 685, p. 936; No. 700, p. 955.

30.   Ibid., No. 543, p. 745; No. 579, p. 805.

31.   Ibid., No. 614, p. 843. This was the 1926 German-Soviet Treaty, extended in 1933 which provided for consultation on joint questions and for neutrality. The applicability of this treaty to the present situation was reviewed by legal expert Nadolny and sent to Schulenburg on July 4, 1939.

32.   Ibid., No. 729, p. 1000.

33.   Ibid., p. 1008.

34.   Ibid., No. 757, pp. 1046-8. Weizsäcker in his memo to the Embassy also mentions the need for speed in view of the political situation. Ibid., No. 759, pp. 1048-49. This exchange is given tragi-comic presence when placed alongside of Ribbentrop's instructions not to show any haste in his conversations with Molotov. Ibid., No. 760, pp. 1049-50.

35. Ibid., No. 758, p. 1048; No. 766, p. 1059.

36. Ibid., VII, No. 14, p. 12. On August 10 Schulenburg reported learning from a reliable source that the British had conceded to the Soviets with regard to moving troops into the Baltic in the event of a direct attack and even in the absence of a request for aid.

37. Ibid., No. 18, p. 17; No. 27, p. 27; No. 50, p. 58; No. 54, p. 61.

38. Ibid., No. 51, p. 59; No. 56, p. 58; No. 71, p. 76; No. 75, p. 84; No. 88, p. 99.

39. Ibid., No. 105, p. 114.

40. Ibid., No. 132, p. 149.

41. Ibid., No. 170, p. 179. For the text No. 159, p. 168.

42. Appendix VIII for the Soviet draft proposal. Appendix IX for the final version.

43. *D.Ger.F.P.*, VII, No. 205; Gaus's affidavit at Nuremburg (*I.M.T. Nuremburg*, X, 312.) Cf. *S.I.A.*, X, p. 500.

44. *D.Ger.F.P.*, VII, No. 213, p. 225 (as recorded by Hencke.) Also *D.I.A.*, 1939, I, pp. 404-8.

45. A. Rossi (*Russo-German Alliance*, p. 208) believes the Soviet Union took the initiative by exploring rapprochement on April 17, by dismissing Litvinov on May 4, by steering the talks to a political plane on May 20 and by Moscow's taking the lead in proposing a pact of non-aggression with a secret corollary, and that talks with the West were continued as reinsurance and to exact a higher price. G. Weinberg, *Germany and the Soviet Union*, p. 17 agrees but places the Russian decision later. E. Wiskemann, *Undeclared War, Introduction*, on the other hand, believes it was Germany who led the way in the negotiations and that the decision regarding Ruthenia paved the way. F. L. Schuman, *Night Over Europe*, p. 233, argues that the whole course of Nazi-Soviet relations took was dependent on the course of negotiations with the West, and that the Soviets favored coming to terms with Germany only if she didn't come to terms with Britain. L. E. Namier, *Europe in Decay* believes the Soviets did not make their decision until the last minute, while G. Hilger, *Incompatible Allies*, pp. 289-91 believes that Hitler's decision was based on his assessment of Soviet strength which would be vastly increased if they came to agreement with the West.

46. In speculating on the nature of the Pact, this is the interpretation given it by U.S. Minister to the USSR, Steinhardt, who wrote on August

24 that territorial compensation would be given to the USSR if there were changes in the status of countries in between. Steinhardt to Secretary of State, No. 93, August 24, 1939, File 761-6211, U.S. National Archives, *G.R.D.S.*, Record Group 59.

47.   The latter assessment was generally agreed upon by the military of all countries who recognized that Soviet action in the Baltic, which was designed to interrupt Swedish iron ore to Germany, could not seriously menace German control of the Baltic Sea. So wrote Kirk to Secretary of State, No. 1108, September 26, 1938, File 760F.62, U.S National Archives, *G.R.D.S.*, Record Group 59.

48.   Phillips to Secretary of State, No. 1160, December 14, 1939, File 740.0011, U.S. National Archives, *G.R.D.S.*, Record Group 59.

49.   *D.Ger.F.P.*, VII, No. 206, p. 211.

50.   Ibid., No. 198, p. 208.

51.   Steinhardt to Secretary of State, No. 111, August 23, File 761. 6211, U.S. National Archives, *G.R.D.S.*, Record Group 59.

52.   Fortier to War Department, January 5, 1940, File 2071-215/20, U.S. National Archives, *Rec.W.D.*, Record Group 165.

53.   Ratay to War Department, December 6, 1939, File 2069-156/22, ibid.

54.   MacMurray to Secretary of State, No. 491, December 6, 1939, File 867.911, *G.R.D.S.*, Record Group 59.

55.   The Russian Naval Attache commented that Germany needed peace with England badly because she needed the help of the Balkan Entente to survive. Hohenthal to War Department, July 22, 1940, File 2657-230-5, U.S. National Archives, *Rec.W.D.*, Record Group 165.

56.   *Nazi-Soviet Relations*, p. 158.

57.   Some authors believe they were destroyed by Ribbentrop in order to press his case. Even in the end, Ribbentrop was more apt to negotiate with Balkan territory than Hitler. According to U.S. wartime documents released September 24, 1979 by the U.S. National Security Agency, on March 17, 1945 Ribbentrop, in a meeting with Japanese Ambassador to Germany, Oshima, suggested that Russia could be brought around to the Axis side by offers of territory in the Balkans because there was some fear that the U.S. and England would attack the Soviet Union to eliminate Communism. Ribbentrop said, "To give my own private opinion, I think Germany would consider it alright to offer Russia all the Balkans, northern

Europe, etc., retaining only old German territory, Hungary and Croatia, and further to support Russia if she wished to penetrate the Dardanelles, or even the Suez." Oshima agreed that the matter could be brought up at the April 17 meeting between the Soviets and Japanese, but Hitler vetoed it.

58. *D.Ger.F.P.*, VII, No. 192, p. 200. In fact, Hitler immediately began to transfer to the Danube route former ocean shipments via Constanza and Hamburg once the war began. Gunther to Secretary of State, No. 179, September 12, 1939, File 508, U.S. National Archives, *P.F.*, Record Group 84.

59. For the press statements, Kirk to Secretary of State, No. 101, August 24, 1939, File 761.6211, U.S. National Archives, *G.R.D.S.*, Record Group 59. For Hitler's, Kordt, *Wahn und Wirklichkeit*, 2nd ed., p. 192. Hitler's later offers to Great Britain for peace illustrates the same thing. Cf. *S.I.A.*, X, p. 503.

60. *Nazi-Soviet Relations*, p. 80-1, or *D.I.A.*, 1939, p. 188.

61. As conveyed by German Ambassador Munters in Latvia on information from his headquarters in Germany. Wiley to Secretary of State, No. 190, September 7, 1939, File 761.6211, U.S. National Archives, *G.R. D.S.*, Record Group 59.

62. *D.Ger.F.P.*, VII, No. 180, p. 188.

63. Lane to Secretary of State, No. 216, August 24, 1939, File 508, .S. National Archives, *P.F.*, Record Group 84.

64. Ciano, *Europa*, p. 374. No doubt the Germans overstated the case somewhat in order to impress on the Italians the need for Italian quiescence in the area.

65. The speech can be found in *Pravda*, September 1, 1939. Extracts in *D.Sov.F.P.*, III, p. 363 and V. M. Molotov, *Soviet Peace Policy, Four Speeches*, (London: Lawrence and Wishart, 1941), pp. 9-20.

66. He was referring to the Anglo-French and American press who criticized the Pact.

67. That they expected war was evident in the heavy Soviet troop concentrations reported by the German military attaches to be at full war strength on the Western front. And in order to protect this line, Molotov requested an amendment to part two of the Secret Protocol revising it to read the Pisa, Warev, Vistula, and San rivers in view of the Soviet realization that the Narev did not extend to the frontier of Prussia, a request promptly approved by the Germans. *D.Ger.F.P.*, VII, No. 413, p. 409; No. 284, p. 195.

68. Steinhardt to Secretary of State, No. 166, September 6, 1939,

File 740.0011, and No. 142, August 28, 1939, File 761.6211; Biddle to Secretary of State, No. 145, August 28, 1939, File 761.6211, U.S. National Archives, *G.R.D.S.*, Record Group 59.

69.   There were swift and strident denials to allegations in the *Daily Herald* to the effect that the Soviets intended to occupy strategic points in Poland at the outbreak of war, (*Mirovoe Khoziastvo*, 1939, p. 11, and *Polish White Book*, p. 187 or *D.Sov.F.P.*, III, pp. 360-62), and statements to the effect that Russian interests were to maintain buffer states and therefore they resented Poland's denials of offers of assistance (Kirk to Secre tary of State, No. 156, August 31, 1939, File 761.6211, U.S. National Archives, *G.R.D.S.*, Record Group 59.)

70.   *D.US.F.P.*, 1939, I, pp. 302-4.

71.   Jovenal writing in the *Paris Soir* based on a conversation with Ribbentrop en route to Moscow. Ibid., p. 367.

72.   Ibid., pp. 342-48 (Steinhardt).

73.   Phillips to Secretary of State, No. 701, August 23, 1939, File 762.65, ibid.

74.   Ciano, *Diaries*, August 22, 1939 entry.

75.   *D.Ger.F.P.*, VII, No. 280.

76.   Even the Poles were optimistic believing the Pact would cause in creasing improvement in Hungarian-Rumanian relations, and improvement in Bulgaria's attitude toward an anti-aggression front in the Balkans. Biddle to Secretary of State, No. 1139, August 38, 1939, File 760.61, U.S. National Archives, *G.R.D.S.*, Record Group 59.

77.   MacMurray to Secretary of State, No. 728, September 2, 1939, Kennedy to Secretary of State, No. 731, September 4, 1939, File 762.65, ibid., and Memo of Conversation MacMurray and Saracoglu, August 24, 1939, File 508, U.S. National Archives, *P.F.*, Record Group 84.

78.   As the Rumanian Foreign Office told Gunther, No. 152, August 24, 1939, ibid.

79.   *D.Ger.F.P.*, VII, No. 361, p. 363; No. 385; No. 482, p. 470.

80.   Opinion of the Rumanian Ambassador in Yugoslavia. Lane to Secretary of State, No. 151, September 4, 1939, File 764.71, U.S. National Archives, *G.R.D.S.*, Record Group 59.

81.   *D.US.F.P.*, 1939, I, pp. 404-5, and Lane to Secretary of State, No. 230, August 31, 1939 and No. 232, September 1, 1939, File 308, U.S. National Archives, *P.F.*, Record Group 84. The Rumanian Ambas sador agreed.

82. *D.Ger.F.P.,* VII, No. 178, p. 187; No. 532, p. 508. The wisdom of Yugoslavia's attitude was also emphasized to U.S. Minister Lane. Lane to Secretary of State, No. 213, August 23, 1939, File 508, U.S. National Archives, *P.F.,* Record Group 84.

83. MacVeagh to Secretary of State, No. 339, September 13, 1939, No. 178, September 19, 1939, and No. 702, September 29, 1939, File 508, U.S. National Archives, *P.F.,* Record Group 84.

84. *D.Ger.F.P.,* VII, No. 289, p. 299, and Gunther to Secretary of State, No. 91, November 21, 1939, File 508, U.S. National Archives, *P.F.,* Record Group 84.

85. Ibid., No. 185, September 13, 1939, and Phillips to Secretary of State, No. 280. Also Montgomery to Secretary of State, No. 296, September 13, 1939, File 740.0011, *G.R.D.S.,* Record Group 59, and Travers to Secretary of State, (as related by the Hungarian Foreign Minister), No. 36, September 5, 1939, File 871.014.

86. *D.Ger.F.P.,* VII, No. 168, p. 177.

87. As related by Kiosseivanov. Millard to Secretary of State, No. 51 and 76, September 1, 1939, and Lane to Secretary of State, No. 252, September 15, 1939, File 508, U.S. National Archives, *P.F.,* Record Group 84.

88. *D.Ger.F.P.,* No. 80, p. 91. August 16 all existing contracts supplying Turkey with German war material were cancelled despite their hope of pressuring Turkey away from the West, (No. 137, p. 154). August 20, German Charge Kroll reported that on information from the Italian military attache, Russia had, during conversations with the West, expressed a desire to participate in the defense of the Dardanelles by a peacetime base on the Sea of Marmora.

89. Ibid., No. 247, p. 260. Papen had seen Hitler at Obersalzburg on August 21 (No. 219), and apparently got this idea from him.

90. Ibid., No. 448, p. 440, and MacMurray to Secretary of State, No. 111, September 16, 1939, U.S. National Archives, *P.F.,* Record Group 84.

91. Ibid., No. 393, p. 389; No. 342, p. 347.

92. *D.I.A.,* 1939, I, p. 193. Also *The Times,* September 2, 1939 and *Hitler e Mussolini,* No. 12.

93. MacVeagh to Secretary of State, No. 3394, September 13, 1939, File 508, U.S. National Archives, *P.F.,* Record Group 84.

94. Ibid.

95. For instance, a *Tass* communique on September 16, 1939 entitled "Violation of the Frontier by German Aircraft." Steinhardt to Secretary of State, No. 545, September 16, 1939, File 761.62, U.S. National Archives, *G.R.D.S.*, Record Group 59.

96. Gunther to Secretary of State, No. 488, September 21, 1939, and Lane to Secretary of State, No. 576, September 23, 1939, ibid.

97. Ibid., Nos. 543, 549, 580, File 761.62. Russian soldiers, in all sincerity and probably knowing nothing different, told the Poles they were marching across Poland to fight Germany and the Poles, according to Ratay, were quick-witted enough to see the joke. (Ratay to War Department, No. 2516, September 21, 1939, File 2069-156/18, *Rec. W.D.*, Record Group 165).

98. MacMurray to Secretary of State, No. 548, September 18, 1939, File 761.621, and Gunther to Secretary of State, No. 383, September 18, 1939, File 740.0011, U.S. National Archives, *G.R.D.S.*, Record Group 59.

99. Phillips to Secretary of State, No. 485, September 23, 1939 and No. 548, September 18, 1939, ibid. The Germans tried to make it seem that Italian neutrality was for the service of "preventing extension of hostilities to the Mediterranean and Balkans." From an article by Kirckner in the Frankfurter *Zeitung* in mid-October. Kirk to Secretary of State, No. 843, October 23, 1939, ibid.

100. *New York Times,* August 26, 1939, 3.7.

101. *D.US.F.P.,* 1939, I, p. 447. Reported by U.S. Minister Lane on information received from the Bulgarian military attache and the Assistant Minister of Foreign Affairs. Also Steinhardt to Secretary of State, No. 102, November 2, 1939, File 771.741, and No. 699, December 12, 1939, File 770.00, U.S National Archives, *G.R.D.S.,* Record Group 59.

102. Gunther to Secretary of State, No. 301, October 4, 1939, File 508, U.S. National Archives, *P.F.,* Record Group 84.

103. Gunther to Secretary of State, No. 257, September 23, 1939 and No. 263, September 25, 1939, ibid.

104. Memo of Conversation Lane and Cinkar-Marković, Lane to Secretary of State, No. 713, September 19, 1939, ibid. Cinkar-Marković also said the Soviet guarantee to Rumania was helpful, though he admitted in view of the Soviet-Polish guarantee that it was probably of little value.

105. For the Rumanian opinion, Gunther to Secretary of State, No. 313, October 7, 1939 and No. 314, October 8, 1939, File 508, U.S. National Archives, *P.F.,* Record Group 84. For the Greek view, MacVeagh

to Secretary of State, No. 219, September 29, 1939, File 761.6211, *G.R. D.S.,* Record Group 59.

106. MacMurray to Secretary of State, No. 122, October 5, 1939, ibid.

107. Ibid., No. 1202, October 13, 1939.

108. Ibid., No. 1238, October 24, 1939, and No. 232, October 5, 1939. Saracoglu told Steinhardt that the Soviets tried to obtain a return of their draft copy but that it had been sent to Ankara. *D.US.F.P.,* 1939, I, pp. 385-86.

109. MacMurray to the President, No. 137, October 27, 1939, ibid.

110. MacMurray to the Secretary of State, No. 126, November 10, 1939, ibid. The Pact provided for aid to Turkey if she were attacked by a European Power, to Great Britain and France if the former were engaged in hostilities resulting from the guarantee to Greece or Rumania, reciprocal aid in the event of war in the Mediterranean, consultation in other circumstances, and a stipulation that Turkey would not be forced to action which might involve her in conflict with the Soviet Union.

111. *D.Ger.F.P.,* VIII, No. 6, p. 5; No. 81, p. 80; No. 91, p. 93.

112. Ibid., No. 116, pp. 114-16.

113. Gunther to Secretary of State, No. 179 and 182, September 12, 1939, File 508, U.S. National Archives, *P.F.,* Record Group 84.

114. *D.US.F.P.,* 1939, I, p. 458. In early October Rumania, Yugoslavia, and Hungary demobilized an additional twenty percent of their forces, but all moved troops to the north to meet a possible Russian threat.

115. Kirk to Secretary of State, No. 687, 211, 212, 213, September 30, 1939, File 740.0011, U.S. National Archives, *G.R.D.S.,* Record Group 59.

116. *D.Ger.F.P.,* VIII, No. 146, p. 151; No. 198, p. 205; No. 202, p. 222.

117. Ibid., No. 175, p. 183; No. 211, p. 236; No. 219, p. 244.

118. Ibid., No. 250, p. 280; No. 268, p. 306. Also Steinhardt to Secretary of State, No. 267, October 20, 1939, File 761.6211, U.S. National Archives, *G.R.D.S.,* Record Group 59.

119. Steinhardt to Secretary of State, No. 270, October 19, 1939, File 761.6211, U.S. National Archives, *G.R.D.S.,* Record Group 59.

120. For the Rumanian view, Gunther to Secretary of State, No. 218, October 16, 1939; for the Bulgarian view, Steinhardt to Secretary of State, No. 248, November 2, 1939; for the Greek view, MacVeagh to Secretary of State, No. 228, October 20, 1939, ibid.

121. *D.US.F.P.*, 1939, I, pp. 460-65. Also Gunther to Secretary of State No. 351, October 23, 1939, and Lane to Secretary of State, No. 713, September 11, 1939, File 508, U.S. National Archives, *P.F.*, Record Group 84.

122. Gunther to Secretary of State, No. 354, October 25, 1939, No. 356, October 25, 1939, and No. 424, December 8, 1939, File 508, U.S. National Archives, *P.F.*, Record Group 84.

123. Steinhardt telegram to Gunther, No. 932, December 6, 1939, Gunther to Secretary of State, No. 424, December 8, 1939, and Steinhardt to Secretary of State, No. 1032, December 6, 1939, ibid. The article was in the *Communist International* to the effect that the British, French and American financial oligarchy was trying to extend the sphere of war in particular to involve the Balkan countries in the struggle against Germany and "in this perspective, against the Soviet Union." The article accused the British of the murder of Calinescu because of his neutral policy and directed attention to Poland as far as the amount of help which could be expected of the allies. At the same time, the article described the "peaceful policy of the Soviet Union" as exemplified in the treaty with Germany and the treaties of mutual assistance with the Baltic states, showing the need for "immediate conclusion of a pact of mutual assistance with the USSR" by Rumania.

124. Hibbard to Secretary of State, No. 445, December 28, 1939, ibid.

125. Phillips to Secretary of State, No. 815, September 19, 1939, File 7600.61, No. 269, October 20, 1939, and No. 94, November 22, 1939, File 761.6211, U.S. National Archives, *G.R.D.S.*, Record Group 59.

126. Lane to Secretary of State, No. 1087, September 27, 1939 and No. 1086, September 26, 1939, File 860H.00, ibid.

127. Millard to Secretary of State, No. 61, September 20, 1939, No. 740, October 24, 1939; No. 76, October 30, 1939; No. 87, December 11, 1939, and No. 87, December 15, 1939, File 508, U.S. National Archives, *P.F.*, Record Group 84.

128. MacVeagh to Secretary of State, No. 3654, December 18, 1939, ibid.

129. Teleki openly showed this map to U.S. Minister Montgomery. Montgomery to Secretary of State, No. 38, December 11, 1939, File 871. 014, U.S. National Archives, *G.R.D.S.*, Record Group 59.

130. Memo of a conversation of Atay and MacMurray, September 23, 1939. Mr. Atay was editor of the semi-official paper ULUS and member of

the Foreign Affairs Committee of Parliament. Saracoglu spoke along the same lines. MacMurray to Secretary of State, No. 1214, October 7, 1939, and MacMurray to the President, No. 137, October 27, 1939, File 508, U. S. National Archives, *P.F.*, Record Group 84.

131. Montgomery to Secretary of State, No. 8, October 20, 1939, No. 170, December 9, 1939, File 764.74, No. 1045, November 17, 1939, File 740.0111, and Bullitt to Secretary of State, No. 62, December 14, 1939, File 761.64, U.S. National Archives, *G.R.D.S.*, Record Group 59.

132. MacVeagh to Secretary of State, No. 3663, November 18 , 1939, File 711.1; No. 243, November 11, 1939, No. 247, November 14, 1939; No. 3663, November 18, 1939, File 508, U.S. National Archives, *P.F.*, Record Group 84.

133. Lane to Secretary of State, No. 342, November 15, 1939 and Millard to Secretary of State, No. 365, November 22, 1939, File 508, ibid.

134. Montgomery to Secretary of State, No. 267, October 9, 1939; Travers to Secretary of State, No. 1944, December 23, 1939; Lane to Secretary of State, No. 365, December 13, 1939, ibid.

135. Ibid., Travers.

136. Steinhardt to Secretary of State, No. 699, December 21, 1939, File 770.00, U.S. National Archives, *G.R.D.S.*, Record Group 59.

137. Gunther to Secretary of State, No. 398, November 22, 1939, File 508, U.S. National Archives, *P.F.*, Record Group 84.

138. Reed to Secretary of State, No. 577, December 2, 1939, ibid. In implementing the new policy, the Italians began to send volunteers to Finland, allow anti-Communist demonstrations, and ready their military development for spring should Soviet action in the Balkans take place.

139. Fortier to War Department, February 16, 1940, File 2071-215/ 22, U.S. National Archives, *Rec.W.D.*, Record Group 165.

Notes to Epilogue

1. Ratay to War Department, No. 2530, December 15, 1939, File 2069-156/26, U.S National Archives, *Rec.W.D.*, Record Group 165.

2. Ibid. According to Ratay, there were detailed inventories in preparation for German evacuation of Bukovina, but not Bessarabia. In addition, carloads of sugar and soybeans destined for Germany were caught by the Russians.

3. Ibid., No. 2546, July 15, 1940, 2069-156/37-42. In fact, this seems to have been exactly what the Germans feared, having no adequate defense of the oil fields and in Ratay's opinion the General Staff had miscalculated Russian intent, believing Russia was in no position to mount a land offensive when in fact bombers, parachutists and air landing troops could have bombed and occupied practically without resistance Bucharest, the oil fields and other important centers. He said the Hungarian General Staff was also taken by surprise.

4. Hohenthal to War Department, File 2657/230-5, ibid.

5. By the cession to Bessarabia and N. Bukovina to Russia, Rumania lost 16.83% of her territory and 2.8 million people; in the cession of Transylvania to Hungary 14.35% of her land and 2.6 million people; in all including the part to Bulgaria, she lost 33% of her population and 34% of her territory.

BIBLIOGRAPHY

Primary Documents (Manuscripts)

General Records of the Department of State, Record Group 59, National Archives, Main Building, Washington, D.C.; contains *Diplomatic Papers* of the Department of State relating to Albania, Balkans, Bulgaria, Germany, Greece, Hungary, Rumania, Turkey, U.S.S.R., Yugoslavia, 1939.

General Records, Post Files, Record Group 84, National Archives, Federal Records Center Building, Suitland, Maryland; contains records for Ankara, Athens, Belgrade, Budapest, Istanbul, and Sofia, but not for Bucharest or Mosocw.

Records of the War Department, General and Specific Staffs, Military Intelligence Division, Record Group 165, National Archives, Federal Records Center Building, Suitland, Maryland.

Primary Documents (Printed)

Baynes, Norman H. *The Speeches of Adolph Hitler* (Oxford: Royal Institute of International Affairs, 1942), Vol. I and II. Cited as *Hitler's Speeches.*

British Blue Book, Documents Concerning German-Polish Relations and the Outbreak of Hostility Between Great Britain and Germany, September 3, 1939, Comd. 6106, (London: HMSO, 1939).

Degras, Jane, ed., *Soviet Documents in Foreign Policy,* Vol. III, 1939-41, (New York: Oxford University Press, 1953). Cited as *D.Sov.F.P.*

Documents on British Foreign Policy 1919-1939, Third Series (1938-9), 9 Volumes, (London: HMSO, 1945-55). Cited as *D.Bri.F.P.*

Documents on German Foreign Policy 1918-1945, Series D, Volumes I-XII, (Washington, D.C.: Department of State, 1949). Cited as *D.Ger.F.P.*

Documents on International Affairs 1928-1938, 13 Volumes (London: Oxford University Press for Royal Institute on International Affairs, 1929). Cited as *D.I.A.*

Documents on International Affairs 1936-1946, Volumes I-III (London: Oxford University Press for Royal Institute of International Affairs, 1951). Cited as *D.I.A.*

Dokumenti i Materiali kanyna ftoroii mirovoii voini, Tom II, Arkiv Dirksena, (Ministerstvo inostranix del SSSR, 1948). (*Documents and Materials on the Eve of the Second World War, Volume III-Archives of Dirksen* (Ministry of Foreign Affairs, USSR, 1948).

Falin, V. M., ed., *Soviet Peace Efforts on the Eve of World War II*, September, 1938-August 1939, Documents and Records (Moscow: Novosti Press, 1973).

Foreign Relations of the U.S.-General, 1939, Volumes I and II (Washington, D.C.: U.S. Government Printing Office, 1956). Cited as *D.US.F.P.*

Foreign Relations of the U.S. Diplomatic Papers—The Soviet Union 1933-1939 (Washington, D.C.: U.S. Government Printing Office, 1952). Cited as *D.US.F.P.-SU.*

French Yellow Book Documents Diplomatiques 1938-1939 (New York: Reynal and Hitchoch, 1940).

German White Book II, (Documents on Events Preceding the Outbreak of War, compiled and published by the German Foreign Office and [translated by] the German Library of Information, New York, Berlin, 1939 and New York, Carnegie Endowment for International Peace, 1950).

The Greek White Book: Diplomatic Documents Relating to Italy's Aggression Against Greece (Washington, D.C.: American Council on Public Affairs, 1943).

Keesing's Contemporary Archives 1937-1940 (London: Goodall, Ltd., Great Britain). Relevant sections.

"La Vie Politique," *Les Balkans*, Vol. XI, (Athñes lllme trimestre, 1939); pp. 112-117 review of the Balkan Entente and sessions of 1939; pp. 312-313 text of Serbo-Croat Agreement; pp. 402-404 text of Anglo-Turkish Agreement.

Molotov, V., *Soviet Peace Policy: Four Speeches* (London: Lawrence and Wishart, 1941).

Nazi Conspiracy and Aggression (A collection of documentary evidence and guide materials prepared by the American and British prosecution staffs for . . . the International Military Tribunal at Nuremburg), 8 vols., (Washington, D.C.: U.S. Government Printing Office, 1946-7).

New Documents on the History of Munich (Prague: Orbis, 1958).

Shapiro, Leonard, *Soviet Treaty Series*, Vol. II (Washington, D.C.: Georgetown University Press, 1955).

Sontag, Raymond J. and James S. Beddie, editors, *Nazi-Soviet Relations 1939-1941 – Documents from the Archives of the German Foreign Office* (Washington, D.C.: Department of State, 1948), Publication 3023. Cited as *Nazi-Soviet Relations*.

Stalin, Joseph, *Problems of Leninism* (Moscow: Foreign Languages Publishing House, 1953).

Stalin, J.V., *Sochineniia*, edited by Robert H. McNeal, 3 vols. (Stanford: Hoover Institution Foreign Language Publications, 1967).

Stalin, J. V., *Works VI, XIII* (Moscow: Foreign Languages Publishing House, 1955).

Trial of Major War Criminals before the International Military Tribunal Nuremburg, 1945-46, 42 Volumes (Nuremburg: International Military Tribunal, 1947-49). Cited as *I.M.T. Nuremburg*.

Memoirs

Beneš, Eduard, *Memoirs of Dr. Eduard Beneš* (Boston: Houghton and Mifflin, 1955).

Ciano, Galeazzo, *Ciano's Diary 1937-38* (London: Metheun and Co., Ltd., 1952).

Ciano, Galeazzo, *Diario 1939-43*, 2 Volumes, 4th ed., (Milan: Rizzoli, 1947), English translation, *Ciano's Diaries 1939-43*, edited by Malcolm Muggeridge, trans. Stuart Hood, (London: Oldhams Press, 1948).

Ciano, Galeazzo, *L'Europa verso la catastrofe* (Milan: Mondador, 1948). English translation, *Ciano's Diplomatic Papers*, edited by Malcolm Muggeridge, trans. Stuart Hood, (London: Oldham Press, 1948).

Davies, Joseph, *Mission to Moscow* (New York: Simon and Schuster, 1941).

Hilger, G. and A.G. Meyer, *The Incompatible Allies: A Memoir History of German-Soviet Relations 1918-1941* (New York: Macmillan, 1953).

Maisky, Ivan, *Memoirs of a Soviet Ambassador* (London: Hutcheson, 1967).

The von Hassel Diaries 1938-1944 (London: Hanish Hamilton, 1948).

Ribbentrop, J. von, *The Ribbentrop Memoirs* (London: Weidenfeld and Nicolson, 1954).

Schacht, H., *Confessions of the Old Wizard* (autobiography), (Boston: Houghton Mifflin, 1956).

Weizsäcker, E. H., *Memoirs* (Chicago: H. Regnery Co., 1951).

Books

Archer, Laird, *Balkan Journal* (New York: W. W. Norton and Co., 1944).

Barker, Elizabeth, *Macedonia, Its Place in Balkan Power Politics* (London and New York: Royal Institute of International Affairs, 1950).

Basch, Antonin, *The Danube Basin and the German Economic Sphere* (New York: Columbia University Press, 1943).

Beloff, Max, *The Foreign Policy of Soviet Russia*, 1929-1941, Vol. I and II (London and New York: Oxford University, Odhams Press, 1947-1949).

Bonnet, Georges, *Fin d'une Europe* (Paris: Hachette, 1946).

Bond, Brian, *British Military Policy Between the Two Wars* (Oxford: Clarendon Press, 1980).

Bullock, Alan, *Hitler—A Study in Tyranny* (New York: Harper, 1952).

Carr, E. H., *German Soviet Relations Between the Two World Wars 1919-1939* (Baltimore: Johns Hopkins Press, 1951).

Cecil, Robert, *Hitler's Decision to Invade Russia 1941* (London: Davis Paynter, 1974).

Churchill, Winston S., *The Second World War,* 6 Volumes (London: Cassell, 1948-54).

Coates, W. P., *A History of Anglo-Soviet Relations* (New York: Lawrence and Wishart and Pilot Press, 1943).

Coulondre, Robert, *De Stalin à Hitler* (Paris: Hachette, 1950).

Craig, Gordon A. and Felix Gilbert, editors, *The Diplomats 1919-1939,* Vol. II (New York: Atheneum, 1965).

Dallin, Alexander, *Soviet Conduct in World Affairs* (New York: Columbia University Press, 1960).

Dallin, David J., *Soviet Russia's Foreign Policy 1939-1942* (New Haven: Yale University Press, 1942).

Davies, Joseph E., *Mission to Moscow* (New York: Simon and Schuster, 1941).

Deutscher, Isaac, *Stalin–A Political Biography* (London: Oxford University Press, 1949).

Fischer, Fritz, *Germany's Aims in the First World War* (New York: W. W. Norton and Co., 1961).

Fischer, Louis, *Men and Politics* (New York: Duell, Sloan and Pearce, 1941).

Fischer, Louis, *Russia's Road From Peace to War: Soviet Foreign Relations 1917-1941* (New York: Harper and Row, 1969).

Fodor, M. W., *South of Hitler* (Plot and Counter Plot in Central Europe) (Boston: Houghton Mifflin, 1937).

Gafencu, Grigoire, *The Last Days of Europe* (New Haven: Yale University Press, 1948).

Gafencu, Grigoire, *Preliminaries de la Guerre a l'Est* (Paris: Egloff, 1944).

Geshkoff, Theodore I., *Balkan Union* (New York: Columbia University Press, 1940).

Hitler, Adolph, *Mein Kampf* (New York: Reynal and Hitchcock, 1940).

Hodža, Milan, *Federation in Central Europe* (London: Jarrolds, 1942).

Hollies, Christopher, *Neutral War Aims* (London: Burns, Oates, 1940).

Hoptner, Jacob, *Yugoslavia in Crisis 1934-41* (New York: Columbia University Press, 1962).

Kaiser, David E., *Economic Diplomacy and the Origins of the Second World War. Germany, Britain, France, and Eastern Europe, 1930-1939* (Princeton: Princeton University Press, 1980).

Kennan, George F., *Russia and the West Under Lenin and Stalin* (Boston: Little, Brown, 1960).

Kerner, R. J. and H. N. Howard, *The Balkan Conferences and Balkan Entente* (Berkeley: University of California Press, 1936).

Kertesz, S. D., *Diplomacy in a Whirlpool: Hungary between Nazi Germany and Soviet Russia* (Notre Dame, Indiana: University of Notre Dame, 1953).

King, W. B., and O'Brian, F., *The Balkans: Frontier of Two Worlds* (New York: A. A. Knopf, 1947).

Korbel, Josef, *Twentieth Century Czechoslovakia* (New York: Columbia University Press, 1967).

Lengyel, Emil, *The Danube 1918-1945* (New York: Random House, 1939).

Litvinov, Maxim. *Against Aggression* (New York: International Publishing Co., Inc., 1939).

Litvinov, Maxim, *Vneshniaia Politika SSSR* (Moscow: Government Publishing House, 1937).

Lukacs, John A., *The Great Powers and East Europe* (New York: American Book Co., 1953).

Macartney, C. A., *Hungary and Her Successors* (London: Oxford University Press, 1937).

Macartney, C. A., *Problems of the Danube Basin* (Cambridge: Cambridge University Press, 1942).

Maser, Werner, *Hitler's Mein Kampf, An Analysis* (London: Faber, 1970).

Molotov, V. M., *The Meaning of the Soviet-German Non-Aggression Pact* (New York: Workers Library Publishers, 1939).

Namier, L. B., *Diplomatic Prelude* (New York: Fertig, 1948).

Namier, L. B., *Europe in Decay* (New York: Macmillan, 1950).

Nikonov, A. D., *The Origins of World War II and the Pre-War European Political Crisis of 1939* (Moscow: Printing House of the USSR Academy of Sciences, 1955).

Packard, Reynolds and Eleanor, *Balcony Empire* (New York: Oxford University Press, 1942).

Ponomarev, I., and Boris Nikolaevich, *Istorii Vneshneii politikoi, 1917-1970* (History of Foreign Affairs, 1917-1970), (Moskva, Akademia Nauk, SSSR, 1966-71) (Moscow: Academy of Sciences, USSR).

Potemkin, V. P., *Istoria Diplomatii III,* (History of Diplomacy) (Moscow: Government Publication of Foreign Literature, 1945).

Pribichevich, S., *World Without End: The Saga of Southeastern Europe* (New York: Reynal and Hitchcock, 1939).

Rehman, M., *Turkish Foreign Policy* (Allahabad: Allahabad Publishing House, 1945).

Ripka, H., *Munich: Before and After* (London: Gollancz, 1939).

Robertson, E. M., *Hitler's Pre-War Policy and Military Plans* (London: Longmans, 1963).

Rossi, A., *The Russo-German Alliance* (London: Chapman and Hall, 1950).

Roucek, J. S., *Balkan Politics: International Relations in No Man's Land* (Stanford: Stanford University Press, 1948).

Rubenstein, Alvin Z., *The Foreign Policy of the Soviet Union* (New York: Random House, 1966).

Sakmyster, Thomas L., *Hungary, the Great Powers and the Danubian Crisis, 1936-1939* (Athens: University of Georgia Press, 1980).

Schevile, F. and W. M. Gewehr, *History of the Balkan Peninsula* (New York: Harcourt Brace, 1933).

Schuman, F. L., *Europe on the Eve: The Crisis of Diplomacy, 1933-1939* (New York: A. A. Knopf, 1939).

Schlesinger, R., *Federalism in Central and Eastern Europe* (London: K. Paul, French, Trubner and Co., 1945).

Schumann, Frederick L., *Night Over Europe* (New York: A. A. Knopf, 1944).

Seton Watson, Hugh, *Eastern Europe Between the Wars* (Cambridge: Cambridge University Press, 1945).

Shotwell, J. T. and F. Deak, *Turkey at the Straits* (New York: Macmillan, 1940).

Southeastern Europe: A Political and Economic Survey (London: Royal Institute of International Affairs, 1939).

Stalin, J. V., *The Great Patriotic War of the Soviet Union* (New York: International Publishers, 1945).

Stavrianos, L. S., *Balkan Federation: A History of the Movement Toward Balkan Unity* (Northhampton, MA: The Department of History of Smith College, 1944).

Sugar, Peter F and Ivo J. Lederer, *Nationalism in Eastern Europe* (Seattle and London: University of Washington Press, 1969).

Survey of International Affairs—1939-1946 I-X (London: Royal Institute of International Affairs, Oxford University Press, 1958). Cited as *S.I.A.*

Taracouzio, T. A., *War and Peace in Soviet Diplomacy* (New York: Macmillan Co., 1940).

Toscano, Mario, *The Origins of the Pact of Steel* (Baltimore: Johns Hopkins Press, 1967).

Weinberg, Gerhard, *Germany and the Soviet Union, 1939-1941* (Leiden, E. J. Brill, 1954).

West, Rebecca, *Black Lombard Grey Falcon: A Journey Through Yugoslavia* (New York: Viking Press, 1941).

Wheeler-Bennett, John, *Munich: Prologue to Tragedy* (London: Macmillan, 1948).

Wiskemann, Elizabeth, *The Rome-Berlin Axis* (New York: Oxford University Press, 1949).

Wiskemann, Elizabeth, *Undeclared War* (London: St. Martin's Press, 1967).

Wolff, Robert Lee, *The Balkans in Our Time* (New York: W. W. Norton and Co., 1967).

Articles

Abramsky, Chimen, ed., "The Initiation of the Negotiations Leading to the Nazi-Soviet Pact: A Historical Problem," *Essays in Honor of E. H. Carr* (Hamden, CN: 1974), pp. 152-170.

"Anglo-Franco-Russian Negotiations of 1939," *U.N. World,* March 1949, p. 224.

Batowski, Henryk, "Proposal for a Second Front in the Balkans in September, 1939," *Balkan Studies* Vol. 9, No. 2, p. 344.

Buzinski, Donald, "Bessarabia: The Thorny 'Non-Existent' Problem," *East European Quarterly,* Vol. XIII, No. 1 (Spring, 1979), pp. 47-74.

Cohen, Barry, Mendel, "Moscow at Munich: Did the Soviet Union Offer Unilateral Aid to Czechoslovakia?" *East European Quarterly,* Vol. XII, No. 3 (Fall, 1978), pp. 341-348.

Dakin, Douglas, "The Diplomacy of the Great Powers and the Balkan States, 1908-1914," *Balkan Studies,* Vol. 3, 1962, pp. 327-374.

Delfiner, Henry, "Vienna Broadcasts to Slovakia 1938-1939: A Case Study in Subversion," *East European Quarterly,* Monograph No. VII, Boulder, 1976).

Funderburk, David Britton, "Nadir of Appeasement: British Policy in the Demise of Albania April 7, 1939," *Balkan Studies,* Vol. 11, 1967, pp. 299-304.

"Germany and the USSR," *International News,* Vol. XVI, 1939, Part II, p. 845.

"Germany's Trade Offensive," *The Economist,* November 3, 1938, pp. 262-267.

Gratke, Charles E., "Behind Russo-German Rapprochement," *Christian Science Monitor,* September 2, 1939, pp. 3 and 15.

Howard, Harry N., "The Balkans after Munich," *World Affairs,* June, 1939.

Johnson, Robert H., "Tradition Versus Revolution: Russia and the Balkans 1917," *East European Quarterly Monograph,* No. XXVIII, (Boulder, 1977).

Komjathy, Anthony Tihamer, "The Crises of France's East Central European Diplomacy 1933-1938," *East European Quarterly*, Monograph XXI, (Boulder, 1976).

Kosinski, Leszek A., "Secret German War Sources for Population Study of East-Central Europe and the Soviet Union," *East European Quarterly*, Vol. X, No. 1, (Spring, 1976), pp. 31-34.

Macfie, A. L., "The Straits Question: The Conference of Montreux (1936)," *Balkan Studies*, Vol. 13, No. 12, 1972.

Oldson, William O., "Rumania and the Munich Crisis Aug.-Sept., 1938," *East European Quarterly*, Vol. XI, No. 2, pp. 177-190.

Polowitch, K. S., "Yugoslav British Relations 1939-1941 as Seen From British Sources," *East European Quarterly*, Vol. XII, No. 3, (Fall, 1978), pp. 309-339.

Patch, Buel, W., "Nazi Objectives in East Europe," *Editorial Research Reports*, January 10, 1939, pp. 19-32.

Poole, DeWitt, C., "Light on Nazi Foreign Policy," *Foreign Affairs*, October, 1946, p. 141.

Roucek, Joseph S. and Jeri Skvor, "Beneš and Munich: A Reappraisal," *East European Quarterly*, Vol. X, No. 3, (Fall, 1976), pp. 375-385.

Stoddard, Lothrop, "The Portents of Prague," *Barrons*, March 20, 1939, p. 9.

Tucker, Robert C., "The Emergence of Stalin's Foreign Policy," *Slavic Review*, Vol. 36, No. 4, (December 1977), pp. 563-589.

Urban, Laszlo K., "German Property Interests in Poland during the 1920s," *East European Quarterly*, Vol. X, No. 2, (Summer, 1976), pp. 181-221.

Winchester, Betty Jo, "Hungary and the Austrian Anschluss," *East European Quarterly*, Vol. X, No. 4 (Winter, 1976), pp. 409-425.

Woytak, Richard A., "Polish Hungarian Relations and the Carpatho-Ukrainian Question in October, 1938," *East European Quarterly*, Vol. X, No. 3, (Fall, 1976), pp. 367-374.

Newspapers

Izvestia—Relevant issues.
Mirovoe Khoziastvo—Relevant issues.
New York Times—Relevant issues.
Pravda—Relevant issues.

Unpublished Papers

Quinlan, Paul D., "The Tilea Affair: A Further Inquiry," Presented at the
New England Historical Association. At the office of *East European
Quarterly*, Boulder, Colorado.

Rainkin, Spas T., "Bulgaria and the Macedonian Nationality," Associate
Professor of History, E. Stroudsburg State College, presented at the
History Forum at Duquesne University, Pittsburgh, PA, October 26,
1971.

Wrigley, W. David, "The U.S. and the Italian Influence in Albania—6 Diplomatic Documents 1928-1939." At the office of *East European Quarterly*, Boulder, Colorado.

Bibliographies

Degras, Jane, *Calendar of Soviet Documents on Foreign Policy 1917-1941*
(London and New York: Royal Institute of International Affairs, 1948).

Kinshevich, Leo O., *U.S. History and Historiography in Post-War Soviet
Writings 1945-1970—A Bibliography* (Santa Barbara, CA: Clio Press,
1976).

APPENDICES

Appendix I
British Interim Guarantee to Poland, March 31, 1939.

. . . His Majesty's Government have no official confirmation of the rumors of any projected attack on Poland and they must not therefore be taken as accepting them as true.

I am glad to take this opportunity of stating again the general policy of His Majesty's Government. They have constantly advocated the adjustment, by way of free negotiation between the parties concerned, of any differences that may arise between them. They consider that this is the natural and proper course where differences exist. In their opinion there should be no question incapable of solution by peaceful means, and they would see no justification for the substitution of force or threats for the method of negotiation.

As the House is aware, certain consultations are now proceeding with other Governments. In order to make perfectly clear the position of His Majesty's Government in the meantime before those consultations are concluded, I now have to inform the House that, during that period, in the event of any action which clearly threatened Polish independence, and which the Polish Government accordingly considered it vital to resist with the national forces, His Majesty's Government would feel themselves bound at once to lend the Polish Government all support in their power. They have given the Polish Government an assurance to this effect.

I may add that the French Government have authorised me to make it plain that they stand in the same position in this matter as does His Majesty's Government.

Cf. *S.I.A.*, X, pp. 92-93. For complete text see *House of Commons Debates*, 5th Series, Volume 345, Col. 2415.

Appendix II
British Guarantee to Greece and Rumania, April 13, 1939.

I have given the House in some detail the history of what may be called the Corfu rumors. How they arose I do not pretend to know, but the fact that they should have been current and widely believed illustrates the general uneasiness created by recent events. Although this particular story has now been discredited, yet as I have said on a previous occasion, once confidence has been roughly shaken it is not so easily re-established and H.M. Government feel that they have both a duty and a service to perform by leaving no doubt in the mind of anybody as to their position. I therefore take this opportunity of saying on their behalf that his Majesty's Government attach the greatest importance to the avoidance of disturbances by force or threat of force of the status quo in the Mediterranean and the Balkan Peninsula.

Consequently they have come to the conclusion that in the event of any action being taken which clearly threatened the independence of Greece or Rumania, and which the Greek or Rumanian Government respectively considered it vital to resist with their national forces, H.M Government would feel themselves bound at once to lend the Greek or Rumanian Government, as the case might be, all the support in their power. We are communicating this declaration to the Governments directly concerned and to others, especially Turkey, whose close relations with the Greek Government are known. I understand that the French Government are making a similar declaration this afternoon. I need not add that the Dominion Governments, as always are being continuously informed of all developments.

Cf. *Keesing's Contemporary Archives 1937-1940* (Goodall Ltd., GB), p. 3527. Full text in *House of Commons Debates,* 5th Series, Vol. 345, Col. 13.

Appendix III
Anglo-Turkish Declaration, May 12, 1939.

1. His Majesty's Government . . . and the Turkish Government have entered into close consultation and the discussions which have taken place between them and which are still continuing have revealed their customary identity of view.

2. It is agreed that the two countries will conclude a definite long-term agreement of a reciprocal character in the interest of their national security.

3. Pending the completion of the definitive agreement, His Majesty's Government and the Turkish Government declare that in the event of an act of aggression leading to war in the Mediterranean area they would be prepared to co-operate effectively and to lend each other all aid and assistance in their power.

4. This declaration, like the proposed agreement, is not directed against any country, but is designed to assure Great Britain and Turkey of mutual aid and assistance should the necessity arise.

5. It is recognized by the two Governments that certain matters, including the more precise definition of various conditions which would bring the reciprocal engagements into operation, will require closer examination before the definitive agreement can be completed. This examination is proceeding.

6. The two Governments recognize that it is also necessary to ensure the establishment of security in the Balkans and they are consulting together with the object of achieving this purpose as speedily as possible.

7. It is understood that the arrangements above mentioned do not preclude either Government from making agreements which other countries in the general interest of the consolidation of peace.

8. A similar declaration is being made in Ankara this evening.

Cf. *S.I.A.*, 1939, X, p. 120. Full text in *House of Commons Debates*, 5th Series, Vol. 347, Col. 953.

Appendix IV
The Balkan Entente Pact, February 9, 1934.

The Balkan Entente Pact
A. The Pact of Balkan Entente
(Between Greece, Rumania, Turkey, and Yugoslavia,
signed at Athens, February 9, 1934)

The President of the Hellenic Republic, His Majesty the King of Rumania, the President of the Turkish Republic, and His Majesty the King of Yugoslavia, being desirous of contributing to the consolidation of peace in the Balkans:

Animated by the spirit of understanding and conciliation which inspired the drawing up of the Briand-Kellogg Pact and the decisions of the Assembly of the League of Nations in relation thereto;

Firmly resolved to ensure the observation of the contractual obligations already in existence and the maintenance of the territorial situation in the Balkans as at present established:

Have resolved to conclude a
"Pact of Balkan Entente"

And for that end have designated their Plenipotentiaries, to wit:

The President of the Hellenic Republic, His Excellency Mr. Demetre Maximos, Minister of Foreign Affairs;

His Majesty the King of Rumania, His Excellency Mr. Nicholas Titulescu, Minister of Foreign Affairs;

The President of the Turkish Republic, His Excellency Mr. Revfik Rüstü Bey, Minister of Foreign Affairs;

His Majesty the King of Yugoslavia, His Excellency Mr. Bogolioub Jevtich, Minister of Foreign Affairs.

Who, have exchanged their full powers, found in good and due form, have agreed upon the following provisions:

Article I
Greece, Rumania, Turkey, and Yugoslavia mutually guarantee the security of each and all their Balkan frontier.

Article 2

The High Contracting Parties undertake to concert together in regard to the measures to be taken in contingencies liable to affect their interests as defined by the present Agreement. They undertake not to embark upon any political action in relation to any other Balkan country not a signatory of the present agreement without previous mutual consultation, nor to incur any political obligation to any other Balkan country without the consent of the other Contracting Parties.

Article 3

The present agreement shall come into force on the date of its signature by all the Contracting parties, and shall be ratified as rapidly as possible. It shall be open to any Balkan country whose accession thereto is favourably regarded by the Contracting Parties, and such accession shall take effect as soon as the other signatory countries have notified their agreement.

In the faith whereof of said Plenipotentiaries have signed the present Pact.

Done at Athens, this ninth day of February, nineteen hundred and thirty-four, in four copies of each having been delivered to each of the High Contracting Parties.

D. MAXIMOS
DR. T. RÜSTÜ
N. TITULESCU
B. JEVTICH

B. The Protocol-Annex

In proceedings to sign the Pact of Balkan Entente, the four Ministers for Foreign Affairs of Greece, Rumania, Yugoslavia, and Turkey have seen fit to define as follows the nature of the understandings assumed by their respective countries, and to stipulate explicitly that the said definitions form an integral part of the Pact.

1. Any country committing one of the acts of aggression to which Article 2 of the London Conventions of July 3rd and July 4th, 1933, relates shall be treated as an aggressor.

2. The pact of Balkan Entente is not directed against any Power. Its object is to guarantee the security of the several Balkan frontiers against any aggression on the part of any Balkan State.

3. Nevertheless, if one of the High Contracting Parties is the victim of aggression on the part of any other non-Balkan Power, and a Balkan State associates itself with such aggression, whether at the time or subsequently, the Pact of Balkan Entente shall be applicable in its entirety in relation to such Balkan State.

4. The High Contracting Parties undertake to conclude appropriate Conventions for the furtherance of the object pursued by the Pact of Balkan Entente. The negotiations of such Conventions shall begin within six months.

5. As the Pact of Balkan Entente does not conflict with previous undertakings, all previous undertakings and all Conventions based on previous Treaties shall be applicable in their integrity, the said undertakings and the said Treaties having all been abolished.

6. The words "Firmly resolved to ensure the observance of the contractual obligations already in existence," in the Preamble of the Pact, shall cover the observance by the High Contracting Parties of existing Treaties between Balkan States to which one or more of the High Contracting Parties is a signatory party. Balkan Entente is a defensive instrument; accordingly, the obligations of the High Contracting Parties which arise out of the said Pact shall cease to exist in relation to the High Contracting Party becoming aggressor against any other country within the meaning of Article 2 of the London Conventions.

8. The maintenance of the territorial situation in the Balkans as at present established is binding definitely on the High Contracting Parties. The duration of the obligations under the Pact shall be fixed by the High Contracting Parties, in the source of the two years following the signature of the Pact, or afterwards. During the two years in question the Pact cannot be denounced. The duration of the Pact shall be fixed at not less than five years, and may be longer. If, two years after the signature of the same, no duration has been fixed, the Pact of Balkan Entente shall ipso facto remain in force for five years from the expiry of the two years after the signature thereof. On the expiry of the said five years, or of the period on which the High Contracting Parties agreed for its duration, the Pact of Balkan Entente shall be renewed automatically by tacit agreement for a period for which it was previously in force, failing denunciation by any one of the High Contracting Parties, one year before the date of its expiry; provided always that no denunciation or notice of denunciation shall be

admissable, whether in the first period of the Pact's validity (namely seven or more than seven years) or in any subsequent period fixed automatically by tacit agreement, before the year preceding the date on which the Pact expires.

9. The High Contracting Parties shall inform each other as soon as the Pact of Balkan Entente is ratified in accordance with their respective laws.

Athens, this ninth day of February, nineteen hundred and thirty-four.

D. MAXIMOS
DR. T. RÜSTÜ
N. TITULESCU
B. JEVTICH

Cf. Theodore S. Geshkoff, *Balkan Union,* (New York: Columbia University Press, 1940), Appendix 13.

Appendix V
Agreement Between the Balkan Entente and Bulgaria at Salonika, July 31, 1939

prenant en considération:

Que la Bulgarie est attachée à la politique de reaffermissement de la prix dans les Balkans et qu'elle est animée du désire d'entretenir avec les Etats balkaniques des relations de bon vosiinage et de confiant collaboration, et

Que les Etates de l'Entente balanique sont animés à l'égard de la Bulgarie du même esprit pacifique et du même désir de coopération,

Les soussignés:

Son Excellence M' le Dr' Georges Kiosséivanoff, Président du Conseil des Ministres, Ministre des Affaires étrangères de Bulgarie, d'une part, et

Son Excellence M. Jean Métaxas, President du Conseil des Ministres, Ministre des Affaires étrangères de Grèce, en sa qualité de Président en exercice du Conseil permanent de l'Entente balkanique, agissant au nom de tous les membres de l'Entente balkanique, d'autre part,

Déclarent au nom des Etats qu'ils représentent que ces Etats prennent l'engagement de s'abstenir dans leurs relations mutuelles de tout recours à la force, conformément aux accords que chacun de ces Etats a souscrits en matiere de non-aggression, et qu'ils conviennent, en ce qui les concerne, à renoncer à l'application des dispositions contenues dans la Partie IV (Clauses militaires, navels et aériennes— du Traité de Neuilly ainsi que des dispositions militaires, navales et aeriennes) du Traité de Neuilly ansi que des dispositions contenues dans la convention concernant la frontière de Thrace signée à Lausonne de 24 juillet, 1923.

Fait a Thessalonique, en double exemplaire, le 31 juillet 1938

G. Kiosséivanoff

J. Métaxas

Cf' *D.I.A.,* 1938, I, pp. 287-288.

Appendix VI
Communique of the Bled Agreement Between the Little Entente and Hungary, August 23, 1939.

The negotiations which have been in progress since last year between Hungary on the one hand and Rumania, Yugoslavia, and Czechoslovakia on the other, and which were inspired by the common desire to rid their mutual relations of everything which could impede the development of good neighbourliness between Hungary and these three States, have resulted in provisional agreements. These agreements include the recognition by the three States of the Little Entente of Hungary's equality of rights as regards armament, as well as the mutual renunciation of any recourse to force between Hungary and the States of the Little Entente.

During the conversations which preceded this agreement, all questions the solution of which might favourably affect relations between the Danube States were discussed in detail and in a friendly spirit. It had been intended to issue declarations embodying the views of the above-mentioned countries on these questions. It was not, however, possible to draw up these declarations in final form. It is hoped that when these difficulties have been overcome, the negotiations will be succesfully concluded, and that the completed agreements and the above-mentioned declarations will be published simultaneously.

Cf. *D.I.A.*, 1938, I, p. 284.

Appendix VII
Anglo-Franco Draft Agreement to the Soviet Union, May 25, 1939.

The Governments of Great Britain, France and Russia, desiring in their capacity as members of the League of Nations to give effect to the principles of mutual support embodied in the Covenant of the League of Nations, have reached the following agreement:

1. If France and the United Kingdom are engaged in hostilities with any European power in consequence of (1) aggression by that power against another European state which they had in conformity with the wishes of that state undertaken to assist against such aggression, or (2) assistance given by them to another European state which had requested such assistance in order to resist violation of its neutrality, or (3) aggression by a European power against either France or Great Britain, Russia acting in accordance with the principles of article XVI, paragraphs 1 and 2, of the Covenant of the League of Nations, will give France and Great Britain all support and assistance in its power.

2. Sets forth the identical obligations as in 1 above on the part of France and Great Britain to the Government of Soviet Russia.

3. The three contracting Governments will concert as to methods by which such mutual support and assistance could in case of need be made effective.

4. In the event of there arising a threat which would call their undertakings of mutual support and assistance into operation, the three Governments will immediately enter into consultations with each other. The methods and scope of such consultations will at once be the subject of further discussions between the three Governments.

5. The obligation of rendering support and assistance in the cases outlined in preceding articles is without prejudice to the rights and position of other powers.

6. Each of the three Governments will communicate to the others the terms of any undertakings to which they are now committed, referred to in paragraphs 1 (1) and 2 (1) above, and before taking on any similar obligations in the future each of the three powers will consult with the others.

7. The agreement is to continue for 5 years and the three Governments will consult as to the desirability of renewal, with or without modifications, not less than 6 months before its expiration.

Cf. *D.US.F.P.,* 1939, I, pp. 262-263. For official text, see *Documents on British Foreign Policy,* 1919-1939, 3d Series, Vol. 5, Doc. No. 624, p. 679

Appendix VIII
The Soviet Draft for a Non-Aggression Pact with Germany, August 19, 1939.

The German Ambassador in the Soviet Union (Schulenburg)
to the German Foreign Office
Telegraph

VERY URGENT   Moscow, August 19, 1939–11:30 p.m.
SECRET
No. 190 of August 19
Supplementing my telegram No. 189 of August 19.
The Soviet nonaggression pact draft reads as follows:

"The Government of the U.S.S.R. and the German Government, desirous of strengthening the cause of peace among the nations and proceeding from the fundamental provisions of the Neutrality Agreement that was concluded in April 1926 between the U.S.S.R. and Germany, have reached the following accord:

ARTICLE 1.   Both High Contracting Parties obligate themselves to desist reciprocally from any act of violence and any aggressive action whatsoever toward each other, or from an attack on each other individually or jointly with other powers.

ARTICLE 2.   Should one of the High Contracting Parties become the object of an act of violence or attack by a third power, the other High Contracting Party shall in no manner whatever give its support to such acts of that power.

ARTICLE 3.   Should disputes or conflicts arise between the High Contracting Parties with regard to questions of one kind or another, both parties obligate themselves to settle these disputes and conflicts exclusively by peaceful means through mutual consultation or if necessary through the creation of suitable arbitration commissions.

ARTICLE 4.   The present Treaty shall be concluded for a period of five years with the proviso that insofar as one of the High Contracting Parties does not denounce it one year before the expiration of the term the validity of the Treaty shall automatically be extended for another five years.

ARTICLE 5.   The present Treaty shall be ratified in as short a time as possible, whereupon the Treaty shall enter into force.

Postscript. The present Treaty shall be valid only if a special protocol is signed simultaneously covering the points in which the High Contracting Parties are interested in the field of foreign policy. The protocol shall be an integral part of the Pact.

SCHULENBURG

Cf. *Nazi-Soviet Relations,* pp. 65-66.

Appendix IX
The Non-Aggression Pact and Secret Protocol, August 23, 1939.

Treaty of Non-Aggression between Germany and the Union of
Soviet Socialist Republics

The Government of the German Reich and the Government of the
Union of Soviet Socialist Republics, desirous of strengthening the cause
of peace between Germany and the U.S.S.R., and proceeding from the
fundamental provisions of the Treaty of Neutrality, which was concluded between Germany and the U.S.S.R. in April 1926, have reached the
following agreement:

Article I

The two Contracting Parties undertake to refrain from any act of violence, any aggressive action and any attack on each other either severally
or jointly with other Powers.

Article II

Should one of the Contracting Parties become the object of belligerent
action by a third Power, the other Contracting Party shall in no manner
lend its support to this third Power.

Article III

The Governments of the two Contracting Parties will in the future maintain continual contact with one another for the purpose of consultation in
order to exchange information on problems affecting their common interests.

Article IV

Neither of the two Contracting Parties will join any grouping of Powers
whatsoever which is aimed directly or indirectly at the other Party.

Article V

Should disputes or conflicts arise between the Contracting Parties over
questions of one kind or another, both Parties will settle these disputes or
conflicts exclusively by means of a friendly exchange of views or if necessary by the appointment of arbitration commissions.

Article VI

The present Treaty shall be concluded for a period of ten years with the proviso that, in so far as one of the Contracting Parties does not denounce it one year before the expiry of this period, the validity of this Treaty shall be deemed to be automatically prolonged for another five years.

Article VII

The present treaty shall be ratified within the shortest possible time. The instruments of ratification will be exchanged in Berlin. The treaty shall enter into force immediately upon signature.

Done in duplicate in the German and Russian languages.

Moscow, August 23, 1939

For the Government
of the German Reich
V. Ribbentrop

With full power of the
Government of the U.S.S.R.:
V. Molotov

SECRET ADDITIONAL PROTOCOL

On the occasion of the signature of the Non-Aggression Treaty between the German Reich and the Union of Soviet Socialist Republics, the undersigned plenipotentiaries of the two Parties discussed in strictly confidential conversations the question of the delimitation of their respective spheres of interest in Eastern Europe. These conversations led to the following results:

1. In the event of a territorial and political transformation in the territories belonging to the Baltic States (Finland, Estonia, Latvia, Lithuania), the northern frontier of Lithuania shall represent the frontier of the spheres of interest both of Germany and the U.S.S.R. In this connection the interest of Lithuania in the Vilna territory is recognized by both Parties.

2. In the event of a territorial and political transformation of the territories belonging to the Polish State, the spheres of interest of both Germany and the U.S.S.R. shall be bounded approximately by the line of the rivers Narev, Vistula, and San.

The question whether the interests of both Parties make the maintenance of an independent Polish State appear desirable and how the frontiers of this State should be drawn can be definitely determined only in the course of further political developments.

In any case both Governments will resolve this question by means of a friendly understanding.

3. With regard to South-Eastern Europe, the Soviet side emphasizes its interest in Bessarabia. The German side declares complete political desinteressement in these territories.

4. This Protocol will be treated by both parties as strictly secret.

MOSCOW, AUGUST 23, 1939.

For the Government of   With full power of the
the German Reich: Government of the U.S.S.R.:
V. Ribbentrop   V. Molotov

Cf. *D.Ger.F.P.*, VII, Nos. 228, 229, pp. 245-247.

Appendix X
Correction to the Secret Protocol, August 26, 1939.

The Ambassador in the Soviet Union
to the Foreign Ministry

Telegram

MOST URGENT   MOSCOW, August 25, 1939—11:37 p.m.
SECRET   Received August 26—6.45 a.m.

Molotov sent for me this evening and said that, because of the great haste with which the Secret Additional Protocol had been drawn up, an obscurity had crept into the Text. As the end of the first paragraph of point two (two) it should read "bounded by the line of the rivers Pisa, Narev, Vistula and San," in accordance with the . . .(grouping missing)[1] held here.

The inadequacy of the maps[2] used during the conversations gave rise to the mistaken impression among all those taking part that the upper reaches of the Narev extended to the frontier of East Prussia, which is . . .(two groups missing)[3] the case. Although there is no doubt as to the meaning of the agreement reached, he asked as a matter of form (sic)[4] the sentence in question by the insertion of the names of the rivers Pisa, San (sic)[5] which could be done by an exchange of letters between him and me.

I request authorization to agree with Molotov on the desired addition . . .(two groups missing)[6] accuracy.

SCHULENBURG[7]

1. The Moscow draft (695/260289-90) reads: "conversations."
2. The Moscow draft reads: "map."
3. The Moscow draft reads: "not in fact . . ."
4. The sentence in the Moscow draft reads: ". . .he asked as a matter of form that the sentence in question be supplemented by the insertion of the name of the river Pisa, which could . . ."
5. The name "San" is a deciphering error; it does not appear in the Moscow draft, see fn. 4 above.
6. The Moscow draft reads: "in the interests of . . ."
7. Marginal note in Weizsäcker's handwritting: "To be kept in special safe (*Sekretieren Kassette*)."

Cf. *D.Ger.F.P.*, VII, No. 284, pp. 295-296.

INDEX

EAST EUROPEAN MONOGRAPHS

The *East European Monographs* comprise scholarly books on the history and civilization of Eastern Europe. They are published under the editorship of Stephen Fischer-Galati, in the belief that these studies contribute substantially to the knowledge of the area and serve to stimulate scholarship and research.

21. *The Crises of France's East-Central European Diplomacy, 1933–1938.* By Anthony J. Komjathy. 1976.
22. *Polish Politics and National Reform, 1775–1788.* By Daniel Stone. 1976.
23. *The Habsburg Empire in World War I.* Edited by Robert A. Kann, Bela K. Kiraly, and Paula S. Fichtner. 1977.
24. *The Slovenes and Yugoslavism, 1890–1914.* By Carole Rogel. 1977.
25. *German-Hungarian Relations and the Swabian Problem.* By Thomas Spira. 1977.
26. *The Metamorphosis of a Social Class in Hungary During the Reign of Young Franz Joseph.* By Peter I. Hidas. 1977.
27. *Tax Reform in Eighteenth Century Lombardy.* By Daniel M. Klang. 1977.
28. *Tradition versus Revolution: Russia and the Balkans in 1917.* By Robert H. Johnston. 1977.
29. *Winter into Spring: The Czechoslovak Press and the Reform Movement 1963–1968.* By Frank L. Kaplan. 1977.
30. *The Catholic Church and the Soviet Government, 1939–1949.* By Dennis J. Dunn. 1977.
31. *The Hungarian Labor Service System, 1939–1945.* By Randolph L. Braham. 1977.
32. *Consciousness and History: Nationalist Critics of Greek Society 1897–1914.* By Gerasimos Augustinos. 1977.
33. *Emigration in Polish Social and Political Thought, 1870–1914.* By Benjamin P. Murdzek. 1977.
34. *Serbian Poetry and Milutin Bojic.* By Mihailo Dordevic. 1977.
35. *The Baranya Dispute: Diplomacy in the Vortex of Ideologies, 1918–1921.* By Leslie C. Tihany. 1978.
36. *The United States in Prague, 1945–1948.* By Walter Ullmann. 1978.
37. *Rush to the Alps: The Evolution of Vacationing in Switzerland.* By Paul P. Bernard. 1978.
38. *Transportation in Eastern Europe: Empirical Findings.* By Bogdan Mieczkowski. 1978.
39. *The Polish Underground State: A Guide to the Underground, 1939–1945.* By Stefan Korbonski. 1978.
40. *The Hungarian Revolution of 1956 in Retrospect.* Edited by Bela K. Kiraly and Paul Jonas. 1978.
41. *Boleslaw Limanowski (1935–1935): A Study in Socialism and Nationalism.* By Kazimiera Janina Cottam. 1978.
42. *The Lingering Shadow of Nazism: The Austrian Independent Party Movement Since 1945.* By Max E. Riedlsperger. 1978.
43. *The Catholic Church, Dissent and Nationality in Soviet Lithuania.* By V. Stanley Vardys. 1978.
44. *The Development of Parliamentary Government in Serbia.* By Alex N. Dragnich. 1978.
45. *Divide and Conquer: German Efforts to Conclude a Separate Peace, 1914–1918.* By L. L. Farrar, Jr. 1978.
46. *The Prague Slav Congress of 1848.* By Lawrence D. Orton. 1978.
47. *The Nobility and the Making of the Hussite Revolution.* By John M. Klassen. 1978.
48. *The Cultural Limits of Revolutionary Politics: Change and Continuity in Socialist Czechoslovakia.* By David W. Paul. 1979.
49. *On the Border of War and Peace: Polish Intelligence and Diplomacy in 1937–1939 and the Origins of the Ultra Secret.* By Richard A. Woytak. 1979.
50. *Bear and Foxes: The International Relations of the East European States 1965–1969.* By Ronald Haly Linden. 1979.

51. *Czechoslovakia: The Heritage of Ages Past.* Edited by Ivan Volgyes and Hans Brisch. 1979.

52. *Prime Minister Gyula Andrassy's Influence on Habsburg Foreign Policy.* By Janos Decsy. 1979.

53. *Citizens for the Fatherland: Education, Educators, and Pedagogical Ideals in Eighteenth Century Russia.* By J. L. Black. 1979.

54. *A History of the "Proletariat": The Emergence of Marxism in the Kingdom of Poland, 1870–1887.* By Norman M. Naimark. 1979.

55. *The Slovak Autonomy Movement, 1935–1939: A Study in Unrelenting Nationalism.* By Dorothea H. El Mallakh. 1979.

56. *Diplomat in Exile: Francis Pulszky's Political Activities in England, 1849–1860.* By Thomas Kabdebo. 1979.

57. *The German Struggle Against the Yugoslav Guerrillas in World War II: German Counter-Insurgency in Yugoslavia, 1941–1943.* By Paul N. Hehn. 1979.

58. *The Emergence of the Romanian National State.* By Gerald J. Bobango. 1979.

59. *Stewards of the Land: The American Farm School and Modern Greece.* By Brenda L. Marder. 1979.

60. *Roman Dmowski: Party, Tactics, Ideology, 1895–1907.* By Alvin M. Fountain, II. 1980.

61. *International and Domestic Politics in Greece During the Crimean War.* By Jon V. Kofas. 1980.

62. *Fires on the Mountain: The Macedonian Revolutionary Movement and the Kidnapping of Ellen Stone.* By Laura Beth Sherman. 1980.

63. *The Modernization of Agriculture: Rural Transformation in Hungary, 1848–1975.* Edited by Joseph Held. 1980.

64. *Britain and the War for Yugoslavia, 1940–1943.* By Mark C. Wheeler. 1980.

65. *The Turn to the Right: The Ideological Origins and Development of Ukrainian Nationalism, 1919–1929.* By Alexander J. Motyl. 1980.

66. *The Maple Leaf and the White Eagle: Canadian-Polish Relations, 1918–1978.* By Aloysius Balawyder. 1980.

67. *Antecedents of Revolution: Alexander I and the Polish Congress Kingdom, 1815–1825.* By Frank W. Thackeray. 1980.

68. *Blood Libel at Tiszaeszlar.* By Andrew Handler. 1980.

69. *Democratic Centralism in Romania: A Study of Local Communist Politics.* By Daniel N. Nelson. 1980.

70. *The Challenge of Communist Education: A Look at the German Democratic Republic.* By Margrete Siebert Klein. 1980.

71. *The Fortifications and Defense of Constantinople.* By Byron C. P. Tsangadas. 1980.

72. *Balkan Cultural Studies.* By Stavro Skendi. 1980.

73. *Studies in Ethnicity: The East European Experience in America.* Edited by Charles A. Ward, Philip Shashko, and Donald E. Pienkos. 1980.

74. *The Logic of "Normalization:" The Soviet Intervention in Czechoslovakia and the Czechoslovak Response.* By Fred Eidlin. 1980.

75. *Red Cross, Black Eagle: A Biography of Albania's American Schol.* By Joan Fultz Kontos. 1981.

76. *Nationalism in Contemporary Europe.* By Franjo Tudjman. 1981.

77. *Great Power Rivalry at the Turkish Straits: The Montreux Conference and Convention of 1936.* By Anthony R. DeLuca. 1981.

78. *Islam Under the Double Eagle: The Muslims of Bosnia and Hercegovina, 1878–1914.* By Robert J. Donia. 1981.

79. *Five Eleventh Century Hungarian Kings: Their Policies and Their Relations with Rome.* By Z. J. Kosztolnyik. 1981.
80. *Prelude to Appeasement: East European Central Diplomacy in the Early 1930's.* By Lisanne Radice. 1981.
81. *The Soviet Regime in Czechoslovakia.* By Zdenek Krystufek. 1981.
82. *School Strikes in Prussian Poland, 1901–1907: The Struggle Over Bilingual Education.* By John J. Kulczychi. 1981.
83. *Romantic Nationalism and Liberalism: Joachim Lelewel and the Polish National Idea.* By Joan S. Skurnowicz. 1981.
84. *The "Thaw" In Bulgarian Literature.* By Atanas Slavov. 1981.
85. *The Political Thought of Thomas G. Masaryk.* By Roman Szporluk. 1981.
86. *Prussian Poland in the German Empire, 1871–1900.* By Richard Blanke. 1981.
87. *The Mazepists: Ukrainian Separatism in the Early Eighteenth Century.* By Orest Subtelny. 1981.
88. *The Battle for the Marchlands: The Russo-Polish Campaign of 1920.* By Adam Zamoyski. 1981.
89. *Milovan Djilas: A Revolutionary as a Writer.* By Dennis Reinhartz. 1981.
90. *The Second Republic: The Disintegration of Post-Munich Czechoslovakia, October 1938-March 1939.* By Theodore Prochazka, Sr. 1981.
91. *Financial Relations of Greece and the Great Powers, 1832–1862.* By Jon V. Kofas. 1981.
92. *Religion and Politics: Bishop Valerian Trifa and His Times.* By Gerald J. Bobango. 1981.
93. *The Politics of Ethnicity in Eastern Europe.* Edited by George Klein and Milan J. Reban. 1981.
94. *Czech Writers and Politics.* By Alfred French. 1981.
95. *Nation and Ideology: Essays in Honor of Wayne S. Vucinich.* Edited by Ivo Banac, John G. Ackerman, and Roman Szporluk. 1981.
96. *For God and Peter the Great: The Works of Thomas Consett, 1723–1729.* Edited by James Cracraft. 1982.
97. *The Geopolitics of Leninism.* By Stanley W. Page. 1982
98. *Karel Havlicek (1821–1856): A National Liberation Leader of the Czech Renascence.* By Barbara K. Reinfeld. 1982.
99. *Were-Wolf and Vampire in Romania.* By Harry A. Senn. 1982.
100. *Ferdinand I of Austria: The Politics of Dynasticism in the Age of Reformation.* By Paula Sutter Fichtner. 1982
101. *France in Greece During World War I: A Study in the Politics of Power.* By Alexander S. Mitrakos. 1982.
102. *Authoritarian Politics in a Transitional State: Istvan Bethlen and the Unified Party in Hungary, 1919–1926.* By William M. Batkay. 1982.
103. *Romania Between East and West: Historical Essays in Memory of Constantin C. Giurescu.* Edited by Stephen Fischer-Galati, Radu R. Florescu and George R. Ursul. 1982.
104. *War and Society in East Central Europe: From Hunyadi to Rakoczi—War and Society in Late Medieval and Early Modern Hungary.* Edited by János Bak and Béla K. Király. 1982.
105. *Total War and Peace Making: A Case Study on Trianon.* Edited by Béla K. Király, Peter Pastor, and Ivan Sanders. 1982
106. *Army, Aristocracy, and Monarchy: Essays on War, Society, and Government in Austria, 1618–1780.* Edited by Wayne S. Vucinich. 1982.
107. *The First Serbian Uprising, 1804–1813.* Edited by Wayne S. Vucinich. 1982.

108. *Propaganda and Nationalism in Wartime Russia: The Jewish Anti-Fascist Committee in the USSR, 1941-1948.* By Shimon Redich. 1982.

109. *One Step Back, Two Steps Forward: On the Language Policy of the Communist Party of Soviet Union in the National Republics.* By Michael Bruchis. 1982.

110. *Bessarabia and Bukovina: The Soviet-Romanian Territorial Dispute.* by Nicholas Dima. 1982

111. *Greek-Soviet Relations, 1917-1941.* By Andrew L. Zapantis. 1982.

112. *National Minorities in Romania: Change in Transylvania.* By Elemer Illyes. 1982.

113. *Dunarea Noastra: Romania, the Great Powers, and the Danube Question, 1914-1921.* by Richard C. Frucht. 1982.

114. *Continuity and Change in Austrian Socialism: The Eternal Quest for the Third Way.* By Melanie A. Sully. 1982

115. *Catherine II's Greek Prelate: Eugenios Voulgaris in Russia, 1771-1806.* By Stephen K. Batalden. 1982.

116. *The Union of Lublin: Polish Federalism in the Golden Age.* By Harry E. Dembkowski. 1982.

117. *Heritage and Continuity in Eastern Europe: The Transylvanian Legacy in the History of the Romanians.* By Cornelia Bodea and Virgil Candea. 1982.

118. *Contemporary Czech Cinematography: Jiri Menzel and the History of The "Closely Watched Trains".* By Josef Skvorecky. 1982.

119. *East Central Europe in World War I: From Foreign Domination to National Freedom.* By Wiktor Sukiennicki. 1982.

120. *City, Town, and Countryside in the Early Byzantine Era.* Edited by Robert L. Hohlfelder. 1982.

121. *The Byzantine State Finances in the Eighth and Ninth Centuries.* By Warren T. Treadgold. 1982.

122. *East Central European Society and War in Pre-Revolutionary Eighteenth Century.* Edited by Gunther E. Rothenberg, Bela K. Kiraly and Peter F. Sugar. 1982.

123. *Czechoslovak Policy and the Hungarian Minority, 1945-1948.* By Kalman Janics. 1982.

124. *At the Brink of War and Peace: The Tito-Stalin Split in a Historic Perspective.* Edited by Wayne S. Vucinich. 1982.

125. *The Road to Bellapais: The Turkish Cypriot Exodus to Northern Cyprus.* By Pierre Oberling. 1982.

126. *Essays on World War I: Origins and Prisoners of War.* Edited by Peter Pastor and Samuel R. Williamson, Jr. 1983.

127. *Panteleimon Kulish: A Sketch of His Life and Times.* By George S. N. Luckyj. 1983.

128. *Economic Development in the Habsburg Monarchy in the Nineteenth Century: Essays.* Edited by John Komlos. 1983.

129. *Warsaw Between the World Wars: Profile of the Capital City in a Developing Land, 1918-1939.* By Edward D. Wynot, Jr. 1983.

130. *The Lust for Power: Nationalism, Slovakia, and The Communists, 1918-1948.* By Yeshayahu Jelinek. 1983.

131. *The Tsar's Loyal Germans: The Riga German Community: Social Change and the Nationality Question, 1855-1905.* By Anders Henriksson. 1983.

132. *Society in Change: Studies in Honor of Bela K. Kiraly.* Edited by Steven Bela Vardy. 1983.

133. *Authoritariansim in Greece: The Metaxas Regime.* By Jon V. Kofas. 1983.

134. *New Hungarian Peasants: An East Central European Experience with Collectivization.* Edited by Marida Hollos and Bela C. Maday. 1983.

135. *War, Revolution, and Society in Romania: The Road to Independence.* Edited by Ilie Ceausescu. 1983.

136. *The Beginning of Cyrillic Printing, Cracow, 1491: From the Orthodox Past in Poland.* By Szczepan K. Zimmer. 1983.

137. *Effects of World War I. The Class War After the Great War: The Rise of Communist Parties in East Central Europe, 1918-1921.* Edited by Ivo Banac. 1983.

138. *Bulgaria 1878-1918. A History.* By Richard J. Crampton. 1983.

139. *T. G. Masaryk Revisited: A Cirtical Assessment.* By Hanus J. Hajek. 1983.

140. *The Cult of Power: Dictators in the Twentieth Century.* Edited by Joseph Held. 1983.

141. *Economy and Foreign Policy: The Struggle of the Great Powers for Economic Hegemony in the Danube Valley, 1919-1939.* By György Ránki. 1983.

142. *Germany, Russia, and the Balkans: Prelude to the Nazi-Soviet Non-Aggression Pact.* By Marilynn Giroux Hitchens. 1983.

143. Guestworkers in the German Reich: The Poles in Wilhelmian Germany. By Richard Charles Murphy. 1983.

144. *The Latvian Impact on the Bolshevik Revolution.* By Andrew Ezergailis. 1983.

145. *The Rise of Moscow's Power.* By Henryk Paszkiewicz. 1983.

146. *A Question of Empire: Leopold I and the War of the Spanish Succession, 1701-1705.* By Linda and Marsha Frey. 1983.

147. *Effects of World War I. The Uprooted: Hungarian Refugees and Their Impact on Hungarian Domestic Policies, 1918-1921.* By Istvan I. Mocsy. 1983.

148. *Nationalist Integration Through Socialist Planning: An Anthropological Study of a Romanian New Town.* By Steven L. Sampson. 1983.